Genovese and Steckenrider provide a timely and important look at the women who have held top political positions around the world while at the same time asking the important question, "when will America elect its first woman president?" In answering that question, this book takes a critical look at how women are defined as leaders based on gender, and more importantly, why that matters for women pursuing top political leadership positions in the United States and other countries as well.

—**Lori Cox Han**, Ph.D., Professor of Political Science,
Chapman University, Orange, CA, USA

Genovese and Steckenrider weave together a wide-ranging collection of cases to shed light on the manner in which context, biography, leadership, and performance intersect with gender, as well as how these dynamics vary cross-culturally and cross-nationally. This is a must-read for scholars and students interested in the growing number of female heads of state. And it is a stark reminder of how far we remain from true gender parity in political institutions across the globe.

—**Jennifer L. Lawless**, Associate Professor of Government and Director
of the Women & Politics Institute, American University, USA

These timely and important essays contain fascinating and genuine insights. The determinative importance of context in the rise to power, family background, the range of leadership styles shown, and the diversity of policies pursued by women leaders such as Benazir Bhutto, Indira Ghandi, Golda Meir, Angela Merkel, Margaret Thatcher, and others are critically assessed. The result is intelligent scholarship of distinction.

—**Professor Angus Hawkins**, FRHistS, Oxford University, UK

D0970019

WOMEN AS POLITICAL LEADERS

In this new volume in the *Leadership: Research and Practice* series, the editors and expert contributors provide a clearer understanding of the impact of gender on political leadership by examining the lives and careers of women who became heads of government: Corazon Aquino of the Philippines, Benazir Bhutto of Pakistan, Violeta Chamorro of Nicaragua, Indira Gandhi of India, Golda Meir of Israel, Isabel Perón of Argentina, Margaret Thatcher of Great Britain, Gro Harlem Brundtland of Norway, Ellen Johnson Sirleaf of Liberia, and Angela Merkel of Germany. These women are not the universe of women heads of government in the past 60 years, but were selected because they illustrate a variety of paths to power, offer examples of both very short and very long tenure in office, are drawn from countries with greatly differing levels of economic and political development, and experienced varying degrees of success in office. Analysis and comparison of their careers contribute to identifying the central questions to be addressed as research continues. Students, academics, and researchers in the fields of leadership studies, political science, women and gender studies, management, and international relations will find this new volume of interest.

Michael A. Genovese holds the Loyola Chair of Leadership and is Professor of Political Science at Loyola Marymount University, where he directs the Institute for Leadership Studies. Genovese is the author of over 30 books, including (with Thomas E. Cronin) *Leadership Matters: Unleashing the Power of Paradox* (2012) and *A Presidential Nation: Causes, Consequences, and Cures* (2013).

Janie S. Steckenrider is Associate Professor of Political Science at Loyola Marymount University and focuses on the areas of gender politics and political gerontology. She is the coauthor (with Tonya Parrott) of *New Directions in Old Age Policies*. Her work has been published in the *Journal of Women and Politics*, *Journal of Health and Human Services Administration*, *Southwest Journal of Aging*, and *Journal of Alzheimer's Disease*.

Leadership: Research and Practice Series
A James MacGregor Burns Academy of Leadership Collaboration

Series Editors

Georgia Sorenson, Ph.D., Research Professor in Leadership Studies, University of Maryland, and Founder of the James MacGregor Academy of Leadership and the International Leadership Association.

Ronald E. Riggio, Ph.D., is the Henry R. Kravis Professor of Leadership and Organizational Psychology and former Director of the Kravis Leadership Institute at Claremont McKenna College.

Scott T. Allison and George R. Goethals
Heroic Leadership: An Influence Taxonomy of 100 Exceptional Individuals

Michelle C. Bligh and Ronald E. Riggio (Eds.)
Exploring Distance in Leader-Follower Relationships: When Near Is Far and Far Is Near

Michael A. Genovese and Janie S. Steckenrider (Eds.)
Women as Political Leaders: Studies in Gender and Governing

Jon P. Howell
Snapshots of Great Leadership

Aneil Mishra and Karen E. Mishra
Becoming a Trustworthy Leader: Psychology and Practice

WOMEN AS POLITICAL LEADERS

STUDIES IN GENDER AND GOVERNING

EDITED BY

Michael A. Genovese

Loyola Marymount University
California, USA

and

Janie S. Steckenrider

Loyola Marymount University
California, USA

Routledge
Taylor & Francis Group

NEW YORK AND LONDON

First published 2013
by Routledge
711 Third Avenue, New York, NY 10017

Simultaneously published in the UK
by Routledge
27 Church Road, Hove, East Sussex BN3 2FA

Routledge is an imprint of the Taylor & Francis Group, an informa business

Library of Congress Cataloging-in-Publication Data
Women as political leaders : studies in gender and governing / edited by Michael
A. Genovese, Janie S. Steckenrider.
     p. cm. — (Leadership : research and practice)
   1. Women heads of state—Case studies.   2. Women—Political activity—Case
studies.   I. Genovese, Michael A.   II. Steckenrider, Janie S., 1954–
HQ1236.W63762   2013
306.2082—dc23   2012037134

ISBN: 978-1-84872-991-9 (hbk)
ISBN: 978-1-84872-992-6 (pbk)
ISBN: 978-0-203-12290-7 (ebk)

Typeset in Minion
by Apex CoVantage, LLC

To Gaby
      —Michael

To TJ
      —Janie

Contents

Series Foreword

This far-reaching and important book spearheaded by two political scientists delivers what has been agonizingly missing from public discourse—a deliberate, research-based analysis of women heads of state, one that drills down into the complexity of this elusive democratic ideal.

Fifty-nine women from 45 countries have been elected or appointed to serve as heads of state, and Genovese and Steckenrider's work provides a close look at a representative and diverse sample of this rarified group. Rather than the usual biographical generalizations, the chapter authors, most of whom are political scientists as well, are directed by a framework of five research questions, namely: What *biographical* factors were important to this leader's rise? What *path to power* did the leader take? What *leadership style* was employed? How well or poorly did the leader *perform*, and why? And finally, to what extent, and how, did gender matter in this leader's rise and performance?

The resulting leitmotif is instructive because it lays out an overview of the recurring barriers impeding politically ambitious women in different contexts and offers details about the strategies some women leaders have used to neutralize barriers to power.

True, some of the women leaders studied surmounted these odds and got elected, but the real question remains: so what? Do women heads of state advance women's condition? Did their election make any discernible difference to other women?

In some cases, yes; others, no. Norway's Gro Harlem Brundtland won a plethora of groundbreaking policies to promote gender equality, ranging from political leadership to child care and parental leave policies. After her presidency, she continued to advance women's equality on the world stage. On the other hand, Margaret Thatcher rejected, even vilified, the women's movement, and firmly denounced policies aimed at women's equality. As Genovese wryly observes in his chapter on Thatcher, the "nascent women's movement created the opportunity for Margaret Thatcher to be a politician. It was a debt that she would not repay."

While this book's reach is clearly global, it begins and ends with what the editors call "the U.S. problem," the reluctance of Americans to support a woman for president. While many other countries have elected women heads of state, some twice over, the United States has yet to elect a woman president or vice president.

The presidential cycle yielded two firsts: a prominent and experienced woman from New York who entered the presidential race for matters of principle and power; an eloquent African American man who took a strong stand at the convention for equal rights. Many were hoping for a joint ticket but it was not to be. (Harvey, 2009; Connole and Sorenson, 2010.) It was certainly a bold move and at the forefront of women's leadership emancipation, and observers suggested that the next election would be poised for success.

But the year was 1872, and the "convention" was held in Seneca Falls, where women first gathered to press for equal treatment under the law. The controversial Victoria Woodhull ran for president on the Equal Rights Party ticket and she selected the iconic abolitionist leader Frederick Douglass as her running mate. While he declined the nomination as her vice president, it was Frederick Douglass who engineered the Declaration of Sentiments most radical resolution, a demand for women's right to vote.

This elegiac goal would take another 50 years, and more than another century would pass before a second remarkable woman from New York emerged to challenge the "U.S. problem." This book goes a long way in our efforts to understand the current dystopian presidential narrative of the world's oldest surviving democracy, and to shine the light on other countries more enlightened in matters of gender equality.

Georgia Sorenson
University of Maryland
Maryland, USA

Ronald E. Riggio
Claremont McKenna College
California, USA

Preface

For years, studies of political leadership have been remarkably non-gender specific. This is due primarily to a tacit assumption, usually made by male scholars, that leaders are men! Historically, there is of course a good deal of validity to this assumption—almost all political leaders *have been* men. To refer to a generic head of state as "him" may thus be understandable, if inaccurate.

Recently, however, the number of women who have served or are serving as heads of governments has risen to the point where the word *leader* is losing its gender reference point. In the post-World War II period, the resurgence of the women's movement and the emergence of women as heads of governments have given us the opportunity to examine the performance of women as political leaders, and to ask, Does gender matter? Do men exercise power in a manner different from women? Is *gender, institutional structure, role, environment,* or some other variable key to understanding executive performance? When women govern, do they promote "women's issues," and do they appoint more women to important posts; do they open doors for other women?

This study is an attempt to grapple with the difficult and controversial questions relating to gender and leadership. This work is not all-inclusive. Some women who have served as heads of government are not included. The selection here is designed to be representative, and to serve as theory-building (or pre-theoretical) steps in our understanding of the impact of gender on political leadership at the national level.

An earlier and shorter version of this book was published in 1993. At that time we could literally name all the women who headed governments. Now, 20 years later, the number has increased dramatically. In developed and less-developed countries, a woman heading a government is no longer unusual, and in most countries, hardly noticed and rarely commented on.

Equality? No. But real, measurable progress. Even in the United States, a woman (Hillary Clinton) came close to winning the nomination of one political party, and several women (Sarah Palin and Michelle Bachmann) were among the front-runners in the other party.

It is time to reexamine and reassess. In the past 20 years, so much has happened, but how much has really changed? To examine women in political power, we reprise the case studies from the 1993 edition: Golda Meir of Israel (1969–1974), Indira Gandhi of India (1966–1977 and 1980–1984), Margaret Thatcher of England (1979–1990), Isabel Perón of Argentina (1974–1976), Corazon Aquino of the Philippines (1986–1992), Benazir Bhutto of Pakistan (1988–1990), and Violeta Chamorro of Nicaragua (1990–1996); and for this new edition, we have added Gro Harlem Brundtland of Norway (1981, 1986–1989, and 1990–1996), Ellen Johnson Sirleaf of Liberia (2006–), and Angela Merkel of Germany (2005–).

In an effort to develop a truly comparative study of women leaders, all authors were asked to focus their case studies on common questions: What was the *context*—the political, social, and economic situation—at that point in time? What *biographical* factors were important to this leader's rise? What *path to power* did the leader take? What *leadership style* was employed? How well or poorly did the leader *perform*, and why? And finally, to what extent, and how, did gender matter in this leader's rise and performance? It is our hope that, by answering these questions, this collection of cases can avoid the common criticism that case studies are "idiosyncratic" and thus "lack . . . utility for theory-building" (Thomas, 1983, p. 50).

Betty Glad (1990–1991), in defending the use of case studies, argued, "Detailed case studies . . . enable the researcher to explore a wide variety of complex relationships. From such studies, one can begin to delineate those factors which transcend the case at hand, as well as those which are specific to the particular decision or outcome being studied" (p. 13). Our goal, and that of the contributors, is to use these case studies as a preliminary step in theory building on gender and leadership issues.

It is customary for authors and editors to preface their books with claims that the work was more arduous and difficult than first imagined, or that the research and writing of a book were grueling and painful. But we say that, in many respects, putting this book together was a real joy ("Blasphemy!" our fellow authors are screaming). How is this possible? No doubt we can attribute this to the good fortune of choosing chapter authors who were remarkably courteous and generous, and extremely punctual. From discussions with others who have assembled edited works with original pieces, we know how unusual this sounds, and we deeply thank all the authors in this book for their professionalism and their care.

Allow us also to thank our research assistants, Rebecca Hartley, Matt Candau, and Brianna Bruns for their tireless efforts; Mackenzie Burr for her project supervision; and typist Brian Whitaker for his outstanding work (and for their patience). We very much appreciate their contributions.

Michael A. Genovese and Janie S. Steckenrider

REFERENCES

Genovese, M. (Ed.) (1993). *Women as national leaders*. Newbury, CA: Sage Publishing.

Glad, B. (1990–1991). The idiosyncratic presidency: Contingency and the use of case studies and synthetic proofs in scientific analysis. *Presidency Research Group Newsletter, 13*(1), 6–20.

Thomas, N. (1983). Case studies. In G.C. Edwards & S.J. Wayne (Eds.), *Studying the presidency* (pp. 50–78). Knoxville: University of Tennessee Press.

About the Editors

Michael A. Genovese received a PhD from the University of Southern California in 1979. He currently holds the Loyola Chair of Leadership Studies, is Professor of Political Science, and Director of the Institute for Leadership Studies at Loyola Marymount University. In 2006, he was made a Fellow at the Queens College, Oxford University. Professor Genovese has written over 30 books, including *The Paradoxes of the American Presidency* (coauthored by Thomas E. Cronin), Oxford University Press, 4th ed. 2013; *The Presidency and the Challenges of Democracy* (coedited with Lori Cox Han), Palgrave, 2006; *The Presidency and Domestic Policy* (with William W. Lammers), CQ Press, 2000; *The Power of the American Presidency 1789–2000*, Oxford University Press, 2001; *The Presidential Dilemma*, Transaction, 3rd ed. 2011; *The Encyclopedia of the American Presidency*, Facts-on File, 2nd ed., 2010 (winner of the New York Public Library "Best of Reference" work of 2004); *Memo to a New President: The Art and Science of Presidential Leadership*, Oxford University Press, 2008; *Contending Approaches to the American Presidency*, CQ Press, 2012; and *Leadership Matters* (with Thomas E. Cronin), Paradigm: 2012. He has also written a cookbook, *Me and Mach: Food Fit for the Prince* (currently under review), and *Shakespeare's Politics* (Paradigm, edited with Bruce Althusler, forthcoming). His articles and reviews have appeared in the *American Political Science Review, The Times Literary Supplement, Public Opinion Quarterly, Presidential Studies Quarterly, White House Studies, The Journal of Leadership Studies,* and elsewhere. Genovese has won over a dozen university and national teaching awards, including the Fritz B. Burns Distinguished Teaching Award (1995), and the Rains Excellence in Research Award (2011). Professor Genovese frequently appears as a commentator on local and national television. He is also Associate Editor of the journal, *White House Studies,* is on the Editorial Board of the journals, *Rhetoric & Public Affairs,* and the *International Leadership Journal,* has lectured for the United States Embassy abroad, and is editor of Palgrave Macmillan Publishing's *The Evolving American Presidency* book series. Professor Genovese has been The Washington Center's scholar-in-residence at three Democratic national political conventions, and the 2008 presidential inauguration, and will serve as scholar-in-residence at the 2012 Republican National Convention. In 2004–2005, Professor Genovese served as President of the Presidency Research Group of the American Political Science Association. He is currently on the Advisory Boards of The Washington Center, The Center for the Study of Los Angeles, and the Foundation for International Education.

Janie S. Steckenrider received a PhD from the University of Southern California and is Associate Professor of Political Science at Loyola Marymount University where she is Associate Director of the Institute for Leadership Studies. Dr. Steckenrider's research and teaching are focused in the areas of political gerontology and women's studies. Her publications include a book, *New Direction in Old Age Policies* (coauthored with Tonya Parrott, SUNY Press) and articles in *Journal of Alzheimer's Disease, Journal of Health and Human Services Administration, Southwest Journal of Aging,* and *Journal of Women and Politics.* Dr. Steckenrider has been a Research Consultant to the National Council on Aging, a recipient of Administration on Aging grants, and has served on the Boards of Directors of a hospital, a skilled nursing facility, and a municipal senior commission.

About the Contributors

Nancy Fix Anderson is Professor Emerita of History at Loyola University New Orleans. She has published widely on Victorian and British imperial history. Her most recent books are (ed.) *Annie Besant*, in the *Lives of Victorian Political Figures* series (2008), and *The Sporting Life: Victorian Sports and Games* (2010). Her current research focuses on Victorian social history and British women in India under the Raj.

Jeanne-Marie Col is Associate Professor at John Jay College. She received her Ph.D. from the University of South Carolina in 1977. Her research interests include development and administration, and women in government. She served as Special Technical Adviser to the United Nations Department of Economic and Social Development.

Jana Everett is Professor of Political Science at the University of Colorado at Denver. Her publications examine various aspects of gender, politics, and development in India and globally. In 2005 she was a Fulbright research scholar in India studying the impact of reserving one-third of the seats in *panchayats* (rural councils) for women. She received her M.A. from Mount Holyoke College in 1969 and her Ph.D. in political science from the University of Michigan in 1976.

Richard L. Fox teaches and researches in the areas of U.S. Congress, elections, media and politics, and gender politics. He has completed, with Jennifer L. Lawless, *It Still Takes a Candidate: Why Women Don't Run for Office* (Cambridge University Press, 2010). He is also coeditor of *Gender and Elections: Shaping the Future of American Politics* (Cambridge University Press, 2010). His work has appeared in such journals as *Political Psychology, The Journal of Politics, American Journal of Political Science, Social Problems, PS: Political Science and Politics*, and *Politics and Gender*. He has also written op-ed articles, some of which have appeared in the *New York Times* and the *Wall Street Journal*.

Sarah L. Henderson is Associate Professor of Political Science at Oregon State University. She is the author of *Building Democracy in Contemporary Russia: Western Support for Grassroots Organization* (Cornell University

Press, 2003) and the coauthor (with Alana Jeydel) of *Women and Politics in a Global World: Participation and Protest* (Oxford University Press, 2009), in addition to a variety of book chapters and articles. She works in the areas of democratization, civil society, women's political participation, and Russia and Central and Eastern Europe. Her research has been funded by the National Council for East European and Eurasian Research, the Smith Richardson Foundation, the American Political Science Association, and the National Security Education Program.

Farida Jalalzai is an Associate Professor of Political Science at the University of Missouri, St. Louis. Her research analyzes gender in politics worldwide. She has published several articles about women prime ministers and presidents, some appearing in *Women, Politics and Policy*, *Politics & Gender*, *German Politics*, and the *International Political Science Review*. She also has a forthcoming book on this topic entitled *Shattered, Cracked or Firmly Intact? Women and the Executive Glass Ceiling Worldwide* (Oxford University Press, 2013).

Zoe M. Oxley is Professor of Political Science at Union College. Her research interests include women in electoral politics, gender stereotyping, and the effects of the media on public opinion. She is the coauthor (with Rosalee A. Clawson) of *Public Opinion: Democratic Ideals, Democratic Practice*, and *Conducting Empirical Analysis: Public Opinion in Action*. Her work has also been published in the *American Political Science Review*, *Journal of Politics*, *Politics & Gender*, *Political Research Quarterly*, *Political Behavior*, and *PS: Political Science and Politics*.

Michelle A. Saint-Germain is Professor of Public Policy and Administration and Director, Program Renewal and Assessment, at California State University at Long Beach. She received her Ph.D. in public administration from the University of Southern California in 1983. Her research interests focus on women and politics in Central America.

Seth Thompson is Emeritus Professor of Political Science at Loyola Marymount University. His chapter on Golda Meir combines his work on the Middle East with his work in political psychology.

Sara J. Weir has been a member of the Political Science Department at Western Washington University since 1989. She has served as the

Department Chair since 2001, while continuing to teach a variety of classes in her role as Associate Professor. In addition, she is the Director of WWU's Munro Institute for Civic Education, a position she has held since 2005. After completing her B.A. and M.A. at Ball State University, Dr. Weir received a Ph.D. from the University of Washington in 1988.

1

Introduction

Women as Political Leaders: Does Gender Matter?

Michael A. Genovese

> Her wings are clipped and it is found deplorable she does not fly.
>
> **Simone de Beauvoir**

The study of political leadership has made great strides in recent years. A variety of "maxims" have emerged that materially advance our understanding of leadership in society. Among these maxims:

leadership is largely contextual

leadership is different than power

leadership requires followers

leadership emerges in all organized groups

leadership can be learned (though not always mastered)

good judgment is the key to good leadership

leadership is aspirational and goal oriented (usually group goals)

Armed with these maxims, scholars can begin the pre-theoretical theory-building efforts that will more fully lead us to understanding and prediction in the complex world of politics and leadership studies.

An area where we are especially lacking in accepted maxims is the study of gender and leadership. One reason is that until recent years, very few women headed governments. Today, no such "small N" problem exists. Dozens of women have headed governments across the globe, and it is now time to search for verifiable generalizations, or maxims, about gender and leadership that can advance theory building.

Leadership refers to more than mere office holding. It is a complex phenomenon revolving around *influence*—the ability to move others in desired directions. Successful leaders are those who can take full advantage of their opportunities and their skills. Institutional structures, the immediate situation, the season of power, the political culture, regime type, the dynamics of followership, and partisan factors define the opportunities for the exercise of leadership. The leader's style, political acumen, character traits, and personal attributes provide a behavioral repertoire, a set of skills. Opportunities and skill interact to determine the success or failure of attempts to lead and influence.

WOMEN IN POLITICS

To begin, comparatively few women rise to a position of political leadership; it is perhaps the last political taboo. In a cross-cultural comparison of political leaders, Jean Blondel (1987) concludes that leaders "are overwhelmingly male" (p. 25). In Blondel's study of world leaders, less than .005% of all leaders were women (pp. 116–117). As Linda K. Richter (1990–1991) writes, "Male dominance has been legitimized in law and custom. Politics or the public life of the polity has been presumed to be a natural sphere for men while for women, to the extent they had a space or turf to call their own, the 'natural' sphere was presumed to be private" (p. 525).

   In recent years, this has begun to change (Dolan, Deckman, & Swers, 2010). Scholars cite three factors that lead to underrepresentation of women in public office: political socialization, situation/structural factors, and active discrimination against women (Hedblom, 1987, pp. 14–15). These, and perhaps other factors, have kept women at the margins of political power (Han, 2007, chap. 1).

WOMEN AS LEADERS

The above notwithstanding, some women have risen to become the chief executives of their countries in the post–World War II era. The number of such cases and the fact that they have occurred in diverse systems and societies under varying political conditions lead, we believe, to two conclusions. The first is that despite the persistence of barriers at individual and national levels, women will continue to emerge as chief executives in a growing number of countries and types of systems. That political fact leads to the second conclusion: that the rise of women to positions of power, their performance in office, and their impact on their societies is ripe for scholarly analysis and deserves careful attention from political scientists.

The study of women in leadership positions, particularly at the highest levels of decision making in a society, promises to contribute to our understanding of both *gender* as a politically defined and politically relevant variable and the politics of the dynamics of *leadership*. The potential for contributions to multiple realms of inquiry is typical of the general fields of gender studies and women and politics (Sapiro, 1983).

When the person who achieves a top leadership role is female, the political and personal biography both allow and force attention to the interplay of perceptions, expectations, interpretations of life experiences, and myths that make up the social definition of reality and "appropriate" gender roles (Baxter & Lansing, 1983; Conway, Bourke, & Scott, 1989). The lives and careers of women who have headed nations offer a unique vantage point on the role of gender in political life. The prevalence of gender distinctions becomes clearer as one recounts the challenges and opportunities that leaders have faced in their climb to the top. The depth and tenacity of gender stereotypes become clear when they continue to affect individuals even after they have achieved the ultimate political position.

The ascent of any person to power within society is, almost by definition, a rare and extraordinary event. The political leader's biography and career can help identify and highlight key features of a political system. Further, when a leader is sharply different in an important and obvious way from her predecessors, it allows an instructive test of propositions about the enduring features of a particular political system and about the necessary conditions for leadership in general. The emergence of a woman head of government may be both effect and cause of social change and fundamental shifts in the distribution of political power between men and women (Ford, 2010, chap. 1).

A focus on the impact of a person's gender on a political career can also help clarify and refine the potential contribution of gender to understanding political behavior within a system. The story of a woman's rise to power traces her encounters with the obstacles, restrictions, and deterrents that face any ambitious person in her society as well as the resources that may be available and skills that may be acquired to circumvent them. But her life will also illuminate the distinctive barriers faced because of marginality (Githens & Prestage, 1977, pp. 6–7) and perhaps her skill at developing gender-specific resources or strategies to overcome them (LeVeness & Sweeney, 1987). Every political system limits opportunity and access to elite roles by tacitly or overtly erecting a set of initial hurdles based on background or demographic traits. The careers of successful women can illustrate the extent to which gender itself, directly or indirectly, is a limiting condition in a particular society. To the extent that these ascriptive traits serve a gatekeeper function and discriminate against everyone who shares them, they are gender neutral. Any aspirant for a leadership position must develop a strategy to overcome them. And some of the preconditions for political success in a system are relatively gender neutral. There are, for example, class, ethnic, religious, and regional biases operative in many societies that restrict access to political power and careers.

Some of the preconditions for success in a system may appear applicable to aspirants, but have differential effects on men and women. For example, in the United States voters show a clear preference for candidates with presentable spouses and one or more children. This is a consideration for both male and female candidates, and thus can be seen as a systematic factor. At the same time, given the still-prevailing expectation that women have the major responsibility for child rearing and family maintenance, the bias in favor of "good family people" as candidates imposes an additional, gender-based constraint on the politically ambitious woman (Carroll & Fox, 2009).

Those aspects of a society that discriminate directly on the bias of gender are often thrown into clear relief by the experiences of those women who face them. The most obvious cases involve overtly sexist attitudes that disparage women as public officials, leaders, or decision makers. Other social institutions have similar effects.

If the implicit rule in a culture is that politics is "really" a man's world, or the experience of other ambitious women suggests that there is a glass ceiling allowing a woman to rise so far but no further, any woman who aspires to the top is subversive of the established order. The woman who does reach the top must have found a way around or over the exclusionary bias and thus potentially undermines it.

The impact of the successful woman's career on beliefs and expectations about gender will vary directly with the extent to which it resembles that of her male predecessors in power. If a woman is already at or near the top of the elite as she begins her political career because she inherited her position and status from her parental family, or because she has acquired it through close association with her husband, then observers with a conscious or unconscious interest in preserving gender bias in the political system may discount her as merely an anomaly unlikely to be repeated or attribute her success to family or spouse rather than her own skills and efforts. But the more closely the woman leader's career resembles those of her male colleagues, the more difficult it is for observers to avoid interpretations that challenge exclusionary assumptions.

The career of a woman who becomes a head of government will thus be affected by and have an effect upon her contemporaries' expectations and stereotypes. A politically ambitious woman cannot escape the consequences of social beliefs that gender differences are politically relevant. She must come to some understanding of herself as a person and as a political figure that resolves, manages, or represses the tensions between her emerging self-view as capable of functioning effectively at the highest political levels and the generalized social view that neither she nor any other woman has that competence. Regardless of how she handles the internal impact of gender roles, she must also develop strategies for dealing with them as a strategic aspect of her career, because others may react to her in terms of gender. At times that will mean overcoming or circumventing restrictions. If one hallmark of the ultimately successful political leader is the ability to transform apparent liabilities into assets, then we might expect to see her manipulate traditional stereotypes of women to outflank or disarm opponents.

We must remember that successful women political leaders are not a recent phenomenon. Throughout history, even when women in general have been excluded from political power, some individuals have exercised great influence. Several queens are central figures in the histories of their countries, there have been a handful of extraordinary women warriors (Fraser, 1988), and there have been consorts who wielded immense power through their relationships to kings or emperors. But those women experienced success by using well the opportunities and resources offered by socially defined and sanctioned gender roles, or could be defined by contemporaries as unique individuals in extraordinary times.

In contrast, the careers of those women who have occupied the highest positions in their respective political systems in the 20th and 21st centuries, with few exceptions, represent a distinctive phenomenon: Their achievement of power challenges existing definitions of gender roles. This has enhanced their political visibility and, arguably, salience to students of politics (Henderson & Jeydel, 2009).

Elizabeth I, for instance, was an important and influential figure in British history because she capitalized on the resources inherent in her position and her considerable political skills as she presided over a profound transformation of Britain's world role and domestic economy. But her presence on the throne was fully consonant with traditional British values and assumptions and did not represent an extraordinary or even particularly unusual event. She came to power in the usual way, fully in keeping with both the explicit and the tacit rules of the game. Her success did not call any basic social assumptions into question.

Margaret Thatcher's residence at 10 Downing Street, on the other hand, makes her an extraordinary figure. During the rule and reign of Elizabeth I, access to the apex of the system, the throne, was a function of birth order; chromosomes and socially defined roles were irrelevant. By the reign of Elizabeth II, access to the apex of the system had long since become the ultimate prize in a much more open and cutthroat political competition. But that competition had been explicitly restricted to males, and at the highest levels was still tacitly exclusive. Margaret Thatcher did not come to power in quite the usual way, and her success necessarily has implications for the future of some salient aspects of the British political system.

UNDERSTANDING GENDER AND LEADERSHIP

Developing an understanding of how social definitions of gender affect a political career will ultimately lead to two sets of conclusions: one concerning the barriers impeding politically ambitious women, the other concerning the strategies some women use to neutralize these barriers (Wolbrecht, Beckwith, & Baldez, 2008; Lawless & Fox, 2010).

Trying to disentangle systematic, situational, and personal variables in explaining the behavior of any political actor is a daunting task, and it is even more so when the actor occupies one of the central positions in a system. A simplistic model that casts gender as *the* independent variable and a particular decision-making style or issue position as the dependent variable is not likely to be very useful (Kelly & Burgess, 1989). However, gender can be expected to have a significant impact on performance in two ways.

Gender will have an effect on the leader's performance in office to the extent that others, allies and adversaries, perceive it as salient and change their own behavior accordingly (Sapiro, 1983). The impact of gender on the 1971 Indo-Pakistan War may be a particularly powerful example. The fact that Indira Gandhi was prime minister of India seems to have had a significant impact on President Yahya Khan of Pakistan. It is possible that Pakistan would have been less bellicose and rigid if the Indian government had been headed by a male (Stoessinger, 1990, pp. 135–136). The more common effects may be more subtle, but they are nonetheless important. Anyone who rises to the top of a political system will have developed a set of strategies and a repertoire of behaviors for dealing with both challenges and opportunities. For the successful woman, the strategies she has developed and her style will inevitably be shaped and influenced by her society's definitions and expectations of gender. She will have learned how to cope effectively with, and even turn to her advantage, the fact that she is a woman in "a man's world." The results of her interaction with her gender may not show in each decision she makes, or even necessarily be evident in any particular case. But a review of a range of decisions or her entire tenure in office should illustrate the relevance of gender to this leader at this point in her country's history.

The focus on women at the highest levels of officeholding provides a useful vantage point for isolating some key variables. For example, there is a generally held belief, and some ambiguous evidence, that the mode for women on some dimensions of management style and decision making differs from the mode for males. One difficulty in evaluating such studies is the existence of potential confounding effects of role definitions and institutional constraints. For example, some studies suggest that women managers are more concerned with interpersonal relationships than are their male counterparts (Bass, 1990, p. 724). However, if women who are leaders or managers are disproportionately clustered in positions whose occupants are expected to be responsible for maintaining group dynamics or are concentrated in firms or industries with institutional cultures that place greater emphasis on group unity and cohesion, the apparent link between gender and management style is spurious, and the useful explanation is gender bias.

The study of political leaders must ultimately be comparative. Whether one is attempting to rank American presidents along the "greatness" continuum or identifying the central components of a model of leadership, understanding the role and contribution of one leader requires understanding others as well. One comparative question is, which factors or variables affect all leaders; and which are specific to a particular leader, a particular point in time, or a particular political system? Studies of women who achieve leadership roles in various political systems can contribute important clues that may help to answer these questions.

Comparing political executives in a single system over time can help elucidate the relatively permanent features of the system. A key issue in studies of the executive institution in a particular political system is identifying those variables that can be used to explain the performance and impact of any incumbent and differentiating them from accidental conditions or constraints. The arrival in office of a person whose background or career is sharply discontinuous from the immediate past creates a quasi-experimental situation. One salient factor that had been a constant for all preceding officeholders can now be understood as a variable, and one can ask what else has changed and what has continued to remain constant. Given the importance of gender roles in a wide range of social interactions, their apparent persistence over time and across social groups, and the role they play in establishing both personal and social identity, when a woman becomes prime minister it clearly represents a significant departure from the past. Her relationship to, and impact upon, various elements of the government and broader political system provides evidence about the extent to which some systemic features are institutionalized and constant, and others vary with the identities of the players. For example, as long as the American presidency continues to be a male preserve, one cannot be certain that observations about the relationship between the presidency and other institutions or actors are relatively permanent features of the system that transcend the particulars of the occupant of the White House. When a woman sits in the Oval Office, her experience will provide an instructive test.

One can also compare political leaders across national and cultural boundaries. At some level, beneath the vagaries of time and place, there are certain constants in the fundamental political relationships between leaders and followers. Those cases of women who have made it to the top of their political systems come from advanced capitalist societies and Third World countries at different stages of development, and from established parliamentary systems, nascent democracies, authoritarian regimes, and the turmoil of revolutionary or postrevolutionary situations. They have been career politicians and inheritors of political roles relatively late in life. They have enjoyed long tenures, and they have presided over short-lived regimes.

One thing they do have in common is that they have made it to the top despite significant gender bias. Their success suggests that social constraints are not absolute and may well be changing. The presence of a woman as chief executive may be an indicator that social change has occurred. At the same time, the performance of the leader during her tenure in office and the ways in which she is evaluated by her contemporaries have implications for other women, not only in politics but in a broad range of social roles (Whitaker, 2010).

The woman leader who is perceived as highly effective undermines negative stereotypes; the woman leader who is deemed to have failed may reinforce them. One dimension for evaluating the legacy of the woman who has led her country is what effect her tenure in office had on definitions of gender in her society.

All women who have come to political power have arrived in societies where the fundamental political relationship has been between male leader and his followers. Case studies of women in power can help isolate the dynamics of the relationship between the leader and the leader's relationship to followers. Case studies of women who govern may indicate whether it is fruitful to think about examining four possible relationships: female or male leader and male or female followers. For example, does a social bias against women in leadership positions in general translate into a specific political liability for a woman chief executive? Will she receive some level of generalized support from the egalitarian or feminist sectors of society, irrespective of her political philosophy, party, or program?

Women still occupy a marginal majority in societies. By focusing on women who have served in leadership roles, we may, as Richter (1990–1991) notes, also come to a deeper understanding of leadership in general: "The experience of . . . politically prominent women offers empirical 'reality checks' on theories of leadership derived almost exclusively from the experiences of men" (p. 527).

Do men and women lead differently? Is the dominant, assertive, top-down, competitive approach a male style and a relationship-orientated, consensus-building, approach to leading a feminine style? Virginia E. Schein (1989) notes the implications of these potential differences:

> That woman would lead or govern differently is not new. Women's leadership has been linked with enhancing world peace, reducing corruption, and improving opportunities for the downtrodden. If women, as keeper of the values of social justice, nurturance, and honesty, are put in charge, then the conflicts, corruption and greed around us will go away—or so say proponents of this view. The maximalist perspective within the now fragmented feminist movement supports this idea. It argues for innate or highly socialized gender differences and views women as more likely to exhibit cooperative, compassionate, and humane types of behaviors than men. (p. 154)

Male-centered theories of leadership may indeed need to be reexamined in light of the rise of women in leadership positions in both the public and corporate worlds, perhaps in search of an "androgynous" style, blending the best of traditionally male and female characteristics. On the other hand, Bernard Bass (1990) notes:

> Because situational changes are rapidly occurring for women in leadership roles, earlier research may need to be discounted. Despite the many continuing handicaps to movement into positions of leadership owing to socialization, status conflicts, and stereotyping, progress is being made. Some consistent differences remain between boys and girls and less so, among adult men and women managers and leaders. Characteristics that are usually linked to masculinity are still demanded for effective management. Nevertheless, most differences in male and female leaders tend to be accounted for by other controllable or modifiable factors, although women will continue to face conflicts in their decisions to play the roles of wives and mothers as well as of managers and leader. (p. 737)

While some early research into gender differences suggested that men and women were different in their styles of leadership, more recent research, especially that coming from neuroscience, paints a more complex and nuanced picture. Yes, there are biological differences between men and women that do lead to some differences in how boys and girls behave (Gray, 2004). These differences—nature—often lead to an exaggerated sense of gender distinctness and often elicit responses from adults that reinforce and grow these differences—nurture. What begin as biological instincts and biases in brain function, which culturally germinate and grow, are amplified over time by stereotyping and gender role expectations, thereby making differences more pronounced (Gilligan, 1993). As Alina Tugend (2001) writes, "What start as innate differences lead us to treat boys and girls differently, which then exacerbates the divide" (p. 173).

Further, several key gaps between men and women are closing. Women participate in sports at an increasing rate, more women go to college and graduate than men, more women are going into "the professions" than ever before. And more women hold visible public positions than in the past (presidential candidates, Supreme Court Justices, CEOs, etc.). Given the plasticity of the brain, these and other changes can only serve to break down gender stereotypes and the import of nature, and over time, further erode gender biases (Eliot, 2010).

In this volume, we attempt to gain a clearer understanding of the impact of gender on political leadership by examining the lives and careers of women who became heads of government: Corazon Aquino of the Philippines, Benazir Bhutto of Pakistan, Violeta Chamorro of Nicaragua, Indira Gandhi of India, Golda Meir of Israel, Isabel Perón of Argentina, Margaret Thatcher of Great Britain, Gro Harlem Brundtland of Norway, Ellen Johnson Sirleaf of Liberia, and Angela Merkel of Germany. These women are not the universe of women heads of government in the past 60 years, but were selected because they illustrate a variety of paths to power, offer examples of both very short and very long tenure in office, are drawn from countries with greatly differing levels of economic and political development, and experienced varying degrees of success in office. Analysis and comparison of their careers should contribute to identifying the central questions to be addressed as research continues.

You will note that no women from the United States are included on this list. That is because of the simple fact that no woman has as yet become president. In 2008, Senator Hillary Clinton came very close to winning the Democratic Party nomination, and in 2012, Minnesota Representative Michelle Bachman, and former Alaska Governor Sarah Palin were seen as contenders for the Republican Party nomination. And yet, Americans remain a bit reluctant to support a woman for president (Streb, Burrel, Frederick, & Genovese, 2008). We have attempted to deal with the "U.S. problem" in a separate chapter in this volume.

The women discussed in this book led fascinating lives and accomplished a great deal in their careers. They form the basis around which serious discussions can be conducted about how women govern and how gender impacts leadership.

REFERENCES

Adams, J., & Yoder, J. D. (1985). *Effective leadership for women and men*. Norwood, NJ: Ablex.

Bass, B. M. (Ed.). (1990). *Bass & Stogdill's handbook of leadership: Theory, research, and managerial applications* (3rd ed.). New York: Free Press.

Baxter, S., & Lansing, M. (1983). *Women and politics: The visible majority*. Ann Arbor: University of Michigan Press.

Blondel, J. (1987). *Political leadership: Towards a general analysis*. London: Sage.

Burn, J. M. (1978). *Leadership*. New York: Harper & Row.

Carroll, S. J., & Fox, R. L. (2009). *Gender and elections: Shaping the future of American politics*. Cambridge: Cambridge University Press.

Conway, J. K., Bourke, S. C., & Scott, J. W. (1989). *Learning about women*. Ann Arbor: University of Michigan Press.

Darcy, R., Welch, S., & Clark, J. (1987). *Women, elections, and representation*. New York: Longman.

Dolan, J. A., Deckman, M. M., & Swers, M. L. (2010). *Women and politics: Paths to power and political influence*. New York: Longman.

Eliot, L. (2010). *Pink brain, blue brain: How small differences grow into troublesome gaps—and what we can do about it*. New York: Mariner Books.

Ford, L. E. (2010). *Women and politics: The pursuit of equality*. Florence, KY: Wadsworth.

Fraser, A. (1988). *The warrior queens*. New York: Vintage.

Gertzog, I. (1984). *Congressional women*. New York: Praeger.

Gilligan, C. (1993). *In a different voice: Psychological theory and women's development*. Cambridge, MA: Harvard University Press.

Githens, M., & Prestage, J. L. (1977). *A portrait of marginality*. New York: D. McKay.

Gray, John. (2004). *Men are from Mars, women are from Venus*. New York: Harper.

Greenstein, F. I. (1967). The impact of personality on politics: An attempt to clear away underbrush. *American Political Science Review, 61*, 629–641.

Han, L. C. (2007). *Women and American politics*. Boston: McGraw-Hill.

Hedblom, M. K. (1987). *Women and power in American politics*. Washington, DC: American Political Science Association.

Henderson, S., & Jeydel, A. (2009). *Women and politics in a global world*. New York: Oxford University Press.

Jones, B. D. (Ed.). (1989). *Leadership and politics*. Lawrence: University Press of Kansas.

Kelly, R. M., & Burgess, J. (1989). Gender and the meaning of power and politics. *Women and Politics, 9*(1), 1–43.

Lawless, J. L., & Fox, R. L. (2010). *It still takes a candidate: Why women don't run for office*. Cambridge: Cambridge University Press.

LeVeness, F. P., & Sweeney, J. P. (1987). *Women leaders in contemporary U.S. politics*. Boulder, CO: Lynne Reiner.

Lovenduski, J. (1986). *Women and European politics: Contemporary feminism and public policy*. Amherst: University of Massachusetts Press.

Richter, L. K. (1990–1991). Exploring theories of female leadership in South and Southeast Asia. *Pacific Affairs, 63*, 524–540.

Sadker, M., & Sadker, D. (1995). *Failing at fairness: How our schools cheat girls* (4th ed.). Boston: Scribner's.

Sapiro, V. (1983). *The political integration of women*. Urbana: University of Illinois Press.

Schein, V. E. (1989). Would women lead differently? In W. Rosenbach and R. Taylor (Eds.), *Contemporary issues in leadership* (pp. 134–160). Boulder, CO: Westview Press.

Stoessinger, J. (1990). *Why nations go to war*. New York: St. Martin's Press.

Streb, M. J., Burrel, B., Frederick, B., & Genovese, M. A. (2008). Social desirability effects and support for a female American president. *Public Opinion Quarterly, 72*(1), 76–89.

Tugend, A. (2001). *Better by mistake: The unexpected benefits of being wrong*. New York: Riverhead Books.

Whitaker, L. D. (2010). *Women in politics: Outsiders or insiders?* (5th ed.) New York: Longman.

Wolbrecht, C., Beckwith, K., & Baldez, L. (2008). *Political women and American democracy*. Cambridge: Cambridge University Press.

2

Managing Softly in Turbulent Times

Corazon C. Aquino, President of the Philippines

Jeanne-Marie Col

The media reported that an ordinary housewife was challenging a 20-year dictator for the presidency of the Philippines. They were engaging in a kind of hyperbole that attracts readers and viewers, but may distort the truth. This ordinary housewife had been tutored in politics from an early age, first in a "politically orientated" family and later by a husband with considerable political instinct, ambition, and accomplishment. While appearing to be a shy, silent student and partner, this housewife gradually developed the perspectives and skills befitting a presidential candidate, if not also a president. What a surprise to her opponent, who suggested that she more properly belonged in a bedroom than in the chief executive's office. Perhaps Corazon Aquino herself was surprised at the extent to which she asserted herself effectively in the political arena. In her decision to focus on redemocratization as her presidential priority, Corazon Aquino made a significant contribution to the welfare of the Filipino people, many of whom expressed the need for a new and genuine model of participatory governance.

Aquino assumed the presidency in 1986 in a bloodless "people power" revolution in which a diverse group of Filipinos emerged in massive nonviolent rallies to defend the election results, as reported by the "quick count" poll watches, and as defended by key military leaders who refused to assist incumbent President Ferdinand Marcos in suppressing the demonstrators. Aquino and her advisers pursued a nonviolent strategy to mobilize popular support and to isolate Marcos. The contrast between Marcos and Aquino was striking. Marcos denigrated his woman opponent as appropriate only for the bedroom, and threatened to use military force, as he had often done in the past, to put down any popular uprising. Aquino accused her male opponent of a track record of martial law, repression, cronyism, and corruption. The military joined the people in manifesting popular impatience with old-style politics and governance. Forces external to the Philippines supported the prodemocracy, anti-Marcos movement. Aquino was handed the victory by the military and the demonstrators that she had apparently won in the popular election. The tasks of redemocratization and rebuilding were hers.

Aquino served as both head of state and chief executive of the government: president, prime minister, and queen combined. And she developed a style in marked contrast to her predecessors. Did Aquino set an example for women and girls? Did she establish a new pattern of democratic government for future presidents? As the first female president of the Philippines, and one of the few women presidents in modern history, did she contribute to our understanding of the performance of female presidents and prime ministers?

The Philippines is a complex, plural society with democratic roots often modified by authoritarian tendencies during several colonial and nationalist periods. While colonial and independent governments have sought to instill national unity, this process has been frustrated by the immense diversity and even fragmentation emanating from factors such as religion, urbanization, isolation, ethnicity, linguism, and regionalism. At the time, it was a society buffeted by natural disasters—not the least of which were a recent volcanic eruption, an equally devastating earthquake, and a normal complement of typhoons. With the populace looking to the government to ameliorate the disastrous consequences of these problems, as well as the everyday social and economic issues of a developing society, any leadership would have been under considerable pressure. The Aquino government was especially pressured by the enormous popular expectations emanating from 14 years of repressive marital law. With these issues and expectations, did the simple housewife serve as an effective president?

Although women have always played an active role in Philippine society, their participation in politics is "most concealed" (Tancango, 1990, p. 323). Marcos's sentiment that Aquino could best participate in the bedroom might have been shared by a wide spectrum of Filipinos. Women, who constitute 49.83% of the Philippine population, are expected to be involved in the nurturing tasks of education and service, while men are expected to be in the forefront of leadership and decision making in politics ("The Status of Women," n.d., p. 15). According to several academic studies, precolonial Filipino culture supports an equal and partnership model of male-female relationships, in which women had equal roles not only in the family and the economy but also in decision making in the important social processes of the bigger community (Rodriquez, 1990, p. 18). The influence of the Spanish and American regimes relegated women to a more "Victorian" confinement to family and home (Estrada-Claudio, 1990–1991; Tapales, 1988). Based on centuries of mixed traditions and encouraged by global trends, tension between the gender equality and female limitation models continues in all institutions in the Philippines. This tension was reflected in Aquino's actions as president as well as in the ambivalent interpretations of her performance.

THE PHILIPPINES AT A CROSSROADS

When Corazon ("Cory") Aquino assumed the position of president of the Philippines, the country had been subjected to an accumulation of natural and devised disasters. From earthquakes, volcanoes, and typhoons to the authoritarian dictatorship of Ferdinand Marcos, the Philippines had more than a few distractions from steady economic growth and increasing social and political harmony and maturity.

Inhabiting an archipelago of 7,107 islands scattered across 500,000 square miles, with a land area of 114,672 square miles and extending almost 1,150 miles from north to south (Steinberg, 1990, p. 12), the 60 million Filipinos are mostly Malay in origin, later mixing extensively with Chinese immigrants and Spanish conquerors, creating the largest current group of Filipinos, which is the racially mixed mestizos. Later, the Chinese and Spanish legacy was mixed with American political and educational culture based on 48 years of American colonial rule and a strong emphasis on education as a means of achieving equality and democratization, thereby creating the now-large category of the *ilustrado elite*, who have university degrees. According to Steinberg (1990), "The Philippines has, in effect, an aristocracy based on economic and education criteria—a privileged upper class and a gap between the entitled few and the masses that is comparable to that in eighteenth-century France" (p. 50).

Anthropologists claim there are 111 different cultural and racial groups in the Philippines, speaking some 70 different languages, from Muslim Malays in the southern islands of Sulu to Episcopalian Igortos in the cordillera mountains of Luzon ("The Philippines," 1988). The most significant cleavages are religious, with respect to the Muslim south; and cultural, involving upland tribes (Komisar, 1987, p. 19). Filipinos are family oriented in their personal relations, and family-style relations are represented in politics by patron-client relations.

Political culture in the Philippines is situated on an axis of democracy and authoritarianism. It has been contended that:

> Filipino political cultural has a superstructure of attitudes and values of Western origin, resting on a definitely indigenous infrastructure. From the West comes individualism and a high respect for achievement and for the rule of law, whereas indigenous values stress primary-group (i.e., family) loyalty and a particularistic view of public affairs. (Wurfel, 1988, p. 43)

According to Corpuz (1969), "The consultative decision making of the ancient barangay, the pragmatic bargaining of interpersonal relationships, and the ability to acquire political status through achievement are traditional traits that provide underpinning for modern democracy" (p. 15). Arcellana (1969) has stated that "child rearing in the Philippines teaches very forcefully that elders, and others in positions of power and authority, must be respected and followed, not challenged" (p. 38).

The use of authoritarian and democratic styles in the presidency created dilemmas for other politicians, the bureaucracy, and the public. Expectations were necessarily confused, and a particular style might need to be stated or modeled very explicitly in order to create understanding and appropriate learning and response. There was a question as to whether Aquino expressed her "soft," democratic style of leadership in as clear a manner as necessary to communicate to citizens how they could assume full responsibility for their lives, their development, and their government. Perhaps such clarity of expression could not have been achieved because of the ambivalence of her cabinet and bureaucratic colleagues, who shared her views in differing degrees. Cariño (1987a) has noted that "the contradictions in the society were reproduced in the bureaucracy: it was authoritarian and participatory, developmentalist and nationalistic, corrupt and committed" (p. 272).

The democratic, open, and more participatory style of government championed by Aquino was consistent with and of benefit to women seeking to overcome the inherited role of being generally relegated to a family-oriented and less public role. Although Filipinas had been influential in their homes and often important in the economy, they had been largely excluded from politics. The few early examples of women leaders were striking, and their legacy continued. In the late 1700s, Gabriela Silang, for whom a women's umbrella group was named, carried on the leadership of a rebellion led by her husband, who was assassinated by Spanish authorities (Tancango, 1990, p. 326).

In the 1980s, many women's organizations emerged in anticolonial struggles, in humanitarian work, and in the promotion of women to local governments. Prominent among these was the Asociacion Feminista Filipina (Feminist Association of the Philippines), the first women's volunteer organization, founded in 1905 and dedicated to both humanitarian objectives and the advancement of women in society (Tancango, 1990, p. 326). A year later, the Associacion Feminista Ilonga (Association of Ilonga Feminists) was formed to work for women's suffrage (Tancango, 1990, p. 327). During pre- and post-independence periods, women formed many organizations for social, religious, civil, business, and political objectives. The Malayang Kilusan ng Bagong Kababaihan (Free Movement of Women), known as MAKIBAKA (struggle), was formed in the 1960s in order to organize both urban and rural women, but was banned during the martial law period that began in 1972. A National Commission on the Role of Filipino Women (NCRFW), formed by the Marcos regime during the United Nations International Decade for Women, confined its activities to studying legal inequities and providing income-generating and welfare projects for women.

After the removal of martial law, many more women's organizations were formed, and in 1984, many coalesced into the alliance known as GABRIELA, after the 18th-century heroine. Other women's groups included, for example, Women for the Ouster of Marcos (WOMB); Stop, an organization that aimed to counter sex trafficking; and KALAYAAN, which exposed sexism within the family, the educational and political systems, and other institutions (Tancango, 1990, p. 329). In December 1985, 250 women who were either relatives or friends of Aquino met with her to assure her of their votes and to signify their intention to help her in the presidential campaign. These women then signed up both professionals and the masses, launching an organization, known as Cory's Crusaders, that eventually became a people's movement (Tancango, 1990, p. 345). They raised money, produced campaign materials, and participated in rallies and other activities. Cory's Crusaders were revitalized during a later senatorial campaign to assist in electing Leticia Ramos-Shahani (Tancango, 1990, p. 360). Although Filipina women were known historically to participate actively in political affairs during revolutionary times, fighting side by side with Filipino men, only to retreat to their homes during peace, the record of Cory's Crusaders and other women's organizations indicated that gender stereotypes may have increasingly shifted to reflect a more consistently active and influential role for women.

Evolution in the political role of women in the Philippines was taking place in the context of wider sociocultural and economic patterns. For instance, income distribution was skewed in favor of a definable elite. The top one-fifth of the population received half the country's income, with famous family names—Lopez, Laurel, Romulo, Soriano, Zobel, Cojuangco, Ayala, Aquino—ever present in political and economic arenas ("The Philippines," 1988). This elite evolved from various immigrations of Chinese traders who visited the Philippines centuries before either Islam or Christianity, subsequently establishing substantial business interests. Muslims established sultanates in Sulu and on Mindanao by the mid-15th century.

The Spanish arrived in 1571 and left a legacy of Catholicism and indirect rule through the Filipino elite. Building upon the Spanish colonial base, Americans exerted considerable cultural, economic, and political influence from 1946, continuing into the 1990s with the presence of U.S. military installations. After the 1869 opening of the Suez Canal and the subsequent increase in travel to Europe, ideas of nationalism and liberalism began to permeate the society.

Rebellion against the Spanish continued through the Spanish-American War in 1898, in which the Philippines were ostensibly sold to the United States for $20 million (Komisar, 1987, p. 19). Like the Spanish, the Americans ruled through the Filipino elite until partial independence in 1935. Foreshadowing future political fragmentation, national political rivalries delayed acceptance of a national constitution and partial inpendence for five years (Komisar, 1987, p. 21). Full independence from the United States occurred in 1946, after the Japanese occupation from 1941 to 1945.

Independence politics has been characterized as "guns, goons and gold," indicating the mobilization of political power through private armies for personal gain through patronage and largess (Komisar, 1987, p. 21). These localized political machines connected to the landed elite and paramilitary groups defended an increasingly unequal accumulation of land and other resources. Peasant uprisings in the 1920s and 1930s led to the militant tenant unions and eventually to the People's Anti-Japanese Army, *Hukbulahap*, better known as the Huks (Komisar, 1987, p. 21). Both the Catholic Church and U.S. officials discouraged these and other peasant movements, solidifying polarization between the educated, city-based elites and the poor, landless cultivators. From the 1920s, the tenant farmers had been demanding not land reform, but only a larger share of the harvest; during the 1940s, their demands escalated to redistribution of the land. From 1946, when the Philippines achieved complete independence, the "Huk rebellion" emerged into a serious guerilla war, with thousands of Huk troops (Komisar, 1987, p. 23). By the 1950s, Communists began to dominate the Huks in some areas, thereby exploiting the extreme income disparities to gain political support in a context of already fragmented political fiefdoms.

During the 1950s, the Philippines was recognized as the most developed nation in Southeast Asia ("The Philippines," 1988). Possessing vast natural resources such as timber, coconut, sugar, bananas, rubber, and minerals, and even oil being discovered, the Philippines developed an economy based on export of raw agricultural materials while establishing industries for import substitution. During the oil crisis, and with rising population and increasingly militant insurgencies, these economic strategies could not sustain economic development. The Philippines failed to create export-oriented industries and failed to develop agricultural productivity ("The Philippines," 1988). Nepotism and "crony capitalism" resulted in large foreign debt and much personal profit invested outside the country.

The political and economic situation in the Philippines worsened in the 1980s, characterized by capital flight, factory closings, rising unemployment, bank closings, devaluation of the peso by 38%, rising prices, and the collapse of world prices of sugar and coconut oil (Komisar, 1987, p. 51). Following the assassination of Ninoy Aquino, Cory's husband, rallies and disruptions were held not only by peasant/worker movements but also by clergy and Makati business persons. Cory was in great demand as a speaker, and was increasingly consulted during negotiations among opposition leaders. The period from 1983 to 1986 was characterized as the "parliament of the streets," in which interests were articulated in popular modalities. Aquino herself joined, but not, at this point, leading (Gonzales-Zap, 1987, p. 78). In the 1984 elections, the opposition gained 56 out of 183 seats in the National Assembly, despite massive vote rigging ("The Philippines," 1988). Momentum for change was building.

While Marcos delayed in announcing elections, 11 potential presidential candidates struggled among themselves for prominence, with Aquino at the sidelines, repeating that she hoped they would agree on a candidate and that she did not want to be considered.

> Although Aquino quickly became the symbol of the struggle, no one in those early days thought of her as a potential leader. Nor did she envision such a role for herself. She was never the political neophyte that some of the pros took her for—at their peril. However, she lacked such leadership qualities as experience, ambition, and confidence, which other opposition personalities possessed in excess. (Burton, 1989, p. 138)

A convener group composed of Lorenzo Tanada, Jaime Ongpin, Aquino, and a national unification council composed of Salvador Laurel, Homobono Aelaza, and Cecilia Muñoz-Palma attempted to bring together different opposition groups in order to forge an agreement about candidates and platforms, under the so-called umbrella of the Bayan or National Democratic Alliance. This conciliatory strategy floundered for months under the continuing arguments, and competition between groups as varied as leftists closely allied with Communists and guerillas and conservatives, including Salvador Laurel, who had worked with Marcos as recently as 1982.

On November 3, 1985, Marcos called "snap elections" for February 7, 1986. Political pressure for increased democracy mounted, and foreign allies, including the United States, sent envoys to urge speedy elections. Unemployment stood at 20%, underemployment at 40%, and inflation was approaching 25% (Komisar, 1987, p. 81). Believing in Aquino's potential to mobilize the electorate, some opposition leaders continued to press her to contest the presidency. Aquino insisted that she preferred not to be a candidate, but would relent in the face of popular demand. She set a seemingly difficult condition: the collection of a million signatures on petitions requesting her to run for the presidency (Gonzales-Zap, 1987, p. 99). When more than a million signatures were obtained, Aquino considered her decision. As was her practice when needing to make difficult decisions, she made a one-day retreat at a Manila convent. On December 3, 1985, Aquino declared her candidacy, with Laurel reluctantly agreeing to serve as her running mate, after having been a contender for the nomination himself. Aquino agreed to lead the challenge against Marcos, and support from all strata and sectors joined the anti-Marcos movement.

CORY "PREPARES" FOR POLITICS

Corazon Aquino had a long political apprenticeship. She grew up in a political family and married into another political family. After years of contentment on the sidelines, she was thrown into the political arena when her husband Benigno Aquino was imprisoned by President Ferdinand Marcos. During that imprisonment, her husband literally tutored her in politics as she served as a link between his ideas and experiences and the outside world. The tutoring continued in family discussions during his exile. Later, after Benigno's assassination, Corazon Aquino evolved into a political actor and was drawn in by circumstances to compete for the presidency. Her initial shyness and dislike of politics were overcome by her increasingly sophisticated political skills and her strong commitment to save her country from the dictator she believed had been responsible for the assassination of her husband and severe political oppression.

Born Maria Corazon Sumulong Cojuangco on January 25, 1933, Cory, as she was nicknamed, was the fourth of five children in a large, landed, well-educated, and political family. On her father's side, she descended from ethnic Chinese immigrants who made their fortune in trading and land (Komisar, 1987, p. 13). Her father, "Don Pepe," became a congressman, and his father was a senator. In her mother's family, her grandfather was a senator, a vice presidential candidate, and a member of the U.S.-sponsored Philippine Commission, which exercised both executive and legislative powers for the islands (Brunstetter, 1989, p. 31).

In her nuclear family, Don Pepe was patient, considerate, soft spoken, and introverted, while her mother Demetria, know as "Doña Metring," was a strong disciplinarian. Doña Metring enthusiastically supported the political efforts of her family through monetary contributions and campaigning (Crisostomo, 1986, p. 12). Apparently, Cory was a quiet child and did not participate in any family political campaigns (Komisar, 1987, p. 13).

Education was highly valued in Cory's household. Especially significant was that her mother had earned a bachelor's degree in pharmacy. Education of girls is correlated with the education of fathers, but especially highly correlated with the education of mothers. Cory followed this tendency, attending St. Scholastica's, a private girls' elementary school run by Benedictine nuns for the children of the wealthy, where she excelled in mathematics and English and graduated first in her class.

Cory's post-primary education continued at religious-based schools and with considerable academic success. Begun at Assumption Convent High School in Manila, her secondary education was interrupted by the Japanese invasion, during which her family moved to the United States, where she attended Raven Hill Academy in Philadelphia and eventually Notre Dame Convent School in New York. At the College of Mount St. Vincent in New York, Cory majored in French and math, and was known as very religious, attending mass often and participating in the Sodality of Our Lady, a religious society that studied liturgy. This religious school focused on imparting traditional values, including the responsibility of wives to support their husbands' wishes at the expense of their own (Brunstetter, 1989, p. 32). According to a friend of Cory's, they were told "that you must never do anything where your husband would lose face. If there was an argument, you gave in, because it's much more difficult for a man to back down than a woman, you never spoke against your husband publicly; you never did anything that would embarrass him" (Komisar, 1987, p. 14).

Although Cory entered law school at Far Eastern University in Manila after graduating from college in the United States, she left after only one term in order to marry Benigno ("Ninoy") Aquino. They were married on October 11, 1954, after a long courtship but a short engagement. Since the time when they were both nine years old, they had met periodically at gatherings of their families, who were friends. On her return to Manila, they began to date regularly and were married when they were 21.

Moving his new family to his home town of Concepción, in Tarlac, Ninoy immediately became both a political and business success, laying the foundation for future activities. He became the youngest elected mayor at 21, then the youngest elected provincial governor at 28, and eventually the youngest elected senator. During each of these campaigns, Cory was an uncomfortable bystander, appearing in public only when absolutely necessary. During this early political period, Cory was concentrating on bearing and raising children. Indeed:

> Ninoy the politician never demanded much from Cory but made it clear from the start of their marriage that her first priority would be their children. Her primary role as his wife would be that of a mother of their children—and a housewife. . . . Thus, throughout her husband's political career she would stay in the background, never making any public utterance or political statement. She preferred to stay away from the limelight and deliberately tried to avoid close scrutiny by the public. At political rallies, whenever she had to be present, she would decline a seat on the stage, [and] stay at the back of the audience, incognito, and listen to what her husband told [her] non-stop far into the night. (Crisostomo, 1986, p. 14)

During her presidency, when reflecting on her role, her husband, and her marriage, Cory was quoted as saying:

> My husband, well, he was a male chauvinist. He never wanted it said that I was influencing him in anything. I didn't mind. Really, because mine was a very private role. And I figured, "Look, you can do what you like in public life; I'm going to make sure that these children of ours will turn out to be good and responsible citizens." And so we managed very well. . . . If you think your husband is really worthwhile, then you just have to accept. (Sheehy, 1986, p. 5)

With these words, Cory seemed to be revealing that the counsel of the nuns at college had been extremely influential in defining her relationships within her family. Only later, when her family was shaken by assassination, and she was no longer overshadowed by a charismatic husband-leader, did she finally move into a more public role.

Ninoy used each of his visible, political positions as a forum for exposing weaknesses of political situations. During years of increasing political activity, Ninoy worked with the Huks and even sold the farm in Concepción to the tenants (Komisar, 1987, p. 34), thereby establishing radical political credentials. By 1972, then-President Ferdinand Marcos had declared martial law—under false pretenses, it is now known ("The Philippines," 1988)—and was able to arrest and detain vocal "critics" such as Ninoy. Even while in prison, Ninoy contested elections and developed the slogan "*Laban*," meaning "Fight." Tortured and traumatized, Ninoy experienced a religious awakening that sustained him during his incarcerations of seven and a half years, during which Cory was forced into an assertive, public role that increasingly encompassed political dimensions. According to *Time* correspondent Sandra Burton (1989):

> While Ninoy was experiencing his epiphany, his wife was undergoing a crash course in realpolitik. Martial law had forced shy, sheltered Cory to shed the comfortable anonymity of housewife and mother and assume the sensitive role of liaison between her husband and the outside world. For the first time since their marriage, she had become an integral part of the political milieu he inhabited. As she and Nena Diokno canvassed the military bureaucracy for news of their husbands and petitioned the Supreme Court to produce them, she encountered firsthand the arbitrary power wielded by those who administered the vast martial law apparatus. (p. 92)

During this difficult period, Cory developed confidence in her ability to analyze politics and to speak for a political agenda. Her sustenance came from tutoring sessions with her husband and her close relationship with the Catholic Church. She was especially affected during his hunger strike and the time when he was sentenced to death. Eventually, Marcos offered him freedom if he would leave the country, an offer that he did not take up until he needed triple bypass surgery. During their exile from 1980 to 1983, while living with their children in the United States, Ninoy and Cory continued their "study" of politics. Deciding to contest the parliamentary elections declared by Marcos in 1984, Ninoy returned to the Philippines on August 21, 1983, to be met by an assassin's bullet. Cory would now begin her personal political odyssey, driven by her commitment to represent the ideals and perspectives that she shared with her husband.

When organizing Ninoy's funeral and the events surrounding it, Cory illustrated considerable political acumen by suggesting that "she would refuse to accept [Marcos's condolences] unless he released all political prisoners as proof of his sincerity" (Burton, 1989, p. 139). This was the strategy of a savvy politician, which, no doubt, by now she had become.

THE FIRST WOMAN BECOMES PRESIDENT

However much Aquino had been prepared for a "background" role in the political arena, she was catapulted into the limelight during her campaign and presidency. Based on a feudal political culture in which there is a "cult of personality" (Abinales, n.d.) surrounding a leader, Aquino groomed herself to present an image that was compatible with her personality and her perceived need of the people. During the presidential campaign, Aquino was seen in the Catholic Philippines as "almost a Madonna, a saint in contrast to the wily, corrupt Marcos" (Richter, 1990–1991). In terms of imaging herself, she was charged by some detractors with wanting only to be "mother" of her nation, but she did, from time to time, take positions on strategic policy issues (Cariño, 1987b, p. 1). According to U.S. Representative Stephen Solarz, Aquino was a "woman who has a steel fist inside a velvet glove" (quoted in Gonzales-Zap, 1987, p. 223).

During the campaign, Aquino emphasized her commitment to such values as democracy, equity, fairness, and efficiency, but Marcos replied by saying that "women should confine their preaching to the bedroom" ("The Philippines," 1988). Marcos often accused her of having no experience in running a government. Aquino replied with statements such as, "I admit that I have no experience in lying, cheating, stealing, killing political opponents" (Gonzales-Zap, 1987, p. 107).

> Cory electrified the populace. It is said that even the famous campaign of Ramon Magsaysay paled in contrast with hers. In a country obsessed with stars, she became the country's newest superstar. Her simplicity, forthrightness and inner strength turned out to be her biggest assets. Cory is adored because she is the antithesis of the infamous family. (Lallana, 1992)

During the campaign she emphasized general issues of justice and fairness but also mentioned specific positions, including amnesty for guerrillas, dismantling of monopolies controlled by Marcos and his friends, release of political prisoners, negotiations with the Communists, a cease-fire with rebels, and "true land reform" (Komisar, 1987, p. 80).

In addition to the issue differences, the process of her campaign was in strong contrast to that of Marcos. Aquino personally visited 68 of 73 provinces and held more than a thousand rallies, but used no television commercials. Marcos visited only 22 provinces and held only 34 rallies, but made extensive use of television. It was also reported that the Catholic bishops told their poor parishioners to take money offered by the Marcos politicians, but to vote their consciences in the actual balloting (Komisar, 1987, p. 92).

During the elections themselves, NAMFREL, the National Citizens' Movement for Free Elections, which was backed by the Catholic Church, business organizations, and labor and civil groups, organized poll watching and a "quick count" process. Although the official Election Commission announced Marcos the winner, its computer officials walked out, saying that the announced tallies did not reflect the computer totals (Gonzales-Zap, 1987, p. 114). After NAMFREL announced Aquino as the winner, Marcos declared himself the president, and widespread political reactions occurred. Boycotts and strikes followed, as did large rallies of up to 2 million people each. The Marcos regime had been under pressure before and had always been able to suppress dissent. What made this situation escalate into a successful "revolution"?

Both external and internal factors, in addition to the character and the image of the standard-bearer, Cory Aquino, led to the eventual exile of Marcos and the installation of Aquino as president. Global visibility of persistent problems and lack of popular political participation in the Philippines encouraged allies to bring pressure for change, as well as strengthened national forces for change. In particular, the United States, formerly an unwavering ally of Marcos, sent signals that Marcos might be assisted in gracefully leaving. Internally, it was apparent that Aquino was not just another politician wanting power, but an innocent and inured party within a rambunctious political scene, seeking the presidency for popular purposes and with a style and message that depended less on money than on genuine popularity, representing personal appeal as well as resonance with the felt needs of the people.

The now-famous "people power" revolution included diverse participants. Fittingly, Aquino described the February epic as "a revolution where the nun and the soldier have equal place" (Gonzales-Zap, 1987, p. 198). The EDS (Epifanio de los Santos Avenue) demonstrations, which took place along three kilometers between two army camps, lasted four nights and days. Three recorded testimonials indicate a middle-class bias to the EDSA events:

(1) If we clearly analyze the people who've been there, we can clearly tell that they were not farmers or fishermen; they were students, teachers, religious people, businesspersons, employees, etc. . . . people from the lower stratum of our society were not there and were not represented . . .

(2) The poor couldn't be very "active" because they have their own lives to support. They do not have extra money to spend for rallies and food to keep them overnight in the streets. When I interviewed vendors, they said that they were there for the business . . .

(3) The revolution entailed costs like sandwiches, flowers, etc. to be given away and that is something the masses do not have. Second, the leadership of Mrs. Cory Aquino is identified mainly as middle class because of her degree of intellectual growth, wealth and social position. (Cruz, 1989, pp. 246–248)

Thus, factors greater than Aquino assisted in her victory, but her character, her platform, and her ability to mobilize people made her an ideal standard-bearer for a renewal of Philippine politics.

<hr>

THE "CORY AGENDA": FROM PEOPLE POWER TO PEOPLE'S POWER

During her presidency, Aquino emphasized process not policy. Specifically, she sought to present a dramatically different model of the exercise of presidential power from that of President Marcos. By developing a "soft" leadership process based on reconciliation and representation, Aquino articulated in word and deed a sharp contrast to the confrontational and personal regime of Marcos. Within a few months of her victory, commentators noted that her program seemed to be "against dictatorship," rather than "for developing the country" (De Dios, 1986, p. 1). Other matters were delegated to her ministers. Throughout her presidency, Aquino articulated policy goals but seemed to lack skills to work effectively with technical people to forge plans of action. Many studies and elegant concepts were not sufficiently transformed into practical programs for development. Aquino's three priorities were chosen in order to establish a framework for development based on rule of law, peace, and participation.

During Aquino's presidency, especially because of the dramatic political shifts that led to her election, there were opportunities not only to establish a new style of leadership but also to create a new political and policy agenda. There were many government committees, commissions, and reports. It is unclear to what extent Aquino exercised control or influence over these agenda-setting exercises. A comparison of her expressed values and her public pronouncements with the recommendations of these reports indicates that she exercised considerable influence, though not complete control, over these reports. This assessment supports the concept of a "soft" leadership style.

Early in her presidency, Aquino had to deal with the complex problem of holdovers from the Marcos era in the legislature, the judiciary, and the bureaucracy. Although some interpreted her desire for "reconciliation, not revenge" as a "soft" inability to move swiftly and decisively, she dismissed and requested resignations from key people at all levels of government, appointing transitional caretakers until elections could be held under the soon-to-be formulated and ratified constitution. The "wholesale firing of more than 70 provincial governors, 1,600 mayors and more than 10,000 council members set off a storm of bitter protests" (Komisar, 1987, p. 132) that continued nearly a year.

Although during the campaign Aquino promised, in a long letter to the bureaucracy, "I will uphold the security of tenure of the civil service. Those of you who have performed your duties competently will be protected" (Cariño, 1987a, p. 271), she gave her government full authority to purge all elected and appointed officials under the authority of the transitional Freedom Constitution. This purge, lasting for one year and until ratification of the new constitution, resulted in severe morale problems for two reasons: Not every removal was justified, and removals went beyond and below positions of authority (Cariño, 1987a, p. 273). Although Aquino cultivated the personal image of being understanding and conciliatory, she armed her ministers with powerful weapons of arbitrary power, which they apparently used unevenly. "More than one-third of career executive service officials (CESOs), the highest civil service level, lost their positions" (Cariño, 1987a, p. 274).

The first Report of the Presidential Commission on Government Reorganization (PCGR) emphasizes five guiding principles that deal primarily with process issues, with strong emphasis on wide political participation:

   (1) promotion of private sector initiatives

   (2) decentralization of authority and responsibility to local governments

   (3) cost effectiveness through elimination of gaps and overlapping functions among government organizations

   (4) popular participation in government, especially in increased efficiency in delivery of public services

   (5) public accountability (Iglesias, 1988)

In the following six years, these principles, in fact, did serve as guidelines for public policy decision making. Unfortunately, application of principles sometimes went awry, as in one case when four agencies were abolished, but nine were created (Cariño, 1987a, p. 277). Aquino relied heavily on private sector executives for advice on government policy, sometimes including them as volunteers in government without pay, but claiming expenses far beyond civil servant salaries. Popular participation was reflected in a renewed emphasis on local governments, including elections at the local level, encouragement of regionalization, and government cooperation with nongovernmental organizations (NGOs) in service delivery and even sponsorships of the development of grassroots organization, such as the Kabisig or Linking Arms Movement, designed to stimulate local democracy, economic development, and probably methods to circumvent regular politics and government ("Congressmen Agree," 1990).

    For a substantive agenda, Aquino emphasized economic development and peaceful resolution of long-standing internal conflicts, the latter oriented toward improvement of both process and outcomes in politics. Although neither economic development nor peaceful resolution of rebellions can be viewed as fully successful, there have been both progress and reversals in both economic and political arenas, largely dependent on occurrence of expensive disaster relief programs and of periodic coup attempts and increases in insurgency activities.

    In the area of peace, Aquino did grant amnesty to guerrillas, and some took advantage of it, leaving the hinterlands, giving up their arms, and becoming part of the normal populations in their areas. She also repeatedly declared cease-fires with the rebels and attempted reconciliation. While this strategy was often at odds with the advice of her military leaders, she persisted in believing that a peaceful solution could be possible. She released political prisoners, some of whom were absorbed into normal society and some of whom were rearrested for subversive activity. These conciliatory actions created a sense of healing among the people, but this feeling could not be maintained without significant economic progress. When economic prosperity was not forthcoming, rebels and guerrillas were able to continue their localized rebellions, especially on Mindanao, where the people diverge from the national norms ethnically, linguistically, and religiously. And, of course, generating economic development under these tense and distant conditions was especially difficult.

In the economic arena, Aquino encountered strong resistance from the economic elite, as well as from the bureaucracy. Her economic advisers were largely from the ranks of activist business persons who joined the opposition in the last years of the dictatorship (Tolosa, 1987, p. 38). Their preference for economic liberalization was consonant with the self-interest of many Aquino allies, including Aquino-related families. But privatization extended to only a few sectors. The swift dismantling of the sugar and coconut trading monopolies stands as one of the few decisive economic policies of the Aquino presidency (Komisar, 1987, p. 175). Further efforts to privatize hundreds of government corporations, including banks, resorts, and industries, were blocked by the bureaucracy, perhaps seeking to preserve their jobs. Aquino actively sought foreign investment, but issues of debt repudiation delayed actions to improve foreign trade and investment relationships.

Aquino's presidency resembled an uneasy coalition, reflecting the hodgepodge collection of political forces that came together to oust Marcos. After the euphoria of victory, these groups, as well as the "people's revolution" allies, reverted to deep divisions among themselves, based not only on personalities but also on policies. For instance, the military, led by Juan Ponce Enrile, was considered, by and large, loyal to him and to prefer a militant stance against the Communists and rebels. Aquino stated that she wanted to stop the fighting and to reach agreement. Middle-class businesspersons wanted protection of property and investments. Encouraged by the rhetoric of the campaign, mass groups and special interest groups felt that they could express their interests openly, including by taking part in disruptive workers' strikes. Tension evolved between the goals of improving the investment climate and improving social justice. Aquino provided inspiration to many groups, including workers, businesspersons, military, and students, but she was not able to create productive working relationships among them. Temporary electoral coalitions were typical of Philippine politics, often resulting in a conglomeration of strange bedfellows in a coalition government.

The plight of rural farmers was particularly problematic. With fewer than 20% of farmers owning their own land, land reform or redistribution was a perennial social and economic issue. Since the Huk rebellion beginning in the 1920s, there had been agitation for improvement of tenants' rights. Communists took advantage of the skewed ownership patterns in order to organize support in the rural areas. Marcos had started a process of distribution of land for corn and rice. Aquino continued land distribution for corn and rice, but ultimately failed to include other crops or additional land, even though the Aquino campaign led to a shift in emphasis from tenancy rights to redistribution of ownership (Komisar, 1987, p. 179). Some successes encouraged farmers. In 1986, fertilizer prices dropped by a third, and prices of copra at the farm gate almost doubled ("The Philippines," 1988). The Aquino administration could claim some successes, amid controversy about moving too fast and moving too slowly, and represent typical results of coalition politics within a context of strong and vocal interest groups.

Opportunities to pursue social justice goals were limited by pressure from unexpected budgetary needs. For example, an avalanche of natural disasters—the Baguio earthquake, the Mt. Pinatubo volcanic eruption, and repeated typhoons—unduly taxed the capacity of the national budget to provide economic development opportunities. These natural disasters required mobilization of government bureaucracies, reallocation of funds allocated for other purposes to relief funds, and attention to emergency management rather than long-term economic reform and development. Continuing political uprisings or rebellions in the south also caused attention to be diverted from economic development concerns.

An assessment after the first 1,000 days, or what can now be viewed as the midterm of her presidency, gave Aquino a mixed review. While economic elites continued to find opportunities for income and wealth generation, the poor and landless were little better off. A survey released by the Philippine *Inquirer* of Manila residents "gave Aquino an overall grade of 73%, with failing grades for her efforts in law enforcement, political stability, counterinsurgency, government services and her administration's anti-corruption drive. Her best score, a 77, was awarded for her efforts to revive the economy" (Lerner, 1988).

On the positive side, in just two years:

> A freedom constitution was proclaimed so that Aquino could rule by decree and sweep away the corrupted constitution and political institutions of the Marcos era; a national plebiscite overwhelmingly approved a new, transparently democratic constitution; a new Senate and House of Representatives were chosen in the first truly free elections since before martial law; and towns throughout the country elected their own local governments. ("The Philippines," 1988)

On the other hand, internal "leftist" critics accused Aquino of ignoring human rights abuses in order to placate the military, and of abandoning genuine land reform by signing a watered-down bill to appease the big landowners. Critics on the right faulted her for lack of determination to defeat the Communist insurgency and to end rampant graft and corruption (Lerner, 1988). With the large number of unresolved problems and the relatively disruptive transition from Marcos cronyism, it was remarkable that Aquino achieved even a small measure of progress.

AGENDA PRIORITY: DEMOCRATIC LEADERSHIP STYLE

During the campaign, it was alleged that in response to an army offer to take over militarily and install Aquino as president, Aquino said, "I am not here for power. I want to know if the people really support me, so we must go through with this election" (Burton, 1989, p. 381). Repeatedly, Aquino asserted that she did not seek absolute and arbitrary power, but rather hoped to create a framework for institutional sharing of legitimate power. Her goal of redemocratization and her style of leadership reflected this viewpoint.

The Filipino political structures and bureaucracy historically were centralized, a tendency that was exacerbated by Marcos. For instance, during martial law, Marcos decreed an integrated reorganization plan, including the creation of the National Economic and Development

Authority (NEDA), which consolidated central planning, resource allocation, and implementation functions that had been performed or shared by different agencies. Although Marcos chose to chair this body (Endriga, 1989, p. 313), which continued as a key coordinating body in Filipino government, Aquino took a more hands-off approach, leaving operational leadership to her ministers:

> Centralization in a person who does not enjoy exercising power can immobilize government. When everyone wants the personal attention of Cory Aquino, she may postpone decisions indefinitely, unless forced by oncoming events. The May 1st (1986) proclamations on labor waited practically up to the end of the year before they were substantiated by executive order. (Cariño, 1987a, p. 281)

Although Aquino tried to model a "softer" version of executive leadership, it was uncertain whether she fully communicated the potential efficacy of a more limited presidential role. Did she give strong-enough direction to government and to the people?

During the transition-to-constitution period, Aquino had access to wide-ranging powers as president, but she exercised those powers in favor of redemocratization, through reestablishing freedom of the press and access to information and releasing all political prisoners. The 1987 constitution, representing the third Filipino experience in redemocratization after 1899 and 1935, guaranteed local autonomy, separation of powers, and public accountability. It drastically restricted the powers of the presidency in matters of monetary policy, treaty making, appointments, nepotism, and conflict of interest, and included a provision limiting the president to one term of six years, without possibility of reelection (De Guzman, 1988, pp. 278–280).

Aquino's emphasis on process over policy resulted in great importance being placed on leadership style. Attempting to encourage the development of a new political culture, one characterized by rule of law, tolerance, and participation, and in sharp contrast to that of Marcos, Aquino deliberately made decisions slowly and only after elaborate and lengthy consultations with as many people and groups as feasible. Although accused of weakness and delay, Aquino did not waiver from her decision that the most important legacy of her presidency would be her presidential leadership style. This commitment often led to situations in which the content of policy decisions took a subordinate role to the process of achieving those decisions.

For example, within her newly formed cabinet, Aquino established an open style of discussion and:

> encouraged debate so that she could hear different views before making her own decisions. She did not pretend to know everything, but could not be easily swayed or forced to come up with a quick answer. She would sit and listen. When she reached a decision and said, "This is what I feel," the discussion would stop. (Komisar, 1987, p. 129)

Most policy making was delegated to the ministries involved, and Aquino did not like to become involved in policy debates among ministers, preferring for them to develop compromises or decisions among themselves. On the other hand, she "would get involved immediately where there was a question of personalities rather than issues and try to smooth over the conflicts" (Komisar, 1987, p. 129). With a cabinet of diverse and often conflicting ministers, each of whom had considerable expertise and experience, this strategy, which appeared to be akin to that of settling disputes among children, might have been successful. On the other hand, this style of conflict management may have given undue emphasis to a congenial family-like atmosphere in the cabinet over needed arguments and decisive stands on controversial policy issues.

Although Aquino encouraged debate, she was occasionally exasperated by the fractiousness of the cabinet. It has been reported that during one particularly heated turf battle, Aquino said, "I'm the one who makes the decisions . . . I've had it, I just have to remind you I'm the president, and if you cannot respect me, there's no way we can work together" (Komisar, 1987, pp. 129–130). Apparently she was neither authoritarian nor entirely carefree about running meetings, and perhaps cabinet ministers had difficulty associating the authority of her position with her nonauthoritarian style, occasionally requiring her to remind them. Critics have charged that, rather than building or strengthening a real coalition of political forces in the cabinet, she relied on close family members for counsel.

Aquino's style as president evolved from her sense that the country needed assurance and the continued symbol of freedom. She gave frequent speeches and made appearances before civic and professional organiza-tions, as well as traveling to the other islands often to "meet with local labour, church, farm and business leaders in well stage-managed and pub-licized 'consultations'" (Komisar, 1987, p. 135). Because the presidency was virtually the only national political institution during the year of transition to constitution, Aquino was determined to use her visibility to reassure the Filipino people concerning stability, reconciliation, and democracy. Al-though her frantic travel and speaking pace left her relatively less time to work on policy development, she placed peace and democratization above substantive policy as her higher goals.

The unique relationship between Aquino and the Filipino public could have been exploited more thoroughly through an early and planned pro-gram of citizen mobilization. Although she need not have mobilized them in favor of a particular issue, she could have mobilized them just to discuss issues. People were looking to her for cues, but she did not lead adequately (Lallana, 1992). Later, in 1990, in a last-ditch effort to capitalize on her popularity, she launched the Kabisig movement for development efforts based on local NGOs and movement-style organizations. It was likely that the real power of the "people power revolution" would eventually be realized by workers, religious activists, and the urban and rural poor, who might be mobilized for action in the future (Doronila, 1988) through something like Kabisig, the Linking Arms Movement ("The Philippines," 1990), organized from the top, or modeling a bottom-up movement from the historical precedent of February 1986.

Early in Aquino's presidency, her office was criticized for delay in issu-ance of executive orders, which, at that time, during the interim Freedom Constitution, had the force of law (Iglesias, 1988). For instance, at a time when officials and the people at large were eager for direction, the PCGR, which was given 90 days (from March 12 to June 12), submitted its report on June 27, securing cabinet approval on August 13. Given the magni-tude of the task, additional days of consultation seem reasonable (Iglesias, 1988). Within nine months, the PCGR produced 2 reports, 45 executive orders, and 13 administrative orders.

But 18 months after the "revolution," Aquino was still beset by delays and somewhat defensive, but honest about the problem. Addressing a group of businesspersons, Aquino confronted the audience, saying, "The issue that really brought you here. The question you all really want to ask, is: Can she hack it? Isn't she weak?" (Clad, 1987, p. 22). She said further:

These are the questions that were asked by all those who have openly challenged my power, authority and resolve, and who have suffered for it. I speak of the shame-faced officers who have abandoned their followers . . . and the failed politicians who made the last places in the last elections and are now trying to find a backdoor to power . . . Well they can forget it. Although I am a woman and physically small, I have blocked all doors to power except elections in 1992. ("The Philippines," 1988)

Another indication of Aquino's fluctuating strength and decisiveness was in relation to the cabinet, which originally was filled with people to whom she owed political debts from the campaign and before. Tensions between the Right and the Left, between the ideologues and the technocrats, and between those with and without a Marcos-era history generated much discussion, few decisions, and often public confusion concerning the direction of government. From November 1986 to September 1987, Aquino engineered several cabinet shuffles and departures, ending up with a team that "makes pretensions to cohesion and efficiency, and was therefore reasonably acceptable to the two groups, the military and business, who had grown most exasperated with Aquino's indecisiveness" ("The Philippines," 1988). Two years later, and more than three years after assuming the presidency, Aquino continued in a similar vein, "I hope that you will be patient with us because we are in a transition period. . . . I promise that this day we will unite and do a better job in serving you" (Brunstetter, 1989, p. 44).

Aquino was also accused of weak substantive leadership. Some policies appeared to be applied inconsistently because some cabinet members deliberately followed strategies opposite to her stated policies. For instance, while she was on a trip abroad, Enrile, apparently with cooperation from Laurel, organized a massive military initiative against the Communists. Although such actions caused Aquino considerable embarrassment both internally and externally, she did not discipline the two men. The ability to endure "many tongues" and even real insubordination might be a sign of humble tolerance, but in a president to whom people look for guidance and leadership, it can appear to be weakness and indecision (Komisar, 1987, pp. 193–195).

Aquino's emphasis on developing a "soft" managerial style based on commitment to democratic participation and openness both with the Filipino people and with her cabinet and senior government officials presented a definite contrast to Marcos's style of authoritarian secrecy and repression. On the other hand, some situations and issues, especially land reform, begged for greater decisiveness, which was not always forthcoming.

SUCCESS IS LEAVING THE PRESIDENCY TO OTHERS

By her own count, Aquino made 93 denials concerning her possible interest in running for the presidency again (Coloma, 1991). But she waited months before finally endorsing a candidate, namely Fidel Ramos, her army chief of staff, and the eventual winner, on January 25, 1992, less than three months before the scheduled election. Even after this announcement and her repeated denials, speculation continued that she would contest. Apparently presuming that a woman incumbent would want to or need to run in order to defeat a "famous and female" Marcos, commentators increased pressure on her after Imelda Marcos declared her candidacy. In fact, Uduardo ("Dandling") Cojuangco, Aquino's estranged cousin, ably represented the Marcos faction and outpolled Imelda Marcos.

It was significant that Aquino decided to support a limited six-year term for president in the 1987 constitution and to abide by the provision when her term was nearing completion. Unlike many other national leaders, she yielded neither to party nor to popular pressure. This decision reflected her commitment to democratic processes and her belief in sharing power, rather than holding on to it tenaciously. While she assumed the "umbrella" candidacy for president reluctantly, she campaigned enthusiastically, and with considerable political interest and acumen. Once president, she governed thoughtfully and deliberately, but avoided developing the perspective that she was all-powerful or indispensable. Her respect for sharing power and the rule of law must be considered a major legacy to the redemocratization of the Philippines.

In describing her post-presidency plans, Aquino stated that she would work with NGOs, which she believed were able to deliver services to the people in a more cost-effective and more personal manner than government organizations (*Economist*, February 1, 1992). Although Aquino was certainly financially comfortable and had a large and supportive family, she was ably setting an example of how a former president could look forward to contributing to her country and its development. Examples of peaceful transition between presidents should not be taken for granted; they have been relatively rare and must be valued by those interested in promoting democratic ideals.

GENDER ISSUES IN THE AQUINO PRESIDENCY

On balance, Aquino made an important contribution to the experience of women leaders, not so much in the policies that she pursued as in the style of governance that she modeled. She did not follow a traditional feminist or pro-woman substantive agenda. She did not champion issues of divorce, birth control, or reproductive freedom. Her personal and political relationship to the Catholic Church seemed to have prevented her from pursuing policies in support of such issues. The church assisted in the struggle against Marcos and in the settling of issues of candidacy for president (Youngblood, 1987). Although her personal opinions were not easily disentangled from the views of her church, Aquino was clearly not antiwoman. In the end, however, she did not actively pursue any courses of action that focused on modern women's issues.

On the other hand, many of the proclaimed policy priorities of her government likely had a positive impact on women, considering that she attempted to focus attention on the poor, and the empowerment of the poor, through her campaign and her development of the Kabisig movement to bring power and resources to local NGOs and movements. Land reform, loans to small enterprises, and social services all benefited women, as they are among the poorest of the poor.

Aquino's biggest contributions were found in the open and democratic style of government that she insisted upon in the 1987 constitution; in her own behavior with her cabinet and with the public; and, as often as possible, in her appointed and elected government colleagues. This style of open and democratic governance had two important meanings for women. First, in more open and democratic systems, those previously denied access to public decision making, such as women, were more able to gain positions and influence. In fact, in the 1992 elections, two candidates for the presidency were women and one of them, Miriam Santiago, achieved a relatively close second place to the eventual winner.

Second, a "softer" style of leadership is more typical of that learned by women in their families and often practiced by women in institutions in which they work, thereby encouraging women to be more comfortable in government positions of power and influence. Aquino appointed many women to executive positions in her government. Many, though not all, of them assisted in empowering other women and in democratizing the bureaucratic culture in which they worked. The Chair of the Civil Service Commission, Patricia Santo Tomas, was one executive who worked to promote qualified women and to open up decision-making processes to workers of all levels in the bureaucracy. Santo Thomas encouraged her staff to develop organization-wide strategic and operational planning, to pioneer onsite child care, and to develop positions of "equality advocates" to monitor and deal with gender-related grievances at centers in regional offices. When Aquino's political appointees, both male and female, pursued policies that were pro-woman, Aquino did not object. She had delegated authority to her appointees.

The legacy of "softly" managing in government for six years during periods of insurgency, coups, natural disasters, difficult economic times, and often chaotic politics is one that left a lasting impression and strong expectations for democracy in the future.

In her final "state of the nation" address on July 22, 1991, Aquino recalled the trauma of Ninoy's murder and the martial law and corruption of the Marcos regime. She chronicled the economic difficulties and natural disasters that had befallen the country during her six-year presidency. But most of all, she emphasized her effort to redemocratize the country— to bring openness and cooperation to the political arena, at both central and local levels. In the face of difficult circumstances, she persisted in her commitment to democratic methods of governance. In spite of slowness and compromises that were often criticized by political opponents, neutral observers, and even staunch sympathizers, she persisted in her pattern of open consultation and deliberate delegation and decentralization. For Aquino's unwavering commitment to democracy for the country and openness and consultation in government, her presidency will be remembered.

REFERENCES

Abinales, P.N. (n.d.). *The post Marcos regime, the non-bourgeois opposition and the prospects of a Philippine "October."* Unpublished manuscript.

Arcellana, E.Y. (1969). Indigenous political institutions. In J.V. Abueva & R. De Guzman (Eds.), *Foundations and dynamics of Filipino government and politics* (pp. 38–42). Manila: Bookmark.

Brunstetter, M.P. (1989). *Women in power: Meir, Thatcher and Aquino.* Paper presented at the annual meeting of the American Political Science Association, Washington DC.

Burton S. (1989). *Impossible dream: The Marcoses, the Aquinos, and the unfinished revolution.* New York: Warner.

Cariño, L. (1987a). *The Aquino government and the civil service: Lessons for future regime bureaucracy interaction, A Filipino agenda for the 21st century: Solidarity conference.* Manila: Solidaridad.

Cariño, L. (1987b). *A year after the people power revolution: The shotgun marriage between the Aquino government and the bureaucracy.* Paper presented at the Asian and Pacific Development Centre, Kuala Lumpur, Malaysia.

Clad, J. (1987, November 5). Cory comes out fighting. *Far Eastern Economic Review.*

Coloma, Roberto. Peril ebbs, but time running out for Aquino. 25 February 1991. *Chicago Sun Times.*

Congressmen agree to shun Kabisig. (1990, June 28). *Daily Globe* (Manila).

Corpuz, O.D. (1969). The cultural foundations of Filipino politics. In J.V. Abueva & R. De Guzman (Eds.), *Foundations and dynamics of Filipino government and politics* (pp. 15–17). Manila: Bookmark.

Crisostomo, I.T. (1986). *Cory: Profile of a president.* Manila: J. Kriz.

Cruz, I.R. (1989). People power Kuno. In W.V. Villacorta, I.R. Cruz, & M.L. Brillantes (Eds.), *Manila.* Manila: De Le Salle University Press.

De Dios, E.S. (1986, August 28). *Can there be recovery without reforms?* Paper presented at the Mid-Year Economic Review.

De Guzman, R.P. (1988). Towards redemocratization of the political system. In R.P. De Guzman & M.A. Reforma (Eds.), *Government and politics of the Philippines* (pp. 267–282). Singapore: Oxford University Press.

Doronila, A. (1988, November 13). Understanding what people power can and can't do. *Manila Chronicle.*

Endriga, J.N. (1989). Bureaucracy in an authoritarian political system: The case of the Philippines. In R.B. Jain (Ed.), *Bureaucratic politics in the Third World.* New Delhi: Gitanjli.

Estrada-Claudio, S. (1990–1991). The psychology of the Filipino woman. *Review of Women's Studies, 1*(2), 1–9.

Gonzales-Zap, M. (1987). *The making of Cory.* Quezon City: New Day.

Iglesias, G.U. (1988). *Government reorganization under Aquino: Issues and problems.* Paper presented at the Northern Luzon Conference on Public Administration, Baguio City, Philippines.

Komisar, L. (1987). *Corazon Aquino: The story of a revolution.* New York: George Brazillar.

Lallana, E.C. (1992). *Rethinking the February revolution.* Quezon City: Kalitran.

Lerner, M. (1988, November 22). After first 1,000 days, Aquino gets mixed grades. *Washington* (D.C.) *Times.*

Richter, L.K. (1990–1991). Exploring theories of female leadership in South and Southeast Asia. *Pacific Affairs, 63*, 524–540.

Rodriguez, L.L. (1990). Patriarchy and women's subordination in the Philippines. *Review of Women's Studies, 1*(1), 15–25.

Sheehy, G. (1986). The passage of Corazon Aquino. *Springfield Journal-Register*, "Parade."

Steinberg, D.J. (1990). *The Philippines: A singular and plural place.* Boulder, CO: Westview Press.

Tancango, L.G. (1990). Women and politics in contemporary Philippines. *Philippine Journal of Public Administration, 34*, 323–364.

Tapales, P. (1988). *The role of women in public administration in the Philippines.* Unpublished doctoral dissertation, Northern Illinois University.

The Philippines. (1990, July 5). *Far Eastern Economic Review.*

The Philippines: A question of faith. (1988, May 7). *Economist.*

The status of women in the Philippines. (n.d.). *Philippine Values Digest, 3*(2).

Tolosa, B.T., Jr. (1987). Constraints on democratic consolidation and the economic ideology of the Aquino government. In. R.J. Bonoan, A.C. Condon, & S.S. Reyes (Eds.), *The Aquino government and the question of ideology.* Quezon City: Phoenix.

Wurfel, D. (1988). *Filipino politics: Development and decay.* Manila: Ateneo de Manila University Press.

Youngblood, R.L. (1987). The Corazon Aquino miracle and the Philippine churches. *Asian Survey, 27*, 1240–1255.

3

Gro Harlem Brundtland of Norway

Sarah L. Henderson

Gro Harlem Brundtland, to many observers, seems larger than life, possessing extraordinary political powers to achieve the miraculous. She was once described by a journalist as a "Viking warrior incarnate, smiting others down not with the sword but with the strength of her beliefs" (O'Hanlon, 1994). And when Brundtland was preparing to meet fellow Prime Minister Margaret Thatcher, the British press portrayed it as a battle between "The Iron Lady versus the Super Woman" (Brundtland, 2002, p. 253). Back in Norway, she was such a dominant force in national politics that many cartoonists merely drew her shoes and ankles, with other tiny politicians scurrying around her feet (BBC News, 1998). At the same time, most Norwegians refer to her simply by her first name, Gro, which is Brundtland's preference, or affectionately as "landsmoderen," or "mother of the nation," a reflection of her enormous popularity, lack of ostentation, egalitarianism, and desire to create better lives for all of Norway's citizens. These values have driven her in her long and successful career in politics at the national and international levels.

Gro Harlem Brundtland was a multifaceted trailblazer. In 1981, at the age of 41, Brundtland became Norway's first female prime minister, as well as its youngest, heading Norway's Labor Party. She was to serve three more terms (1986–1989; 1990–1996), shepherding Norway through turbulent economic waters in the 1980s and 1990s. Through her advocacy on environmental issues, Brundtland put Norway, a small, Nordic country, on the international map through her leadership on the World Commission on Environment and Sustainability and Development. Their resulting report, *Our Common Future*, put now-commonplace international concerns on the global agenda: sustainable development, energy consumption, population problems, and global poverty. Throughout all of her work, she maintained her fierce commitment to social democracy, a vision of society that combines support for a market economy with a strong role for the state in providing generous social safety nets as antidotes to socioeconomic inequality. She viewed the state as an agent of progressive change at all levels of governance—local, national, and international and helped cement Norway's global reputation as an affluent yet socially progressive society.

Even in an egalitarian society such as Norway, as a woman, Brundtland shattered a number of glass ceilings. A staunch feminist, Brundtland developed groundbreaking approaches to promote gender equality across a wide array of areas, ranging from political leadership to child care and parental leave policies. Through personal example and designing proactive policy, she paved the way for other women to join her or follow her, taking their own paths to power. She advocated for gender equality at the international level, emerging as a powerful voice for women at UN-sponsored international conferences in Cairo and Beijing. In addition, and unlike many other female political leaders, she "managed to carve out a full personal life—a long, strong marriage and four children. Privately as well as publicly, the message of her career has been that you can be a woman, especially concerned about women, and no less whatever else you may be—businessperson, professional, national leader" (Matthews, 1996, p. A21). When she voluntarily resigned as prime minister at the peak of her popularity and power in 1996, she did not quietly retreat from the political realm. She is one of the few female politicians (along with former Chilean president Michelle Bachelet) to leave a career in national politics only to take up a very successful second career in international politics, as head of the World Health Organization from 1998 to 2003 and then as UN General Secretary BanKi-moon's Special Envoy on Climate Change. She currently serves on the Council of Elders, an international nongovernmental organization of public figures noted for their diplomatic abilities to work on solutions for seemingly insurmountable problems such as climate change, gender inequality, poverty, and conflict resolution. Over her long political career, Gro Harlem Brundtland successfully juggled multiple roles—political leader, diplomat, and mother—and led Norway through turbulent waters at home and dramatically reshaped Norway's position in the global arena.

CONTEXT

Norway is one of four Scandinavian countries (along with Denmark, Finland, and Sweden) that constitute, in the words of one scholar, "a social laboratory for the Western World" (Einhorn & Logue, 2007, p. 65). These four countries in the post–World War II era pioneered policies that presented a "third way" between free market capitalism and authoritarian statism, and they currently share a distinct identity as countries that combine economic wealth with generous and extensive welfare systems, creating societies of relative equality and broadly shared prosperity. In addition, Scandinavian countries are characterized by high levels of gender equality; women make up a significant proportion of the general workforce, and they have some of the highest levels of political representation in the world. Politically, the Scandinavian model is a social-democratic one; political equality can only be achieved in the presence of some level of socioeconomic equality between classes and sexes, and their countries' parliamentary systems are built around vigorous coalitions that govern based on a political culture that values consensus and compromise in building this vision. In the international arena, Scandinavian countries, though small, have leveraged their size to maximum benefit, and have taken leading roles in collaborative governance through international organizations such as the United Nations, focusing on issues such as environmental sustainability, poverty reduction, conflict prevention and reconciliation, and the promotion of democracy and human rights as universal values. Nonetheless, the Scandinavian model is not static nor free of conflict, and since the 1970s, the Scandinavian model has faced challenges. Changing global and regional economic pressures (such as the discovery of oil in Norway and the expansion of the European Union), new social challenges such as the growing presence of non-Western European immigrants and demographic changes have led to voter realignment, increased changes in government, and recalibrations of the famed welfare edifice in all countries. In the Norwegian case, throughout the 1980s and 1990s, Gro Harlem Brundtland led the Labor Party and, for much of that time, the nation, through this process of recalibration, helped the country to successfully weather a number of political, economic, and social transformations in an increasingly globalized world. Let's now turn to Norway's evolution within this larger Scandinavian picture.

Although the era of the Vikings is long past, echoes of these feared, seafaring warriors battling against hostile climates and communities reverberate still in the 21st century in terms of shaping Norway's national identity. As Europe's northernmost country, Norway's terrain is rugged, dotted with high plateaus, steep fjords, mountains, and fertile valleys; and, except for a border with Sweden, surrounded by sea. Two-thirds of the country is tundra, rock, or snowfields, and only about 3% of the land is arable and, combined with its northern location, the country experiences a very short growing season. Further, despite its lengthy coastline (over 13,000 miles), Norway is a small, sparsely populated country; it is roughly the size of New Mexico, with a population of just under 5 million people (similar to the state of Colorado). Norway's population density is just 16 people per square kilometer, compared with Germany's rate of 233 per square kilometer. Norway's land of snow and ice, bountiful coast, extreme climatic conditions, and thinly populated land all make it more than just a traveler's paradise; these factors have all shaped the national psyche. To paraphrase the great Norwegian playwright Henrik Ibsen, if one wishes to understand Norwegians, one must know Norway. Norwegians are hardy, self-sufficient, independent people comfortable with isolation. At the same time, they are also (along with the other Scandinavian countries) uniquely homogeneous in linguistic, religious, ethnic, and racial terms. Thus, the main social division in Norwegian society is that of economics or class, unlike other patterns of social cleavage that have complicated the politics of many Western European nations. This homogeneity, many argue, has facilitated Norway's consensual, solidaristic, social-democratic model.

Norway is a constitutional monarchy, one in which the king has mainly symbolic value. Although the 1814 Constitution grants significant executive powers to the king, in practice, Norway operates as do most other parliamentary systems; power rests primarily with the Norwegian legislative body, known as the Storting. The leader of the party or bloc of parties that controls a majority of seats is asked by the monarch to form a government and is appointed prime minister. If elections do not produce a clear majority to any party or coalition (a result that happens in Norway with increasing frequency), the leader of the party most likely to be able to form a government is appointed prime minister. The prime minister and his or her cabinet form the Council of State, and members are formally appointed by the king. However, in practice, the Council has to maintain the confidence (support) of the legislature.

Maintaining a government and/or the confidence of the legislature can be difficult as a result of Norway's electoral system. Elections to the now 169-member Storting are held every four years, and seats are distributed according to the logic of proportional representation (parties get legislative representation that is roughly commensurate with the percentage of the vote they receive).[1] In practice, this means that even the parties that "win" the elections by receiving the most votes rarely win a majority of the seats needed to pass legislation (instead, they get a plurality). Therefore, the winning party, whose leader usually makes the first attempt at forming a government, needs to build a parliamentary majority in order to pass legislation and maintain the confidence of the Storting. One option is to formally go into a coalition with ideologically similar parties; participating parties in the coalition usually get to head several key ministries, or push a particular legislative agenda. Another option is to form a "minority" government; the ruling party decides to rely on informal coalitions or shifting alliances with other parties to pass its platform. In Norwegian politics, both scenarios have been common; while Labor Party governments have often maintained minority governments and relied on the informal support of other parties to retain the necessary parliamentary votes, most non-Labor governments have been coalitions.

Yet, even a party that wins the most votes may not end up forming the government, as party leaders may not be able to cobble together a coalition (formal or informal) that can endure, and sometimes a party that comes in second in the elections forms a government, if that party leader is able to muster more broad-based support among other parties in the Storting. For example, in 1981 (an election that turned Brundtland out of office), the Labor Party received the most votes (37.2%) and seats (66); yet, it didn't have enough leftist and centrist allies to form a government, while the second-place Conservative Party did. Further, unlike legislatures in some parliamentary systems, the Storting cannot be dissolved, and there is no opportunity to call for new elections within the four-year election term. Therefore, the possibility that a government will fall if it cannot hold together its coalition or maintain the confidence of the Storting is a reality of Norwegian politics, and increasingly so in the past three decades. This can result in a change in leadership without elections, as elections are fixed, but parliamentary agreements between parties often are not. For example, between 1970 and 1990, Norway held five general elections but was ruled by 10 governments. This rigidity in the election cycle but flexibility in terms of government stability can, in the ideal situation, facilitate compromise, since new elections are not an option, but it also can sometimes lead to gridlock and stalemate, as parties struggle to form support for their legislative policies in the absence of a fresh popular mandate derived from electoral outcomes.

This delicate dance of formal and informal coalition politics has been performed by about 6 of the 13–15 political parties spread across the political spectrum that regularly contest Norwegian elections. The dominant party in this dance in the post–World War II era has been the Norwegian Labor Party, which is a center left party committed to social-democratic values, such as support for a large welfare state and redistributionist policies that reflect its motto, "work for everyone." It has been the largest party in the Storting since the 1927 elections up to the most recent 2009 elections. When Gro Harlem Brundtland first assumed office in 1981, Norway had been ruled by Labor governments in all but six years from 1945 (the three periods were 1963, 1965–1971, and 1972–1973). In particular, the two decades following World War II are widely seen as the Labor Party's "golden era"; Einar Gerhardsen served as Norway's prime minister for two decades, and from 1945 to 1961, the Labor Party controlled a majority (rather than a plurality) of seats in the Storting.

The main center right party, and historically the second-largest party in Norwegian politics, has been the Conservative Party. Like many other center right parties, the conservatives are advocates of economic liberalism and a reduction in taxes and government spending. In addition, the Norwegian Conservative Party has consistently been pro–European Union, supporting Norwegian membership during the 1972 and 1994 referendums. Unlike some other conservative parties, the Norwegian Conservative Party is not socially conservative, and it currently supports policies such as gay adoption rights and gay marriage. It has been a leading voice in Norwegian politics, but a consistent second to the Labor Party. From 1945 to 2009, the party participated in 7 governments, leading 4 of them. (In comparison, the Labor Party has participated in 15 governments, leading all 15.)

Although the Labor Party has continued to play a leading role in forming governments after its "golden era," since the 1960s both the Labor and Conservative parties have been unable to single-handedly form majority governments, and coalition and minority governments have become the norm, rather than the exception. Further, many of these governments have been maintained by a very narrow majority, sometimes of one vote (the result of the 1985 elections, for example). Thus, even though Norway leans left at election time, the Labor Party no longer can claim the mandate that they once had after World War II; and, in fact, both the Labor Party and the Conservative Party have been struggling to redefine their constituencies. In particular, the Labor Party began to lose votes to the right in the 1970s and also has been challenged by parties further to the left, such as the Socialist Left Party, which tend to maintain a more statist approach to the economy and differ with the Labor Party on foreign policy issues such as EU integration and NATO membership.[2] The conservatives also began to lose their traditional constituencies in the 1990s. Other parties, such as the farmer-based Center Party, the Christian Democratic Party, and the Liberal Party have carved out critical (and increasingly larger) constituencies and, as a result, played decisive roles in cementing formal and informal coalitions. In particular, the right-wing Progressive Party, which first emerged as a contender in the 1973 elections, has built a powerful base from its antitax, libertarian, and anti-immigrant rhetoric. Regardless of whether a ruling party chooses to form a majority government or a minority one, smaller parties increasingly have the power to make or break governments, as happened in 1986 and 1990, when the Conservative-led government collapsed after smaller parties quit over policy disagreements.

Labor's enduring if weakening role in nearly every post–World War II government has had a significant impact on the economic and social structure of postwar Norway. It was the architect of Norway's version of the Scandinavian model discussed earlier in this section, the "third way," which successfully combines economic growth with a focus on an expansionist welfare state and tolerant social values to promote high qualities of life for a very high percentage of its citizens. The Labor Party created a welfare state that is one of the most extensive in the world, with free medical care and higher education, along with generous pension and unemployment benefits. The Norwegian state has been able to combine market efficiency and growth with relatively nonconfrontational labor markets, fair distribution of income, and social cohesion. It is this delivery of better quality of lives for its citizens in the post–World War II era that helped cement the Labor Party as the largest and most popular party, not only in Norway, but in other Nordic countries as well.

Further, the Labor Party helped cement a distinct political culture, shared by other political parties, which emphasized compromise as a political virtue, along with empirically based, consensual policy making. In this system, ideology, while never completely absent, nonetheless takes a backseat to facts. In a parliamentary system that is often ruled by coalitions or narrow majorities, the political incentives are to build policies that many across the political spectrum can tolerate. The fact that Norway, as a sparsely populated country, is ruled by a small political elite, in which many are personal friends across party lines, also helps facilitate this. Further, Norway's high levels of interest group organization, particularly in terms of labor organization, means that their views are often incorporated into making and implementing national policy through a routinized process of consultation before, rather than after, legislative initiatives are passed. This method of policy making, called corporatism, has further helped build a political process based on exhaustive fact finding, data collection, extensive consultation and input, deliberative consensus building, and gradual change, rather than extreme shifts in policy.

However, the discovery of offshore oil and gas deposits in the late 1960s wrought dramatic change to Norway and is something that sets it apart from its Scandinavian neighbors. As of 2010, Norway was the second-largest net exporter of natural gas and the seventh-largest exporter of oil in the world. It produces much more than it consumes domestically, and most of the oil and gas is sold abroad, with many of the proceeds pumped back into government coffers and accounting for nearly a third of state income (U.S. Department of State, 2011). The oil and natural gas revenues, which started flowing in the 1970s, have helped transform Norway from one of Europe's poorest countries to one of its richest. This influx of oil revenue also allowed Norway to expand its already generous social welfare system. Wages rose, budget deficits were wiped out, and unemployment fell by 1981 to under 2% of the workforce (Downie, Jr., 1981, p. A26).

However, this much reliance on a natural resource can be a mixed economic blessing in terms of coping with "windfall wealth" and rising expectations, not just in Norway, but in any country whose wealth is based on natural resources. The massive influx of foreign currency can cause the value of domestic currencies (in this case, the kroner), to rise, thereby making other exports uncompetitive, and can also lead to inflation. The dramatic increase in revenues can prompt a large spending (and lending) spree, both in the public and private sectors, as expectations rise over the promise of continued profits. Thus, for example, in the 1970s, in anticipation of growing need (and increasing funds), the Norwegian government increased domestic investment and increased construction of hospitals, schools, and roads. It also borrowed heavily to fund this spending, as there was a significant time lag between the discovery of oil and developing the technology and infrastructure to pump it out and/or refine it. These behaviors, in Norway and elsewhere, may be sustainable if oil revenues continue to pour in; however, prices for natural resources on the international market can be quite volatile, and a significant drop in oil prices can bring dramatic swings in economic performance, as we shall see was the case in Norway in the 1980s. There was also enormous political debate over how quickly Norway should develop its oil production, with business leaders, some trade unionists, and Western European countries pushing for maximizing production (for their consumption habits), while farmers, fishermen, environmentalists, and leftists pushed for lower production goals. As we shall see, one of the country's most contentious political issues has been managing the potential destabilizing effects of this massive influx of dollars into the economy as well as debating what to do with the money.

The impact of oil is not just economic, and many in Norway initially worried that the development of the oil industry in the 1970s would also tear apart traditional Norwegian society, fearing that oil production in the south would lure Norwegians out of industries in small towns in the north. Traditional life, which Norwegians prized, would be altered beyond recognition. Trygve Bratteli, Norway's prime minister (1971–1972; 1972–1976) voiced a common Labor Party concern when he commented: "When I first visited the United States in 1949 I was so impressed by the economic efficiency, high productivity, big cars, high standard of living. The problem for us is how to get similar efficiency without running into the stress, the kind of life where people are sitting in cars for hours to get to work, the crowded subways, always rushing, never taking life easy" (Weintraub, 1975). For a country that perceived itself as a nation of fishers and lumberjacks, the promise of oil wealth was both alluring and destructive.

The discovery of oil also further spurred significant shifts in the country's political allegiances, a shift that was also taking place in many other European countries throughout the 1970s. As mentioned previously, the Labor Party had solidly dominated politics for much of the postwar era. However, by the 1970s, the Labor Party began to lose voters, particularly younger ones, in part due to the larger changes the oil money had wrought in Norwegian society. The oil industry brought with it higher wages (and nicer houses, cars, and vacations) for many, which conflicted with Norwegian traditions of egalitarianism and worker's solidarity of the union-based

Labor Party. Wage inflation also pushed many Norwegians into higher tax brackets of a tax system that already was very progressive, and many younger, affluent Norwegians felt they were not personally reaping the financial benefits of Norway's oil wealth. These younger voters, who were often born into the terms of Norway's generous welfare state, began to resent paying such high taxes to support it.

This created throughout the 1970s a swing to the parties of the political right, particularly among younger voters. As one Norwegian journalist commented about this voter realignment in 1981: "The young born into the affluent welfare state are leaving the [Labor] party. Sons of union workers are now university professors and other well-paid professionals with ski chalets and beach houses. They don't march in May Day parades. They want six-hour days, five-week vacations, lower taxes and take home pay" (Downie, Jr., 1981, p. A26). These younger voters remained committed to the welfare state but also wanted to see lower taxes, a reduction of what they saw as unnecessary public spending, and less government interference in business. As voters began to realign to more centrist and center right parties in the 1970s, the Labor Party struggled to respond cohesively to this shift. Even though the Labor Party continued to lead governments throughout the 1970s, it was in disarray; and by the end of the decade, it was headed by a seemingly indecisive and ill party leader and Prime Minister Odvar Nordli, who struggled to resolve the split between various factions about a number of issues.

Yet, although oil and gas had dramatically reshaped Norway's economic, political, and social landscape in the 1970s and 1980s, fishing remains a small but critical component of Norway's economy. The North Sea, Norway's coastal waters, the Barents Sea, and the Norwegian Sea polar front are all important fishing grounds for Norway, and almost all of Norwegian fish is exported, representing a small (compared to oil) but critical percentage of Norway's income. Norway's fish industry has enormous emotional resonance for Norwegians and is a central component of Norwegians' self-image. In fact, the attachment to this self-image is one of the main reasons why Norway's repeated bids to join the European Union have failed, first in 1972 and later under Brundtland's leadership in 1994.

The decades following the end of World War II were also ones of dramatic change for Norway in the realm of international politics, and the country sought a "third way" in international relations similar to its efforts to design a unique "third way" of social democracy in the domestic arena. Norwegians have traditionally been protective of their sovereignty and wary of integrationism. The country became independent in 1905 after 400 years of Danish rule and another 90 years of union rule with Sweden. During World War II, Norway was invaded by the Germans and occupied, and in the immediate years after liberation, Norway maintained a low profile in foreign policy, with the intention of staying out of conflicts between the major powers as well as any bloc formations. Initially, Norwegians hoped that UN membership, particularly under the leadership of its first secretary general, fellow countryman Trygve Lie, would be sufficient to guarantee security. However, it was impossible to avoid the politics of the Cold War, particularly given that Norway was geographically wedged between the competing sides, and the Soviet Union was a powerful, ideologically driven neighbor with nuclear capabilities. East–West tensions quickly mounted, particularly in the wake of the Communist takeover of Czechoslovakia in 1948, and the Soviet Union's proposal for a defensive alliance similar to the pact it had with Finland triggered a strong reaction in Norway. After a failed attempt to form a Nordic defense alliance, Norway embraced the idea of collective security and was one of the founding signers (along with Denmark) of NATO in 1949, which put Norway firmly in the camp of Western Europe. At the same time, Norway had to engage in a delicate dance between its commitment to NATO and engaging constructively with the USSR, with whom they shared common borders and concerns (such as pollution, management of fishing rights, and the Barents Sea). Norway also consistently made nuclear disarmament a top priority and maintained a principle of nondeployment in the country's territory of nuclear weapons and foreign bases. These principles came head to head with the realities of NATO membership during the height of the Cold War and, as we shall see, controversy over this issue helped propel Gro Harlem Brundtland into a leadership position in 1980.

Norway's relationship with Europe was also a key issue in the 1970s. Was Norway part of the emerging united Europe or should it stay distinct, either in a bloc with other Nordic countries or completely on its own? In the early 1970s, Norway joined Britain, Denmark, and Ireland in negotiating membership of what was then the Six (Belgium, France, Italy, Luxembourg, Netherlands, and West Germany). But in 1972, Norway's membership to the Common Market was put to a referendum and rejected by Norwegian voters (54% to 46%). Similar to the discovery of oil, the debate over membership triggered a much larger issue of what it meant to be Norwegian. Proponents of membership argued that Norway would be "left behind" the rest of Europe, both in terms of trade and economic development as well as in having a voice about international affairs that impacted Europe. NATO membership was not enough to guarantee that Norway would remain central to European politics and economics. Others argued for integration, but with other Nordic economies (Denmark, Sweden, Finland, and Iceland). Similar to the emerging battles over NATO membership, the ruling Labor Party was also split with the left-wing unionists campaigning for a no vote as a way to signal opposition to the increasingly market-driven European economies. The small but influential farming interests argued that membership would mean the destruction of traditional agriculture, for Norway had higher farm prices than those already in the Common Market, and officials estimated that farmers' income would drop by 40% to 50% as a result of membership (*The New York Times*, 1971, p. 1). And the fishing industry feared what EC (European Commission) membership would mean for fishing rights and access to the sea, and how they would fare against competition from EC member fleets. Underneath the economic concerns were the fundamental questions about Norwegian identity as a country of hardy, isolated communities living different kinds of lives than those emerging in Western Europe. One Labor Party politician commented that it was the closest that the country has ever come to a civil war without violence. The voters' decisive rejection led to the downfall of the Labor government, led by then-Prime Minister Trygve Bratteli. The Labor Party was further punished in the general elections the following year in 1973; it lost 12 of its 74 seats in the Storting and most of them to parties further to the left. Although the Labor Party was still able to form a government, it was a sign of future troubles to come— Labor was under assault from all directions, and the golden years of Labor Party dominance were over.

As Labor Party leader and prime minister through parts of the 1970s to the 1990s, Gro Harlem Brundtland was at the helm of steering Norway through these rough waters of shifting political allegiances, increased economic challenges at home and abroad, and shifting geopolitics. Brundtland's biggest challenges were maintaining Norway's distinct "third way" in economic, social, and international policy, as well as the Norwegian political policy making of consensual, open, rationalistic, and deliberative practices given the shifting sands of a changing world in the 1980s and 1990s.

BIOGRAPHICAL SKETCH

Gro Harlem Brundtland was born April 20, 1939, four months before World War II broke out. Literally from birth, Labor Party politics were central to her life. Brundtland' s parents were active in left-wing politics, and when Germany invaded Norway in April 1940, Brundtland' s mother fled to her homeland Sweden with baby Gro. However, her mother returned to Norway to assist her father in their work in the resistance, and Brundtland spent her early years, along with her younger brother Erik, raised by her Swedish grandmother, a trailblazer in her own right who at the age of 24 left her husband to pursue her aspiration to become a lawyer (in the early 1930s, she became the first female lawyer ever to hold public office in Stockholm). By 1945, the Brundtland family had reunited in Norway and, after the war years, her father, a doctor by training, moved from the underground resistance to part of the government and served as a Labor Party cabinet member, first as Minister of Social Affairs (1955–1961) and then as Minister of Defense (1961–1965). As a daughter of an extremely political active family, Gro also became deeply steeped in Labor Party politics, as her family residence was often the center of evening and late-night gatherings of Labor Party luminaries; and politics was a popular discussion topic at all hours of the day. By the age of 7, she had joined the Progress Group, the Labor Party–inspired organization for children, where she also socialized with other children of Labor Party activists and politicians. These informal connections and friendships, as well as the exposure to the ideology and framework of Labor Party politics from an exceedingly early age, would benefit her tremendously, if indirectly, later on in her adult political career.

Another key constant throughout her life was medicine; her father was a doctor, and Brundtland's family moved to the United States for a year when she was 10 to accompany her father, who had won a Rockefeller scholarship to study. Several years later, the family again accompanied their father overseas when he accepted a position in Egypt as an expert on rehabilitation. At university, Brundtland followed in her father's footsteps and received a Doctor of Medicine degree. She also married Arne Olav Brundtland, a fellow student interested in international affairs. Several years later, accompanied by her husband and growing family (she eventually had four children), she departed for Cambridge, Massachusetts, where she received a Master of Public Health degree from Harvard University, writing a thesis on patterns and benefits of breastfeeding for women and children in various cultures around the world. After completing her studies, she worked for Oslo's Department of Social Services as the assistant medical director of the Oslo Board of Health, where she focused on children's health issues such as breastfeeding, cancer prevention, and other diseases. While not directly involved in national politics at the time, she was involved in Labor Party politics and was a key figure in the campaign to legalize abortion in the 1970s. Her background in medicine also later provided a firm platform from which to address political problems. As she noted, "As a doctor and as a politician, you have to first ask: What is the problem? Then, how can we prevent and cure this problem? Who needs to become involved? How shall we act together to reach common goals?" (Brundtland, 2002, p. 471). Her medical background also enhanced her abilities to make later, far-reaching connections between public health, environmental degradation, and development, which stood her in good stead when she helped coin the phrase "sustainable development" as part of her work as chair of the World Commission on Environment and Development.

Many of the qualities, values, and characteristics for which Brundtland later became famous were evident at a very young age. Perhaps due to her upbringing, Brundtland developed the social-democratic values espoused by the Labor Party early; writing of her grade school years, she noted "There were big class differences in our class and in the school. We noticed it. We could see that it wasn't right that Liv should have to wear old clothes when children from wealthier areas got whatever they wanted" (Brundtland, 2002, p. 12). She remembers that "from an early age I had strong opinions and a large vocabulary," in part from listening to political discussions among friends and family (Brundtland, 2002, p. 9). She also exhibited early leadership qualities; by high school she served on national party youth committees and then again at the university level (although in her memoirs, she always expressed surprise at being asked to take a leadership position). Nor was she uncomfortable with having to stake out and maintain potentially unpopular positions; even during her youth, she noted, she would find herself in a minority of one, but that this would not deter her from holding on to her beliefs. All of these attributes, developed at a precocious age, would serve her well in her adult career.

Her family continued to play a central life in her political career in adulthood; for many years she continued to rely on her father for advice, and her mother spent her entire professional career in the Storting, serving as a secretary to the Labor Parliamentary Group, working under Brundtland' s predecessor Prime Minister Bratteli before working under her daughter. When Gro married, her husband also became a pillar of support and political advice. Many outsiders thought this unusual, for Arne Olav Brundtland, a renowned expert on international relations, eventually became a prominent member of the Conservative Party, the opposition to Brundtland's Labor Party. However, they always stressed their shared love of politics; and in an interview he commented, "My field is analysis of international relations. Her field is doing international relations. That makes for very good morning seminars" (Gibbs, 1989). Brundtland's marriage was also seen as somewhat unorthodox in the sense that the division of labor between her and her husband was somewhat unusual for the social mores of the time. The Brundtlands had four children, Knut, Kaja, Ivar, and Jorgen, at the same time that Brundtland was rising up the ranks of the Labor Party.

While it may be common for a male politician to have multiple children (and a wife to take care of the domestic front), it is less common for aspiring female politicians to successfully juggle the demands of a political career, often involving long hours, late nights, and travel away from home. Either they are unwilling to take that on or are unable to do so, due to a complex mix of social norms, expectations, and rules of behavior. As Brundtland's career began to take off, she and her husband had to make difficult decisions about raising their four children. Eventually, they decided that he would serve as the logistical anchor of the family, managing the household and the family schedule on a daily basis, serving as the physical constant in contrast to Brundtland's hectic schedule. In her memoirs, she writes of the painful decision to grant him the last word on household matters as something in the best interests of their family. At the same time, her family was never far from her thoughts even while she was in office, and she writes of taking weekend political calls in the basement of her busy (and noisy) house, so that she could shut the door to receive a bit of silence. Her husband was an invaluable help to her in all aspects, from the critical to the seemingly mundane, and one telling anecdote in her memoirs relays how he ironed her dress while she shampooed her hair before her induction into office in 1986. In politics, it is still rare for husbands to serve in the "wife" position in a political relationship, and Brundtland's political success could not have been possible without the love and loyalty of her family, particularly her husband.

In sum, Brundtland's formative years are central in understanding who she became as an adult. She grew up in an extended family in which all members, men as well as women, were deeply committed to high-level political and medical work, pursing public service with the dedication of a calling. Raised by strong, professionally accomplished women in their own right, Brundtland grew up in a household where biological sex did not determine one's destiny; rather, hard work, perseverance, and dedication did, for women could achieve anything that men could. At the same time, her social-democratic values led her to appreciate that social norms and economic conditions could deeply stratify society, whether by sex, class, or some other delineation, and she spent her career fighting to eradicate these stratifications. With the unstinting support of her family and friends, her basic egalitarianism blended with a sense of social responsibility powered her long and illustrious career in Norwegian politics.

PATH TO POWER

Brundtland had a relatively quick ascent up the ladders of political power (although it depends on when one starts counting, since her informal political internship literally began in the womb). However, her political trajectory up the rungs of the Labor Party accelerated dramatically when she left her job as the assistant medical director of the Oslo Board of Health in Norway's public health system to serve as Norway's Environmental Minister from 1974 to 1979. In 1975, she became deputy party leader for the Labor Party, and in 1977, she won her first seat in parliament. In February 1981, in the wake of the abrupt resignation of Prime Minister Ordli (also of the Labor Party), she was appointed prime minister. At 41, she was both the youngest person as well as the first woman to hold that office in Norway. Although her first government would not last out the year, she would return as prime minister again, in 1986–1989 and 1990–1996.

In 1974, Brundtland' s professional life shifted significantly when she was offered a cabinet position as minister of the environment. Norway was the first country in the world to create such a cabinet post in 1972 and, as a new ministry, it was one of the least powerful. Nonetheless, any cabinet position is a critical stepping stone for a young, ambitious politician looking to ascend the ranks of institutionalized political power, and for Brundtland, 35, this was a crucial test of her emerging political skills. Although she did not immediately see herself as an environmental specialist, her father, a former defense minister (whose primary expertise was not initially in defense) convinced her to try it. Further, through her own work as a doctor, she was increasingly convinced of the link between health and environment. During her time as environmental minister, she focused on issues such as acid rain and land preservation. In particular, she established the Hardangervidda wilderness, Europe's largest continuous mountain plateau, as a national park, despite significant opposition from proponents of hydropower and the farmers' union. One of her biggest political challenges during her tenure involved managing the blowout at the oil platform Bravo in the Ekofisk field, the largest such catastrophe in the North Sea. Brundtland earned national and international praise for effectively coordinating recovery efforts, making decisions that limited the environmental damage, and managing communication with the international media.

Less than a year after she had been appointed minister of the environment, she was approached by the then-minister of education about running for the deputy leader position in the Labor Party. Given her youth and relatively brief experience, this was an unusual request, for the deputy leadership position is part of the central leadership group and, as such, the person would be considered a future candidate for party leader and prime minister. Brundtland, who already had significant responsibilities as a relatively new minister, at first declined. However, the women's secretariat of the party contacted her and also urged her to take the post, which convinced a reluctant Brundtland. As she remembered, "I couldn't say no. How could we hope to achieve equality if the women said no?" (Brundtland, 2002, p. 80). And two years later, she agreed to run for parliament as a representative from Oslo, cementing her political resume as a potential future prime minister.

This resume was put to the test in February 1981, when Prime Minister Odvar Nordli abruptly resigned. The official reason was for health issues; after five years in office, Nordli was suffering from severe stress, likely due to Labor Party divisions over Norway's decision, as a member of NATO, to stockpile U.S. weapons on Norwegian soil. It is hard to remember a time in which concerns over the Cold War drove other country's domestic politics, but Norway's position in NATO was a deeply divisive national issue by the late 1970s. Even though Norway was a founding member of NATO, nonetheless, historically Labor-led governments had always fought to limit defense spending and the presence of NATO military and weapons on Norwegian soil. In 1980, the United States and NATO military increased their pressure on Norway to allow the Pentagon to deploy artillery, tanks, and other heavy equipment for a U.S. brigade of the marines on Norwegian soil in the event of a Soviet attack. This request was deeply unpopular with the Norwegian public, who saw this as violating Norway's sovereignty and emblematic of the hubris of large powers, such as the United States, who were endangering world peace and security with their seemingly needless arms race.

The ruling Labor Party was also badly split over this issue. The left wing of the Labor Party advocated negotiation of a treaty with the Soviet Union to keep Scandinavia free of NATO nuclear weapons if the Soviets reduced their nuclear arsenal near Norway, which caused a great amount of concern in other NATO capitals. Others within Labor advocated allowing the stockpiling while drawing the line at nuclear weapons. This issue pitted "old" Labor, represented by the unions and long-time party activists against "new" Labor (such as Brundtland), which advocated more centrist policies on a wide array of issues, in addition to NATO policy. Further, the Labor-led government maintained a one-seat majority at this time, and Labor's parliamentary allies (the socialists and the communists) threatened to upend this one-seat majority in response to Labor Party decisions to support nuclear stockpiling, increase defense spending, and invest in costly energy projects such as the hydroelectric power station in the Northern Alta Valley. While the Storting eventually approved the prime minister's plans to permit stockpiling of American military hardware in Central Norway, 600 miles from the Soviet border, in readiness for war, it was a potentially costly "victory" for the Labor-led government, particularly with less than a year to go before general elections. Nordli's early resignation was probably a calculated move; if he stepped down before the general elections, the decision about who would succeed him could be made internally by the Labor Party. A different, more dynamic Labor Party leader might be able to turn around the fortunes in the party before the following year's general elections. Gro Harlem Brundtland, as deputy leader of the party, was one of several contenders to replace Nordli as prime minister. She emerged victorious, perhaps because she was quickly building for herself a reputation as a young, energetic, decisive leader willing to take Labor in new directions to re-win disaffected voters. After an internal party battle, Brundtland was named the new prime minister, in the hopes that she could stave off electoral loss in the looming general elections.

How did she go from being a physician in Norway's public health system to leading the country in little over five years? This rapid rise up the ranks was somewhat unusual. Party leaders, official and unofficial, tended to be male and at least a decade older, representing a generation of people born well before World War II. They had worked their way up through the party, usually serving in a variety of leadership posts and cabinet positions to build their political network and experience. Often, they had experience either as a factory worker or had close ties to the unions. They tended to be "reluctant Europeans," questioning the utility of NATO or European Community membership. In contrast, Brundtland had served as minister of the environment for less than nine months when she became deputy leader.

Even though Brundtland's formal ascent was relatively quick, she was no outsider; Brundtland had been active in Labor Party politics virtually since birth, so her "apprenticeship" into the workings of a life in politics began at a very young age. Even though she received her political appointments through her own emerging skills, she was also born into a dense network of Labor Party insiders. One photo from Brundtland' s memoirs depicts a 7-year-old Gro marching in a youth Labor event behind the son of then-Prime Minister Einar Gerhardsen (Brundtland, 2002, p. 246). It also probably did not hurt that the Prime Minister Trygve Bratteli, who appointed her environmental minister, was a friend and former colleague of her father's (Vinocur, 1981, p. A6). However, even though she was born into a political network, as a relatively young woman she also represented a generational change in terms of shaking up the "old boys' network" culture of party politics. And when Prime Minister Nordli resigned, as a potential candidate to replace him she was not met with open arms by all members of the party, particularly the older guard, and by the outgoing prime minister in particular, who had indicated preference for another long-time party activist. She represented the younger, more moderate wing of the Labor Party that wanted to change some of the party's positions to rekindle voters' enthusiasm (and allegiance). As she wrote of that era, she wanted to find "new approaches" to "old issues," and saw a need for "new thinking and a critical attitude towards many established 'truths'" (Brundtland, 2002, p. 88). In sum, she was both political insider and outsider, and she was able to quickly rise through the ranks of a Labor Party that was deeply divided in the 1970s over how to respond to a changing international context, the rapid changes wrought by the discovery of oil, and a rapidly changing (and realigning) voter constituency. However, nine months in office was not enough to turn around the Labor Party's political fortunes, and the October 1981 general elections returned a victory to the conservatives. Nonetheless, Brundtland did not stray far; for the next 15 or so years, she continued to lead, either in opposition or as prime minister. What was she like as a leader?

LEADERSHIP STYLE

Scandinavian politics have been described as the politics of compromise (Einhorn and Logue, 2007). This is, in part, because of the disappearance of single-party majorities in parliament and the increasing reliance on coalitions and minority governments. But it is also a reflection of Scandinavian political culture and a shared belief that good policy is policy in which all major players have had a chance to provide input into policy design. Thus, major legislative proposals often begin with commissions composed of politicians, interest organization representatives, and academics, and the resulting reports are expected to be based on evidence and facts rather than ideological abstracts. This approach has been described as the "CORD model," or consensual, open, rationalistic, and deliberative policy making (Einhorn and Logue, 2007, p. 69). And while politics in Norway are certainly not conflict free or nonideological, nonetheless, political leaders are groomed in this culture of compromise and fact-based policy making.

Brundtland's leadership style reflects this general description of CORD policy making. She was known for her will to go deep, her refusal to give up before all aspects of complex and controversial problems were examined, and her commitment to sitting down with the relevant policy actors to work toward a solution. Her training as a doctor may have also reinforced the CORD approach. Her approach to designing policy involved building teams of well-qualified people, and gathering facts and expertise presented from as many viewpoints as possible in order to identify weaknesses of reasoning or logic. As she wrote, "Tempo is important in politics. But it must be linked with respect for facts and quality. Otherwise society loses time and strength, and resources are wasted" (Brundtland, 2002, p. 153). Decisions made on momentary intuition, she believed, could lead to poor long-term policy. Her comprehensive approach to problem solving was matched by her conviction that a solution could be found, even for the most seemingly intractable problems. In reaching these common goals, Brundtland's work ethic and commitment to public service were legendary; she was known for working 14- to 16-hour days.

However, Brundtland's belief in solidarity and working together does not mean that she was uncomfortable with disagreement, conflict, or serving as the final arbiter for difficult decisions. She commented, "When you become a leader, you have to reach out. You must listen to all aspects of a problem and try to comprehend as well as any of the experts the totality of the case. That is the role of the leader. There's no point in being scared. You must put the experts to work for you, respect their expertise, but never forget that any problem worthy of your time is neither simple nor unequivocal. You must ask the critical questions. Nobody else takes that role if you as a leader do not" (Brundtland, 2002, p. 153). She recognized that as the leader, it was also her job to guide the process, ask the hard questions, and sometimes make the difficult decisions.

Various journalistic profiles of Brundtland over the years portray a driven, committed, and passionate politician. Two reporters once wrote, "her success has been the victory of the dogged virtues determination, perseverance, application, and industry" (Hattersley & Henley, 1996, p. 20). Another profile described her as "tireless . . . friends say she laughs easily, but tells few jokes. Struggles with a fiery temper. Demanding and compassionate, she has few interests outside politics" (Sholdice, 1996, p. 12). She was also perceived as frank, honest, and upfront, known for clear and unambiguous communication, a strategy she developed, she wrote, as a way to clearly negotiate with older, male colleagues who were used to veneration and getting their way after a long career of service. This frankness and habit of plain speaking was on international display when, at the UN-sponsored Cairo conference on international population and development (1994), she challenged countries' hypocritical morality that allowed women to suffer and die from unwanted pregnancies, illegal abortions, and miserable living conditions. While this statement was greeted with consternation by the Catholic Church and many Muslim majority countries, it is comments like these that indicate her comfort level with speaking her beliefs plainly and clearly.

All of these traits depict an extremely dedicated, efficient, and plainspoken leader, but they do not quite explain Brundtland's popularity with her people, which exceeded that of the Labor Party, with approval ratings ranging from 70% and sometimes soaring to over 90% (Hattersley & Henley,

1996, p. 20). In addition to her policy performance (discussed later in the chapter) and personal authority, Brundtland also exuded an infectious energy that made people believe she could accomplish the unimaginable. Her state secretary for personal relations described her first days in office in 1981: "Gro was something completely new at the Prime Minister's office. It was not only that she is a woman. She was glowing with a fighting spirit and willingness to work. It seemed that there could be no task so difficult that it would scare her away from taking it on right away with the conviction that she would find a solution." Brundtland herself, upon assuming office and leadership of a party in disarray, seemed unfazed by the turmoil, commenting, "This will all be fun" (Brundtland, 2002, p. 139). She inspired her coworkers to give their best, often through her own personal example. Her secretary noted, "Some of us, to our own surprise, were able to excel more than we thought possible" (Brundtland, 2002, p. 151). And despite media descriptions of her as dogged, with few interests outside politics, at the same time this is a person who at the end of her run as prime minister in 1996, after formally handing in the keys to her office, was met by her husband in their car, packed with clothes, tools, "and a case of light beer" for some time away from the spotlight at their winter cottage at Lake Mylla. As she commented, "For what is most important in life beyond one's job? Family, and being outdoors with one's closest" (Brundtland, 2002, p. 428). Her strong work ethic, combined with her keen appreciation of nature and reliance on a close network of friends and family, fit in well with Norway's hardy, taciturn population. And while she took her job extremely seriously, she never felt the urge to compromise solely in order to hold onto her position of power in politics. She noted she always had a solid fallback if her political career dissolved—she could always go back to being a medical doctor! Perhaps the public sensed her devotion to public service and the good of the whole, and respected it, even if they didn't always politically agree with her policy sentiments.

KEY ISSUES

Gro Harlem Brundtland guided Norway through a decade and a half, either as prime minister or as leader of the opposition. Her time in office in the 1980s and 1990s was during an era in Norwegian politics in which governments alternated between minority Labor governments and conservative-led center right coalition governments. The center right governments gained power in three out of four elections during this period (1981, 1985, 1989), while Brundtland's Labor Party toppled these governments twice between elections (1986, 1990) and stayed in power after one election (1993). By the time she resigned as prime minister in 1996 (at the peak of her popularity), she had served four terms spanning more than 10 years as prime minister.

As discussed previously, Brundtland's appointment as prime minister and party leader in 1981 were not enough to stave off electoral defeat in the general elections later that year, and the conservatives ruled under party leader Kare Willoch, first as a minority government, and in 1983 expanded to a majority coalition with two other supporting parties—the Center Party and the Christian Democratic Party. The general elections in 1985 returned this center right coalition to power, although under diminished circumstances. The Conservative Party lost the popular vote (which Labor won), although it was able to maintain a majority of one seat in the Storting with its coalition partners. Brundtland's Labor Party, although still in opposition, was able to make significant electoral gains by critiquing the quality of the welfare state (such as health care), particularly given the enormous influx of oil money into the economy. In contrast, significant policy differences quickly emerged in the ruling coalition and, from the outset, a conservative-led full term was seen as a "miracle" (Feder, 1985, p. A12). And the crash of oil prices in the international market in the mid-1980s certainly did not help matters. Few were surprised when, less than eight months after the election, the government was forced to step down after losing a parliamentary vote of confidence on a rise in gas taxes, part of an unpopular austerity package (the Progress Party, a right-wing party, refused to support the measure).

Brundtland, as leader of the opposition Labor Party, stepped in to serve as prime minister for her second stint in office in May 1986 until the general elections in 1989 (which Labor lost). She promptly made history by ensuring that 40% of her cabinet was comprised of women, the highest rate in the world at the time. She was handed a thankless tangle of economic problems resulting from the crash in oil prices, along with a host of politically unpalatable options to pull Norway out of its economic problems. Yet, rolling up her metaphorical sleeves, Brundtland, along with her administration, dug in with a host of unpopular but necessary austerity measures, deftly using her reputation as a straight talker to wring concessions out of business, labor, and the general population in the general interest of restoring vigor to the Norwegian economy. This may have earned her respect from the population, but it did not earn her Labor Party new converts, and the 1989 elections turned Labor out of office and returned the previous three-party coalition to power, although this time under the leadership of conservative leader Jan P. Syse. However, the coalition was short lived, and the government collapsed by November 1990 over the issue of Norwegian membership into the European Economic Area. (The Center Party opposed membership, while the conservatives supported it.)

For the third time, as Labor Party leader Brundtland stepped into the position of prime minister, a position she would keep through a successful 1993 election until her abrupt resignation in 1996. She continued to build Norway's international profile as chair of the UN World Commission on Environment and Development, host of the 1994 Winter Olympics in Lillehammer, and through her championship of increased financial support to international challenges such as global poverty reduction and development. At the domestic level, she continued to focus on stabilizing Norway's economic footing through increased integration with the European Union and expanding the reach and improving the quality of the welfare state. When she stepped down in 1996, many predicted her "retirement" would be short-lived; a politician as able as she could only continue to move upwards in international politics. We now turn to looking at some of the issues she faced in greater depth.

Managing the Economy

As discussed previously in the chapter, while the discovery of oil offshore in the late 1960s helped make Norway one of the wealthiest countries in Europe over the ensuing decades, it also dramatically altered the economic, social, and political underpinnings of the country. The Norwegian state and citizens alike, newly affluent in the 1970s, dramatically increased their spending and became accustomed to economic growth, budget surpluses, full employment, and extensive welfare provisions. However, the 1980s was a decade of overproduction of crude oil worldwide. The world price of oil, which had peaked in 1980 at over $35 per barrel, fell in 1986 from $27 to below $10. Given Norway's reliance on oil revenues to fund its activities, this drop in price had dramatic effects on the Norwegian economy. The economy had been booming, growing at 5% in 1985, with high levels of consumption, prices, wages, and consumption to match. When the price of oil collapsed, so too did the economy.

In 1986, the conservative-led coalition, already hanging by a legislative thread of a one-seat majority, was the next institution to be swept to the wayside in the economic collapse after it lost a vote of confidence on an "Easter package" of emergency budget measures. Brundtland, as opposition leader, was asked to form a government, since the center right coalition could not hold. She was confronted with a large number of economic problems as well as a laundry list of extremely unpopular reforms to bring some austerity back into Norway's spending habits. Implementing any kind of austerity plan is never politically palatable and, in this case, was particularly hard. Brundtland was presiding over a minority government, which meant that she could not consistently count on majority control of the legislative agenda, and she served as head of a party that historically and ideologically tended to advocate for increases, rather than reductions, in government spending.

Her prescription was the implementation of a series of neoliberal reforms that were anathema to the left wing of her party. A strict regime of cuts was enforced. In an agreement between government, employers, and employees, wages and prices were scaled, and wage growth was halted at 4%. Interest rates were raised in order to curb spending. Her government raised taxes 2% on the higher incomes, and the Norwegian currency, the kroner, was devalued by 12% to encourage export earnings. Many considered these measures political suicide, although they were economically effective. By 1989 (another election year), inflation had been curbed, the budget was showing a surplus, and foreign trade was booming. But this did not come cost free; unemployment had also doubled to almost 5%, a high figure for a small country used to full employment. This, in part, explains why the Labor Party experienced a reversal of fortunes in the 1989 elections, dropping over 6 percentage points (to 34%) in the popular vote from 1985. The Conservative-led coalition briefly returned to rule, although they proved no more adept at maintaining their coalition in 1989 than they did in 1985, and the following year Brundtland was back in power. Unemployment peaked at 6% in 1993 and remained a significant policy issue for her government until the end of her fourth term.

Brundtland's government did not solely rely on austerity, however, to pull Norway out of its economic crisis; she was a staunch supporter of Norway's large welfare state. As she noted, "As a social democrat I strive to change society in such a way that it is healthy for people, enhances equality and distributes primary needs in an honest way" (Ribberink, 2006, p. 72). At the same time, she recognized the limits placed on welfare state spending by the volatility of the oil economy, and maintained that "we must never forget that we have to pay for our efforts" (Brundtland, 2002, p. 426). This commitment to the welfare state and budgetary restraint sometimes put her at odds with the Labor Party's traditional base of support—the labor unions. At the same time, many credit her deft repositioning of her party to more centrist economic measures with Norway's ability to maintain its generous welfare state. And her initial austerity measures, combined with higher taxes, helped engineer a budget surplus in 1994 and 1995. This, in turn, allowed to her to invest in state spending to battle unemployment and the dislocation created by the previous decade's economic instability (Ribberink, 2006).

Managing the economic fallout from the collapse of oil prices was thrust on the Brundtland governments; they certainly did not choose to implement austerity. And much of the political conversation in Norway since has revolved around ways to respond to this devastating vulnerability to external price volatility. This may be one of the reasons that prompted the Norwegian government to found the petroleum fund, the Government Pension Fund Global, in 1990 in order to save and invest the state's earnings from oil and gas revenues. Since its creation, the size of this fund has grown substantially (as of October 2010, it was valued at over $500 billion). This will help address Norway's looming demographic crisis. By 2030, the percentage of pensioners will have increased by over a third, while the numbers of workers supporting them will have decreased. This is a problem faced not only by Norway, but also by many industrialized countries that face aging populations supported by dwindling numbers of workers.

Promoting Gender Equality

Gro Harlem Brundtland repeatedly addressed the issue of gender equality by proactively implementing government policies to improve the position and status of women in Norwegian society and abroad. In the 1970s, Norway had already begun to address women's lack of political power; several political parties, such as the Socialist Left Party and the Liberal Party, had laid the groundwork for increasing women's political representation by mandating voluntary and self-imposed gender quota systems in nominations to elections. Further, in 1978, Norway enacted an act pro-hibiting the differential treatment of men and women, stipulating that women must be given equal pay and equal access to education, and estab-lished that 40% of the members of all public bodies with more than four individuals must be women (Pande & Ford, 2012). When Brundtland first assumed power, she took this charge seriously and in 1983, in part due to Brundtland's leadership, the Labor Party reformed from within, mandat-ing a minimum of 40% of each sex in all elected positions, and in forth-coming elections, were successful in that goal for the Labor Party in all elections but one. Quotas have been mandated in other areas to increase women's representation at all levels of power in politics, economics, and society. For example, in 1981 a quota system was introduced for public appointed committees, boards, and councils because previously only 11% of the representation of such assemblies was female. Since 1988, there has been a requirement that representation be a minimum of 40% of each gen-der, a goal which the government had achieved by 1997 (Royal Embassy of Norway, 2012). When Brundtland assumed power a second time in 1986, she made history by appointing women to 8 out of 18 ministerial positions, which at the time was a world record. This use of quotas has increased women's political representation; at the time that Brundtland won her first seat on the Storting (1977), women comprised 24% of the parliament; by the time she left office in 1996, that number was just shy of 40% (Interparliamentarian Union). This approach of quotas, voluntary as well as mandatory, has been used in other Nordic countries to great success and is a major factor in explaining why these countries rank as the world's leaders in terms of levels of gender equality.

Brundtland also focused on putting policies into place to help parents balance the demands of raising children with working outside of the home. In 1993, Norway's paid maternity leave was extended to a year. Further, in the government's efforts to encourage both parents to take leave (in most countries, leave is overwhelmingly taken by the mother), four weeks were reserved in particular for the father in a "use or it lose it" scheme. (When leave is formally gender neutral in that either parent can take it, in prac-tice the mother usually takes it. It is only when measures are specifically targeted to fathers do men take the leave in significant percentages.) The number of fathers who took advantage of parental leave skyrocketed from 4% to 70% in over three years. Brundtland's government also instituted more flexibility in its leave policy, allowing parents to use it over a period of years rather than all during the child's first year. Instead, a parent can take full leave in the first six months and then work six-hour days (receiving full pay) until the child is almost three. And because it is hard for both parents to choose to work if there is not affordable or available care, Brundtland's government pledged a spot in (state-subsidized) nursery school for every child. By 2000, Norway had achieved 90% coverage for children below five. Brundtland's government also added a year of schooling to every child's education, starting at six rather than seven, which also, in addition to helping children's development, enables working parents to balance work and family life (Brundtland, 2002, p. 424).

International Relations

Brundtland also worked tirelessly to push Norway from the periphery to a more central place in the international arena, somewhat to Norwegians' consternation. In addition to pushing for continued NATO integration (a debate that originally launched Brundtland into her first term as prime minister), Brundtland revived the debate over Norway's relationship with Europe and specifically the question of EU membership, a divisive issue that had brought down a previous Labor government in 1972 when Norwegian voters returned a "no" vote in a popular referendum. In 1992, two decades after the previous failure to secure membership, she submitted Norway's second application. Once again, Oslo and the political elites were in favor of membership, while much of the countryside and the coastal regions were opposed. Brundtland' s own Labor Party was divided. The pressures for membership were primarily economic, and desire for membership was in part driven by a concern about diversifying an economy heavily reliant on oil revenues. By the mid-1990s, Norway was the world's second-largest producer of oil behind Saudi Arabia (Barbash, 1996, p. A27). Yet, Brundtland and others maintained that revenues generated from a nonrenewable resource such as oil could not last indefinitely and that they were inherently unstable due to price volatility. Further, Norway as a large but underpopulated nation on the edge of Europe simply could not afford to remain outside. Staying out of the Union, many feared, would make the Norwegian economy even more uncompetitive and less likely to attract the kind of foreign investment that could support the kinds of industry that could diversify the economy. Norway's membership was the best possible way to spur diversification of the economy.

The argument, advanced by the "no" side, was equally impassioned. Some no proponents argued that Norway was blessed with abundant natural resources that ensured that it was economically strong enough to go it alone. Further, the development of natural gas fields in the 1990s created optimism that even if oil could not last indefinitely, natural gas could be an additional massive income generator for the Norwegian state (and people). Others worried that Norway's higher standard of living and more exacting standards, ranging from environmental protection to its generous welfare state, would diminish as a result of EU membership. It made no sense to them to pay money to join an organization with lesser standards. Brundtland was also opposed by the fishing industry, which did not want to yield fishing rights and quotas. The image of big foreign trawlers wiping the Nordic seas clean of fish was a powerful one, in 1972 as well as in 1996. Few proponents could argue that membership would be a benefit to Norway's fishing and farming communities, two areas of the economy that played a larger-than-life significance in the Norwegian psyche and self-image. EU membership represented more than just economic changes; it entailed, to some, the destruction of a traditional Norwegian lifestyle. A leader of the anti-EC campaign explained this resistance:

> They call us gnomes sitting on boulders. Well, Norway is full of boulders. Only 3 per cent of it is cultivated, but we are proud of what we have achieved. We have survived. We have learned to use our resources, and to build our society. We don't want Norway to degenerate into a few densely populated areas. If we let it collapse it will not be possible to build it up again.

After a fierce campaign, the voters returned a similar verdict to the one delivered in the 1972 referendum; by 52% to 48%, voters returned a "no" verdict, splitting from its Nordic neighbors Sweden, Finland, and Denmark and remaining, along with Switzerland and Lichtenstein, the only states in Europe outside the union.

The Labor Party emerged relatively unscathed from this loss; unlike Prime Minister Bratteli in 1972, Brundtland did not link the outcomes of the vote with a vote of confidence in her leadership; nonetheless it was a blow to her political prestige. However, the Brundtland administration had not put all of their eggs in one policy basket; in addition to pursuing an EU application, Norway had also submitted an application to the European Economic Area, which allows non-EU member countries such as Iceland,

Liechtenstein, and Norway to participate in the EU's Internal Market without a conventional EU membership. In exchange, they are obliged to adopt all EU legislation related to the single market, except laws on agriculture and fisheries. Membership to this, which went through in 1994 (two years before the EU referendum), grants Norway, in practice, full access to the European market. While Brundtland did not achieve her goal of full EU membership, she did succeed in ensuring that Norway would integrate more deeply into the European economy.

Although Norwegians are "reluctant Europeans," nonetheless Brundtland continued to focus on expanding Norway's presence in international politics; increasing its global reputation; and, as a result, ability to affect the outcome of international negotiations. When Brundtland stepped down as prime minister in 1981 (but staying on as leader of the Labor Party, now in opposition), she was approached by bureaucrats within the UN to use her environmental and leadership expertise to head a newly formed World Commission on Environment and Development. Formed in 1983, the commission's mandate was to examine natural constraints on continued economic growth in the Third World. Known as the Brundtland Commission, the group put sustainable development on the international agenda with the publication of their report *Our Common Future*. This report resulted in the 1992 Rio Earth Summit, which established the framework that eventually evolved into the Kyoto Protocol, an international treaty on reducing greenhouse gas emissions. In addition, she traveled exhaustively to promote the ideas behind the report, which ensured "buy in" from many developing countries who might have otherwise perceived it as another report issued by the global North issuing a "to do" list for cash strapped countries in the global South. She also increased Norway's "soft" power by helping to win the 1994 winter Olympics for the Alpine town of Lillehammer.

PERFORMANCE EVALUATION

Brundtland's professional career was overshadowed by personal tragedy; in 1992, her youngest son Jorgen committed suicide after a long struggle with depression. Recognizing the difficulties of maintaining her previous levels of commitment to her work while focusing on her family, later that year she resigned as Labor Party leader but pledged to stay in office as prime minister at least until the general elections in September 1993. The Labor Party claimed victory in that election, and she stayed in office to complete her work on Norway's EEA and EU membership. However, in 1996, upon consultation with her husband, she decided to resign as prime minister. She timed it with the 1997 general elections in mind; her resignation in 1996 would give Labor Party leader Thorbjorn Jagland time to develop a reputation as prime minister with voters. Although some speculated that she resigned to campaign for the position of Secretary General of the United Nations (General Secretary Boutros Boutros-Ghali's term was set to end at the end of 1996), she herself maintained that she simply needed a break from a career that demanded the totality of one's attention at a time when she needed to devote more to her family. She stepped down at the height of her popularity, leaving behind a successful record of policy accomplishments.

Political analysts uniformly praise Brundtland's deft handling of Norway's economic crisis in the latter half of the 1980s, although some in the Labor Party mourn her decision to move its ideology closer to the center in terms of advocating a social market economy, allowing for some privatization of government-held assets, as well as reducing income tax progressivity.

Brundtland shattered the glass ceiling of Norwegian politics by becoming the country's first female prime minister and then quickly putting into place policies to ensure that she would not be the last. She made history (and raised eyebrows) by ensuring that 40% of her cabinet were women; only 15 years later, when she relinquished power, her successor, Thorbjorn Jagland, would not consider a cabinet with fewer than 40% women. This promotion of women in politics is not solely confined to the Labor Party; even by the 1993 elections, in addition to Brundtland's Labor Party, two other parties contesting elections were led by women. After she left office, Norway continued to pass progressive legislation to promote the position and status of women; in 2003, Norway enacted a law requiring companies to fill 40% of corporate board seats with women by 2008 (Reier, 2008, p. 15). And Norway was the first country to decouple the appointment of Minister of Children, Equality, and Social Inclusion with gendered norms and expectations. In many countries, this ministry is given to a female bureaucrat under the implicit assumption that women are more interested or fit to make policy on children's issues; however, Auden Lysbakken, a member of the Socialist

Left Party, became Norway's first male Minister of Children, Equality and Social Inclusion in 2009 (Reistad-Long, 2009). Brundtland created a ripple effect of gendered policies that she proactively worked to foster.

Brundtland also increased Norway's international prominence through her tireless international work. When she announced that she was stepping down as prime minister, the Norwegian News Agency NTB commented, "She has been Norway's face abroad in an entirely different way from that of her predecessors. Her involvement in international affairs has led to her being known in countries that scarcely would have been aware of Norway otherwise" (Hattersley & Henley, 1996, p. 20). In particular, analysts praise her leadership on the World Commission on Environment and Development, which opened up a number of other international opportunities for Brundtland and Norway. Further, thanks to her successful bid for the Winter Olympics held at Lillehammer in 1994, Norway became fixed in the global public's mind as the hope of a thriving population and pristine landscape. This is significant not just in terms of attracting tourists; this has been an effective tool for increasing Norway's power and influence in the international arena without having to use methods such as military might and the use of force. Rather, Norway has worked hard to use its soft power, or its ability to attract and co-opt rather than coerce and force as a means of persuasion. In terms of geopolitics, Norway has replaced the strategy of the Vikings (pillage and conquer) with strategies to promote peace and reconciliation, often through multilateral institutions and the distribution of generous amounts of overseas development assistance.

Brundtland's biggest policy failure was Norway's "no" vote on EU membership, something for which Brundtland had campaigned vigorously, although she did not make it a vote on citizen's confidence in the Labor Party. Yet, she emerged personally unscathed from this loss; her popularity remained undiminished, despite her staunch support for the EU and her country's ultimate rejection of membership. And she was able to secure Norway's membership to the EEA, which brings similar economic benefits to EU membership. This was a major feat in its own right, since that same issue had caused the collapse in 1990 of Norway's Conservative-led coalition. However, this policy defeat does have a cost; Norway cannot effectively influence the EU's other governing bodies. Norwegian diplomats can cajole, persuade, ask, and proclaim about policy in the EU, but they cannot vote on it, and that policy has a dramatic impact on European economic and political affairs from fisheries to labor relations.

In her own view, she felt she had done "a reasonably good job for a number of years" ("Brundtland to Resign as Prime Minister," 1996, p. 12). She felt her policies "created results that truly mattered for most people. That makes political work worthwhile" (Brundtland 2002, p. 427). Evidently, Norwegians, whether Labor Party voters or not, agreed with this assessment for she remained through all the ups and downs of her leadership tremendously popular with the public.

GENDER

Brundtland commented that her election as Norway's youngest and first female prime minister in 1981 was a cultural shock for most Norwegians. Reflecting on her first few months in office, she recalled that "it was very tough in 1981. In the worst of times I always thought, if you get through this, it will be much better for the next woman" (Gibbs, 1989). Having a female prime minister and party leader seemed to be a challenge for the national and international media. Brundtland herself noticed this arguing that, "Women leaders are criticized more, and differently, than their male colleagues. You cannot defend yourself against such tactics. Your only option is to try to look past them" (Brundtland, 2002, p. 153). Over the years, clothing, hairstyle, speech, gait, and manner of leadership all came under the scrutiny of the media, whether through headlines, critical articles, or the ways of presenting photographs. If she exhibited qualities that were seen as typically "female," like crying or tearing up, as she did more frequently when she first achieved national prominence as party leader and prime minister, she was criticized for being too emotional. Yet, if she was assertive and confident (typically "male" behaviors), she could be labeled as strident, too brisk, not "human" enough. For example, in 1996, *The Economist*, responding to the news of her resignation and speculating on possible future plans for a bid for the secretary general position of the UN, predicted she would be an "effective, albeit humourless, head of the UN" ("Post-Brundtland Norway," 1996, p. 65). Was Kofi Annan judged by these same standards? And if a man had made similar policy decisions as Ms. Brundtland, would it have been evidence of that leader's humorlessness or a sign of his resolve? Upon her announcement that she would step down as prime minister in 1996, *The Observer*, under the headline "Earth Mother," wrote of one of Europe's most successful and internationally well-known politicians: "The definitive description is 'sturdy'... sturdy in appearance, character, and intellect" (Hattersley & Henley, 1996, p. 20). The *Irish Times* referred to her as "feisty," an adjective that rarely gets applied to male politicians known for their tenacity and energy ("Brundtland to Resign as Prime Minister," 1996). One reporter, aware of this standard, asked her, "Is it only men who describe you as rock-hard, strong-willed, and obstinate?" Brundtland herself stated, "I would prefer 'dedicated to producing results'" (Brundtland, 2002, p. 150).

The fact that she played the "male" role as political leader also was a subject of fascination with the media and the population. Her husband, a prominent political analyst in his own right, served the "decorative spouse" role in politics accompanying her on state visits, taking care of the domestic arrangements, and serving as the primary caretaker of their four children. While this is often not remarked on with male politicians, this arrangement was treated as highly unusual (which, in all truth, it was). But the media and public often questioned why her husband needed to accompany her on official trips as a spouse, wondering why he was there, and who paid for his trip, when it is often rarely questioned when wives accompany their husbands on similar trips. And when Brundtland appeared in public with her family, she was judged doubly as a prime minister and as a mother, based on how well behaved her children were in the public spotlight.

Finally, Gro Harlem Brundtland's leadership style stands out in stark contrast to Europe's other female prime minister at the time, Margaret Thatcher. Perhaps all they had in common was their biological sex; in terms of ideology and political positions, they were worlds apart. While Brundtland made gender politics a central component of her platform, Thatcher studiously ignored it. When the two leaders met during Margaret Thatcher's official visit to Norway in 1986, Brundtland raised the issue of women in politics, asking what Thatcher was doing to increase the number of women in British government. But Thatcher showed little interest in that conversation, maintaining that very few women were qualified. Brundtland commented, "I got the message. She was Prime Minister because she was the best. If other women were the best, they would certainly manage what she had managed" (Brundtland, 2002, p. 255). As a leader, she represented an alternative—a consensus and coalition builder rather than a hierarchical top-down leader; gender aware rather than gender averse. Yet both women, simply by fact of their sex, were outsiders to some extent, despite climbing the traditional, insider route to power. Thatcher ignored this fact, while Brundtland used her gender awareness and her leadership style to consciously change the path for future women to lead.

CONCLUSION

It is hard to think of Gro Harlem Brundtland as "stepping down" from her career as prime minister, since after a break from politics she "stepped up" at the international level to serve as Director-General of the World Health Organization from 1998 to 2003. Despite her desire to be close to her family (which now included multiple grandchildren), she was almost immediately committed to making a bid for the leadership position of the WHO, in part to avoid the temptation to become a backseat driver in Norwegian politics. As she wryly noted, "avoiding comment . . . would be easier if I had an international responsibility to take care of and was living abroad" (Brundtland, 2002, p. 433). She was inspired to take up the charge also, in part, because the World Health Organization was in crisis, poorly organized, underfunded, and tainted with charges of corruption and lack of results. During her tenure, her decisive actions helped avert a global outbreak of SARS (severe acute respiratory syndrome) in 2003, an accomplishment for which she was awarded the Policy Leader of the Year Award from the *Scientific American Magazine*. She also worked on specific WHO campaigns such as the Tobacco Free Initiative, Roll Back Malaria, and the Stop Tuberculosis Initiative as part of her larger efforts to combat poverty, famine, and other communicable diseases. In addition to implementing her passion for public health and poverty issues, she reformed the organizational structure of WHO into nine clusters, each with an executive director or minister. Similar to her priorities during her tenure as prime minister, she left a legacy of female leadership in WHO by appointing a wide array of female executive directors.

Brundtland was also a founding member of the Elders, an international organizational of elder statespeople drawn together by Nelson Mandela to use their tremendous wealth of diplomatic experience to help resolve contentious issues. For example, in her capacity as elder, she was part of a delegation to Israel and the West Bank in 2009 to support efforts to advance Middle East peace. She traveled to Greece, Turkey, and Cyprus to facilitate peace negotiations between the leader of Greek Cypriot and Turkish Cypriot communities. She visited the Korean peninsula to advocate for better sanitation and health conditions for North Koreans, and in 2011 she was in sub-Saharan Africa to advocate the end of child marriages. In recognition for her work, she has received numerous international awards, such as the Third World Prize in 1988, Indira Gandhi Prize in 1989, the Earth and Onassis Prizes in 1992, the World Economy Award and Global Leadership Prize in 2001, and the Four Freedom Award in 2002. Despite her retirement from national politics, she shows few signs of slowing down; in 2012, she was a featured speaker at the Rio + 20 Earth Summit and was blogging from India about her work with the Elders in addressing the undervaluation of girl children. She once noted that "women power is a formidable force," and this quote applies as much to her as it does to the women she was addressing (Brundtland, 1995).

NOTES

1   The size of the Storting has expanded several times in the latter half of the 20th century. Thus, you may see different numbers cited throughout the chapter, depending on the era under discussion.
2   For example, the Socialist Left Party has garnered anywhere from 4% to 13% of the national vote since it was founded in 1973.

REFERENCES

Barbash, F. (1996, October 25). No deficit, but no joy, in Norway; Riches of petroleum encourage caution. *Washington Post*, A27.
BBC News. (1998, January 27). World profile: Gro Harlem Brundtland. http://news.bbc.co.uk/2/hi/51080.stm.
Brundtland, G.H. (1995). Closing address by Prime Minister Gro Harlem Brundtland. *Women's International Network News*, 21(4), 18.
Brundtland, G.H. (2002). *Madame prime minister: A life in power and politics*. New York: Farrar, Straus and Giroux.
Brundtland to resign as PM. (1996, October 24). *The Irish Times*, 12.
Downie, Jr., L. (1981, September 14). Conservatives favored as Norwegians vote. *The Washington Post*, A26.
Einhorn, E.S. & Logue, J. (2007). Scandinavia. In C. Hay and A. Menon (Eds.), *European Politics*. New York: Oxford University Press.
Feder, B.J. (1985, September 11). Close vote puts Norway's coalition in doubt. *The New York Times*, A12.
Gibbs, N. (1989, September 25). Norway's radical daughter. *Time Magazine*.

Hattersley, R. & Henley, J. (1996, October 27). The Observer profile: Earth mother. *The Observer*, 20.

Matthews, J. (1996, October 28). Norway's woman of influence. *The Washington Post*, A21.

Norway's cabinet judging premier, who admits lie. (1971, February 28). *The New York Times*, 1.

O'Hanlon, L. (1994, September 11). Profile: Too big for her roots: She made enemies in Cairo, but the world may need Norway's leader: Gro Harlem Brundtland. *The Independent*. http://www.independent.co.uk/opinion/profile-too-big-for-her-roots-she-made-enemies-in-cairo-but-the-world-may-need-norways-leader-gro-harlem-brundtland-1448170.html.

Pande, R. & Ford, D. (2012). Gender quotas and female leadership. Washington, D.C.: World Bank.

Post Brundtland: Norway. (1996, October 26). *The Economist*, 65.

Profile of Gro Harlem Brundtland. http://people.brandeis.edu/~dwilliam/profiles/brundt land.htm.

Reier, S. (2008, March 22). Women on board: Norway's initiative leads to a new model of corporate governance. *The International Herald Tribune*, 15.

Reistad-Long, S. (2010, March 9). Investing in equality is profitable. *Forbes*.

Ribberink, A. (2006). Gro Harlem Brundtland: A true social democrat. *Social Europe: The Journal of the European Left*, 2(2), 72–77. http://www.social-europe.eu/fileadmin/user_upload/journals/SocialEurope-6.pdf.

Royal Embassy of Norway. The official site in the United Kingdom. http://www.norway.org.uk/

Sholdice, D. (1996, October 24). Gro Harlem Brundtland. *The Irish Times*, 12.

U.S. Department of State. (2011). Background note: Norway. www.state.gov/r/pa/ei/bgn/3421.htm.

Vinocur, J. (1981, February 4). Woman in the news: The woman at the helm in Norway. *The New York Times*, A6.

Weintraub, B. (1975, September 28). Norway will curb production of oil. *The New York Times*.

Women in national parliaments. http://www.ipu.org/wmn-e/world.htm.

4

Benazir Bhutto and Dynastic Politics

Her Father's Daughter, Her People's Sister

Nancy Fix Anderson

When Benazir Bhutto (1953–2007) was first elected prime minister of Pakistan in December 1988, she became the first woman to head a modern Muslim state. Thirty-five years old, she was also the youngest head of a democratic government, and, when she had her second child in January 1990, she became the first elected chief executive to give birth while in office. Her rise to power is especially remarkable in that the history of Pakistan has been characterized by the dominance of the military and of conservative Muslims.

Intelligent and ambitious, Bhutto was able to assert herself in Pakistani politics through her own strengths, but more so because she was the daughter of charismatic powerful Zulfikar Ali Bhutto (1928–1979), president and then prime minister of Pakistan from 1971 to 1977. Deposed in a military coup and executed in 1979 by General Muhammad Zia-ul-Haq, Zulfikar became all the more exalted in the popular mind by his martyrdom. When Zia, after ruling under martial law for 11 years, allowed the return of parliamentary government and free elections in 1988, Benazir Bhutto campaigned as the daughter and heir of her martyred father and as the caring sister of her oppressed people. These emotional appeals, successful at the polls in 1988 and again in 1993, did not lead to success in office. Unable to overcome entrenched resistance to her gender and to her liberal policies, her tenures as prime minister were generally considered, even by her supporters, as failures. She was, however, perceived as enough of a threat to the reactionary forces in Pakistan, that when she campaigned for a third term as prime minister in 2007, she was assassinated.

PAKISTAN: A HISTORICAL OVERVIEW

The country over which Benazir Bhutto ruled was a relatively new nation, created in 1947 when the British granted independence to their Indian colony and partitioned it along religious lines, creating the new state of Pakistan as Muslim, and India as predominantly Hindu. Pakistan was composed of five (later four) provinces and four federally administered areas, with diverse and often conflicting ethnic identities. The most problematic was East Pakistan, a Bengali province separated from West Pakistan by 1,000 miles.

The one unifying force in Pakistan, and indeed its raison d'être, is Islam. At least 95 percent of all Pakistani are Muslim. The founding father of Pakistan, Muhammad Ali Jinnah, wanted Pakistan to be a secular state, with clear distinction between political and religious authority, views shared by his later successors, Zulfikar Bhutto and daughter Benazir. After Jinnah's death, and especially since the rise of Islamic fundamentalism in the late 1970s, the power of Islamic radicalism in Pakistan has increased. When Muslim-based political parties have been in power, they have attempted with some success to make state law conform to the Islamic religious code, the Shariah. When the more secularist Bhuttos, father and then daughter, were in office, Muslim fundamentalists were among their most virulent opponents.

Founded as a dominion in the British Commonwealth (renamed soon thereafter as the Commonwealth of Nations), Pakistan became a constitutional republic in 1956, with a bicameral parliamentary form of government. The prime minister, leader of the largest party in the lower house, the National Assembly, held the executive authority, and a president had a more ceremonial role as head of state. Pakistani political history has been characterized by the repeated overthrow of civilian parliamentary governments and the establishment of military dictatorships. In 1958, Field Marshal Ayub Khan declared martial law, suspending the constitution and assuming full authority, just as General Zia later would do in a similar situation in 1977 and General Pervez Musharraf in 1999.

A strong army has been seen as essential under civilian governments as well as military dictatorships because of the concern about national security. Pakistan's main enemy has been India, with whom it has waged three unsuccessful wars: in 1947, 1965, and 1971. The major point of contention has been disputed possession of the state of Kashmir, a region in the Himalayan mountains bordering both countries. Kashmir has a majority Muslim population, but at the time of independence, it had a Hindu princely ruler and it was therefore ceded to India, a decision Pakistan has never accepted.

The military has also been seen as an effective means of dealing with internal ethnic conflict. The army was unable, however, to quell the secessionist struggle of the Bengalis in East Pakistan. With Indian assistance, East Pakistan successfully rebelled in 1971 and established independence as the nation-state of Bangladesh. The government in power as well as the Pakistani army was discredited in this humiliating defeat, which led to the appointment as president and then as prime minister of the populist, strongly nationalist Zulfikar Ali Bhutto in December 1971.

ZULFIKAR ALI BHUTTO, 1929–1979

Born in 1928 in the province of Sindh, Zulfikar Bhutto came from a wealthy, politically prominent landowning family. As did many ambitious South Asian men of means, Bhutto had a Western education, attending the University of Southern California, University of California at Berkeley, and Oxford University. Affirming his Asian identity, he would say, "his mind was Western, but his soul Eastern" (quoted in Bhutto, F., 2010, p. 42). Despite his enormous wealth, living as a feudal lord on the rents from tenants on his vast estates in Sindh, in his political career Bhutto was committed to improving the lives of the poor. In 1967, he founded the populist Pakistan People's Party (PPP), which had as its slogan, "*roti, kapra aur makan*" ("bread, clothes, and housing"). When he was in power, he introduced socialist reforms, including the nationalization of industries and banks and the establishment of educational programs to improve the very low literacy rate.

Bhutto's secular Westernized lifestyle, which included such practices as drinking alcohol, angered traditional Muslims, but his answer was that, although he had a drink occasionally, "unlike other politicians, I do not drink the blood of the people" (quoted in Bhutto, B., 1989, p. 20). Although willing to pander to orthodox religious forces when necessary, he privately scorned Muslim conservatives as "damned beards" (quoted in "In Pakistan, the Making of a Martyr," 1979). Committed to gender equality, he was willing to risk the ire of fundamentalists with measures to eliminate discrimination against women.

Bhutto's adoring daughter Benazir praised him as "the first to bring democracy" to Pakistan: "The six years of his government had brought light to a country steeped in stagnant darkness" (Bhutto, B., 1989, pp. 16–17). Although espousing democratic principles, Zulfikar Bhutto ruled in as authoritarian a manner as any of his predecessors. Described as an "arrogant, charismatic, brooding, and suspicious politician who governed with great flair and ruthlessness" (Weisman, 1986b), he was a populist demagogue who established a personality cult that became known simply as "Bhuttoism."

Befitting his demagogic leadership, Bhutto was determined to strengthen Pakistan's prestige and power. Representing Pakistan at the United Nations Security Council meetings in December 1971 that were convened to discuss the issue of secession of East Pakistan, he passionately argued against the dismemberment of Pakistan. When the Security Council ruled in support of the new Bangladesh, Bhutto stormed out of the session in protest.

Propelled by his strong position into the prime ministry that same month, in 1972 he took Pakistan out of the Commonwealth of Nations because of its recognition of the independence of Bangladesh. At a historic meeting with the Indian Prime Minister Indira Gandhi in the Indian hill town of Simla, also in 1972, he was able through skillful diplomacy to restore national pride by negotiating a settlement with India that met all of the Pakistani demands except for the recovery of East Pakistan. All Pakistani prisoners were returned, and Pakistan recovered the West Pakistani territory seized by India in the 1971 war. Not depending on diplomacy only, Bhutto wanted Pakistan to achieve nuclear capability, and remarked, with strange words for a populist leader, that Pakistan should develop nuclear weapons, even if the people had to eat "grass or leaves" or "even go hungry" (quoted in Talbot, 2009, p. 238).

Zulfikar Bhutto was overthrown in July 1977 in a military coup led by General Zia-ul-Haq. Accused of complicity in the murder of an opponent, Bhutto was tried and convicted. Zia could have let him go into exile, but Bhutto refused to disavow his determination to return to power (Lieven, 2011, p. 76). Therefore, seeking a final solution to the threat from Bhutto, Zia ordered his execution in April 1979. Zia established martial law and, through his treatment of Bhutto and his own repressive policies, helped create the mystique of Zulfikar Bhutto as a martyred hero. Thinking that he had eliminated Bhuttoism by executing Bhutto, Zia found an equally formidable adversary in the person of Bhutto's oldest daughter, Benazir.

THE MAKING OF A MUSLIM WOMAN LEADER, 1953–1984

Twenty-five years old when her father was executed, Benazir Bhutto was born in 1953 in Karachi, the capital of Sindh and Pakistan's largest port. Her privileged background as part of a wealthy powerful family gave her a sense of confidence and entitlement that both enhanced and undermined her later attempts at leadership. Benazir's mother, Nusrat Bhutto, was a Shiite Muslim of Iranian descent in predominantly Sunni Pakistan. This sectarian difference was not important in the secularized Bhutto household. Showing his lack of regard for traditional Muslim customs, Zulfikar did not mourn the birth of a daughter. He was reportedly delighted when his first child, Benazir ("without equal"), was born. He thought that she, who later so identified with him, looked just like him (Bhutto, B., 1989, p. 204).

Although two sons were subsequently born, Murtaza in 1954 and Shahnawaz in 1958, as well as another daughter, Sanam in 1957, Benazir claimed that she was her father's favorite, and she in turn worshipped him. For emotional and as well as political reasons, throughout her life she extolled him as a saint (Jack, 1986, p. 73). As the irreverent historian Christopher Hitchens (2011) commented, Benazir Bhutto "had the largest Electra complex of any female politician in modern history" (p. 472). It was perhaps easier to idealize him because he was away on diplomatic missions during most of her youth—she later said that she saw her father as often in the newspapers as in person. He kept in touch with her, however, through lengthy letters of advice and encouragement (Bhutto, B., 1988, p. 3).

Benazir's mother was a constant but more ambivalent presence in Benazir's life. College educated and raised in relative social freedom, when Nusrat married, even though to the liberal Zulfikar Bhutto, she entered the traditional Muslim woman's life in secluded *purdah* with her husband's sisters. When Benazir reached puberty, her mother wanted her to wear a *burqa* when she traveled, the black full-body covering that traditional Muslim women wore for modesty. When her father learned about it, he said that his daughter did not have to cover herself. Nusrat then decided that neither would she (Bhutto, B., 1989, pp. 46–47). In her later political life, Benazir did always wear the traditional *dupatta*, a scarf covering the head, to appease traditional Muslims as well as to assert her own identity as a Muslim woman.

The language spoken in the Westernized Bhutto home was English. Benazir was later handicapped politically because although she could speak Urdu, the national language of Pakistan, she did so with grammatical errors that were often mocked by her enemies. She barely spoke Sindhi, the language of her native province. She began her education with an English governess, and later at an English-speaking convent school. At the young age of 15, she completed with distinction her secondary-school graduating "O-level" examinations, prompting her father to write to her that he was proud to "have a daughter who is so bright that she is doing O-levels at the young age of 15, three years before I did them. At this rate, you might become the president" (quoted in Bhutto, B., 1989, p. 52).

Providing for his daughters the same educational opportunities as his sons, Benazir's controlling father carefully chose what university she would attend and what she would study. Following his path of doing his undergraduate education in the United States, but eschewing California as too distracting an environment, he selected the prestigious Radcliffe College, then a women's college in Cambridge, Massachusetts, that integrated with Harvard University in the early 1970s. Only 16 years old when she entered the university, and from a completely different world, Benazir experienced severe culture shock when she first arrived in Cambridge. Accustomed to domestic servants and chauffeurs, she had difficulty learning to cope for herself. She was also shocked by the easy heterosexual mixing. She said that she never even danced, for fear her father would find out. He may have been a Westernized liberal, but there were limits to what he would tolerate in his daughter. And she obeyed him, even at long distance. "I respected him so much. I didn't want to fall in his eyes" (quoted in Jack, 1986, pp. 71, 73).

Benazir soon adapted to American university life in the heyday of the radical 1960s and early 1970s. She shed the traditional Pakistani female clothing and started wearing jeans and a sweatshirt. She became involved in the nascent women's rights movement, and delighted in being with women who refused to be hampered by their gender: "My fledgling confidence soared and I got over the shyness that had plagued my earlier years" (Bhutto, B., 1989, p. 49).

Benazir joined the antiwar movement that was stirring students across the nation in protest against the U.S. war in Vietnam. She was not a pacifist, but, echoing her father's views, she believed that the United States should not engage in military action in Asia. Ironically, her first political speech was in opposition to Asian people seeking freedom. In response to a Harvard professor's criticism of Pakistan for trying to crush the nationalist movement of the Bengalis in East Pakistan, she blindly endorsed her father's position on the right of Pakistan to control the Muslim territories in the East (Bhutto, B., 1989, p. 53). Her stance was reinforced when Zulfikar Bhutto came to New York to the United Nations in December 1971 to plead against the independence of East Pakistan. He asked his daughter to come down from Cambridge to join him there and to act as his assistant, giving Benazir her first taste of serving as her father's apprentice.

Several years later, when she was at Oxford University, Benazir lobbied ardently to have the university give an honorary degree to her father, an alumnus of the university. There was too much opposition, because of the brutal atrocities, reportedly directed by Zulfikar, against the East Pakistani Bengali nationalists. A leader of the protest, Shyam Bhatia (2008), who later became her friend, said that Benazir, who "idolized her beloved 'Papa' and visibly basked in his affection," was "totally blind to his limitations" (pp. 8, 16–17). Many years later, she acknowledged that East Pakistan had been exploited as a colony by the western part of the country. Seeking absolution, she claimed that she had so many times "asked God to forgive me for my ignorance" (Bhutto, B., 1989, p. 63).

In those apprentice years, Benazir accompanied her father in 1972 to the historic summit in Simla with Indira Gandhi, to work out the agreement after the 1971 war. At this conference, Benazir was able to see firsthand an example of a strong South Asian female political leader in the person of the prime minister of India, who, as Benazir would later, came to power on the coattails of her father, the first prime minister of India, Jawaharlal Nehru.

After Benazir graduated from Radcliffe with honors in government in 1973, Zulfikar Bhutto decreed that she should continue her studies at his alma mater, Oxford University, and focus on politics, philosophy, and economics. Her being there, he wrote to her, gave him "a strange sensation in imagining you walking in the footsteps I left behind at Oxford over twenty-two years ago" (quoted in Bhutto, B., 1989, p. 80). At Oxford, Benazir proved that she was indeed a Bhutto by her extraordinary achievement of being elected president of the prestigious male-dominated university debating society, the Oxford Union. In the race for president, Benazir campaigned so vigorously that official complaints were lodged. Her friends later commented that she wanted to be president so much to please her father (Jack, 1986, p. 73). As president, she delighted in picking such provocative debate topics as the double-entendred "This house likes domineering women" (Hall, 1984).

Completing her postgraduate studies at Oxford in June 1977, Benazir returned to Pakistan ready to begin what she thought would be a career in the foreign service. Two weeks after her return, however, after Zulfikar Bhutto's resounding victory at the polls earlier that year, he was overthrown and incarcerated in General Zia's military coup. Significantly, Bhutto immediately instructed his sons, 23-year-old Murtaza and 19-year-old Shahnawaz, to leave Pakistan and seek safety elsewhere, with the assumption that his sons were more vulnerable to political reprisals in patriarchal Pakistan than were his wife and daughters. Not long before his death, as Murtaza's daughter Fatima Bhutto (2010) later reported, Zulfikar placed a heavy burden on his sons by writing to them that "if you do not avenge my murder, you are not my sons" (p. 169).

Murtaza and Shahnawaz went first to nearby Kabul, Afghanistan, and later to Syria, where they lived under the patronage of their father's close friend, President Hafez al-Assad. Establishing the Save Bhutto Committee, they campaigned vigorously to arouse international pressure to force Zia to free their father. After his execution, following his instructions for revenge, they turned to violent methods to challenge Zia's rule. Founding Al-Zulfikar, soon to be labeled a terrorist organization, they trained troops to carry out acts of sabotage and assassination. Murtaza himself admitted that his agents had made five unsuccessful attempts to kill Zia (Bhatia, 2008, p. 20).

The most dramatic and far-reaching act reportedly of Al-Zulfikar was the hijacking in 1981 of a Pakistani airliner, which was forced to land in Kabul. After a 13-day stalemate, the Zia regime agreed to Al-Zulfikar's demands to release PPP and other opposition political prisoners. Death warrants in Pakistan were issued for Murtaza and Shahnawaz, and they could therefore not return to Pakistan without the threat of arrest. Fatima Bhutto, as ardently loving and defensive a daughter to Murtaza as was Benazir for her father, claimed that her father was innocent, citing the testimony of one of the passengers who said, after his release, that "the whole thing was maneuvered by General Zia! He wanted an explosion in front of the world that would destroy the Bhutto boys" (Bhutto, F., 2010, p. 227). A reporter interviewing Murtaza later in Syria, however, said that he "came close to accepting responsibility for such acts" (Kamm, 1994a).

When Zulfikar Bhutto was first imprisoned in June 1977, with her brothers out of the country and her younger sister Sanam still in school at Harvard University, Benazir, along with her mother Nusrat, remained in Pakistan, protected at least for a while by the seeming innocuousness of their gender. By September 1977, however, General Zia, recognizing the danger that the female Bhuttos represented to his regime, had Benazir and Nusrat placed under house arrest and sometimes in jail. Even under those conditions, Benazir had what her brothers did not, access to visit her father when the authorities permitted. Those two years of his imprisonment, receiving his counsel and watching him suffer, and then experiencing the horror of his execution on April 4, 1979, were traumatic to the young Benazir. She grieved that the day before his death, she had only "half an hour to say goodbye to the person I love more than any other in my life" (Bhutto, B., 1989, p. 20), and her idolization of him only increased with his martyrdom. Even into her fifties, she would cry when she talked about his sufferings in prison (Bhatia, 2008, p. 9).

The two years during her father's imprisonment and then death forged in the young Bhutto daughter the determination to continue in his footsteps as his chosen political successor:

> On the day my father was arrested, I changed from a girl to a woman. He would guide me over the next two years. . . . On the day he was murdered, I understood that my life was to be Pakistan, and I accepted the mantle of leadership of my father's legacy and my father's party. (Bhutto, B., 2008b, pp. 187–188)

Framing this role as one that she had not chosen but which was "thrust upon my shoulders after my father's murder" (Bhutto, B., 2007), Benazir nevertheless fought fiercely when her brother Murtaza as the oldest male child claimed the right of leadership. Emphasizing that she and not Murtaza was with their father in those dark days of his imprisonment and execution, she claimed that Zulfikar had made clear that she was his designated political heir. Murtaza responded with the argument that their father sent his sons out of Pakistan when he was arrested to protect them as his successors. Rejecting her brother's claim based on his gender, Benazir repeatedly insisted that sex discrimination was not part of the family heritage:

> Among Bhuttos, sons and daughters were equal. And when the time came to pick up my father's mantle and legacy and lead the Pakistan People's Party, I as his eldest *child* present in Pakistan, led the struggle for democracy. . . . It is the gender equality in Islam under which I was brought up. (Bhutto, B., 2008b, p. 39)

As confirmation of her claim, a family friend reported that when he visited the Bhuttos in 1971, he was struck with the deference Zulfikar showed his young daughter, only half-jokingly referring to her as "my first son." The friend concluded, "it was clear that Benazir . . . was meant to carry the mantle of the political dynasty that he hoped to start" (Taheri, 2007).

Benazir's claim to leadership was strengthened by the sufferings that she herself experienced under Zia's brutal rule, when she became, as her father had been, a symbol of resistance to the military regime (Shafqat, 1996, p. 657). Although her mother was allowed to leave the country for medical treatment in 1982, Benazir remained in various degrees of detention for almost seven years. The most difficult time came after the 1981 hijacking of the Pakistani airliner, when she was sent for six months to the Sukkur prison in the remote Sindh desert, in solitary confinement and under conditions that were so horrible that even mere survival was a struggle. In the extreme heat and dirty cell, "my skin split and peeled, coming off my hands in sheets. More boils erupted on my face. The sweat dripped into them, burning like acid. My hair, which had always been thick, began to come out by the handful" (Bhutto, B., 1989, p. 200).

Benazir's friends in the United States and elsewhere tried to arouse international concern about her harsh treatment. Zia's repressive military regime was protected, however, from official Western, especially American, criticism because of the Soviet invasion of Afghanistan in December 1979, which increased U.S. reliance on Pakistan's support. For Zia, the invasion "was a godsend. Soviet occupation changed everything. Zia became Washington's best friend against communist expansionism" (Bhatia, 2008, p. 45). Finally, in January 1984, after pressure from the United States, organized by her Harvard friend Peter Galbraith, who was on the staff of the Senate Foreign Relations Committee, Zia agreed to release Benazir from prison and allow her to leave the country for medical care. In poor health from the terrible conditions under which she suffered, she said that Zia "did not want to face the international uproar of having yet more Bhutto blood on his hands" (Bhutto, B., 2008b, p. 191).

Zia had imprisoned Benazir Bhutto to break her spirit, but in fact the ordeal only intensified her determination to challenge his rule. Each incarceration, she said while imprisoned, "is just adding another layer of anger" (Bhutto, B., 1989, p. 36). Peter Galbraith said that she "was transformed by the fights in those difficult years. . . . Nothing in her background suggests that she would have had such courage to see it through" (quoted in Weisman, 1986b). She was toughened, certainly, but as Steven Weisman (1986b) asked, did the experience strengthen her or "transform her into a distrustful imperious loner striving for vindication?"

PARTY LEADER IN EXILE, 1984–1986

After her release, Benazir Bhutto flew to London, where she told reporters that she was not in permanent exile, but had come only to seek medical treatment for conditions suffered while in prison. "I was born in Pakistan and I'm going to die in Pakistan. My grandfather is buried there. My father is buried there. I will never leave my country" (Bhutto, B., 1989, p. 259). In a message released in Pakistan, she explained that in London she would be able to work with exiled members of the Pakistan People's Party campaigning against Zia's regime, and in that way, "your Sister hopes to play [a role in the] redemption of the lost rights of the people" (Bhutto, 1988, p. 65).

The inexperienced Bhutto soon experienced conflict with PPP members. Largely because of the mystique of her family name and her own suffering under General Zia, she was elected head of the party. Idealistic and single minded, she was irritated by the factionalism and politicking of her associates (Bhutto, B., 1989, p. 273). They, in turn, had trouble accepting the leadership of a young woman whom they had known as a child (Gupta, 1986). In choosing her, they assumed, as had the Indian Congress party when it chose Nehru's daughter as their leader, that she would serve primarily as a symbol. (The Congress Party, according to Benazir, called Indira "'a dumb doll' behind her back. But this silk-and-steel woman had outmaneuvered them all") (Bhutto, B., 1989, p. 72). Similarly, the PPP treated Benazir, a colleague observed, "like a little punk girl" (quoted in Weisman, 1986b). She resented the party's patronizing attitude, and readily dismissed these men she called her "uncles" from party positions and replaced them with her own followers, whose loyalty and deference to her authority were unquestioned.

The resolve of Bhutto and the PPP to overthrow General Zia was intensified because of his program to completely Islamicize Pakistani government and law. From his own religious convictions as well as his political judgment that it was Islam that held the country together, Zia had state laws revised to bring them in accordance with the Islamic religious law, the Shariah (Lieven, 2011, p. 76). The major focus of Zia's Islamization was regulation of social and, especially, female behavior. Inspired by the triumph of Khomeini and Islamic fundamentalism in Iran in 1979, Zia's Shariah courts issued most notoriously the Hudood ordinances, which punished crimes such as adultery and rape in strict accordance with Islamic law. This meant that four Muslim men were required as witnesses to prove a woman's charge of rape. Without the witnesses, a woman bringing a charge of rape could be accused of adultery and stoned to death if married, or receive 100 lashes and imprisonment if unmarried. In another codification of the Shariah, the Law of Evidence decreed that a woman's testimony would be worth only half as much as the testimony of a man.

As part of the restriction of women in the name of Islam, Zia's government idealized the image of woman as faithful to *chador our char diwari* (remaining veiled and within the confines of the four walls of one's house) (Weiss, 1990, p. 438). Although many women, of course, did not return to *purdah*, traditional symbols of modesty reappeared. Female newscasters on television were required to cover their heads with *dupattas* or be dismissed. The requirement that all female teachers wear *dupattas* was expanded in 1982 to require them to wear the heavier opaque veil, the *chador*. Many women began wearing the full-body covering of the *burqa* again. Women's field hockey teams were required to keep their legs covered, which eliminated them from international competition. During the Seoul Olympics in 1984, the Pakistan television screens went blank every time a female swimmer did a flip-turn (Walsh, 1989).

Bhutto had another personal grievance against Zia with the death in 1985 of her beloved younger brother, Shahnawaz. The family, in scattered exiles, had gathered for a reunion in Nice, France. While there, amid marital strife and other familial conflicts, Shahnawaz mysteriously died of poisoning. It was never determined if it was suicide, or perhaps, as the authorities suspected, the act of his wife. Bhutto was convinced that Zia had personally ordered the murder (Bhatia, 2008, p. 10). She courageously decided to take his body back to Pakistan for burial, demanding that the Zia government allow her the right to bury him according to proper Muslim rites. Probably bothered by the cheering crowds that greeted Bhutto's arrival, Zia had her detained briefly after the funeral, but then released her to return to London (Bhutto, B., 1989, pp. 295–304).

Later that same year, in December 1985, with the apparent failure of the Soviet campaign in Afghanistan, the United States felt free to pressure its ally Zia to lift martial law and restore the constitution. Zia complied, but protected his power by securing the passage of the Eighth Amendment, which specified that acts, ordinances, and decrees passed under martial law could be undone only with a two-thirds majority of both houses of the legislature. The president also was given the right to dissolve the National Assembly anytime he judged that an appeal to the electorate was necessary. With these safeguards, Zia allowed political parties to once again operate openly and legally, which meant the return to Pakistan of Benazir Bhutto and the Pakistan People's Party.

BHUTTO'S RETURN TO PAKISTAN TO CAMPAIGN FOR ELECTION, 1986–1988

Benazir Bhutto returned to Pakistan in April 1986, ready to take on the Zia government in the elections. When she arrived, she was greeted by huge, cheering crowds at the airport and along her route to a rally. Strikingly attractive and charismatic, Bhutto won the hearts of the Pakistanis with her long suffering under Zia and her unwavering resistance to his repressive regime. Playing the politics of suffering by dramatizing her own experiences, she reminded the Pakistani people that, "I have willingly taken the path of thorns and stepped into the valley of death" (Bhutto, B., 1989, p. 329). In the words of the historian Ian Talbot (2009), "it is almost impossible to exaggerate the weight of expectation which her return aroused" (p. 293).

Bhutto was well aware that the major source of her popularity came from the memory of her martyred father. The constant cry that she heard from the crowds was *"Jiye Bhutto"* (long live Bhutto) (Bhatia, 2008, p. 21), suggesting the hope that the revered leader had returned in the person of his daughter. In her campaign for the return of the PPP to power, therefore, with herself as prime minister, she referred repeatedly to her father in her speeches and always had his picture in the background of her official portraits. As she exclaimed to the crowds in a campaign rally, "Seeing you, the people, makes me feel that Bhutto is alive before my eyes. He told me at our last meeting at Rawalpindi jail that I must sacrifice everything for my country. This is a mission I shall live or die for" (quoted in Weisman, 1986a).

Bhutto also emphasized her familial role as the sister of the people. It was not a big hurdle, she said, for her as a woman to be a leader in a Muslim country: "People didn't think of me as a woman. If anything, they thought of me as a sister" (quoted in Hall, 1984). When she arrived back in Pakistan, she reminded the welcoming crowds, "I am the daughter of martyr Zulfikar Ali Bhutto, the sister of martyr Shahnawaz Khan Bhutto, and I am your sister as well" (Bhutto, B., 1989, p. 333).

As an unmarried woman, Bhutto did have difficulty dealing socially with her male colleagues. "I must always maintain a certain degree of formality. . . . I can't develop the kind of camaraderie that exists between men" (quoted in Jack, 1986, p. 135). Thirty-three-years old when she returned to Pakistan, she told curious reporters that she did not have time for marriage, because she was totally dedicated to her political mission (Jack, 1986, p. 134). Being unmarried became, however, a political liability. She bemoaned the fact that men can remain unmarried without being questioned, while single women are somehow "suspect" (Bhutto, B., 1989, p. 353).

In 1987, therefore, Bhutto made the fateful decision to marry, to a man chosen by her family. Seeing it as an act of self-sacrifice, she said it was "the price in personal choice I had to pay for the political path my life had taken" (Bhutto, B., 1989, p. 350). Although arranged marriages are the accepted norm in South Asian society, her decision shocked her Western friends. She explained that in her high-profile life she had no opportunity to meet an appropriate man, and that "for me as leader of a Muslim party, it would just not do to marry for love. . . . It would be detrimental to my image" (quoted in Bennett, 1987). An arranged marriage, she would often argue, is no different from computer matchmaking sites. "When it's difficult to find a man, for whatever reason, one has to look for mediation" (quoted in Dreifus, 1994). Her mother and aunts interviewed possible candidates, and it is surprising that they chose Asif Ali Zardari, who was also from a Sindhi landowning family but whose father was owner of the rundown Bambi cinema in Karachi. Two years younger than Benazir, Zardari was much below her not only socially and economically, but also intellectually. In contrast to her Harvard and Oxford education, he went to a minor London commercial college. A stylish dresser who loved fancy cars, his main passion was apparently polo (Bhatia, 2008, p. 4). Bhutto nevertheless agreed to the marriage. Making the commitment for the sake of her career, the marriage ironically turned out to be a political disaster, with many damaging legal charges through the years brought against Zardari for his boundless greed and corruption.

Bhutto's supporters worried (and her opponents hoped) when they heard of her marriage plans that she would give up politics. As she traveled around the country, she reassured the people "that I was their sister and would always be their sister, and that my marriage would have no bearing on my political career" (Bhutto, B., 1989, p. 358). Significantly, she retained her father's name, Bhutto. (Her antagonistic brother, Murtaza, would sometimes taunt her by calling her "Mrs. Asif Zardari" and claim that she was not a Bhutto. She would retort that she was a feminist, and had therefore kept her own name [Bhutto, F., 2010, p. 311].)

Repeatedly criticized by her opponents as being too Western, Bhutto used her arranged marriage to emphasize her identity as an Asian woman. She pointedly entitled her first memoirs, published in 1988 to coincide with the parliamentary campaign, *Daughter of the East*. (The book was published in the United States in 1989 with the modified title *Daughter of Destiny*.) The image of her as a (somewhat) traditional Muslim bride did confuse those who knew her in her earlier radical days. As a London *Times* writer put it, "The metamorphosis of Benazir Bhutto, impassioned sari-wearing leader of the Pakistan People's Party, into demure fiancée of Asif Zardari . . . is, to western eyes, one of the most impressive transformations in a career already full of contradictions" (Bennett, 1987).

Hardly demure, but with the cloak of respectability as a married woman, Bhutto campaigned vigorously for the elections of 1988. When asked whether she would have children, she replied that that would have to wait (Preston, 1988, p. 47). She did, however, immediately get pregnant. She tried to hide her pregnancy from Zia, knowing that he would then schedule the election at the time of her due date. It was easier to hide a pregnancy with the loose South Asian women's clothing, but Zia learned about it, and, as she had feared, scheduled the election at her due date in September. It was "the first election to be timed for gynecological considerations" (Singh, 1988, p. 45).

In an extraordinary twist of fate, General Zia, the murderer of her father and perhaps also her younger brother, and the focus of Bhutto's political attacks from the time of her father's arrest in 1977, was killed in a plane crash on August 17, 1988, the cause of which was never determined. Bhutto's reaction was one of frank joy: "I can't regret Zia's death. . . . People think it's too good to be true" (quoted in Gupta, 1988, p. 13). In political terms, it was not good, in that his death eliminated the major thrust of her campaign. However, she was helped when Ghulam Ishaq Khan, the leader of the Senate who became the new president, postponed the elections until November. Giving birth to her son Bilawal in September, she was soon back on the campaign trail, working tirelessly to promote the PPP agenda.

BHUTTO AS PRIME MINISTER, 1988–1990, 1993–1996

The PPP won 92 of the 203 contested seats in the National Assembly. Bhutto claimed that her party would have won many more seats if Zia had not earlier decreed that all voters must have identity cards, which many of her supporters, especially poor women, did not have (Bhutto, B., 1989, pp. 390–391). Although not a majority, the PPP was the largest party in the National Assembly, and therefore on December 2, its leader, Benazir Bhutto, was appointed prime minister, making history by becoming the first woman to head a modern Muslim state.

The euphoria over Bhutto's return was augmented all the more by her election. As her new minister of state for information extravagantly proclaimed, "After eleven years of darkness a woman leader has come to power who is brave, bright, brilliant, gracious, to overthrow the forces of darkness" (quoted in Lieven, 2011, p. 235). The more reasoned Voice of America described Bhutto as "a breath of fresh air," and "a symbol of the new democratic Pakistan" (quoted in Ziring, 2003, p. 213). These extravagant expectations worked to Bhutto's disadvantage, because they inevitably led to severe disappointment and disillusionment when political realities kept Bhutto from carrying out her promises. With a plurality but not a majority in the National Assembly, and with a Senate that was dominated by anti-PPP parties, she could not get any reform legislation passed. After barely 20 months in power, President Khan used the powers of the Eighth Amendment to remove her from office, on the charges of corruption, abuse of power, and ineptitude. New elections were called, and this time the winner was Nawaz Sharif, the head of the Pakistan Muslim League (PML). Bhutto assumed the position of leader of the opposition.

Bhutto was imperial even in defeat, demanding that she, as leader of the opposition, be allowed to appoint the national election commissioner, and that all judicial appointments and the selection of the four provincial governors be cleared by her. Sharif refused, replying that "in no country in the world" did the opposition leader have such powers (quoted in Gargan, 1993a). He received more opposition than just from Bhutto, and Sharif in turn was removed from office in 1993 for the same reasons as given for Bhutto's removal in 1990.

New elections in 1993 brought Bhutto and the PPP back into power, although on a more moderate platform that seemed hardly different from that of Sharif's. As *The New York Times* reporter Edward Gargan (1993b) assessed her victory, he concluded that "the electoral achievement of Ms. Bhutto, a striking, almost glamorous woman in a deeply male-dominated society, appears to be testimony more to her phenomenal campaign personality before a mostly illiterate electorate than to any of her party's policy pronouncements."

Again Bhutto had only a plurality. She was, however, more realistic and experienced the second time around, and more willing to cooperate with opposition parties. This time the president, Farooq Leghari, was a member of her own party (Talbot, 2009, p. 333). Nevertheless, she still faced formidable obstacles, and was again unable to govern effectively. A friend reflected that "the fight seemed to go out of Benazir during her second term. Whether it was the 1988–1990 experience that soured her, or whether she lacked the mental stamina necessary to run the country, there was a sense of drift throughout her second term" (Bhatia, 2008, pp. 99–100). Her second prime ministry was generally judged as much a failure as her first one, and so President Leghari, having lost confidence in her, dismissed her government in 1996.

THE CHALLENGES AND OBSTACLES TO BHUTTO
AS PRIME MINISTER

Benazir Bhutto's tenures as prime minister were bitter disappointments to those who had had such high hopes for a new era in Pakistani politics. There were some achievements that she would point to with pride. One of her first acts as prime minister was to order that all death sentences be commuted to life imprisonment and that all women prisoners except those convicted of murder be released (in that most had been imprisoned under the Zia's oppressive Shariah laws.) She lifted the ban on trade unions and student organizations. She allowed greater freedom of speech, including in the media. This freer environment, however, allowed the opposition to criticize her without restraint and to work openly to undermine her rule. Pakistanis were not accustomed to such public criticism of their government, so it was commonly interpreted that she was weak and had lost control (Weiss, 1990, p. 435).

She brought Pakistan back into the Commonwealth of Nations, and, in the spirit of the times, she began the process of the privatization of industries and banks that had been nationalized by her socialist father. There were some efforts to improve the lives of especially poor women, with the establishment of women's banks and all-women police stations, and the appointment of women judges. Greater social freedom for women was reflected in the renewed participation of Pakistani women in international sports competitions (Bhutto, B., 2008b, p. 200).

Bhutto's achievements were seen as meager, however, in the light of all her promises and the popular expectations. Among the many obstacles that she faced, some were of her own making, including her own leadership style and the blatant corruption during her tenures, whereas others, such as the power of the military and of the Muslim fundamentalists and the forces of patriarchy in general, were endemic to the Pakistani political culture, and would have been difficult to overcome even with the most skilled leadership.

Bhutto's Leadership Style

Benazir Bhutto had a positive reputation in the West and especially in the United States as a liberal democrat, committed to fighting oppression, and her image among the Pakistani masses remained strong. Among those with whom she worked, however, she was seen as of authoritarian and intolerant of dissent, characteristics all the more fatal because of her own political inexperience. As Saeed Shafqat (1996) concluded, "Although as a female leader she confronted enormous but by no means insurmountable odds, she showed a poor grasp of the workings of government. . . . She persisted in establishing personal supremacy but without creating conditions that strengthened her party" (p. 667).

Some critics have attributed her sense of imperiousness to her privileged upbringing, making her, in the words of William Dalrymple (2007), "a feudal princess with the aristocratic sense of entitlement that came with owning great tracts of the country and the Western-leaning tastes that such background tends to give." The historian Lawrence Ziring (2003) suggested that she was modeling herself on her authoritarian father. "Her intemperate behavior revealed how wounded she was by her father's execution and how closely she resembled the character of her father, who had shown a total inability to work with people who disagreed with him" (p. 212). Strong women are often criticized as domineering, whereas strong men are praised as capable. Bhutto's poor record as prime minister, however, suggests that, unlike such powerful female leaders as Indira Gandhi and Margaret Thatcher, Bhutto's authoritarian personality undermined rather than facilitated her political leadership.

The Military

A formidable obstacle to Bhutto's effectiveness as a political leader came from the powerful Pakistani army. Mistrustful of her as a woman, and seeing her as too Westernized, the generals were especially concerned that, as a member of the PPP and using rhetoric of peace in the campaigns, she would be too soft on the archenemy, India (Gupta, 1986, p. 14). In fact, as her father's daughter, Bhutto was a strong nationalist. Recognizing the power of symbolism, she typically wore green and white clothing, the colors of the Pakistani flag. When the military scorned her for her youth, she could play the martyr's card by saying that she had "seen too much pain and repression" to be young (quoted in Gupta, 1988, p. 21). She also cleverly used her youth as an advantage. Unlike the generals born before Partition in 1947, she had "never been an Indian. I had been born in independent Pakistan" (Bhutto, B., 1989, p. 72).

As a strong nationalist, out of conviction as well as of political expediency, Bhutto maintained the hard line on Kashmir. In her speeches and writings, she unequivocally insisted that Kashmir, with its Muslim majority, belonged to Pakistan. Although there was no war with India during her tenures, she did encourage pro-Pakistani Kashmir militants to attack Indian officials (Bhatia, 2008, p. 61).

Bhutto also continued her father's policy of developing nuclear-weapons capability. In a 2003 interview, she said that she "cannot take credit for our nuclear programme, that goes to my father, but I am the mother of the missile programme." She admitted what had long been suspected, that she secured the missile technology in an exchange deal with North Korea. She said that on a trip to North Korea she had worn an overcoat with the "deepest possible pockets" into which she put the CDs containing the scientific data about uranium enrichment that the North Koreans wanted. She then brought North Korea's missile information back with her on CDs to Pakistan. As the interviewer remarked, "The idea of the Pakistani Prime Minister acting as a female James Bond was simply incredible" (Bhatia, 2008, pp. 39, 42).

Despite her passionate nationalistic rhetoric and actions, the army never trusted Bhutto, and, working through the far-reaching Inter-Service Intelligence (ISI), it tried to prevent her election and then to sabotage her governments. During her first government, the ISI conducted what they called "Operation Midnight Jackal," bribing members of the PPP to defect, and spreading rumors, well before it actually happened, that the president was about to sack her, and tried to convince her ministers and the PPP members of the National Assembly to switch sides to keep their positions (Lieven, 2011, p. 211). To prevent her reelection in 1990, according to the testimony of the-then director of the ISI in a court proceeding, the agency was ordered by the army chief of staff to provide "logistic support" for the distribution of funds to Bhutto's opponents (Jones, 2002, p. 240). This kind of harassment continued to plague Bhutto throughout her political career.

Islamic Reactionaries

Bhutto's governments were also undermined by conservative Muslims. Despite her efforts to accommodate traditional religious forces, such as making a pilgrimage to Mecca before taking office and by always covering her head with a *dupatta*, she could not overcome the religious prejudice against her for being a woman. Throughout her life, in her speeches and writings, she argued, as have other Muslim feminists and scholars, that Islam does not discriminate against women, and that the prophet Mohammed affirmed sexual equality. She repeatedly emphasized the glorious history of Muslim women who had successfully performed public roles: "People think I am weak because I am a woman. Do they not know that I am a Muslim woman, and that Muslim women have a heritage to be proud of?" (Bhutto, B., 1989, p. 332). Such appeals fell on the deaf ears of her reactionary opponents.

Muslim stalwarts also targeted Bhutto because of her secularist political platform, with a major theme, especially in her 1988 campaign to repeal the civil laws based on the Shariah. Of particular concern were the Hudood ordinances and the Law of Evidence, and other laws that discriminated against women. Intensifying religious opposition because of these promises, she received the bitterest recriminations from women's rights advocates because of her failure in office to do so. Some former supporters blamed her lack of commitment and resolve, and accused her of being more interested in power than women's rights (Thomas, 1989). A member of the Pakistani Human Rights Commission commented during Bhutto's second term that, "The fact remains that Benazir does not have the courage or sometimes the support to do away with laws that actually encourage men to commit crimes against women" (quoted in Bhatia, 2008, p. 2). Given the realities under which she ruled, however, it is hard to imagine that, even with skilled courageous leadership, she could have gotten the controversial repeals passed through the recalcitrant legislature.

Economy

Bhutto was blocked from fulfilling her campaign promises to improve the lives of the poor, not so much because of political opposition but because of economic constraints. She inherited from Zia a dismal economy, marked by an enormous national debt, unemployment, and inflation. Her efforts to improve the economy through the privatization of industries and other sectors were, her critics said, ill conceived and poorly implemented (Shafqat, 1996, p. 665). Dependent on foreign loans just to keep the government afloat, and weighted down with the heavy cost of the large military and the drain on public funds of rampant corruption, the Pakistani government under Bhutto simply did not have the money to spend on health and education and other social services.

Ethnic Violence

One of the most difficult situations that Bhutto had to confront was the violent ethnic conflict in her native province of the Sindh, especially in its major city, her home city, Karachi. Sindh is the home to two quite different ethnic groups: the indigenous population, who spoke primarily the regional language of Sindhi; and the *mohajirs* (in Arabic, "immigrant"), Muslims who fled from India to Pakistan after the 1947 Partition. Settling primarily in the Sindh, the *mohajirs* spoke the national language of Urdu and did not have a sense of Sindhi identity. Despite their religious commitment to endure extreme hardships and danger to immigrate to Pakistan, they were seen as unwelcome outsiders by the native Sindhi.

To protect their rights, activist *mohajirs* formed the Mohajir Qaumi Movement (MQM), to undermine, sometimes through militant acts, the PPP-dominated Sindhi provincial government. The Sindhi police responded with harsh reprisals. As violence escalated in Karachi in the 1990s, making it one of the most dangerous cities in the world, in 1994 Bhutto launched Operation Clean-up, to try to crush the unrest. This meant targeting primarily the MQM, which Bhutto, herself an ethnic Sindhi, was "categoric and emphatic in saying was a terrorist organization" (Shafqat, 1996, p. 671). The government's methods included eliminating suspected terrorists by summarily executing them, without judicial proceedings. Bhutto's niece Fatima, always hostile to her aunt and holding her responsible for whatever problems there were in Pakistan, called Operation Clean-up a "genocidal strike" against the ethnic *mohajirs* (Bhutto, F., 2010, p. 373). The less-prejudiced Amnesty International concurred, accusing Bhutto's government of having "one of the world's worst record of custodial deaths, killing and torture" (Dalrymple, 2007).

Motherhood

In contrast to military, Islamic, economic, and ethnic problems, one area of Bhutto's life that did not apparently handicap her ability to rule was motherhood. She barely missed a beat with the birth of her babies: her son

Bilawal, born during her first election campaign in September 1988; her daughter Bakhtawar, born in January 1990, during her first term; and a second daughter, Asifa, born in February 1993, while Bhutto was leader of the opposition and not long before her campaign for reelection later that year. Although the failures of her governments were not due to pregnancy and childbirth, a popular joke after her first daughter was born in 1990 was that "all she had been able to deliver as prime minister was a baby" ("Miss Bhutto's Distractions," 1990).

When her babies were little, she often took them with her on official trips. A *New York Times* reporter commented in 1994 that:

> In all the world there cannot be another plane quite like the official jet of the Prime Minister of Pakistan, Benazir Bhutto: The front section is a kind of office-cum-nursery, jammed with toys, briefcases, newspapers, nannies and Bhutto's children. . . . It is both jarring and interesting to see soldiers saluting a woman with children on her lap. It is wildly surreal to be discussing nuclear weapons with a head of state while her 4-year-old hands her candy hearts. (Dreifus, 1994)

When Bhutto did have to leave her children behind, she suffered the maternal guilt familiar to many working women. As she was preparing to go on a government trip, for example, her children were watching cartoons on television, which she did not like, but she caved in because of her departure. Her 7-year-old daughter, Bakhtawar, asked her to come back soon. "I ask her what she means. 'I am your mother. I am stuck to you like that arm of yours for life.' 'But Mama, my arm keeps going away'" (Bhutto, B. 2008a, pp. 251–252).

Asif Zardari and Corruption

Unlike motherhood, Bhutto's role as wife to Asif Zardari was severely damaging to her career and reputation. Throughout her terms as prime minister, Zardari notoriously amassed a large fortune through bribes and kickbacks in exchange for government contracts. In a world in which corruption by government officials was standard operating procedure, Zardari "went beyond patronage and limited corruption into outright kleptocracy" (Lieven, 2011, p. 79). With the common knowledge in Pakistan of his practice of using his wife's position to demand payments, he was sarcastically nicknamed "Mr. Ten Percent" (Jones, 2002, p. 235).

Although Bhutto insisted that the charges were unfounded and politically motivated, there was sufficient evidence against him and possibly her also. The charges could be seen simply as political attacks by Bhutto's enemies, but not so the conclusion of the Swiss government. With Zardari keeping large stashes of money in Swiss bank accounts, Swiss officials launched an inquiry, and found "damming evidence" of illegal gains. The ruling magistrate charged Zardari with money laundering, had his bank accounts frozen, and recommended that the Pakistani authorities indict him. Zardari was arrested and imprisoned in 1996. In 1999, the Pakistani High Court lodged additional charges against Zardari and this time Bhutto also, fining them eight million dollars and sentenced them to five years in prison. Zardari was already in prison on the earlier charge, but Bhutto was able to flee abroad before she could be arrested (Jones, 2002, p. 235).

The validity of the charges were questioned when it was revealed that the outcome of the High Court trial had been fixed (Jones, 2002, p. 235). It was hard to deny, however, the results of a 1998 *New York Times* in-depth investigation, which resulted in John Burns's scathing report, "House of Graft," documenting Zardari's corruption. Burns (1998) revealed that Zardari got more than 1.5 billion dollars in illegal profits through kickbacks "in virtually every sphere of governmental activities." He detailed Zardari's extravagant purchases with his illegal gains, including a £4 million estate outside of London, properties in France and elsewhere, and expensive jewelry.

Burns (1998) was ambiguous about whether Bhutto herself was implicated. He did quote her former press secretary who explained that Bhutto so identified herself with Pakistan, that "in her mind, she was Pakistan, so she could do as she pleased." Denying the charges, but so tainted by them, Bhutto continued to insist that her husband also was innocent. When presented with evidence of his shady financial deals, she retorted that "he is a businessman" (quoted in Bhatia, 2008, p. 34). When Zardari was imprisoned, she proclaimed that "time will tell if he is the Mandela of Pakistan" (quoted in Burns, 2007). Although in prison for eight years, Zardari did not suffer the deprivations of Mandela. He had a separate room, with an attached bathroom; air-conditioning; two servants; and, as one visitor said, the best of food (Perlez, 2008).

Murtaza and Filial Rivalry

Finally, fighting charges of corruption throughout her public life because of her husband, Bhutto also confronted painful familial conflict with her brother Murtaza. As politically ambitious as his sister, and claiming the prerogative of leadership as their father's oldest son, Murtaza sought to replace his sister as head of the PPP and as prime minister. Although in exile in Syria and labeled a terrorist, unable to return to Pakistan under threat of arrest, in 1993 Murtaza nevertheless used a quirk in the Pakistani law to run from outside of the country for a seat in the National Assembly. Actually contesting 24 seats, as the law allowed, he won only one. He assumed his sister, reelected as prime minister, would have the charges against him removed so he could return to Pakistan and take his seat. She refused, saying she could not interfere in the judicial process (Kamm, 1994b).

Murtaza nevertheless returned to Pakistan at the end of 1993 and was immediately arrested and incarcerated for seven months, then released on bail. Taking up the reins of political activism, Murtaza formed his own breakaway political party, the "Pakistan People's Party (Shaheed [holy martyr] Bhutto)," posing as the guardian of their father's values in opposition to what he saw as his sister's sell-out policies (Talbot, 2009, p. 337). Intensifying for Bhutto the painfulness of the now-public family feud, her mother sided with her son. She told reporters that Benazir "talks a lot about democracy, but she's become a little dictator. . . . She tells a lot of lies, this daughter of mine . . . She has become paranoid about her brother" (Bhutto, F., 2010, p. 349). Bhutto in turn lamented that through all her struggles, "I hoped the day would never come when I would have to battle male prejudice in my own family. It was a cruel stab in my heart when my mother declared that the male should inherit" (quoted in Kamm, 1994a).

The feud came to a tragic climax on September 20, 1996, when the police shot and killed Murtaza and six of his associates and guards outside of his family home in Larkana, Sindh. Bhutto blamed the army for the murder as an attempt to overthrow her government (Bhutto, B., 2008b, p. 209), but Fatima Bhutto was convinced that her aunt had a hand in it. The official investigation concluded that the order for the murders "came from a high level." Zardari, who had quarreled violently with his brother-in-law, was held responsible, and the charge of accessory to murder was added to the charges of corruption leveled against him (Bhutto, F., 2010, pp. 416–417, 422–423). This scandal was the final blow against Bhutto's government, which was dismissed from power in November 1996.

EXILE, 1999–2007

Fleeing arrest on charges of corruption in 1999, with her husband in prison in Pakistan until released on bail in 2004, Bhutto sought refuge first in London, then in Dubai. She lived with her children and also her mother, with whom she had reconciled after her brother's death, a reconciliation aided by her mother's early Alzheimer's disease. Bhutto spent the years in exile traversing the world, giving speeches and writing articles, in defense of her maligned record as prime minister and to restore her image on the international scene. In a world increasingly polarized between the West and Islam, she also passionately articulated an appealing view of Islam as a religion of peace and equality, not the violent patriarchal religion as bastardized by the jihadists and other fundamentalists.

Always maintaining that her heart was in Pakistan where she longed to return, she presented to the world a vision of Pakistan as a democratic country, presumably under her future rule. This vision became all the more evocative when her rival and replacement as prime minister in 1990 and again in 1996, Nawaz Sharif, was overthrown in a military coup in 1999, led by General Pervez Musharraf. The establishment of this military regime intensified Bhutto's campaign for the restoration of democracy in Pakistan. The al-Qaeda terrorist attack on 9/11 and the war in Afghanistan, however, necessitated that the United States work with and prop up Musharraf's repressive military dictatorship, just as it had Zia's regime after the Soviet invasion of Afghanistan in 1979.

RETURN TO PAKISTAN AND ASSASSINATION, 2007

By the spring of 2007, six years into its war in Afghanistan, and uneasy about supporting yet another unpopular military dictatorship, the United States sought to improve the image of General Musharraf, who was facing increasing opposition within Pakistan. The person whom they felt could do this was Benazir Bhutto. Having restored her reputation as an advocate of democratic liberal values and as a moderate Muslim, Bhutto seemed the right choice to balance the military rule in Pakistan. The United States therefore brokered a power-sharing deal between Musharraf and Bhutto, in which he would serve as president and she would be prime minister. Eager to return to Pakistan and to a position of power, but to the dismay of some of her supporters who saw Musharraf as the archenemy, Bhutto agreed to the deal. She did specify that Musharraf had to resign his military position and serve as a civilian president, which he reluctantly agreed to do. Also as part of the agreement, Musharraf issued a National Reconciliation Ordinance, in which all charges of corruption against Bhutto and her husband were dropped, as well as the other charges against Zardari.

In deciding to return to Pakistan and campaign for reelection, Bhutto was fully aware of the dangers that awaited her. It was almost as though she deliberately chose to take the martyr's road. As she reminded everyone, her father also "gave his life for democracy in Pakistan" (quoted in Taheri, 2007). Her husband stayed behind in Dubai so that, she said, if anything happened to her, her children would still have a parent. "Long ago I had made my choice. The people of Pakistan have always come first" (Bhutto, B., 2008b, p. 2). She wrote a political will just before she returned to Pakistan, in which she specified that if anything happened to her, Zardari should succeed her as head of the PPP. A reporter friend who interviewed her just before she left for Pakistan said that Bhutto "was looking much older than I remembered. . . . There was no sparkle in her voice, or her face. Why are you going back, I asked in bewilderment? She muttered something about it being too late to back out" (Bhatia, 2008, p. xi).

On October 18, 2007, when Bhutto stepped down again on Pakistani soil after her long exile, she tried to control her emotions. "Like most women in politics, I am especially sensitive to maintaining my composure, to never showing my feelings. . . . But as my foot touched the ground of my beloved Pakistan for the first time after eight lonely and difficult years of exile, I could not stop the tears from pouring from my eyes" (Bhutto, B., 2008b, p. 1). Forgetting the disappointments of her governments and remembering only the Bhutto mystique, large cheering crowds greeted Bhutto at the airport in Karachi and on the procession through the streets, just as they had on her triumphant return from exile in 1986. Along the way, she saw many thousands of pictures, not just of her, but also huge portraits of her father. "I had an overwhelming sense that he was with me on that truck as we slowly rolled through these millions of supporters" (Bhutto, B., 2008b, p. 7).

The dangers she faced were manifested in a frightening way on that same day of her return when on the procession from the airport, her entourage was attacked by a terrorist bomb. Bhutto escaped injury, but at least 130 of her guards and supporters were killed and hundreds were wounded.

Attributing the attack to Zia's supporters, Bhutto also blamed the Musharraf government for not providing better security for her (Khan, 2008, p. 149). Nevertheless, she continued campaigning over the next 10 weeks for the election, set for January 2008. During this time, she "galvanised the PPP base across the country. . . . At the time of her death, she had re-emerged as the most popular political leader in recent history" (Shafqat, 2011, p. 106).

Her popularity did not prevent, but rather precipitated, the subsequent tragic events. On December 27, 2007, proceeding in an armored car in the streets of Rawalpindi after a rally, she stood up through the sunroof to wave at the cheering crowds, and this time, the assassins were successful. There was gunfire, then a bomb explosion, killing Bhutto and 20 others. It was unclear exactly what the cause of her death was. Blaming the Pakistani Taliban whose modus vivendi was to use bombs, the Musharraf government said that the bomb blast caused her to hit her head on the side of the sunroof and fracture her skull. This conclusion was backed up by a Scotland Yard investigation, even though, on Zardari's orders, there was no autopsy for confirmation. The first medical reports, however, which were later changed, indicated death by a gunshot wound in the head, raising suspicions that it was not the work of terrorists but "rather a calculated plan worked out by individuals within Musharraf's government" (Khan, 2008, p. 153). Bhutto's family blamed Musharraf, whom they say deliberately and in cooperation with the Taliban did not provide her the necessary security that would have prevented the assassination. Under threat of impeachment and criminal charges, Musharraf stepped down as president in 2008 and went into exile.

Amid an outpouring of grief throughout the country, marked by riots and violence, Bhutto was buried next to her beloved father in the middle of the family mausoleum, again with primacy over her brothers, whose tombs were over on the side. The Pakistani government honored Bhutto by renaming the Islamabad International Airport after her, and also many streets and public buildings. The tribute that would have meant the most to her was the resounding victory of the PPP in the elections, postponed until February 2008, and especially the election of her still-unpopular husband, Asif Zardari, as president to replace Musharraf. The assumption was that Zardari would hold power until Bhutto's oldest son, Bilawal, only 19 when his mother was assassinated, completed his studies at Oxford and could pick up his mother's mantle as a blood Bhutto. Graduating from Oxford in 2010, Bilawal returned to Pakistan, and replaced his father as chair of the PPP. He has increased his public exposure and experience by accompanying his president father on international trips, and, as of 2012, is preparing to plunge into the murky waters of Pakistani electoral politics, evoking again the cry of "*Jiye Bhutto*" (long live Bhutto).

REFERENCES

Bennett, C. (1987, July 31). Ideal arrangement? *The Times* (London). Retrieved from www.lexisnexis.com/

Bhatia, S. (2008). *Goodbye, Shahzadi: A political biography of Benazir Bhutto*. New Delhi: Roti Books.

Bhutto, B. (1988). *The way out: Interviews, impressions, statements and messages*. Karachi: Mahmood.

Bhutto, B. (1989). *Daughter of destiny: An autobiography*. New York: Simon & Schuster.

Bhutto, B. (2007, September 20). When I return to Pakistan. *Washington Post*. Retrieved from www.washingtonpost.com/

Bhutto, B. (2008a). One day: June 17, 1997. In S.M. Strong (Ed.), *The maternal is political: Women writers at the intersection of motherhood and social change*. Berkeley, CA: Seal Press.

Bhutto, B. (2008b). *Reconciliation: Islam, democracy, and the West*. New York: Harper Perennial.

Bhutto, F. (2010). *Songs of blood and sword: A daughter's memoir*. New York: Nation Books.

Burns, J. (1998, January 9). House of graft: Tracing the Bhutto millions. *New York Times*. Retrieved from www.nytimes.com/

Burns, J. (2007, December 28). Benazir Bhutto, 54, who weathered Pakistan's political storm for 3 decades, dies. *New York Times*. Retrieved from www.nytimes.com/

Dalrymple, W. (2007, December 29). Pakistan's flawed and feudal princess. *The Guardian/Observer*. Retrieved from www.guardian.co.uk

Dreifus, C. (1994, May 15). Real-life dynasty; Benazir Bhutto. *New York Times*. Retrieved from www.nytimes.com/

Gargan, E. (1993a, July 19). Pakistan government collapses; Elections are called. *New York Times*. Retrieved from www.nytimes.com/

Gargan, E. (1993b, October 8). Bhutto wins plurality and faces a new struggle. *New York Times*. Retrieved from www.nytimes.com/

Gupta, S. (1986, May 15). Interview with Benazir Bhutto. *India Today* (International Ed.), 14–15.

Gupta, S. (1988, September 15). Pakistan after Zia. *India Today*, 10–24.

Hall, C. (1984, April 4). The April of her freedom. *Washington Post*. Retrieved from www.lexisnexis.com/

Hitchens, C. (2011). Benazir Bhutto: Daughter of destiny, Dec. 27, 2008. In C. Hitchens, *Arguably: Essays by Christopher Hitchens*. New York: Twelve.

In Pakistan, the making of a martyr (1979, April 8). *New York Times*. Retrieved from www.nytimes.com/

Jack, I. (1986, May). The destiny of Benazir Bhutto. *Vanity Fair*, 69–73, 134–135.

Jones, O.B. (2002). *Pakistan: Eye of the storm* (2nd ed.). New Haven, CT: Yale University Press.

Kamm, H. (1994a, January 6). Battle among the Bhuttos: From politics to gunfire. *New York Times*. Retrieved from www.nytimes.com/

Kamm, H. (1994b, January 12). Karachi journal: With blood tie sundered, blood divides Bhuttos. *New York Times*. Retrieved from www.nytimes.com/

Khan, A. (2008, January/February). Pakistan in 2007: More violent, more unstable. *Asian Survey, 48*, 144–153. Retrieved from www.jstor.org

Lieven, A. (2011). *Pakistan: A hard country*. New York: Public Affairs.

Miss Bhutto's distractions. (1990, March 3). *Economist*, 31.

Perlez, J. (2008, March 11). From prison to zenith of politics in Pakistan. *New York Times*. Retrieved from www.nytimes.com/

Preston, Y. (1988, March). Bhutto's choice. *Ms. Magazine*, 42–45, 47.

Shafqat, S. (1996). Pakistan under Benazir Bhutto. *Asian Survey, 36*, 655–672.

Shafqat, S. (2011). Praetorians and the people. In Lodhi, Dr. M. (Ed.), *Pakistan: Beyond the Crisis State*. New York: Columbia University Press.

Singh, R., with Sheikh, A. (1988, June 30). A bloodless coup. *India Today*, 44–46.

Taheri, A. (2007, December 29). For Benazir, defying fate was pointless. *The Times* (London). Retrieved from www.lexisnexis.com/

Talbot, I. (2009). *Pakistan: A modern history*. New York: Palgrave Macmillan.

Thomas, C. (1989, October 11). Bhutto's reforms stalled. *The Times* (London). Retrieved from www.lexisnexis.com/

Walsh, M.W. (1989, May 3). At the mercy of men: Pakistan women look to Bhutto to improve a harsh existence. *Wall Street Journal*. Retrieved from www.proquest.com/

Weisman, S. F. (1986a, April 11). A daughter returns to Pakistan to cry for victory. *New York Times*. Retrieved from www.nytimes.com/

Weisman, S. F. (1986b, September 21). The return of Benazir Bhutto: Struggle in Pakistan. *New York Times*. Retrieved from www.nytimes.com/

Weiss, A. (1990, May). Benazir Bhutto and the future of women in Pakistan. *Asian Survey, 30*, 433–455.

Ziring, L. (2003). *Pakistan at the crosscurrent of history*. Oxford: Oneworld Publications.

5

Women in Power in Nicaragua

Myth and Reality

Michelle A. Saint-Germain

On February 15, 1990, Violeta Chamorro was elected president of Nicaragua and became the first woman ever directly elected to the presidency of any Central American nation. Given the prevailing Latin norm that politics is a male domain and the proper sphere of women is the home, three questions come to mind: Why did a woman become president *then*? Why did *this* woman become president? And *what did this* mean for women and leadership?

Addressing these questions requires an understanding of the context of Chamorro's election. Thus, a brief review of the historical development of political culture and gender identity in Nicaragua follows, along with a short biography of Violeta Chamorro. Also provided are the details of the 1990 presidential campaign, where the political culture and the gender identity system collided head-on to produce unique electoral conditions that ultimately resulted in the election of Nicaragua's first woman president. Finally, through an analysis of her first year in office, we can explore what Chamorro's election meant for women in power in Nicaragua: myth or reality?

POLITICAL CULTURE

Politics in Nicaragua has been marked by invasions, civil wars, and violent deaths of heads of state (Barquero, 1945). Until 1990, Nicaragua had never experienced a peaceful transfer of government between the group in power and the opposition. Lacking traditions of democratic institutions and the rule of law, politics was "a violent business to be carried on by force, fraud, and coercion" (Close, 1988, p. 25). This political culture was shaped early on by three colonial powers. Spain and the United States were attracted to the country because it offered the shortest, mostly navigable route between the Atlantic and Pacific Oceans; for Britain, it was part of a strategy to dominate the Caribbean. In the twentieth century, invasions and occupations by U.S. Marines and a 40-year dynastic dictatorship reinforced the tendency for Nicaraguan politics to be dominated by foreign interests.

Beginning with the fourth voyage of Columbus in 1502, colonization by the Spanish was a violent experience that greatly reduced the native population through fighting, slavery, disease, ill treatment, and flight (Radell, 1969; cited in Close, 1988). From the Spanish, Nicaraguans inherited a "patrimonial, corporatist political structure," which emphasized military values, and the Catholic religion, which justified that structure and those values (Close, 1988, p. 7). A corporatist system is not based on checks and balances, laissez faire, or the unfettered competition of interest groups independent of the state. Rather, corporatism is a "system of national organization in which the component social and political groups are organized functionally" in sectors, with the states as the final arbiter of conflict (Wiarda, 1981, p. 90). Corporatism stands in contrast both to liberalism—in that it is not based on individual rights—and to socialism—in that it presumes that conflicts between groups can be mediated. The group is seen as the natural link between the individual and society. Political parties, however, are not seen as natural groups, and such things as a "loyal opposition" have little meaning in a system where harmony of interests is presumed and enforced.

The Spanish established two major cities in Western Nicaragua, and each city developed its own political party that reflected the major economic interests of its region. The conservatives of Granada, on the shores of Lake Nicaragua, represented the big cattle ranchers and traders, while the liberals of Leon, closer to the Pacific Ocean, represented the rival coffee growers and urban business interests (Envío Collective, 1989b, p. 6). When the yoke of Spanish rule was overthrown in 1821, Nicaragua fell almost immediately into a series of civil wars in which each political party was supported by a rival foreign power intent on gaining control of the country in order to build a canal across it.[1] In 1823, U.S. President James Monroe proclaimed the United States's intent to consolidate its influence over Latin America and the Caribbean under the doctrine of "America for the Americas"; by 1850, under the Clayton-Bulwer Treaty, the United States had forced Britain to give up its interests in a Nicaraguan canal, greatly weakening British political power in the region and intensifying U.S. influence over Nicaraguan politics.

The discovery of gold in California in 1848 renewed international interest in Nicaragua, because the swiftest route from the Eastern United States to the West was by boat through Nicaragua. Competition between different U.S. companies for control of the routes across Nicaragua was again played out through hostilities between the Liberal and Conservative Parties. For example, when the conservative government of Fruto Chamorro, a direct ancestor of Violeta's husband Pedro Joaquín, signed a contract with U.S. businessman Cornelius Vanderbilt, the discontented liberals—backed by Vanderbilt's rivals—hired U.S. mercenary William Walker in 1855 to overthrow Chamorro. Walker not only defeated the conservatives but also declared himself president of Nicaragua. Within six months, however, Walker was defeated by a coalition of Nicaraguan conservatives and other Central American forces backed by the Vanderbilt faction (Ramírez, 1989).

The pattern of conflict between liberal and conservative Nicaraguan political parties as surrogates for outside interests continued in the twentieth century. When a U.S.-supported conservative government was threatened in 1912, U.S. Marines invaded Nicaragua and remained there almost continuously until 1932. The Marines supervised the six presidential elections held during this period in Nicaragua, deciding which parties could run, counting the votes, and declaring the winners (Vargas, 1989b).

Presidential politics in Nicaragua was thus nearly always dominated by military forces, either because the president was in the military or because a military force—national or foreign—was in de facto control of the government. Thus, military rather than democratic values prevailed. As in war, in the Nicaraguan political culture, to the victor go the spoils. A patronage system developed that was so extensive that the party in power had nearly total and unlimited access to resources, and the party out of power had virtually none. In addition, the winners, as far as possible, would dismantle anything that the losers had done, including programs, policies, laws, and even the constitution. As a government official put it, "the historic error of this country is that the government of the day ran the country for itself and its people and repressed its enemies with confiscation, jail, and exile.

Nicaraguans like strong governments. The temptation to punish the loser is in our blood" (Boudreaux, 1991, p. 10).

Under these conditions, it is not surprising that most Nicaraguan presidents have attempted to secure their own reelection, or, if reelection was not possible, to rig elections to favor other candidates from their own political parties. Because winning was everything, elections were often marked by massive fraud on the one hand and massive abstention on the other, as the electorate tired of single-candidate elections, dominance by the U.S.-favored candidates, and invasions by U.S. Marines when the designated favorite did not win (Vargas, 1989a). When a popular resistance movement led by August César Sandino fought the U.S. occupation forces to a standstill in 1932, U.S. officials decided to withdraw the Marines and leave behind a surrogate national police force whose purpose was to safeguard U.S. interests by controlling electoral politics so that the levels of violence were reduced. This force, the National Guard, not only failed to establish the basic conditions necessary for free elections, but also ushered in a new repressive era that continued the cycle of violence for another four decades.

In 1932, Anastasio ("Tacho") Somoza García was named head of the National Guard, ostensibly a nonpartisan force that would mediate between the two major political parties. But Somoza had personal political ambitions. First, he arranged for the assassination of Sandino in order to eliminate any prominent political rival. Then he ousted President Juan Bautista Sacasa (his uncle) in a coup, had himself appointed interim president by the National Legislature, and engineered an electoral victory for himself in 1936. The Liberal party was turned into Tacho's personal machinery, and he was continually reelected. Somoza established a type of hereditary dictatorship (Kantor, 1969), followed by sons Luis and Anastasio Jr. (Tachito), controlling the office of the presidency for more than 40 years. During this time, the Somozas added another twist to the Nicaraguan political culture that would affect the 1990 elections.

Under the Somozas, only two political parties were recognized: the historic liberals and conservatives. Past attempts to form other political parties had been generally unsuccessful; Sandino may have been assassinated because he was working on developing a third alternative (Envío Collective, 1989b). As the Somozas rapidly consolidated political and economic power with the Liberal party, the conservatives became increasingly dissatisfied—not so much with the regime as with their share of power. In return for tacitly acknowledging the legitimacy of the Somozas' rule, they were awarded a quota of seats in the National Legislature through various pacts. There was, however, no sharing of power with anyone or any group that disagreed with the Somozas. There was so little tolerance for dissenting opinions that both parties began to splinter into various factions. Splits developed not only over ideological differences but over personality differences and disputes over control of economic resources as well. Given the Nicaraguan preoccupation with legitimacy (perhaps deriving from their history as a conquered people), each splinter group or faction claimed the true heritage of the Liberal or Conservative party. This prevented factions that actually had much in common ideologically from uniting to form alternative (third) parties, because neither conservative nor liberal factions would give up names tracing their historic descent from one of the two traditional parties, the only ones recognized as legitimate power centers.

It was not until 1957 that the Social Christian party emerged, but by 1975 it too had divided into two factions. Even the Sandinista National Liberation Front (FSLN), which formed in 1961, had split into three tendencies by 1975. The Somozas tightly controlled political power, skillfully manipulated economic power, and played the various factions off against one another, successfully preventing the formation of effective coalitions until a popular uprising ousted their regime in 1979. The intolerance of pluralism within political parties enforced by the Somozas, combined with the Nicaraguan insistence on purity of political heritage and reluctance to form new alternatives, has now produced an explosion in the number of political parties. By 1990, there were more than 20 political camps, with 6 parties calling themselves Conservative, 4 Liberals, 4 Social Christians, and 5 Socialist or Communist parties. Intolerance of dissent was so high that some parties consisted of little more than close family members; others were referred to as "microparties" or "merely letterhead" (Envío Collective, 1990f, p. 30).

The Somozas also carried on the Nicaraguan tendency toward government paternalism, in which citizens did not have rights, but rather concession from an arbitrary ruler (Velazquez, 1986, p. 54). The National Legislature, election councils, and municipal governments were all merely facades for the dictator. Any other organizations that attempted political action were forcefully suppressed. Thus, the development of civil political institutions was stifled in Nicaragua. Even with modernization in the 1960s, the Somozas opposed the formation of any independent associations or organizations not aligned with the dictator's political party or the officially sanctioned "opposition" party. The Somozas also retarded the political development of the private sector by playing off competing economic interests against one another (Envío Collective, 1990h, p. 25). The only political qualities rewarded by the Somozas were loyalty and servility; the reaction to disloyalty or dissent was instantaneous, cruel, and exemplary (Velazquez, 1986).

The FSLN emerged as the leader of a national uprising that overthrew the Somozas in 1979. The FSLN was the only political party to reunite its various factions during the insurrectionary period, which gave it more strength than any other political group. The FSLN faced little serious political opposition at the time of the revolution, since there were few organized groups among the private sector that had the experience necessary to take over. The Nicaraguan elite, like other Central American ruling elites, had resisted democratic forms of government that involved power sharing, and no other groups had much experience in running a country except under a strongman or a foreign power (Close, 1988). Conditioned by years of political suppression, coupled with a tradition of appeals to external authorities, the anti-Sandinista opposition turned to the United States rather than organizing internally around their strengths to gain political power under the new situation (Close, 1988, p. 108); the result was the establishment of the counterrevolutionary force known as the *Contras.*

Thus, in 1979, the Sandinistas inherited a political culture in which power was authoritarian, hierarchical, and complete; where negotiation, compromise, and power sharing were either unknown or despised; and where disagreement was experienced as betrayal. Although they attempted to change politics in Nicaragua, the FSLN was to some extent also a product of that culture, and so reforms were often accompanied by politics as usual. While they made some headway, they were also constrained by the traditional pattern of domination of Nicaraguan politics by outside interests, since throughout the 1980s various Nicaraguan political groups continued to be co-opted as surrogates for the interests of either the U.S.-led Western bloc or the Soviet-led Eastern bloc.

GENDER IDENTITY

Nicaragua's desirability as a crossroads also shaped the development of its system of gender identity. The constant migration of early tribal peoples resulted, according to Pablo Cuadra (1987), in the development in Nicaraguans of a "vagabond restlessness," a psychology of transience that is "stamped by nostalgia" (p. 47). These characteristics were later exacerbated by the economic developments that forced peasants off their lands and permanently turned large numbers of Nicaraguans into migrant laborers.

Spanish *conquistadors* brought with them the gender identity system called *machismo*, an exaggerated maleness, sometimes known as the cult of virility. Its characteristics include "an exaggerated aggressiveness and intransigence in male-to-male interpersonal relationships and arrogance and sexual aggression in male-to-female relationships" (Stevens, 1973, p. 90). Maleness is associated with the rapacious women who were conquered. Since Nicaraguans are for the most part mestizos (part Spaniard/part Indian), they have elements of both the conqueror and the conquered. For males, this is said to present a frightening bisexuality (Goldwert, 1985). *Machismo* is "built on weakness—fear of the female and dread of passivity and intimacy" (Kovel, 1988, p. 93).[2]

The female counterpart in this gender identity system, which has been *marianismo*, is rooted in the worship of the Virgin Mary in Catholicism. *Marianismo* is described as a "cult of feminine spiritual superiority, which teaches that women are semi-divine, morally superior to and spiritually stronger than men" (Stevens, 1973, p. 91). Insofar as a woman conforms to the behaviors prescribed by this ideal—abnegation, humility, sacrifice, patience, and submissiveness to the demands of men—she enjoys social approval and veneration. Women who stray from this model are not deserving of respect; rather, they become objects of contempt. "Home is the sphere of the woman, and the ideal woman is a mother ... even today, the proper woman will not leave her house except to run necessary errands or to make family visits" (Levy, 1988, p. 8). Women have their separate sphere, the home, where their authority is recognized; they do not compete with men in the public (political sphere), and are assumed to be in fact apolitical.

Every aspect of life is governed by this dual gender identity system. Girls and boys are educated in a system that promotes distrust of the other sex (Elias, 1988) and reinforces homosociality (the tendency to associate only with members of one's own sex), although some psychoanalysts have explored the specter of homosexuality raised by *machismo* as well (e.g., Goldwert, 1985). Cultural prescriptions for distinctive gender behavior result in spatial separation as well, with women found mostly in the home and men found at work, sports events, bars, and other male-oriented places (Elias, 1988). These pressures are reinforced by economic conditions that promote men's migration in search of jobs and compounded by *machista* norms of virility. It is not unusual for Nicaraguan men to maintain sexual relations with and produce children with more than one woman at a time, drifting from one home to another, leaving the majority of women as de facto heads of household.

Men and women have their clearly defined and separate spheres, but these spheres are not equal. *Marianismo* may lead women to believe that they will be rewarded in the next life for their efforts in the here and now, but the balance of power in temporal terms clearly lies with men. Under this system, women derive their identities through their male relatives—fathers, brothers, husbands, and sons—and achieve their highest fulfillment as wives and mothers. But men are often aggressive, unfaithful, and immature, and frequently absent, so women can expect to experience much suffering at the hands of men and much sadness in life. A strong sense of victimization and resignation seems to pervade women's daily lives. According to Kovel (1988), women in a self-help workshop in Managua described men as, among other things:

> Slothful, womanizing, drunkards, irresponsible, traitorous, humiliators, ingrates, opportunists, abandoners, dishonest, imbeciles, egoistic, shameless, evil, executioners, despised, jokers, offensive, lying, farcical, prideful, loafers, bossy, cowards, wolves, brutes, coarse, vicious, vain, capricious, woman-beaters, and *machista*. (p. 92)

Positive images of men were less numerous, but included "worker, useful, good father, brave, and beloved." Women's positive images of themselves contained references to their "moral qualities having to do with being responsible or caring, . . . bravery, strength, and intelligence." Negative images reflected the women's feelings of victimization:

> marginal, discriminated against, martyred, tricked, unappreciated, wretched, lack prestige, humiliated, exploited, desperate, bitter, miserable, abandoned, needing father for their children, tormented, disconsolate, suffering, abnegated, slaves, objects of commercialization, and sheep. (Kovel, 1988, p. 93)

At marriage (or upon forming a couple), men and women are (rather unrealistically) expected to be able to put aside these feelings and form a stable heterosexual relationship. At this time, however, men and women do not enter a new, gender-neutral world; rather, the man enters the female world of the home, without a symmetrical integration of the woman into the masculine world outside the home. Men become uncomfortable and at first opportunity flee the female-dominated sphere of the home, while the public sphere and its values remain alien to women. The link between male values and the political culture—and their opposition to the sphere of the home is summed up by Díaz (1966):

> A father tends to be seen a free agent rather than as the representative of a nuclear family in reference to the outside world. As a consequence . . . the child sees authority as power shorn of responsibility and clothed in symbols of the male role . . . to be physically strong, careless of consequences and dangers, jealous of one's home and able to enforce one's wishes on others. Power is seen as unpredictable, based on personal whims, shaped by will. (p. 92)

Until now, the values of the public sphere—physical strength, virility, military powers—have dominated Nicaraguan politics, with little acceptance of the values of the private sphere—capacity for caring, sacrifice, and altruism—in the public realm.

BIOGRAPHICAL SKETCH OF PRESIDENT CHAMORRO

Richter (1990–1991) suggests that when exploring women's paths to political power, it is important to examine variables such as social class and lifestyle, historical context (including imprisonment), electoral arrangements, and the prevailing gender identity system. Each of these elements played a role in Violeta Barrios de Chamorro's election. Born in 1929, she grew up as one of six children in a wealthy ranch family; she loved horseback riding. Her childhood ambitions were to learn to type and to become a secretary (Associated Press, 1990). Her father, a graduate of MIT, insisted that she have an education that included attending schools in the United States in order to learn English. But Violeta was not interested in studying, nor was she a particularly good student. At age 19, she returned to Nicaragua after her father's death, where she met Pedro Joaquín Chamorro whom she married a year later. For the next 27 years she was the wife of one of the most active opposition figures in Nicaragua, until his assassination in 1978.

In historical sources, Violeta Barrios is usually mentioned only as the wife, or widow, of Pedro Joaquín Chamorro, slain owner of the newspaper *La Prensa*. Indeed, her own accounts of her life in interviews contain little more than descriptions of the activities of her husband and children. Her work, she said "was to be his wife, to take care of my children, take care of the house, accompany him on trips, take food to him in prison, going to drop off the food, there and back, nothing more" (Uhlig, 1990, p. 62).

The details of her personal life are sketchy; however, her class, health, and religion stand out. She was often been dismissed as "just a housewife," but her role was actually that of a "lady of the house" who directed the smooth running of the household, supervising others who perform the mundane domestic tasks, a nontrivial difference in lifestyle.[3] She experienced considerable ill health. A bout of pneumonia kept her from returning to Nicaragua for a month after her father died. An incompatibility between her own and her husband's blood complicated most of her five pregnancies; four children survived. Her osteoporosis caused numerous broken bones. A devout Catholic, Violeta Chamorro maintained a strong, almost mystical religious faith that she shared with her husband. They were married on December 8, the major religious feast day in Nicaragua that celebrates the conception of the Virgin Mary. Pedro Joaquín experienced premonitions of his death and saw himself as a Christ-like figure sacrificing himself for his country (Edmisten, 1990). Violeta Chamorro also had strong ties to the formal Nicaraguan Catholic Church, which she called the "true" church, as opposed to the church of liberation theology or the popular church (Heyck, 1990, p. 41), and the Catholic cardinal, Miguel Obando y Bravo.

The dominant force in Violeta Chamorro's life, however, continued to be Pedro Joaquín. In Latin America, it is said, the dead do not die. It is clear that, were he alive, Pedro Joaquín Chamorro would have been the choice to be president. The United States considered him a possible challenger to Somoza in the 1970s, but he was assassinated in 1978, an event that precipitated the 1979 armed insurrection and raised him to the status of a national martyr. His legacy was claimed by many of the political parties in Nicaragua (Edmisten, 1990). For example, Daniel Ortega's inauguration as president in 1984 took place on January 10, the date of Pedro Joaquín Chamorro's death.[4] Like her husband, Violeta appeared to be a strong nationalist, and did not flee to Miami after the revolution as did so many others, although, ironically, she was in Miami on a shopping trip with one of her daughters who was about to be married when Pedro Joaquín was killed. After that, she relied heavily for support on her son-in-law, Antonio Lacayo.

After the 1979 revolution, Violeta Chamorro was appointed, as the widow of the slain martyr, to the five-person junta formed to run the country. She resigned a year later, publicly citing health reasons (a broken arm), but privately blaming differences of opinion with the Sandinistas. She returned to her home, which she kept like a mausoleum to the memory of Pedro Joaquín (Edmisten, 1990). She had on display the clothes he was wearing; the car he was driving on the day he was killed was kept on the patio. Another room contained his sailboat. Photographs covered the walls. She visited his grave often, and each night at bedtime, "commends herself to Christ, to the Virgin Mary, to Pope John Paul II, and to her husband, whose spirit is alive within her" (Edmisten, 1990, p. 91).[5]

Violeta Chamorro's status in Nicaraguan society was largely ascriptive. Despite living most of her life at the center of Nicaraguan politics, she never became a politician or a member of any political party. While receiving numerous awards from international organizations as the owner of *La Prensa*, she herself was never active in the newspaper's day-to-day operations or in political or ideological decisions (Envío Collective, 1989b).[6] Yet she achieved the ultimate status that a woman can attain in Nicaraguan society by being the devout widow of a politically correct martyr. Her role was that of the grieving matriarch who can still hold her family together. Of her four children, two were Sandinistas and two opposed the Sandinistas, not unusual in war-torn Nicaragua. However, her ability to get all the family to sit down at Sunday dinner together achieved nearly legendary status, an example par excellence of the proper woman in the proper (private) sphere.

THE 1990 ELECTIONS

The question of why a woman became president of Nicaragua *then* is probably the easiest to answer. It had become commonplace that women in Third World countries could rise to positions of leadership under conditions of change that undermine tradition (e.g., Chaney, 1973). Although women may suffer disproportionately from the violence that accompanies political change in Latin America, war and revolution are seen as creating political opportunity for women (Levy, 1988, p. 9). Violeta Chamorro's election was due in part to the electoral conditions that were a legacy of the Sandinista revolution, including the crisis situation brought on by nine years of aggression from the United States, and in part to challenge the political culture that was mounted by explicitly using the Nicaraguan gender identity system as a weapon in the 1990 campaign.

Electoral Conditions

First, Sandinistas deliberately changed the status of women in Nicaragua. The Sandinista National Liberation Front, unlike its Cuban counterpart 20 years before, developed at the same time as and was influenced by the international women's movement. As early as 1969, the FSLN endorsed the principle of gender equality, promising that the revolution would "abolish the odious discrimination that women have been subjected to compared with men . . . [and] establish economic, political, and cultural equality between women and men" (Molyneux, 1985, p. 238). As many as one third of FSLN combatants were women; several reached the highest ranks.

Upon taking power in 1979, the Sandinistas substantially increased political opportunities for women. Bills were enacted outlawing prostitution and the gratuitous use of women's bodies in advertising. Laws recognized the equal obligations of both parents to support children and do housework. Other statutes provided for 90 days of paid maternity leave and stipulated equal pay for equal work. Under the Sandinistas, women's economic participation grew in a number of fields. Among organized groups, women represented 80% of the health workers union (FESTA-LUD), 70% of the teachers union (ANDEN), 40% of the farm workers association (ATC), and 37% of the Sandinista workers syndicate (CST) (Barricada Internacional, 1990).

In the elections of 1984, 19.7% of the FSLN deputies elected to the Nicaraguan Assembly were women, the highest proportion of any party in Central America. Women held 31.4% of the leadership posts in the FSLN party. Sandinistas appointed a woman as the minister of health and as chief of police, and 15% of ambassadors and international representatives were women, including Violeta Chamorro's daughter Claudia (Barricada Internacional, 1990). AMNLAE, the national women's organization founded by the Sandinistas, grew to a membership of 80,000 at its peak—in a country where before the revolution there were only a handful of women's organizations, most of them upper-class charities or gardening clubs. Women moved into nontraditional occupations and became vocal and active in political associations at all levels. Thus, on the one hand, there was a much greater ability for the Nicaraguan people to accept a woman president than ever before, as 10 years of social change had improved the opportunities for women in politics. On the other hand, the Sandinistas may have tried to move too far too fast, creating a backlash, nostalgia for the past, and preference for a more traditional woman.

Second, the Sandinistas created the conditions for opposition political parties to form, raise funds,[7] campaign, and, if the people so willed, win the election. The Sandinistas guaranteed that the victory would go to whomever was chosen by secret ballot. They waged a massive campaign to register voters and to encourage people to vote on election day, although voting was not compulsory. They invited thousands of international observers to watch over the entire election process, and thousands more journalists to record the event for the entire world to see. Never before had a government in power requested observers from foreign bodies to supervise their elections.

Thus, for only the second time in modern Nicaraguan political history, space was opened up for participation by multiple opposition parties (the first time was for the 1984 election). After many years of suppression of political expression, what emerged was a wild profusion of political parties, some representing traditional political interests, but others with little or no grounding in Nicaraguan reality. In addition, many of these parties had depended for years on a military strategy (i.e., the Contras, funded by the United States) to remove the Sandinistas from power, thus neglecting to develop their political skills or to build up grassroots support. Confronted with the fact that power would be decided in a popular election, the opposition parties scrambled to put together a coalition that would pool their strengths.

The result was the United National Opposition, or UNO, which in Spanish means "one" or "someone." However, as an old Nicaraguan proverb says, someone in general is really no one specific (*uno no es ninguno*). UNO was a loose-knit, constantly shifting coalition of more than a dozen political parties, embracing the entire political spectrum from ultra-right to communist ideology. Voters were faced with two extremes—the FSLN or the anti-FSLN coalition (UNO)—with almost no political parties occupying a middle ground.[8] The emergence of only two major forces strengthened Violeta Chamorro's chances of election significantly over what they would have been with 20 political parties competing separately.

Third, during the Sandinista administration, the economy deteriorated and there were many war deaths, due to the low-intensity war waged against Nicaragua by the United States. The United States vetoed Nicaragua's requests for credit in multinational organizations such as the World Bank and the International Monetary Fund. And the United States trained and financed the Contras, the counterrevolutionary guerrilla army that waged war—in direct violation of U.S. and international law—on the Nicaraguan people for more than nine years. Popular discontent with the economy, the war, and Sandinista administration in general were at high levels. By maintaining their anti-U.S. government stance, however, the Sandinistas appeared to do nothing but further antagonize the Bush administration. Nicaraguans understood that to vote for the Sandinistas was to vote for more of the same.

In contrast, Violeta Chamorro was associated with factions that were pro-United States. For example, her newspaper, *La Prensa*, had received money from U.S. foundations opposed to the Sandinistas (Sharkey, 1986, p. 36). In May 1989, Chamorro was invited to the White House. During her visit, she was reportedly asked by Bernard Aronson, U.S. undersecretary of state for inter-American affairs, whether she would consider being an opposition candidate for president. Shortly after, in October, Marlon Fitzwater stated that she "is our candidate, and the candidate George Bush declared that if UNO won he would lift the embargo against Nicaragua (Envío Collective, 1990a).

At the close of 1989, the Nicaraguan people were searching for a way to put an end to the Contra war, reunite their divided country, and begin to rebuild their economy. To do this they had to seek relief from the wrath of the United States. The two political candidates offered quite different ways to do this, which became clear in the use of the symbols of the Nicaraguan gender identity system in the battle for the presidency.

Gender Symbolism

If the electoral conditions made it more possible for *any* woman to be elected president, the political culture and gender identity system almost ensured that it would be *this* particular woman who was elected. At first, Violeta Chamorro seemed an unlikely choice for a presidential candidate. She was described in the *Miami Herald* as "politically illiterate" (quoted in Taylor, 1989). During her year in government after the revolution, she had been called the "flower" of the junta, but was not known for making decisions (Envío Collective, 1989b). An article in her own newspaper reinforced this perception of Violeta Chamorro as apolitical, describing her as "a beautiful and noble woman, without vanity, without pride, without ambition, a homeloving woman" (*La Prensa*, September 4, 1989).

But symbolism was enormously important in bitterly polarized Nicaragua (Boudreaux, 1991). As the UNO coalition searched for a presidential candidate for the 1990 elections, what seemed to be Violeta Chamorro's political liabilities were turned into political strengths. The multiparty UNO coalition realized that only a political outsider could hold their divisive factions together[9] and possibly hold together the nation as well. Violeta Chamorro was a symbol of the sacrifices that had been made in Nicaragua's bloody political history. She was associated with a popular independence movement as the widow of a respected voice of moderation in Nicaraguan politics. She was a matriarch who held together a divided family, a family that symbolized the divided country. As one of her brothers-in-law said, "We are not looking for someone to run the country. We are looking for someone who represents the ideal [of democracy]" (Boudreaux, 1991,

p. 13). Even Chamorro described herself as "a symbol, a proud symbol that we Nicaraguans have dignity, a symbol that nobody can snatch away from one what one has by right" (*La Prensa*, September 4, 1989). Any person strongly identified with an existing political faction would have had too many political liabilities, no matter what their strengths. A strategist for Violeta Chamorro's campaign said bluntly, "Violeta wasn't chosen for her abilities as president. Violeta was chosen to win" (Uhlig, 1990, p. 72).

Violeta Chamorro, who was reportedly at home listening to the radio when she learned she had been selected, did not actively campaign for the nomination, as that would have appeared unseemly; but her newspaper, *La Prensa*, did so on her behalf. Chamorro was not the UNO coalition's only candidate for president. In fact, it took days of heated debate before a presidential nominee was selected. For some of the factions, Chamorro's demonstrated acceptability to the United States was decisive because it would be translated into the cash needed to conduct a media campaign. This expectation proved correct: In October, after Chamorro's nomination, the U.S. Congress approved an additional $9 million for the UNO campaign (Envío Collective, 1990a).[10] One observer concluded that UNO realistically had a choice only over whom to propose as candidate for vice president (Cortez, 1990).

The reaction to her nomination was mixed. A dominant business coalition publicly doubted Violeta's abilities, and her vice-presidential running mate at one point called her "a useless old bag of bones" (Cortez, 1990, p. 207). Popular reactions were more positive than expected. At her first campaign appearance, when thousands of people unexpectedly turned up to greet her, she became flustered and "ran away" (Preston, 1990). However, she soon became accustomed to the cheers and affection of large crowds. Often during her campaign Violeta said, "I am not a politician, but believe this is my destiny. I am doing this for Pedro and for my country" (Boudreaux, 1991, p. 13); Chamorro stated that she had accepted the nomination "after consulting with God and my dead husband" (*Barricada International*, September 30, 1989). Even Chamorro's daughter Claudia, an FSLN supporter who openly opposed her mother's candidacy, expressed "not the slightest doubts as to [Violeta's] democratic convictions nor as to her genuine desire for Nicaragua's wellbeing . . . less still do I doubt her integrity and personal honesty" (Chamorro Barrios, 1989).

Once the candidates were selected, the campaign swung into high gear. If politics is the conscious and unconscious manipulation of symbols

(Kretzer, 1988, p. 2), the 1990 Nicaraguan elections provided a stunning example. As one writer expressed, in typical poetic style, "Politics [in Nicaragua] breathes with the heart and is expressed in symbols" (Mendoza, 1990, p. 26). With a nontraditional presidential candidate, UNO had no hope of winning the election through a show of strength, military prowess, or any of the other male-associated values of the private sphere into the public arena of politics.

During the campaign, Violeta's image was modeled after that of the Virgin Mary. She was dressed all in white, with a simple gold crucifix to symbolize her almost mystical Catholicism. Chamorro was introduced at political rallies as Nicaragua's "María," the "white dove of peace" (O'Kane, 1990, p. 29). She was paraded around in the back of a pickup truck under a white canopy, much as a patron saint is displayed at festival time. The fact that she had broken her leg in a fall on New Year's Day and was confined to a wheelchair only increased her image as the valiant and suffering mother, perhaps " the most important image in Nicaraguan myth" (Kovel, 1988, p. 102). "Chamorro's maternal and reconciliatory image . . . seemed to exist on a higher plane than traditional politics" (Envío Collective, 1991a, p. 4). It was not necessary for her to speak much, since the Virgin Mary is only an image. As one European diplomat remarked, "She is not really a political figure, she is an emotional and visual figure—an icon" (Preston, 1990).

The symbolism embraced by UNO and its candidate Violeta Chamorro stood in stark contrast to that adopted by the FSLN and its candidate, Daniel Ortega. The FSLN played to the traditional male-orientated values of Nicaraguan political culture: aggression, intransigence, military might, and virility. The FSLN platform contained mostly business as usual, refusing to end the military draft, to change its confrontational attitude to Washington, or to tone down its strongly nationalistic rhetoric. No new economic reforms were outlined. U.S. officials implied that if the FSLN won, there would be a possibility of more aid to the Contras and continuation of economic sanctions—in short, more of the same.

Ortega adopted for his image *el gallo ennavajado*, the fighting cock. He shed his thick, bullet-proof glasses for contact lenses and abandoned his usual green military fatigues for tight jeans and florid shirts open at the waist. In his campaign appearances, he strode back and forth on a flat-bed truck, accompanied by rock music and dancing girls, throwing autographed baseballs into the crowds. To counter Violeta's image of the national mother, Ortega presented himself as the national father. Gigantic billboards of Ortega with Camilla, the youngest of his 10 children, were erected all over the country. His female assistants took thousands of instant Polaroid photographs of Daniel kissing children, to the delight of proud parents. TV spots were accompanied by the Beatles song "All You Need Is Love." Despite U.S. threats, his campaign slogan promised that "everything would be better" (Cortez, 1990, p. 344).

In a campaign of symbols, neither side offered much substance. Other than promising to end the military draft and bring about better relations with the United States (and the hoped-for possibility of billions in U.S. aid), UNO's campaign strategy consisted largely of praising their candidate and attacking the FSLN. At UNO rallies, speakers told the crowds that "Pedro and God were above watching" (O'Kane, 1990, p. 29). Violeta's almost complete identification with Pedro Joaquín Chamorro "reinforced the impression that she would have little else to offer" (Uhlig, 1990, p. 62). The selection of a woman candidate signaled to some that the United States considered this to be a throwaway election. However, Chamorro dismissed criticisms that she was incompetent to lead Nicaragua, on the grounds that her critics were taking the wrong approach. "There's no need to study how to govern a country," she said. "I have accepted the challenge to revive this country with love and peace, according to the dictates of my conscience" (Boudreaux, 1991, p. 13). No one really expected UNO to win, least of all UNO coalition members themselves. Even Chamorro's most ardent supporters were shocked when the election results became clear early on the morning of February 26: their symbol had won. In her acceptance statement, Chamorro remembered her husband Pedro Joaquín and promised to fulfill her commitments "with the help of God and the Blessed Virgin."

The results of the election are shown in Table 5.1. More than 1.75 million Nicaraguans were registered to vote, and—although voting was not obligatory under the law as in many other Latin American countries—86.3% voted. Nicaraguans filled out three ballots on election day: one for presidential and vice-presidential candidates, one for candidates for the National Assembly, and one (since 1990) for candidates for local offices. The majority of the votes for president (54.7%) and National Assembly (53.9%) went to UNO; the FSLN polled 40.8% of the votes for both sets of ballots. The 90 National Assembly seats were apportioned according to the popular vote, with UNO gaining 51 seats, the FSLN 38, and the Social Christian party 1. Losing presidential candidates from the FSLN and the Revolutionary Unity movement who polled the minimum percentage of the popular vote were also awarded seats, bringing the total number of representatives to 92. The actual party affiliations of representatives holding seats under the UNO coalition—a point of heated dispute within UNO—are shown in Table 5.1.

TABLE 5.1

1990 Nicaraguan Election Results

Political Parties	Votes Received		Seats Received National Assembly
	President and Vice President (%)	National Assembly (%)	
FSLN	40.8	40.8	39[a]
UNO	54.7	53.9	51
National Conservative Party			5
Popular Conservative Alliance			6
Independent Liberal Party			5
Constitutionalist Liberal Party			5
Neo-Liberal Party			3
National Democratic Confidence Party			5
National Action Party			3
Nicaraguan Socialist Party			3
Communist Party of Nicaragua			3
Social Democratic Party			5
Nicaraguan Democratic Movement			3
Central American Integrationist Party			1
Conservative National Action			2
Popular Social Christian Party			2
Social Christian Party—YATAMA			1
Revolutionary Unity Movement			1[a]
Total			92

[a] This total includes a defeated presidential candidate—as provided for by Nicaraguan law—in addition to the 90 seats awarded in accordance with the popular vote.

EVALUATION OF CHAMORRO'S FIRST YEAR IN OFFICE

In its 1989 report, the International Commission for the Recovery and Development of Central America (The Sanford Commission) describes Central America as trapped in a vicious circle in which, to paraphrase, violence impeded development, and the poverty resulting from under-development intensified violence. The report concluded that social and economic justice, democratic participation, and international support for the development were not only inseparable but indispensable for peace in the region (Envío Collective, 1990h, p. 31). In the long run, the challenge was complicated for Violeta Chamorro by problems that specifically arise in the case of women leaders (see Richter, 1990–1991). In addition to achieving peace, stabilizing the economy, and institutionalizing democracy, Chamorro had to confront the problems caused by her lack of a stable power base, perceptions that she was only a temporary or stand-in president, and questions about her legitimacy.

Upon taking office, Chamorro addressed the first group of problems, promising to demobilize and repatriate the Contras, to achieve economic stabilization within 100 days, and to consolidate the bases of democracy. Early in her term, Chamorro seemed headed toward some modest successes. By June 1990, most Contras had entered neutral zones set up for them in the Nicaraguan countryside after supposedly handing their weapons over to a special international commission. It appeared that the counterrevolutionary war begun nine years earlier was finally at an end. At the same time, a plan to achieve economic stabilization was set into motion. Bolstered by the electoral support of the Nicaraguan people and confident of receiving U.S. and other international aid, Chamorro's economic team announced its goals: get foreign reserves, encourage exports, and privatize the state productive sector (Envío Collective, 1991c). And an unprecedented transition protocol negotiated by the incoming and outgoing administrations promised to start Nicaragua on the path to institutionalization of democratic principles in the political system.

One year later, the Contras (later dubbed *Recontras*) were re-arming, foreign aid did not materialize, unemployment stood at nearly 50%, and the government was unable to contain political struggle "within a civic framework" (Envío Collective, 1991d, p. 5). In making sense of the year's developments, we must examine how Chamorro attempted to develop a power base, combat the perception that she was only a temporary stand-in, and institutionalize the legitimacy of her presidency.

POWER BASE

As soon as the vote totals were announced, it was clear that there was a widespread lack of agreement on exactly what Chamorro's election meant for Nicaragua. Most conservative and right-wing groups saw Chamorro's election as their chance to put an end to the Sandinistas as a political force and to their revolutionary state, differing only with respect to the speed at which this process should take place and the means that should be used. Some of these groups were characterized as willing to "sink even their own economic and political wellbeing . . . to say nothing of their country's" in order to bring down the FSLN (Envío Collective, 1989a, p. 6). In contrast, the Sandinistas and radical left-wing parties saw Chamorro's election as a chance to regroup and become a major opposition force with an eye to the next elections in 1996, but without giving up any of the important social and economic gains of the revolution—many of which were embedded in the 1987 constitution—or their political power. In a speech made the day after he conceded the election, President Daniel Ortega vowed that the FSLN would "rule from below."

Thus a very important short-run challenge facing Chamorro was to establish the rules of the political game, based on the principle that in a democracy, there are limits on the means that may be used to pursue political ends, whatever those ends may be. To achieve this goal, Chamorro's government would have to be accepted as *the* dominant legitimate political force. But what was Chamorro's power base? Having never belonged to a political party, Chamorro relied on a tiny group of extended family members and close advisers to run the government. Chamorro's faction had no popular base, no party machinery, and no security force of its own. After her election, longtime friend Venezuelan President Carlos Andrés Pérez sent bodyguards to protect Chamorro and consultants to advise her on political and economic matters (Selser, 1990a), compounding perceptions that she was unduly beholden to outside interests. Despite being a sentimental favorite during the election, her later actions did not win her many converts. For example, when a poor man complained that his children were dying of hunger, she responded enthusiastically, "Yes, but they will die in a democracy!" (Boudreaux, 1991, p. 13).

Her inner circle's attempt to keep her out of the mudslinging that goes on among the various UNO factions also backfired to some extent, making her seem uncaring or disconnected from reality. Even Violeta's image as the embodiment of national reconciliation was ridiculed by elites as only "laugh[ing] and hold[ing] her arms out," and by nonelites as a "sophisticated game of kisses and hugs at the top and billy clubs at the [bottom]" (Envío Collective, 1991d, p. 13).

The situation was complicated by the awakening in Nicaraguans of new political expectations. Many Nicaraguans became politically literate and politically active. They had high expectations of government accountability to their needs, more so than in any other Central American country (Jonas & Stein, 1990). As one Nicaraguan peasant woman said:

> Before [1979] we were ashamed, we couldn't even speak. The revolution untied our tongues. That infuriated those who wanted us to remain always like nesting hens. Now, if they don't fulfill their promises, they'll feel those promises around their necks like a yoke on a mule. *Doña* Violeta shouldn't forget that people can throw her out, just like they put her in. She knows now that it's the people who rule. (quoted in Mendoza, 1990, p. 24)

Polls showed that about one third of Nicaraguans were strong FSLN supporters, with another third evenly divided between the extreme right and the extreme left. The final third was considered "in dispute." Some Nicaraguans admitted to casting sympathy votes for Violeta, "a nice lady with her leg in a cast," whom they did not want to see lose too badly (Envío Collective, 1990c, p. 35), and others "identify with the maternal image projected by Violeta Chamorro and with her project as well." For most, however, the overwhelming concern was "peace at . . . any price." This "silent majority" of Nicaraguans was largely passive and would not support anything that smacked of conflict (Envío Collective, 1990k, pp. 8–9), so it was unlikely that they could be politically mobilized to become a base of support for Chamorro.

To counter the lack of a strong popular base, Chamorro turned to the executive branch of government, the branch over which she had the most control. During the campaign, Chamorro often criticized the executive branch as having too much power, but after her inauguration she attempted to transfer functions to the executive from the three other branches—legislative, judicial, and electoral—or otherwise weaken the control of other political groups over these branches. Some of these efforts were not successful. For example, upon taking office, she issued a flurry of decrees, some of which were considered to be unconstitutional because they usurped the function of the legislature (Selser, 1990a). She did succeed in decreasing FSLN control of the Supreme Court by increasing the number of justices from seven to nine and giving the position of chief justice to one of her appointees. In addition, by arranging for the resignation of two of the seven FSLN justices, Chamorro managed to thwart the right-wing's plan to increase the total number of justices to 15 and pack the court with its supporters (Envío Collective, 1990j, p. 5).

PERCEPTIONS OF PERMANENCE

Another factor that complicated Chamorro's ability to act as president was the perception that she was merely a temporary leader, or stand-in. Because of her deeply religious orientation, she was perceived by some as a surrogate for Cardinal Miguel Obando y Bravo, who was reportedly approached before Chamorro as a possible UNO presidential candidate.[11] Her lack of skills was also taken as a sign that she was only a figurehead. Upon assuming the presidency, she knew little about the government or how it worked, and her knowledge of world affairs was also limited. She forgot the names of foreign leaders (like Ronald Reagan) and struggled to remember well-known events (Preston, 1990) or the names of the colleges she attended (Heyck, 1990, p. 44). Her attention span was said to be short. She did not deliver prepared speeches well, but when she talked spontaneously she often made slips of the tongue that later had to be "explained" by her aides. For example, she suggested that she could fund the national educational system by winning the state lottery, and that the budget of the Ministry of Health should be slashed because its efforts could be taken over by international agencies (Envío Collective, 1990g, p. 5). Some of her pet projects seemed petty—for example, a plan to change the uniform of the national police from tan to light blue, the color of the Nicaraguan flag. Staff in the presidential offices was prohibited from calling people *compañero* or *compañera*, the preferred form of address under the Sandinistas. No miniskirts, tight pants, or shorts were allowed, and women who wore sleeveless blouses had to shave under the arms (Cuadra, 1990b). She ordered the elementary school textbooks introduced by the Sandinistas to be thrown out and replaced with texts from Honduras financed by U.S. aid (Jiménez, 1990).

Even members of her own coalition (UNO) treated her as merely temporary. When UNO representatives elected to the National Legislature caucused in April, on the eve of Chamorro's inaugurations as president, to select a slate of candidates for the governing board of the Legislature, some reported being pressured by Vice President Godoy to vote for his slate rather than the Chamorro slate. One delegate reported, "Dr. Godoy threatened me . . . saying that he would be president within a year and would make those of us who did not vote for [his slate] pay" (Envío Collective, 1990d, p. 8).

Portrayed as strong willed, President Chamorro declared upon her election that "under the Constitution, I'm going to be the one in charge. I will be the one who gives the orders" (Hockstader, 1990). She also tended to be stubborn and to divide the world into "them" and "us" (Heyck, 1990, p. 47). But in fact she was not the key decision maker in the government, although she disputed any suggestion that she was not in charge. For example, she was not involved in the development of the UNO platform and its plans for economic renewal. Her son-in-law, Antonio Lacayo, married to Violeta's daughter Cristiana (publisher of *La Prensa*), was the power behind the throne, along with his brother-in-law Alfredo César (a former Sandinista *and* a former Contra regarded by both sides as an opportunist). (Ironically, *Lacayo* translates into English as "lackey.")

The question of whether Violeta Chamorro was a stand-in, and for whom, also complicated the problem of securing international aid. Before the election, a political cartoon showed President Bush flying a Violeta Chamorro doll over Nicaragua (*Barricada International*, September 30, 1989), signifying the switch from a costly military strategy to a cheaper political strategy to defeat the Sandinistas, and, for some, also signifying that the United States felt it could control Chamorro. For other

Nicaraguans, Violeta Chamorro's claim to be the legitimate heir to all that Pedro Joaquín stood for was tarnished when she went on a preelectoral fund-raising trip among his former enemies (ex-*Somocistas*) in Miami. Throughout the campaign, rumors circulated that if Violeta Chamorro won, the United States would pour so many aid dollars into Nicaragua that no one would have to pay utility bills, bank debts, or even bus fare (Envío Collective, 1990c, p. 35). Indeed, it seemed reasonable that Nicaragua could expect to reap its own "peace dividend," with the money that had funded the Contras now funding development projects. But months after Chamorro won the election, there was still no substantial U.S. aid for Nicaragua. Chamorro's personal appeal to President Bush for $40 million in emergency aid was refused (Envío Collective, 1990e, p. 4) in a humiliating manner.

Why was U.S. aid not forthcoming? For one thing, Nicaragua was no longer unique. It was now—along with Panama—just one of many new democracies that had to compete with Eastern European states, the former Soviet Union, and others for U.S. aid dollars. And the United States, itself in deep debt, had no wish or ability to expand its foreign aid program. For another, Chamorro did not comply with U.S. wishes to remove FSLN party member Humberto Ortega as head of the army. During a general strike in the summer of 1990, the U.S. ambassador reportedly pressured Chamorro to step down, ostensibly for health reasons, so that Vice President Godoy—more favorable to U.S. interests—could take over (Envío Collective, 1990j, p. 6). The United States continued to exert strong pressure on the Chamorro government to "accelerate Nicaragua's privatization process, further reduce the size of the army, and withdraw Nicaragua's case against the U.S. [for its illegal Contra war] in the International Court of Justice" (Envío Collective, 1990k, p. 9). An extremely cynical view, but one that makes sense given continued U.S. hostility toward the Sandinista party, was that aid was being withheld so that in the resulting economic and social deterioration the FSLN might commit some tactical error that would weaken popular support for the party (Envío Collective, 1990e, p. 5) or some act that could be used as a pretext for a U.S. invasion to restore order.

Nicaragua's international financial situation was also at a standstill. Until its debts with international lending institutions were paid off, no more credit would be extended to Nicaragua. Lenders were willing to renegotiate these debts, but only if strict austerity measures were imposed, such as cutting utility, transportation, food, education, health, and other subsidies, cuts that disproportionately affected the poor and working classes. But pressure from labor unions and other organized groups in Nicaragua prevented the Chamorro government from implementing these measures. No foreign government was willing to give Nicaragua the cash to pay off those debts so that it could bypass the austerity measures required for renegotiation, because at its current rate of spending, it would soon be back in the same situation, and the government was perceived as lacking the clout to alter the current spending formula.

LEGITIMACY

Threats to Violeta Chamorro's legitimacy as president began on her first day in office. Animosity between Chamorro and Vice President Godoy exploded in a dispute over office space and ended with Chamorro banning Godoy from the presidential office building, giving him no space, staff, or support. Godoy, who led the major group within the UNO coalition, constantly attacked Chamorro's legitimacy. He did not participate in cabinet meetings, nor did he preside over the government in the president's absence as the constitution directed, that duty being taken over by Chamorro's son-in-law Antonio Lacayo, minister of the presidency. A foreign reporter once asked him, "Dr. Godoy, are you in the government?" (Envío Collective, 1990i, p. 26). Godoy's only official assignments were to a task force investigating the revival of the Central American parliament. Godoy, who served for four years as minister of labor under the FSLN, was then seen as a "very embittered man[who] would do anything to get rid of the Sandinistas" (Envío Collective, 1990f, p. 29), apparently even seizing power from his own president if necessary.

Without foreign aid, the two apparent successes of Chamorro's early days—ending the Contra war and restarting the economy—turned to failures that also threatened her government's legitimacy. When the Sandinistas turned over control of the government to the Chamorro administration, and the army was reduced by nearly half, the Contras lost their last reason for continuing hostilities. By June, most fighters had moved into neutral zones from which all regular military and police forces had been banned.[12] The Contras entered the zones in part because the Chamorro government promised to provide "credit, housing, roads, health care, education, running water, and electricity," despite the fact that these services were largely unavailable in any existing towns and the cost would have been enormous. Not surprisingly, given the government's financial crisis, these promises were not kept (Envío Collective, 1991b, p. 20). Thereafter, ex-Contras pressed their demands by taking over both private and state lands, farms, and cooperatives, blockading roads, and clashing with military and police forces outside the special zones. Other than demands for land, most ex-Contras did not appear to have a larger political agenda, and most seemed to be favorably disposed toward President Chamorro personally. However, they represented a potential armed force that could be tapped by factions hostile to the FSLN. For example, Vice President Godoy reportedly used ex-Contras to attack workers who occupied buildings or people who built barricades during the general strike in July 1990.[13]

The net result was a transmutation of the nine-year conflict between the Nicaraguan Army and the counterrevolutionary forces that took place mostly in the remote countryside and border areas into an ongoing conflict between numerous armed groups in cities and towns all over Nicaragua (e.g., FSLN supporters, Godoy faction, several rival groups of ex-Contras, radical ultra-left- and right-wing supporters). The possibility that the country would break into civil war, or further destabilize into a Central American Lebanon, seemed more likely than ever. To maintain order, Chamorro had to depend on the Nicaraguan Army and the National Police, which remained heavily influenced by the FSLN. She was reluctant to do so because her reliance on these forces was used as an excuse by the right win to mount their own "defense forces," since they believed the destruction of the FSLN (and the army and police) should be the primary objective of the new government and for them any sign of cooperation between Chamorro and the FSLN meant that the government had lost its legitimacy because it had been taken over by the FSLN.

As observed by Richter (1990–1991) in Asia, qualities such as tolerance and willingness to compromise—qualities that are necessary for democracy—were perceived in the violent Nicaraguan political culture as signs of personal weakness or timidity that make the bearer unfit for the presidency. Violeta Chamorro's plan for national reconciliation, *concertación*, or a social pact, was perceived by some Nicaraguans as "a cry from those who lost, who need a safety net" (Tellez, 1990), while others saw it as "class suicide" (Selser, 1990b). The very word *pact* "sent shivers up the spines of most honest Nicaraguans," because it historically signified an agreement among elite national (and often international) interests on how to divide power up among themselves at the expense of nonelites (Nuñez, 1990). Politicians on the left and right of Chamorro's middle faction accused her of lacking legitimacy. The right wing said she "betrayed the noble and generous people of Nicaragua by signing a secret pact with the Sandinista mafia" (Envoi Collective, 1990i, p. 27), while the left wing accused her of subverting the election by trying to undo the gains of the revolution by extralegal means. In sum, it was commonly accepted in Nicaragua that toppling the Chamorro government would be easy; what kept most groups from trying to do so was the certain knowledge that the result would only be worse.

IMPLICATIONS FOR WOMEN AND POLITICS IN NICARAGUA

In one sense, a woman president in Nicaragua was as unexpected as Mary, the first queen of England, centuries before. Neither Mary Tudor nor Violeta Chamorro had any "examples of appropriate behavior for them, particularly in the public aspects of their rule" (Levin, 1986, p. 42). In defining her role, Chamorro chose for the most part to act within the boundaries established by the male-oriented values of Nicaraguan political culture and the dual gender identity system of *machismo* and *marianismo*. She neither denied her femaleness by becoming "one of the boys" nor differentiated herself from other women by saying, "do as I say, not as I do." During the campaign, she emphasized that "I act and speak as a woman" (O'Kane, 1990, p. 29). As a woman, mother, and a widow, Violeta Chamorro challenged the stereotype of what a president should be like, but survived by conforming to the typical expectation in Latin American countries that women who become involved in politics will do so as an extension of their role in the home. It is only on their cultural authority as mothers that women can acceptably venture into the political sphere in Latin America, as, for example, in movements of mothers of the "disappeared."

Violeta Chamorro fit this mold quite well. During her campaign, she often spoke of returning women to the home, of strengthening the family, of reestablishing traditional values. In her inaugural speech, and on count-less other occasions, she referred to the country as the Nicaraguan family, a family divided by conflict but one that she would redeem through her abnegation and suffering as the national mother. Other women in poli-tics who did not conform to this mold were treated far more harshly. For example, Miriam Argüello, a career politician who was once jailed by the Sandinistas, who openly campaigned for the UNO nomination for presi-dent, and who was elected to the National Legislature and served as its president, was ridiculed in the popular media for being a spinster. Violeta Chamorro challenged the conception of what a president is or should be by her mere presence; paradoxically, however, her challenge may have been limited by her source of moral authority. As Kovel (1988, pp. 102–104) pointed out, women who historically derived their power through their identity with nature itself, or with a mother image is timeless; it is also out-side history, excluded from the possibility of self-transformation, mythic but passive as a force for change. Chamorro was one of a select group of women who came to power through unique and sometimes tragic circum-stances, often involving the political assassination of a male relative (see Richter, 1990–1991). As such, she did not provide a viable model for most women seeking political power, and faced the difficult challenge of con-verting her moral authority into a positive force for changing the culture of Nicaraguan politics.[14]

Women were more than half the electorate in Nicaragua, but Violeta Chamorro had no specific agenda for women. During the presidential campaign, she repeatedly asserted, "I'm not a feminist, nor do I want to be one. I am a woman dedicated to my home, as Pedro taught me." Fur-ther, she declared that she had been "marked with the Chamorro brand-ing iron" (Cuadra, 1990a)—an image of female subjugation that was seen as excessive even in *machista* Nicaragua. Chamorro did not favor increas-ing the participation of women in politics and gave few political posts to women in her government. There was little in the UNO platform of benefit to women, except indirectly, but ending the military draft and negotiating an end to the war. Rather, analysts feared that "the privatization and state budget cuts called for in UNO's overall economic plan are likely to have disproportionate effect on the female labor force" and to affect women and children by cutting funding for child care centers, health programs, and school milk programs (Envío Collective, 1990b, p. 25).

In this context, changes for women and political power in Nicaragua would probably have to be brought about by women and men identified with other forces. Besides Chamorro, there was another woman candidate for president and another for vice president. Roughly 25% of the 1,632 candidates nominated for National Assembly and municipal council posts were women, with the FSLN nominating 35 women, the Social Christian party 28, and UNO 20 for the 90 seats in the National Assembly (Cuadra, 1990a). Women increased their numbers as deputies in the National Legislature and represented a wide spectrum of parties. For example, Azucena Ferrey, a former Contra, was also in the legislature. And many women rose to positions of power within various political parties.

Other factors, however, had a dampening effect on women's quest for political power. Nicaragua was a poor, dependent, peripheral country, where women did not have the affluence, occupational structure, services (such as child care), or control over fertility that are seen by some as "indispensable" for advancement (Kovel, 1988, p. 107), nor was their economic situation likely to improve soon. With no unique products or services to market, Nicaragua had to compete with other Third World nations to sell its few agricultural exports. Constant cycles of violence discouraged foreign capital investment, and there was no large urban proletariat that could work in assembly plants. A chemical industry did provide employment for highly skilled technicians, but also resulted in massive pollution of the environment.

Another problem, which also occurred in Eastern European nations, was that progressive thinking on women's issues became associated with a party that had recently been turned out of office. While the opposition stressed conservative values and "reconstruction of the family group" (García & Gomáriz, 1989, p. 243), the FSLN championed women's issues, at least at the level of public discourse, so much so that any concerns about child care or reproductive rights were seen as linked to its discredited ideology. It would take Nicaraguan women some time to detach major women's organizations from the FSLN party, make it clear that women's issues transcend partisan politics, and adopt new alternative strategies for putting women's issues on the agenda. A tentative plan for all women representatives in the National Assembly to form an interparty caucus was one hopeful step in this new direction.

A third complication was that Nicaragua women, consistent with their traditional gender role, were repeatedly called upon to sacrifice their demands in the interest of national security, national unity, reconstruction, the economic crisis, or any number of other things that were seen as having precedence. Gender consciousness has been raised a number of times—for example, in the open forums surrounding the framing of a new constitution in 1986—but many of the statutes enacted were not fully enforced. It was difficult to convince women to muster the necessary energy to again take up the cause of women's issues when there were so many disappointments before, and when to do so ran counter to the prevailing standard of selflessness as appropriate behavior for women.

In conclusion, there was no immediate danger that Nicaragua would become a matriarchy. President Chamorro's task, however, was nearly as daunting: to change the political culture (Boudreaux, 1991, p. 10). Her accomplishments—staying alive, staying in power, and keeping the country from full-blown civil war—were by no means trivial. The longer her government lasted, the stronger the democratic tradition and institutions it was establishing would become. As long as she remained in office, Nicaraguan President Violeta Chamorro was certainly worth watching.

NOTES

1 The canal was eventually built across Panama instead, ironically because Nicaragua was deemed too politically unstable.
2 Interestingly enough, although women are obviously *mestizos* as well, the issue of what this dual heritage means for females is almost never explored. That is, men are presumed to have to deal with both their male and female characteristics, while women are presumed to have only female characteristics.
3 She has been compared with Philippine President Corazon Aquino, who was also sometimes dismissed as "just a housewife," but in other respects the two women are quite different. On a visit to Washington, some U.S. officials hailed Violeta Chamorro as another Corazon Aquino, but Aquino, who has her own political history, reportedly declined to have her picture taken with Chamorro (Cortez, 1990, p. 223).
4 Many people who are now Sandinistas were associated with *La Prensa* when it was an opposition newspaper in Somoza's time: for example, Danilo Aguirre Solis, a Sandinista representative in the National Legislature; Sergio Ramírez, former vice president; and Rosario Murillo, a companion of former President Daniel Ortega.
5 Various accounts of her visits to her husband's grave put them at twice a week, once a week, and monthly on the anniversary date of Pedro Joaquín's death.
6 Members of the Chamorro clan run all of the daily newspapers in Nicaragua: Violeta's eldest daughter manages the now pro-government *La Prensa*, her youngest son manages the official Sandinista party newspaper *Barricada*, and her brother-in-law manages the independent *El Nuevo Diario*.

7 Bowing to opposition demands, the electoral code was changed to permit foreign interests to donate money and supplies to Nicaraguan political parties—a practice that is illegal in most countries and a move that clearly favored the coalition of political parties (UNO) supported by the United States.

8 Some political parties did occupy a middle ground but were virtually unknown to voters because they neither had the money to finance their own campaigns nor would join the opposition coalition (UNO) in order to gain access to foreign donations that flowed to the UNO campaign coffers.

9 The difficulty of building a coalition that includes extreme right- and left-wing parties became apparent when members of different factions engaged in shoving matches and fistfights during the campaign and began scrambling for power as soon as the elections were over.

10 The United States had already "spent 12.5 million for the 'promotion of democracy' and election activities, or about $7.00 per [Nicaraguan] voter" (Sharkey, 1990, p. 22); other estimates put total U.S. spending at $25 million (*New York Times*, April 27, 1990).

11 Having a religious orientation, however, was not unusual in Nicaragua. Even Francisco Mayorga, an economist and head of the Central Bank, closed his speeches with the line, "with help from God and the Holy Virgin Mary" (Cuadra, 1990b).

12 Ironically, it was only in defeat that the Contras were able to accomplish their objective of occupying land inside Nicaragua, a goal they were never able to attain during nine years of counterrevolutionary guerrilla warfare.

13 This is according to a personal interview I conducted in Nicaragua during the July 1990 general strike.

14 Still, Chamorro's presidency has reportedly inspired at least one other Central American woman to launch a campaign to become president—Margarita Penón de Arias, wife of former Costa Rican President Oscar Arias.

REFERENCES

Associated Press. (1990, February 26). Dateline Managua, Nicaragua.

Barquero, S.L. (1945). *Gobernantes de Nicaragua: 1825–1947*. Managua: Publicaciones de Ministerio de Instrucción Pública.

Boudreaux, R. (1991, January 6). The Great Conciliator: President Violeta Chamorro Reconciled Nicaragua's Warring Armies. But Can She Deliver Anything Else. *Los Angeles Times*.

Chamorro Barrios, C. (1989, October 27). UNO unites my father's enemies. *Barricada, 10*, 21.

Chaney, E.M. (1973). Women in Latin American politics: The case of Peru and Chile. In A. Pescatello (Ed.), *Female and male in Latin America*. Pittsburgh, PA: University of Pittsburgh Press.

Close, D. (1988). *Nicaragua: Politics, economics, and society*. London: Frances Pinter.

Cuadra, P.A. (1987). The Nicaraguans. In R.S. Leiken & B. Rubin (Eds.), *The Central American crisis reader*. New York: Summit.

Cuadra, S. (1990a, January 20). A vote for equality. *Barricada International, 10*, 11.

Cuarda, S. (1990b, May 19). There's more to politics than meets the eye. *Barricada International, 10*, 6.

Díaz, M.N. (1966). *Tonalá: Conservatism, responsibility, and authority in a Mexican town*. Berkeley: University of California Press.

Edmisten, P. (1990). Nicaragua divided: La Prensa and the Chamorro legacy. Pensacola, FL: University of West Florida Press.

Elías, A. (1988). Los hombres que creen amar a las mujeres. *FEM, 12*(69), 38–40.

Envío Collective. (1989a, June). Nicaragua's electoral process: The new name for the war. *Envío, 8*, 3–10.

Envío Collective. (1989b, October). Navigating the electoral map. *Envío, 8*, 3–14.

Envío Collective. (1990a, January). A thorn by any other name pricks the same. *Envío, 9*, 6.

Envío Collective. (1990b, March/April). UNO plans market economy. *Envío, 9*, 21–27.

Envío Collective. (1990c, March/April). After the poll wars: Explaining the upset. *Envío, 9*, 30–35.

Envío Collective. (1990d, May). On the verge of peace, or civil war? *Envío, 9*, 5–9.

Envío Collective. (1990e, June). Playing with fire. *Envío, 9*, 3–13.

Envío Collective. (1990f, June). UNO's balance of power—on a tight rope. *Envío, 9*, 26–32.

Envío Collective. (1990g, July). From military to social confrontation. *Envío, 9*, 3–8.

Envío Collective. (1990h, July). Two faces of UNO. *Envío, 9*, 24–37.

Envío Collective. (1990i, August/September). UNO politics: Thunder on the right. *Envío, 9*, 26–30.

Envío Collective. (1990j, October). Polarization and depolarization. *Envío, 9*, 3–11.

Envío Collective. (1990k, November). Who will conquer the chaos? *Envío, 9*, 3–10.

Envío Collective. (1991a, January/February). Concertación and counter-concertación. *Envío, 10*, 3–9.

Envío Collective. (1991b, January/February). Rebellion in the ranks: Challenge from the right. *Envío, 10*, 18–27.

Envío Collective. (1991c, March). A year of UNO economic policies: The rich get richer . . . *Envío, 10*, 30–49.

Envío Collective. (1991d, May). Bankers and masses square off: Economic overhaul, social breakdown? *Envío, 10*, 3–15.

García, A.I., & Gomáriz, E. (1989). *Mujeres Centroamericanas: Vol. 2. Efectos del conflicto.* San Jose, Costa Rica: FLASCO.

Goldwert, M. (1985). Mexican machismo: The flight from femininity. *Psychoanalytic Review, 72*(1), 161–169.

Heyck, D.L. (1990). *Life stories of the Nicaraguan revolution.* New York: Routledge.

Hockstader, L. (1990, March 1). Chamorro assails Ortega. *Washington Post.*

Jiménez, M. (1990, May 19). Neo-liberalism in the classroom. *Barricada International, 10*, 8.

Jonas, S., & Stein, N. (1990). The construction of democracy in Nicaragua. *Latin American Perspectives, 17*(3), 10–37.

Kantor, H. (1969). Nicaragua: America's only hereditary dictatorship. In H. Kantor (Ed.), *Patterns of politics and political systems in Latin America.* Chicago: Rand McNally.

Kovel, J. (1988). *In Nicaragua.* London: Free Association.

Kretzer, D.I. (1988). *Ritual, politics, and power.* New Haven, CT: Yale University Press.

Levin, C. (1986). Queens and claimants: Political insecurity in sixteenth-century England. In J. Sharistanian (Ed.), *Gender, ideology, and action: Historical perspectives on women's public lives.* Westport, CT: Greenwood.

Levy, M.F. (1988). *Each in her own way: Five women leaders of the developing world.* Boulder, CO: Lynne Rienner.

Mendoza, R. (1990, October). We erred to win. *Envío, 9*, 23–50.

Molyneux, M. (1985). Mobilization without emancipation? Women's interests, the state, and revolution in Nicaragua. *Feminist Studies, 11*, 227–254.

Nuñez, O. (1990, June 30). Pacts, accords, and alliances. *Barricada International, 10,* 19.

O'Kane, T. (1990). The new old order. *NACLA Report on the Americas, 24*(1), 28–36.

Preston, J. (1990, February 27). Chamorro faces task of reconciling a divided nation. *Washington Post.*

Radell, D. (1969). *The historical geography of western Nicaragua.* Unpublished doctoral dissertation, University of California, Berkeley.

Ramírez, S. (1989). The kid from Niquinohomo (L. Baker, Trans.). *Latin American Perspectives, 16*(3), 48–82.

Richter, L.K. (1990–1991). Exploring theories of female leadership in South and Southeast Asia. *Pacific Affairs, 63,* 524–540.

Selser, G. (1990a, June 16). Slanted justice. *Barricada International, 10,* 5–7.

Selser, G. (1990b, June 30). Social Pact? What Social Pact? *Barricada International, 10,* 3.

Sharkey, J. (1986, September/October). Back in control: The CIA's secret propaganda campaign puts the agency exactly where it wants to be. *Common Cause,* 28–40.

Sharkey, J. (1990, May/June). Nicaragua: Anatomy of an election. How U.S. money affected the outcome in Nicaragua. *Common Cause,* 20–29.

Stevens, E.P. (1973). Marianismo: The other face of machismo in Latin America. In A. Pescatello (Ed.), *Female and male in Latin America.* Pittsburgh, PA: University of Pittsburgh Press.

Taylor, C. (1989, November 11). UNO: Throwbacks and greenbacks. *Barricada International, 9,* 12–13.

Tellez, D.M. (1990, June 16). Who needs a "National Accord"? *Barricada International, 10,* 19.

Uhlig, M.A. (1990, February 11). Opposing Ortega. *New York Times Magazine,* 34–35.

Vargas, O.R. (1989a). *Elecciones presidenciales en Nicaragua, 1912–1932.* Managua: Fundación Manolo Morales.

Vargas, O.R. (1989b, September 30). Elections in Nicaragua (1912–1974). *Barricada International, 9,* 6–7.

Velázquez, J.L. (1986). *Nicaragua: Sociedad civil y dictadura.* San Jose, Costa Rica: Libro Libre.

Wiarda, H.J. (1981). *Corporatism and national development in Latin America.* Boulder, CO: Westview Press.

6

Indira Gandhi and the Exercise of Power

Jana Everett

How do we make sense of Indira Gandhi's role as the central political leader of India from 1966 when she became prime minister to 1984, when she was assassinated by her Sikh bodyguards? Did it matter that she was a woman? Her critics often used gender imagery, as in Salman Rushdie's (1980) description of a prime minister who "aspired to be Devi, the Mother-goddess in her most terrible aspect, possessor of the *Shakti* (female energy) of the gods, a multi-limbed divinity with a center-parting and schizophrenic hair" (p. 522; see also Rushdie, 1985). Yet most commentators have not seen gender as a significant factor in Mrs. Gandhi's governance. For example, *India Today*'s effort to capture her complexity used gender-neutral terms: "Dictator or democrat? Saint or tyrant? Consolidator or destroyer? Peacemaker or warmonger? She was all of these yet none of them. To the final tragic end, the Indira enigma remained intact" (Bobb, 1984, p. 94).

Among the myriad efforts to explain Mrs. Gandhi's policy decisions, leadership style, and political legacies, there are two main theoretical approaches. The first is a Marxist approach that depicts the Indian political economy as directed by a coalition of dominant classes and characterized by structural crises of backward capitalism (Banerjee, 1984, pp. 2028–2031; Roy, 1984, pp. 1896–1897). Writers using this approach interpret Mrs. Gandhi's actions as shaped fundamentally by exacerbating crises and conflicts among the classes. The second is a psychological approach that explains her actions in terms of personality variables leading to a compulsion to dominate (Hart, 1976; Malik, 1988). Within this approach, some writers focus on a sense of insecurity engendered in childhood and others focus on the amoral political culture of the 1960s. Both of these approaches are ultimately unsatisfactory. While the Marxist approach discounts the independent effect of Indira Gandhi as a leader, the psychological approach dismisses the context confronting this leader. Sudipta Kaviraj (1986) offers a more useful approach that takes into account the extent to which domestic and international constraints forced Mrs. Gandhi to work out a "logic of survival" upon becoming prime minister: "Initially, this logic of survival made her act pragmatically, but eventually, these *ad hoc* and individual initiatives altered the basic structure of Indian politics" (p. 1697). Although not addressed by Kaviraj, gender considerations appear to have played a role in Indira Gandhi's survival strategies.

CONTEXT

India may have been the "jewel in the crown" of British colonialism, but under the British, India experienced economic stagnation.[1] Urban Western-education elites, created by the colonial system to work in its administration, began to demand economic and political reforms. The Indian National Congress, formed in 1885, created a mass movement for independence under the leadership of Mohandas Gandhi (1869–1948) and Jawaharlal Nehru (1889–1964). Independence was achieved in 1947, and with it the trauma of partition, as the Muslim majority areas in the Eastern and Western parts of the subcontinent became Pakistan. Nehru presided over the process of constitution making, which established a parliamentary democracy with a prime minister, a federal political system with central and state governments, guarantees of fundamental rights, a largely ceremonial presidency, a Supreme Court with the powers of judicial review, and emergency governmental powers when national security was threatened. Congress transformed itself from a mass movement to a political machine, winning the first three general elections in a one-party dominant political system.

The challenges facing the Indian state were enormous. About half of the citizens were extremely poor. Rural India, constituting the vast majority of the population, was characterized by crop yields among the lowest in the world and by extreme inequalities in landowning: While the top 5% of households (owning 20 acres or more) controlled 41% of the land, 22% of households owned no land, and 39% of households (owning 2.5 acres or less) controlled 8% of the land (Frankel, 1978, pp. 96–97). India has great cultural diversity (Hardgrave & Kochanek, 1986, pp. 4–11); 12 major languages and hundreds of minor ones are spoken in India. Although Hindus make up more than 80% of the population, they are divided into high castes (the Brahmins, Kshatriyas, and Vaishyas), middle castes (the upper *shudras*), "backward castes" (the lower *shudras*, 25% of the population), "scheduled castes" (the former untouchables, 15% of the population), and tribals (mainly counted as Hindus, 7% of the population). Religious minorities include Muslims (11%), Christians (35%), and Sikhs (2%).

Nehru was committed to democratic social transformation, self-reliance, and "a third way," distinct from capitalist or communist approaches in both domestic and foreign policy. In foreign affairs, Nehru was the most distinguished spokesperson for the Afro-Asian world; in advocating non-alignment, he was often at odds with U.S. policy makers who sought to build alliances to contain communism during the Cold War era, including a 1954 mutual defense treaty with Pakistan. Indo-Pakistan relations remained tense, with wars in 1948 and in 1965 over Kashmir, which remained under Indian control. Nehru's prestige suffered in a 1962 war with China over disputed territory, when Indian defenses collapsed.

Scholar Akhil Gupta (1989) notes, "Democratic-capitalist third-world states are characterized by an internal tension because their developmental goals frequently run up against the limits imposed by the private control of productive resources" (p. 790). The coalition of dominant classes—industrial capitalists, rich farmers, and professionals (state, bureaucrats, and intellectuals)—constrained the development strategies of the political elites, who were unable or unwilling to organize the peasantry to promote radical agrarian reform. Under Nehru's direction, India had embarked on a policy of rapid industrialization, with a strong public sector. Nehru favored industrial changes in agriculture—land reform, rural cooperatives—to achieve gains in agricultural productivity necessary for industrial growth. However, state leaders resisted these changes, and the increases in productivity were not forthcoming.

By the mid-1960s, India was dependent on foreign assistance from the United States and the Soviet Union to finance development plans and on imports of food grains to feed its people. Under Prime Minister Lal

Bahadur Shastri (1964–1966), national economic policy shifted toward a larger role for private investment and modern technology to increase agricultural production. Upon taking office in 1966, Mrs. Gandhi's options were severely constrained. India's military and agricultural weakness had created international dependence and domestic crises. The Congress Party organization did not seem able to handle the demands of an increasingly politicized electorate. Mrs. Gandhi herself was dependent on Congress President K. Kamaraj Nadar and other party bosses.

INDIRA GANDHI'S EARLY YEARS

Several themes can be extracted from the stories Mrs. Gandhi and her biographers tell of her childhood, youth, and early adulthood (see Bhatia 1974; Gandhi, 1980; Hutheesing, 1969; Malhotra, 1989; Masani, 1976; Moraes, 1980). National politics permeated her family life. The public invaded the private, absorbing her father, dominating her play, eclipsing her marriage. She did not participate well in student political and academic life in England, the conventional masculine route to political leadership among the nationalist elite. Her route to power would be different, based on being the daughter of a widowed prime minister. Mrs. Gandhi's early career revealed the difficulties she had with being accepted by the male political leaders as an equal. Under the shadow of her father, she was not taken seriously by the politicians and statesmen who met with Nehru, and she had to absorb her husband's hostility over her success. These difficulties would also be seen during her years as prime minister.

Indira Gandhi, the only child of Jawaharlal and Kamala Nehru, was born into the prominent nationalist family on November 19, 1917, in their family home in Allahabad. The Nehrus were Kashmiri Brahmins who had served in the administration of both Mughal and British rulers of India. Indira's paternal grandfather, Motilal Nehru (1861–1931), was a successful lawyer and leader of the moderate wing of Congress. Jawaharlal Nehru had been trained as a lawyer in England but turned to full-time work in the nationalist movement. In 1920 the Nehru family joined Mohandas Gandhi's noncooperation movement, giving up their lavish Westernized lifestyle for *khadi* (handspun and handwoven cloth), simple Indian food, and numerous terms of imprisonment.

With a constant stream of nationalist leaders coming to the Nehru home, Indira had few opportunities to play with other children. She recalled a close relationship with Gandhi: "As a very small child, I regarded him, not as a great leader but more as an elder of the family to whom I went with difficulties and problems, which he treated with the grave seriousness which was due to the large-eyed and solemn child I was" (quoted in Masani, 1976, p. 18). She was separated from her father for long periods during his jail terms. Her schooling was also frequently interrupted, and Indira was primarily taught at home through her 12th year. She would amuse herself by playing political games: lining up her dolls to confront each other as nationalists and police, and delivering speeches to the servants. Exposed to a wide range of books, Indira developed a fascination for Joan of Arc, telling her aunt, "Some day I am going to lead my people to freedom just as Joan of Arc did" (quoted in Hutheesing, 1969, p. 45). In a 1972 interview with Oriana Fallaci, Mrs. Gandhi painted a picture of a lonely, insecure childhood that taught her self-reliance:

> If you only knew what it did to me to have lived in that house where the police were bursting in to take everyone away! I certainly didn't have a happy and serene childhood. I was a thin, sickly, nervous little girl. And after the police came, I'd be left alone for weeks, months, to get along as best I could. I learned very soon to get along by myself. (quoted in Fallaci, 1976, p. 173)

In her extended family household, conflict among the female relatives marked Indira's childhood. Kamala was deeply religious, teaching her daughter the Hindu classics and the Hindi language. The more sophisticated Nehru women, especially Motilal's wife, Swarupani, and her daughter Nan (later Vijayalaksmi Pandit), ridiculed Kamala, who they did not believe was good enough for Jawaharlal. Swarupani, and her daughter, Krishna (later Hutheesing), was more supportive. Indira Gandhi later said of her mother: "I loved her deeply and when I thought she was being wronged I fought for her and quarreled with people" (quoted in Malhotra, 1989, p. 30). Kamala eagerly embraced Gandhi's cause. Indira Gandhi (1980) remembered her mother as "a convinced feminist, a position which I didn't understand then because I felt that I could do what I liked and that it didn't make any difference whether I was a boy or a girl" (p. 23). Throughout Indira's childhood, her mother's health was poor. A diagnosis of tuberculosis led Jawaharlal, accompanied by Indira, to take Kamala to Switzerland for treatment in 1926–1927.

Indira's adolescence was marked by her mother's deteriorating health and separation from her father because of his imprisonment. In 1931, Kamala too was arrested; as president of the Allahabad Congress Committee, she had organized women to picket liquor stores and foreign cloth shops. Left out of the Congress actions because of her age, Indira organized children into the Vanar Sena ("Monkey Army," from the Indian epic *Ramayana*), which served as Congress auxiliaries, bringing water to demonstrators, smuggling messages to Congress leaders, and spying on police stations. Jawaharlal, in prison, supplemented Indira's education with a series of letters later published as *Glimpses of World History*. She was sent to nationalist-oriented schools, first in Poona in 1931 and then in 1934 to Rabindranath Tagore's school in Santiniketan, Bengal. In May 1935, Indira accompanied her mother, whose condition had worsened, to Europe for treatment. Jawaharlal joined them in September after his release from prison. Kamala died in February 1936 in Lausanne, Switzerland.

After her mother's death, Indira went to England to prepare for the Oxford entrance examinations while her father returned to India to assume the Congress presidency. Her schooling was again interrupted, by trips home and to Southeast Asia and Europe with her father, and by ill health. She developed a close friendship with Feroze Gandhi, a student at the London School of Economics who had been a devoted follower of Kamala Nehru. Gaining entrance to Oxford on her second attempt, Indira joined Somerville College in February 1938 to read modern history. She did not stand out in academic work or in the politics of the Indian community in England. An 11-month recuperation in Switzerland followed an attack of pleurisy. Indira returned to India with Feroze in 1941, giving the war and her heath as reasons for abandoning her studies. In 1985, a fellow student revealed that she was forced to leave Oxford because she had failed a Latin examination (Malhotra, 1989, p. 44).

Against the initial objections of her father, Indira married Feroze Gandhi on March 26, 1942, in Allahabad. Nehru was more concerned by Feroze's modest economic background than by the religious differences between them—Feroze belonged to the Parsi or Zoroastrian community, while the Nehrus were high-caste Hindus. Nehru quickly came to their defense when there was a public outcry about her "mixed marriage." Both Feroze and Indira spent time in prison in conjunction with the Quit India movement and then moved into the Nehru family home in Allahabad. Their first child, Rajiv Gandhi, was born in August 1944. At the end of the war, Jawaharlal

Nehru assumed the leadership of the interim government and appointed Feroze managing director of *the National Herald*, a Lucknow newspaper founded by Nehru. Mrs. Gandhi moved to Lucknow with her husband and son, but was soon commuting to Delhi to act as hostess for her father. Her second son, Sanjay, was born in Delhi in December 1946.

On August 15, 1947, Jawaharlal Nehru became prime minister of Independent India. Nehru, Mrs. Gandhi, and her sons moved to Teen Murti House in Delhi, leaving Feroze in Lucknow. According to Mrs. Gandhi (1980), the decision to help her father "wasn't really a choice"; his grief after the assassination of Mahatma Gandhi on January 30, 1948, increased her determination to stay with him (p. 9). Stressing her duty to her father also covered up marital discord brought on by Feroze's difficulties with being "son-in-law of the nation." In 1955, Mrs. Gandhi wrote, "I have been and am deeply unhappy in my domestic life. Now, the hurt and the unpleasantness don't seem to matter so much. I am sorry, though, to have missed the most wonderful thing in life, having a complete and perfect relationship with another human being" (Norman, 1985, p. 28). Her responsibilities grew as she supervised the Nehru household, traveled abroad with the prime minister and on her own, and gradually began to stand in for Nehru at meetings. She became active in the organizational wing of the Congress Party, working in the Women's Department and serving on the Congress Election Committee and Working Committee. In 1959, she was elected Congress president.

Meanwhile, Feroze pursued a political career of his own as a member of Parliament from 1950 to his death in 1960. Moving to Delhi, he occupied housing provided for MPs and also stayed with his wife and children at Teen Murti House. He developed a reputation as an independent Congress backbencher, uncovering a corruption scandal that led to the resignation of the finance minister in 1957. In a 1966 interview, Indira Gandhi described the tensions in their relationship: "When I went into public life and became successful, he liked it and he didn't like it. Other people—friends, relatives—were the worst. They would say, 'How does it feel, being so-and-so's husband?' He would get upset, and it would take me weeks to win him over" (Hutheesing, 1969, p. 137). After Feroze suffered a slight heart attack in 1959, they reconciled, and the family went for a holiday in Kashmir. When he had a second heart attack in September 1960, Mrs. Gandhi rushed him to the hospital and sat up with him all night; she was with him when he died in the early morning. In spite of their estranged relationship,

Mrs. Gandhi wrote shortly after his death: "Up till now I had somebody to whom I could pour out my thoughts—even if there was a lack of attention and sympathy—and with the removal of that outlet I have to look outward" (Norman, 1985, p. 78). Four years later her father would die, and less than two years after that Mrs. Gandhi would become prime minister.

PATH TO POWER

From the perspective of hindsight, the dynastic character of Indian political leadership is apparent: Nehru family members served as prime ministers for 40 of the 44 years of independence. Indira Gandhi groomed her first son Sanjay and then her son Rajiv to succeed her, and after Rajiv Gandhi's assassination at the close of the 1991 election campaign, Congress (I) leaders tried unsuccessfully to persuade his widow, Sonia, to accept the Congress Party presidency. Nevertheless, Indira Gandhi's accession to power was by no means a foregone conclusion. Her status as the only offspring of the widowed prime minister created a political career for Mrs. Gandhi, but her father took no action to indicate he wished her to succeed him in office. Only after his death did any signs of Mrs. Gandhi's ambition to be prime minister surface, and even then her accession to the office did not seem especially likely.

A constellation of factors thrust political leadership upon Indira Gandhi.[2] One factor was the Indian political context in 1966 at the unexpected death of Prime Minister Shastri, a factionalized Congress Party, and party leaders determined to prevent a particular individual, Morarji Desai, from becoming prime minister. Another was the "Appendage Syndrome" (Fraser, 1988, pp. 307–308). Congress President Kamaraj orchestrated Mrs. Gandhi's selection as prime minister because he perceived her to be weak enough that he and the other regional party bosses (known as the Syndicate) could control her, and yet strong enough to beat Desai in a party election because of the high regard for her father. In addition, her lack of association with any party faction meant she had fewer enemies than the other possible candidates. According to Dom Moraes (1980):

> Kamaraj felt that a woman would be an ideal tool for the Syndicate, especially Nehru's daughter. He had watched her, gentle, sedate, obedient to her

father, properly courteous to her elders: her parentage would capture the public imagination, and once she was properly in power the Syndicate could switch profession: from queenmakers to puppetmasters. (p. 123)

Although Prime Minister Nehru asserted publically that he did not want to play a role in choosing his successor, a policy initiative taken by him in August 1963 weakened the prospects of Finance Minister Morarji Desai, who was too conservative in Nehru's view. Known as the Kamaraj plan, this initiative was designed ostensibly to strengthen the party organization by having 12 government officials at the state and national levels resign their positions and devote themselves full time to party work. Both Desai and Home Minister Lal Bahudur Shastri stepped down from the cabinet under the Kamaraj plan. Shastri was brought back into the cabinet in early 1964.

Some, including Desai, have argued that the Kamaraj plan was designed not only to eliminate Desai's chances of becoming prime minister, but also to ensure Mrs. Gandhi's selection (Frankel, 1987, pp. 242–243; Richter, 1990–1991). However, since Nehru neither openly advanced her candidacy nor appointed her to a cabinet office, it seems unlikely that he planned for her to succeed him. When Nehru died of a stroke in May 1964, Mrs. Gandhi was not seriously considered as a candidate for prime minister. Congress President Kamaraj and the Syndicate orchestrated a party consensus behind Shastri as his successor. The Syndicate shared Nehru's distrust of Desai, but for different reasons: They saw him as too individualistic to accept Syndicate control.

Mrs. Gandhi joined Shastri's cabinet as minister of information and broadcasting and became a member of the Rajya Sabha, the indirectly elected upper house of the Indian Parliament. According to Mrs. Gandhi (1980), Shastri insisted "he must have a Nehru in the Cabinet to maintain stability" (p. 101), and he offered her the position of foreign minister, which she refused. This seems unlikely; given her administrative inexperience, her cabinet appointment can be seen as a tribute to Nehru's memory and Shastri's attempt to neutralize her as a political force (Brecher, 1966, pp. 103, 107; Masani, 1976, p. 133; Moraes, 1980, pp. 12–121).

While Mrs. Gandhi apparently performed in a lackluster manner in the conventional parliamentary and cabinet arenas, she found other ways to develop a public following. She moved to 1 Safdarjung Road and continued the Nehru custom of the moving *durbar*—opening her home to the public, who came with petitions or simply to view Nehru's daughter. She criticized the government for drifting to the right and in two instances—during language riots in Madras and at the onset of the 1965 war with Pakistan—gained public admiration for her courage and resoluteness. Arriving in Kashmir at the same time that several thousand Pakistani infiltrators were discovered, Mrs. Gandhi went to the military control room, communicated the seriousness of the situation to Prime Minister Shastri, and helped to maintain morale. Her actions won her the title of "the only man in a Cabinet of old women" (Masani, 1976, p. 136).

BECOMING PRIME MINISTER

On January 10, 1966, Prime Minister Shastri died suddenly of a heart attack in Tashkent, where he had signed a peace agreement formally ending the 1965 Indo-Pakistan War. Succession politics returned, and once again Congress President Kamaraj played the crucial role in the selection process. His choice of Indira Gandhi was initially opposed by the Syndicate because of her perceived leftist leaning, but she gained their support after building a coalition of state chief ministers. This time an open contest for prime minister was unavoidable, because Desai refused to step aside again "for this mere *chokri*" (slip of a girl) (Masani, 1976, p. 139). On January 19, the Congress Parliamentary Party (CPP) elected Indira Gandhi prime minister over Morarji Desai, with a vote of 355 to 169. On hearing of her election, the crowds cried out not only "Long Live Indira," but also "Long Live Jawaharlal" (Moraes, 1980, p. 172).

Looking more broadly at the processes of political succession in India and also elsewhere in South and Southeast Asia, the means by which Indira Gandhi achieved power appear fairly typical of these political systems, which are all characterized by prominent political families and elite factionalism (Richter, 1990–1991). Widows, daughters, and sisters of male leaders have served as prime minister or president in Sri Lanka (Sirimavo Bandaranaike), Pakistan (Benazir Bhutto), Bangladesh (Khalida Zia), and the Philippines (Corazon Aquino), as well as in India. In addition, imprisoned Daw Aung San Suu Kyi, winner of the 1991 Nobel Peace Prize and daughter of Burmese nationalist leader U Aung San, was leader of the Burmese political party that was prevented by the military from taking power after winning elections in 1990. Under conditions of bitter political rivalries, female representatives of political dynasties have played a unifying role, but in some cases they have also raised fears in the military leadership. In India's first two successions, a small group of party leaders decided upon a candidate, but a broad array of institutional interests within the party was involved in the selection process: the Congress Working Committee, the state chief ministers, and the CPP. The contrast in the succession of Rajiv Gandhi—he was chosen by the CPP (executive) and sworn in as prime minster within hours of his mother's assassination—serves as an indicator of the deinstitutionalization of Indian politics and its dynastic character by 1984.

LEADERSHIP STYLE

Commentators have described Mrs. Gandhi's leadership style as pragmatic, reactive, and characterized by extended periods of drift interspersed with periods of decisive action (Carras, 1979, p. 37; Tharoor, 1982, p. 74). Over the course of her tenure in office, she would fashion strategies to increase India's military and economic powers as well as her own. These strategies did not constitute an overarching, deliberate design; they were not ideologically consistent, but they had elements in common. Kaviraj (1986) views Mrs. Gandhi as outwitting her adversaries by acting decisively in a manner characterized by "a disregard for institutional norms" (p. 1700). Although her initiatives increased her personal power, they limited the options available for her to solve future crises. Having eliminated political leaders with independent bases of support from Congress and having almost destroyed the party, Mrs. Gandhi was left to rely on her own presence, state policies, and the agencies of state repression.

Several elements of Mrs. Gandhi's leadership style emerged in 1969 (Brass, 1988; Kothari, 1988; Manor, 1983; Rudolph & Rudolph, 1987, pp. 134–145). As in her college days and in her time in Shastri's cabinet, the conventions of male political behavior did not work for her, so she conceived her own. When rules of the game worked against her, she changed the rules. When the party bosses threatened her, she overthrew them and weakened the party. Using radical rhetoric and championing the needs of the poor, Mrs. Gandhi pursued a populist style to establish a personal relationship with the electorate unmediated by institutions. Elections became referenda on Mrs. Gandhi's rule. The rhetoric was not followed by the implementation of radical change. Under Mrs. Gandhi there was a centralization of power in the party and a breakdown of party organization. Intraparty elections were not held; instead, officials were appointed from the top. Mrs. Gandhi selected chief ministers and other officials on the basis of personal loyalty, not on the basis of their political standing at the local level. State politics lost autonomy through "unprincipled intervention by the center in state politics" because Mrs. Gandhi believed her power depended on this degree of control (Brass, 1988, p. 212). The personalization of power contributed to institutional decay as Mrs. Gandhi overturned commonly accepted procedures, norms, and principles of political competition and governance to achieve political advantage.

Mrs. Gandhi's vision for India (and perhaps also of her own leadership) was articulated in a 1977 interview: "We want India to be self-reliant and to strengthen its independence so that it cannot be pressurized by anybody . . . this cannot be done unless we solve our own problems, and the major problem is poverty and economic backwardness" (quoted in Tharoor, 1982, p. 88). This vision was pursued in isolation; Mrs. Gandhi lacked close ties with other political leaders due to her own past experiences and to additional gender considerations: A woman could not be too intimate with male politicians (Carras, 1979, p. 50). Instead, Mrs. Gandhi relied on a shifting group of personal advisors in the prime minister's secretariat and increasingly on her sons and their families. Rajiv and Sanjay lived with Mrs. Gandhi and, after their marriages, Sonia and Meka joined the Gandhi household. Perhaps partly due to her isolation, Mrs. Gandhi developed a tendency to interpret policy failures and political opposition in terms of conspiracies against her, often with external involvement. In response, she built up the intelligence capability of her office and increasingly resorted to coercive force to put down dissent.

MRS. GANDHI'S AGENDA

The Achievement of Political Survival: 1966–1971

Indira Gandhi's performance during her first few years in office underscored her weak position. She continued Shastri's economic liberalization and green revolution policies. In March 1966, Mrs. Gandhi traveled to the

United States seeking food aid and foreign exchange. She avoided criticism of U.S. policy in Vietnam and agreed to a proposal for a joint Indo-U.S. educational foundation in India. India's dependence on U.S. food aid, the World Bank, and the Aid to India Consortium was symbolized in the announcement to devalue the rupee by 36.5%, made on June 6, 1966. Within 10 days, the United States resumed food aid suspended the previous year at the outbreak of the Indo-Pakistan war. These policies, especially devaluation, were extremely unpopular in India and in the short run were unsuccessful. Devaluation led to a drop in foreign exchange earnings of 8% in 1966–1967, and more generally increasing disparities accompanied economic stagnation (Frankel, 1978, pp. 322–336). Shipments of U.S. food aid were delayed and irregular; the United States put India on a "short tether." Facing the failure of a second monsoon, Mrs. Gandhi was deeply humiliated by this treatment and resolved never to be in such a position of dependence again.

Mrs. Gandhi's credibility as a national leader was seriously compromised by domestic political developments. Political protests, including riots, strikes, student "indiscipline," rural rebellions, and secessionist movements, increased dramatically after 1965 (Rudolph & Rudolph, 1987, pp. 227, 238). The 1967 elections demonstrated a dramatic decline in Congress popularity and power. The Congress share of the Lok Sabha vote declined 4%, to 41%, and, more significantly, alliances among opposition parties led to a 21% decline in Congress seats, leaving a slender majority of 25 (Frankel, 1978, p. 353).[3] Congress lost legislative elections in eight states as the Congress share of the state assembly vote fell 3%, to 42%, and opposition of coalitions took office.

Within the party Mrs. Gandhi found herself generally outmaneuvered by the Syndicate and harassed in meetings of the party organization and Parliament, where she was nicknamed "the Dumb Doll" (Malhotra, 1989, p. 93). After the 1967 elections, supporters of Morarji Desai once again advanced his candidacy for prime minister, charging that government policies and the party bosses (including Kamaraj) that had put Mrs. Gandhi in office had been repudiated by the electorate. Kamaraj was able to work out a compromise, but it involved including Morarji Desai in Mrs. Gandhi's cabinet as deputy prime minister and finance minister. At the end of 1967, Mrs. Gandhi was able to prevent Kamaraj from having another term as Congress president, but the party bosses refused to let her become president, and she was forced to accept S. Nijalingappa, a Syndicate member.

By early 1968, Kamaraj had decided Mrs. Gandhi should be removed as prime minister. In what can be seen as the fashioning of survival strategy, Mrs. Gandhi began to edge cautiously to the left in both foreign and domestic policy, a direction that offered increased autonomy internationally, greater popularity nationally, and the potential to defeat her rivals within the party. She visited the Soviet Union in July 1966 and demanded an unconditional halt to U.S. bombing of North Vietnam, and she hosted a Non-Aligned Summit for Tito and Nasser in October 1966. In 1967, the Indian government dropped the planned Indo-American Education Foundation. The Soviet Union became India's most important arms supplier and increased development aid commitments. While shifting superpower relationships with India reflected international political consideration (primarily concerning China) over which India had little influence, closer ties with the Soviet Union replaced military and economic aid from an unreliable United States and enhanced anti-imperialist rhetoric that built popular support for Mrs. Gandhi.

Domestically, Mrs. Gandhi proposed a reformist 10-point program adopted by the Congress Working Committee in May 1967, but made no immediate move to implement the policies—including nationalization of general insurance, removal of the privileges of the princes, public distribution of food grains, and restriction of industrial monopolies—that were opposed by party conservatives such as Desai. Although party radicals pushed for bank nationalization, Desai was able to get the government to accept a compromise scheme for the "social control" of banking. By 1969, Mrs. Gandhi and Nijalingappa were publically debating policy issues, with the prime minister supporting a strong public sector and the party president criticizing its inefficiencies.

The struggle over power and policy direction within Congress came to a head in the contest for president of India in 1969 (Frankel, 1978, pp. 414–425; Masani, 1976, pp. 196–204). By acting decisively, Mrs. Gandhi was able to win a power struggle and to advance her own policy agenda. The struggle pitted the Syndicate (now seeking to oust Mrs. Gandhi in favor of Morarji Desai) against Indira Gandhi, who was supported by a group of "young Turks" in the Congress Forum for Socialist Action. Mrs. Gandhi abruptly divested Desai of the finance portfolio; opposed the Syndicate choice for president, Sanjiva Reddy (the official Congress candidate); and announced her support for bank nationalization, which was enormous; she had seized the moment with a populist program. When complimented by a friend on the strategic timing of bank nationalization, Mrs. Gandhi responded, "They drove me to the wall and left me with no other option" (quoted in Malhotra, 1989, p. 120).

Since she had lost in the party, Mrs. Gandhi sought to win in the wider national arena. She announced a free vote for president, and her candidate, V.V. Giri, the interim president running as an independent, won a narrow victory based on the support of Communists, Socialists, and regional parties, as well as from approximately one third of Congress legislators. Mrs. Gandhi (1980) framed the conflict in the following terms:

> Whether (a) the Congress should be a mass based organisation or one manipulated by a handful of party bosses, (b) it should adhere firmly to its declared policy of secularism and socialism, and (c) in a democracy the elected head of government could be overruled by a party organisation which is not responsible to Parliament. (p. 133)

The Syndicate portrayed the conflict in terms of party discipline and tried to take action against Mrs. Gandhi for voting against the official party candidate for president. The Congress split, with two rival All India Congress Committees holding meetings in November. Although the Syndicate instructed the CPP to choose a new leader, a majority (310) of the 429 members supported Mrs. Gandhi (Bhatia, 1974, p. 226). (The president is chosen by an electoral college composed of MPs and state legislators.) There were now two Congress parties—Congress (R) (Ruling) and Congress (O) (Organization). Because Mrs. Gandhi's party had lost its absolute majority in Lok Sabha, Congress (R) now depended on the support of the Communist Party of India (CPI), several regional parties, and independents. The Congress split strengthened Mrs. Gandhi's power immeasurably; few questioned the methods she had used.

After the split in Congress, Indira Gandhi pursued a populist program: More industries were nationalized and the privy purses of the former princes were terminated. Conflicts increased between an activist Parliament and a conservative Supreme Court, which struck down much of the legislation on the grounds of unconstitutional interference with private property rights. In order to amend the constitution, Indira Gandhi required a two-thirds parliamentary majority, which she achieved in elections held in March 1971. She campaigned with the slogan "*Garibi hatao*" (Remove poverty), which the opposition alliance countered with "*Indira hatao*" (Remove Indira). Congress (R) won a resounding victory in the 1971 elections, with 43% of the vote translating into the needed two-thirds majority in the Lok Sabha (Frankel, 1978, p. 455). Congress (O) dropped from 65 to 16 seats in the Lok Sabha. Indira Gandhi utilized her increased power base to pass two constitutional amendments to establish parliamentary supremacy over the Supreme Court in the interpretation of fundamental rights.

From the Heights to the Depths: 1971–1975

Shortly after her impressive electoral victory, an international crisis brought on by a struggle for self-determination within East Pakistan confronted Mrs. Gandhi (Frankel, 1978, p. 461; Kissinger, 1979, pp. 853–897; Malhotra, 1989, pp. 134–141; Masani, 1976, pp. 237–247). Following the Awami League sweep of the December 1970 elections based on a campaign for maximum autonomy, the Pakistani army launched brutal military repression in East Pakistan on March 25, 1971. The Awami League went underground, proclaimed Bangladesh independent, and launched a resistance movement. More than 10 million refugees swarmed over the Indian border during the ensuing months, taxing Indian resources. Although the Indian public clamored for intervention, Indian leaders feared Chinese retaliation and were aware of the Nixon administration's "tilt" toward Pakistan.

Mrs. Gandhi devised a carefully constructed strategy to cope with this crisis: launching an international diplomatic initiative to explain the difficulties facing India and to pressure Pakistan to negotiate a settlement, securing support from the Soviet Union in the form of a 20-year Treaty of Friendship, supplying covert aid to the resistance, preparing Indian troops for armed conflict with Pakistan, and building a national consensus for her actions. When Pakistan mounted a surprise air attack on December 3, 1971, the Indian army launched a speedy conquest of East Pakistan; Pakistani forces surrendered on December 16. Through a quick military victory, Mrs. Gandhi was able to head off U.S. efforts to intervene on behalf of Pakistan in the United Nations, and she refused to be intimidated by units of the U.S. Seventh Fleet sent to the Bay of Bengal. Bangladesh had achieved independence, Pakistan had lost its Eastern wing, and India was now clearly the predominant power in South Asia.

State legislative elections held in March 1972 continued the "Indira wave," with Congress winning 47% of the vote and 70% of the seats

(Frankel, 1978, pp. 474–477). Success came at the cost of centralization of power in the party and in the government; Mrs. Gandhi replaced four chief ministers with her own nominees. Factionalism and corruption increased as weak state leaders put in office by Mrs. Gandhi were challenged by rivals. "Black" (illegal) money from corporations and organized crime played a growing role in elections. The taint of corruption touched the Gandhi family in charges against Mrs. Gandhi's son Sanjay for his unsuccessful government-financed Maruti car project. After the Supreme Court once again limited the power of Parliament to amend the constitution and the position of chief justice of the Supreme Court became vacant in April 1973, the government departed from the established convention of seniority and bypassed the three most senior judges to appoint a chief justice favorable to the government's position.

Mrs. Gandhi did not follow up her populist rhetoric with radical policy initiatives on poverty. A number of credit and rural works antipoverty schemes were initiated, but they reached less than one-tenth of the eligible small farmers and rural unemployed (Frankel, 1978, pp. 497–508). Land reform legislation, a campaign promise, was extensively watered down by the time it passed the state legislatures. The state's effort to take over trading in food grains was a complete failure and had to be abandoned.

In 1973, India was again confronted by economic crisis in the form of food shortages and inflation, partly triggered by OPEC oil price rises. Inept chief ministers, preoccupied with staying in power, were unable to cope with these problems (Kochanek, 1976). Mrs. Gandhi responded to the ensuing protests with repression; the army was deployed against civilian unrest 15 times in the period 1973–1975 (Cohen, 1988, pp. 125–126). The 1971 Maintenance of Internal Security Act (MISA) was expanded in scope; it allowed the preventative detention of individuals threatening national security, public order, or essential services. Under pressure from the International Monetary Fund and the World Bank, the government enacted anti-inflation ordinances and certain economic liberalization measures.

Popular uprisings emerged in Gujarat and Bihar against the state governments and coalesced into the nationwide J.P. movement, named after J.P. Narayan, a veteran nationalist leader. Mrs. Gandhi charged that she "had become the target of a conspiracy by 'external elements in India's affairs in collusion with some internal groups'" (Frankel, 1978, p. 527). The government invoked Defense on India Rules (DIR) and MIS to arrest the leaders of a threatened railway strike called for May 8, 1974, and then quickly crushed the strike by arresting more than 20,000 workers (Frankel, 1978, pp. 529–530).[4] Two unrelated policy initiatives during this period appear as diversions from the increasing level of political conflict. In May 1974, India carried out an underground nuclear test, and in April 1975 Sikkim was incorporated into India.

On June 12, 1975, Mrs. Gandhi experienced two serious challenges to her political leadership (Frankel, 1978, pp. 539–540; Hardgrave & Kochanek, 1986, pp. 212–213). The Allahabad High Court ruled that she had committed election code violations by using the services of government officials in her 1971 campaign. This conviction invalidated her 1971 election and barred her from elective office for six years, which meant that she would have to resign as prime minister. The ruling was stayed for 20 days in order to permit an appeal to the Supreme Court. On the same day, state legislative elections in Gujarat resulted in a victory for the opposition coalition, Janata (People's Front), over Congress (R), a massive assault on the prestige of Mrs. Gandhi, who had campaigned hard in the state. Opposition parties and the press called for her resignation, which was vigorously opposed by Congress politicians and especially by Sanjay Gandhi, who at the time was his mother's most influential advisor. A few years later, Mrs. Gandhi explained her thinking at the time to Dom Moraes (1980):

> After my judgment in 1975, what could I have done except stay? You know the state the country was in. What would have happened if there had been nobody to lead it? I was the only person who could, you know. It was my duty to the country to stay, though I didn't want to. (p. 220)

On June 24 the Supreme Court rejected Mrs. Gandhi's application for an absolute stay; she was allowed to continue as prime minister pending consideration of her appeal, but she could not participate in the Lok Sabha. On June 25 there was a mass rally in Delhi led by opposition leaders J. P. Narayan and Morarji Desai, who called for a nationwide movement to depose Mrs. Gandhi.

Emergency and Political Wilderness: 1975–1979

Convinced that her leadership, now gravely challenged, was indispensable to the nation, Mrs. Gandhi acted decisively to maintain her power by transforming the political process from democracy to dictatorship. In the evening of June 25, she informed the president that she planned to invoke the emergency provisions of the constitution in response to the threat to internal security posed by the opposition, and he signed the Proclamation of Emergency, which was issued the next day. Mrs. Gandhi justified the imposition of the emergency in an All India Radio address the morning of June 26: "I am sure you are conscious of the deep and widespread conspiracy which has been brewing ever since I began to introduce certain progressive measures of benefit to the common man and woman of India" (quoted in Hardgrave & Kockanek, 1986, p. 214). Under the emergency, the central government imposed authoritarian rule over the country; the constitutional powers of the states and the guarantees of fundamental rights were suspended. Opposition leaders and Congress dissidents were arrested early the morning of June 26 under MISA. Press censorship was imposed, many political organizations were banned under DIR, constitutional protections against arbitrary arrest were suspended, and more than 110,000 people were jailed without trial (Hardgrave & Kochanek, 1986, p. 215).

Mrs. Gandhi's policies during the emergency centered on constitutional changes to reduce the power of the judiciary and on her "Twenty-Point Program" and Sanjay Gandhi's "Five-Point Program" of social and economic reform. Parliament approved the emergency, and through two retroactive constitutional amendments made declaration of an emergency and electoral disputes involving the prime minister or other national officials nonjusticiable. The most important constitutional change was made by the 42nd Amendment, which took the power of judicial review away from the Supreme Court (Frankel, 1978, p. 570).

The accomplishments of the emergency fell short of the commitments to the basic social change for the poor because of the lack of institutional infrastructure for implementation (Frankel, 1978, pp. 551–556). The Twenty-Point Program promised to implement land ceilings for agriculture, abolish bonded labor, increase agricultural wages, lower prices, prevent tax evasion, take action against smugglers and hoarders, and many other popular policies. While more land was distributed through land ceiling legislation during the emergency than during the previous three years (1.1 million versus less than 62,000 acres), progress in the rural programs was very uneven. More was achieved in the urban areas: direct taxes collected rose 27%, more than 2,100 smugglers were arrested, worker days lost in strikes declined. The inflation rate declined in part due to a good monsoon and record agricultural production. There were some moves toward economic liberalization.

Sanjay, through his leadership of the Youth Congress, assumed a central role in policy making during the emergency and brought criminal elements into the party (Frankel, 1978, pp. 562–566). His Five-Point Program urged people to plant trees, practice family planning, abolish dowry, eradicate slums, and teach illiterate people to read and write. Under his orders, slum demolitions in Delhi were carried out in a heavy-handed manner, resulting in the eviction of 700,000 people and the destruction of their homes: in one case of resistance, six residents were killed by the police. Sanjay concentrated on family planning after the government announcement of a new National Policy in April 1976. Although the new policy did not sanction forced vasectomies, pressure by Sanjay Gandhi and overzealous efforts by government officials trying to ingratiate themselves with the Congress leaders led to coercion, sterilization quotas imposed on local government employees, nearly 2,000 deaths, and widespread rumors of abuses as the target of 7.4 million vasectomies was surpassed (Chadney, 1988, p. 93; Hardgrave & Kochanek, 1986; Weiner, 1978, pp. 25–39).

On January 18, 1977, Mrs. Gandhi unexpectedly called for national elections in March; political prisoners were released, press censorship was relaxed, and other emergency regulations were lifted. She believed that Congress (R) would win because of a good record of economic growth during the emergency, and she also wanted to rehabilitate her image as a democratic leader. The election became a referendum on the emergency; the opposition coalition, the Janata Party, won a resounding victory, with 43% of the vote and 270 seats in the Lok Sabha. With 35% of the vote and 153 seats, Congress was the chief opposition party, but was swept from power in North India (Frankel, 1978, p. 573). The reasons for the anti-Congress vote were the "excesses" of the emergency—forced sterilizations, slum demolitions, arbitrary arrests. Mrs. Gandhi formally lifted the emergency and submitted her resignation. Morarji Desai was chosen as prime minister on March 24. In January 1978, Congress (R) split and a faction became known as Congress (I) (for Indira).

Kiviraj (1986) points out that the Janata period demonstrated how much Mrs. Gandhi dominated Indian politics because "much of its three years in power the Janata government spent in debating what to do with Indira Gandhi rather than what to do with the country" (p. 1706). It appointed the Shah Commission to investigate abuses of authority committed during the emergency and removed many of the emergency measures. Both Mrs. Gandhi and her son Sanjay faced numerous criminal charges.

On December 20, 1977, the Lok Sabha passed a constitutional amendment restoring the Supreme Court's power to rule on the constitutionality of state or central legislation. Mrs. Gandhi reemerged as a political leader warmly received by the people as she traveled across India. In November 1978, Mrs. Gandhi won a Karnatakaby election to the Lok Sabha, but she was expelled from Parliament and jailed during the seven-day session in December on grounds that she had engaged in misconduct and abuse of authority. In 1979, legislation set up special courts to try the senior government officials in charge during the emergency. However, by the summer of 1979, the Janata government collapsed because of infighting among its constituent parties; new elections were called for January 1980, after which all the charges against Mrs. Gandhi and Sanjay were dismissed.

Return to Office: 1980–1984

Mrs. Gandhi campaigned on the theme, "Elect a government that works," and she promised "law and order" and a restoration of stability (Hardgrave & Kochanek, 1986, pp. 223–227). Sanjay played a central role in candidate selection. Congress (I) emerged victorious with 43% of the vote and 351 of the 525 seats in the Lok Sabha. With the disintegration of the Janata Party, Congress (I) was able to win back many of the votes lost in 1977. In 1980 Janata won 19% of the vote and Lok Dal won 9%; the two parties unified in 1977 had won 43% of the vote. In February 1980, Mrs. Gandhi called for new elections in the nine opposition-controlled state legislatures, and Congress was able to win eight of those state elections.

On June 23, 1980, tragedy struck Mrs. Gandhi with the death of Sanjay, who was widely viewed as the "crown prince," in the crash of a small airplane he was piloting. After Sanjay's death, Mrs. Gandhi began to rely on her elder son, Rajiv, who had been a pilot with Indian Airlines. Rajiv was elected to the Lok Sabha from Sanjay's former constituency in a by-election in 1981 and was appointed a party general secretary. Now Rajiv became the "heir apparent." This was resented by Sanjay's widow, Maneka, who felt she should inherit Sanjay's position.

Foreign affairs remained Mrs. Gandhi's sphere of greatest accomplishment. Overall, her policies reflected the response she gave to an American reporter's question about why India always tilted to the Soviet Union: "We don't tilt on either side, we walk upright" (quoted in Malhotra, 1989, p. 265). Mrs. Gandhi faced a difficult situation when the 1979 Soviet invasion of Afghanistan prompted massive U.S. arms buildup when 19 of its 21 divisions were deployed against India (Kapur, 1988, p. 57). After initially condoning the invasion, the Indian government attempted to develop an independent position that both foreign troops and foreign interference in Afghanistan should cease (Dutt, 1990, p. 37). In response to the increased Pakistani military threat, the Indian government modernized its weapons, buying military hardware from France, West Germany, and Great Britain.

In addition, Mrs. Gandhi moved on the diplomatic front to strengthen India's position internationally and in South Asia (Andersen, 1983, p. 120; Hardgrave, 1984, pp. 216–218). Efforts, not noticeably successful, were made to normalize relations with Pakistan and China. Among her 18 trips abroad to 23 countries were trips to both the United States and the Soviet Union in 1982. A compromise was reached on the conflict with the United States over supplying fuel to India's Tarapur nuclear reactor. The United States refused to honor the commitment unless India signed the nuclear nonproliferation treaty, which India viewed as "discriminatory and unfair" (Malhotra, 1989, p. 264). In 1983, the South Asian Association for Regional Cooperation (SAARC) was formed. Mrs. Gandhi served as president of the Non-Aligned Movement (NAM) and hosted the 1983 NAM New Delhi summit, where she called for a restricting of the international economic order and a nuclear freeze.

Mrs. Gandhi continued the economic liberalization begun during the emergency, explaining to a chief ministers' meeting that her government "does not believe in a doctrinaire theories" (Andersen, 1982, p. 124; Kohli, 1989, pp. 308–310). In 1981–1982, India applied for a $5.8 billion loan from the IMF. The liberalization policies that loosened government control of the economy were introduced piecemeal while Mrs. Gandhi continued to voice commitment to the poor and to formulate antipoverty schemes that were initiated with great fanfare. In the new Twenty-Point Program introduced in January 1982, Mrs. Gandhi emphasized expansion of integrated rural development and rural employment (Bhargava, 1988, p. 73).

Center-state relations deteriorated in the 1980–1984 period under conditions of increased centralization and personalization of power. In response to factionalism within governing Congress (I) parties at the state level, Mrs. Gandhi removed chief ministers in five states, selecting four chief ministers in Andhra in three years. Mrs. Gandhi and her son Rajiv campaigned actively in 1983 legislative assembly elections held in Karnataka and Andhra, which were widely viewed as a referendum on her leadership; Congress (I) lost both elections. Centrally appointed governors, acting upon Mrs. Gandhi's orders, invited Congress to form governments in Haryana and Himachal Pradesh in 1982 without ascertaining whether the party commanded a legislative majority and dismissed opposition governments in Sikkim, Kashmir, and Andhra in 1984 for partisan reasons. In one of these states, Andhra, the chief minister flew his 161 legislative majority to Delhi, and the governor had to reinstate him. Mrs. Gandhi began to appeal to Hindu chauvinist sentiments, as she anticipated the main competition to Congress (I) would come from the right-wing Bharatiya Janata Party. According to one report, "In November 1983, she states the religion and traditions of Hinduism were under attack and ought to be defended" (Puri, 1985, p. 149; see also Banerjee, 1984, pp. 2029–2030; Manor, 1988, pp. 80–82).

Religious, caste, linguistic, and ethnic confrontations escalated over the course of Mrs. Gandhi's tenure in office, as did her tendency to respond to these confrontations with repression. The government passed the National Security Act, authorizing preventative detention; and the Essential Services Maintenance Act, banning strikes in many occupations. In 1984, more than 40 million Indians were living under military rule, and the military had been called in to suppress domestic violence 19 times in the period 1980–1984, excluding the ongoing cases of Assam and Punjab (Cohen, 1988, p. 100). These two movements for regional autonomy were perceived by Mrs. Gandhi as threatening the political stability of her government and represented intense grievances felt by both winners and losers in the development process (Kaviraj, 1986, p. 1706).

The issue in Assam, one of the poorest states, was control of resources by the Assamese, 59% of the state's population (Das Gupta, 1988). The Assamese movement demanded the expulsion from the states of all foreigners, who were mainly refugees from Bangladesh. The Assamese movement demanded that these "illegal aliens" be purged from the electoral rolls, but they were a crucial vote bank for the Congress (I), and the government went ahead with 1983 state assembly elections in the face of a massive boycott by opposition parties. Violence erupted, the most serious incident involving the massacre of almost 1,400 Bengali Muslims by Assamese tribals. Although Congress (I) won the election, it was discredited, for less than one-third of the electorate had voted, half of the 1978 voter turnout (Hardgrave, 1984, p. 210).

"Divide and conquer" tactics by Mrs. Gandhi and her advisors to ensure Congress (I) rule in the Punjab played a large role in creating a crisis in the center of the green revolution (Brass, 1988, p. 180; Tully & Jacob, 1985). During 1977–1980, while the Akali Dal, a Sikh political party, was in power in the Punjab, Sanjay Gandhi brought criminals into the Punjab Congress (I) and supported the rise of the Sikh fundamentalist, Sant Bhindranwale, in order to weaken the Akali Dal. Congress regained power in the Punjab with the 1980 state elections in a radicalized atmosphere. When the Akali Dal launched an agitation for increased state autonomy, Mrs. Gandhi's government both refused to make concessions that might undermine her support in the Hindu majority states of North India and failed to control Sikh extremists such as Bhindranwale. In a situation of escalating violence, Mrs. Gandhi imposed president's rule on the Punjab in 1983 after a number of Hindus were killed by Sikh militants. Bhindranwale directed a campaign of terrorism from the Golden Temple, the holiest shrine of the Sikhs. In June 1984, Mrs. Gandhi launched Operation Bluestar, a military assault on the Golden Temple resulting in an official death count of 576 (including Bhindranwale) and considerable damage to the temple.

On October 31, 1984, Mrs. Gandhi was assassinated by two of her security guards who were Sikhs (Hardgrave, 1985, pp. 139–141; Malhotra, 1989, pp. 15–24). Following news of the assassination, there was a wave of violence against Sikhs in Delhi and other cities; research by human right groups indicated the violence was orchestrated by Congress (I) party bosses. Immediately after the assassination, the Congress Parliamentary Board nominated Rajiv Gandhi as the leader of the CCP, and he was sworn in as prime minister. This selection was validated by the Indian electorate in late December 1984, as Rajiv won a massive victory in Lok Sabha elections, winning just under 50% of the vote and 79% of the seats contested.

THE GENDER FACTOR

Gender mattered for Indira Gandhi in complex and contradictory ways. On the surface, Mrs. Gandhi did not identify herself in gender terms and she did little to advance the cause of gender equality. She seemed to operate as an "honorary male," many times asserting that she did not feel handicapped by being a woman: "As Prime Minister, I am not a woman. I am a human being" (Carras, 1979, p. 48; Fraser, 1978, pp. 307, 318). The Indian feminist journal *Manushi* asserted, "No woman could be more alienated from her sex than she is" (Manushi Collective, 1979–1980, p. 4). Mrs. Gandhi did not appoint any women to full cabinet rank or make any special effort to encourage women leaders; and during her tenure in office the conditions of the majority of Indian women worsened, as reflected in literacy and employment rates and the declining sex ratio (Bumiller, 1990, p. 164; Manushi Collective, 1979–1980, pp. 2–5).

On another level, however, Mrs. Gandhi's career path to power, agenda, style of leadership, and overall performance can be seen as profoundly shaped by a patriarchal political system in which women in power "are there in men's terms and for their survival they have to forget that they are women, and that as women they are unequal" (Manushi Collective, 1979–1980, p. 5). Like Mrs. Gandhi, nearly all Indian women in political office are relatives of prominent male politicians; they are members of political families that lack male members of the appropriate age or temperament to continue the family dynasty (Bumiller, 1990, pp. 151–153; Wolkowitz, 1987). As prime minister, Mrs. Gandhi continually encountered male hostility directed at her gender. The disrespect ranged from despair among some Indians over having a woman leader to sexist overtones in the contempt expressed by her critics, as in Salman Rushdie's referring to her as "the widow" in *Midnight's Children* (1980) or Pakistani President Yahya Khan's outburst during the Bangladesh conflict, "If that woman thinks she is going to cow me down, I refuse to take it" (quoted in Malhotra, 1989, pp. 137, 190).

Manushi argued, "To survive [women political leaders] must, on the one hand, make themselves like the stereotypical male—aggressive, competitive, ruthless, authoritarian—and on the other, continue to play the "good woman" role" (Manushi Collective. 1979–1980, p. 3). The male-defined rules of the political game worked against Mrs. Gandhi. In overthrowing them, she behaved in a ruthless and authoritarian manner. Many commentators have identified the above "male" characteristics with Mrs. Gandhi, but in interviews and behavior the "good woman" surfaced as well. She stressed that motherhood was the most important part of her life:

> To a mother, her children must always come first, because they depend on her in a very special way. The main problem in my life was, therefore, how to reconcile my public obligations with my responsibility towards my home

and my children. When Rajiv and Sanjay were babies I did not like the idea of anyone else attending to their needs and I tried to do as much for them as I could. Later when they began school, I was careful to have my engagements during school hours so as to be free when the boys returned home. (Gandhi, 1980, p. 55)

Mrs. Gandhi always dressed modestly, covering her head with her sari, when she traveled within India. Her husband died when she was only 42, but she neither developed any other romantic attachments nor wanted any (Malhotra, 1989, pp. 184–189). Mrs. Gandhi's fishbowl existence precluded such liaisons, but gossip persisted throughout her time in office.

One instance in which Mrs. Gandhi did not play the good women role was when she threw Maneka, Sanjay's widow, out of her home in March 1982, accusing her of being "a willing tool of my enemies" (Malhotra, 1989, p. 241). The nation was entertained by "first family" intrigue after Sanjay's death, and Mrs. Gandhi came across as a shrew. With press photographs of Maneka's luggage dumped outside, Maneka retaliated by comparing her mother-in-law to the goddess Kalie, "who drinks blood," and by forming a political party to oppose Congress (I). Arun Shourie (1983) commented, "The Great Mother image [was] nudged by the stereotype mother-in-law image" (p. 26)

To say that gender did not matter to Mrs. Gandhi herself and that she was victimized by it does not capture the complexity of gender relations for this woman leader, for Mrs. Gandhi also used powerful gender imagery in a purposeful manner. Sometimes, she identified herself as mother of her country, as in a 1967 campaign speech to villagers: "My burden is a manifold because scores of my family members are poverty stricken and I have to look after them" (quoted in Malhotra, 1989, p. 104). Motherhood also became intertwined with dynastic politics as Mrs. Gandhi groomed her sons to succeed her. Rajiv explained his decision to enter politics after Sanjay's death by saying, "Someone has to help Mummy" (quoted in Bobb, 1991, p. 30). One paradox of Indian civilization is the coexistence of traditions of female power alongside extremely patriarchal beliefs and practices. There are Hindu goddesses as well as gods, and several queens ruled after their husbands died. After the Bangladesh war, Mrs. Gandhi was hailed as the Hindu goddess Durga and worshipped as the incarnation of *shakti*, images that she manipulated when needed. A reporter described Mrs. Gandhi reviewing crowds from a balcony in Cochin during her comeback campaign in 1978: "She jammed a torch [flashlight] between her knees, directing the beam upwards to light her face and arms. She rotated the arms as if perfecting the dance of Lakshmi, Goddess of Wealth . . . 'You've no idea how tiring it is to be a goddess'" (Chatwin, 1989, p. 119).

Although Mrs. Gandhi played the game of patriarchal politics only too well, her legacy for feminists was not completely negative. She used gender imagery to empower herself, but she also became an image of women's power. Ela Bhatt, leader of the Self-Employed Women's Association of Ahmedabad, expressed the feeling in the following manner: "Consciously or unconsciously, every woman, I think, feels that if Indira Gandhi could be prime minister of this country, then we all have opportunities" (quoted in Bumiller, 1990, p. 151).

CONCLUSIONS: MRS. GANDHI'S PERFORMANCE

To what extent was Mrs. Gandhi able to achieve self-reliance for India and to solve domestic problems such as poverty and economic backwardness? In what ways did the constraints and opportunities inherent in the context in which she operated shape her strategies and performance in office? What consequences did her strategies have for Indian politics? How did gender figure in?

Contemporaries offer a split verdict on Mrs. Gandhi's performance. A survival strategy approach draws attention to the enormity of the challenges facing Mrs. Gandhi throughout her career and to the high level of political skill she demonstrated in gaining, maintaining, and regaining political power over an 18-year period. Although Mrs. Gandhi would have denied it, a central challenge she faced was that of operating in a male-dominated political system. Sometimes her survival rested on the destruction of male-defined institutions and norms, but she failed to create replacements. A survival strategy approach also draws attention to some of the destructive political consequences of the strategies she devised—political consequences that were later played out in the problems facing India.

There is widespread agreement that Mrs. Gandhi's greatest achievements were in foreign policy—maintaining India's self-reliance, strengthening the military, and helping India become the predominant power in South Asia. The business-oriented *India Today* noted that "foreign policy was to prove her greatest forte and the mark she finally left on the world stage exceeded even her own high expectations" (Bobb, 1984, p. 100). The left-intellectual *Economic and Political Weekly* concurred: "A considerable part of India's current stature is directly attributable to the nimbleness and sense of self-confidence with which Indira Gandhi had directed the nation's external relations" ("Indira Gandhi's Bequest," 1984, p. 1849).

Mrs. Gandhi's economic performance elicits mixed reviews. On the plus side, the green revolution eliminated famines and the dependence on food aid, and bank nationalization made banking relevant to an underdeveloped country. While many commentators criticized economic policies that zigzagged in response to political calculations, India's economy continued to grow, albeit slowly, and the growth rate rose to 5% in 1984. On the minus side was the continued misery of half of the Indian population in abject poverty and increasing disparities among regions and between rich and poor. *India Today* emphasized the central failure "to grasp the growth opportunities presented by a period when new countries emerged on the global economic scene as forces to be reckoned with. India was not among them" (Ninan, 1984, p. 107). *Economic and Political Weekly*, in contrast, emphasized inequality and corruption: "Socio-economic pronouncements . . . do not mean a thing in actuality, the apparatus of the State is all the time being manipulated for the sake of a fractional minority of the population at the top of the social hierarchy . . . for ensuring the accumulation of private hoards" ("Indira Gandhi's Bequest," 1984, p. 1849).

Mrs. Gandhi's leadership style generates the harshest criticism for her contributions to political centralization and deinstitutionalization. Inder Malhotra (1989) has described the emergency as "the body blow to Indian democracy she chose to deliver and from which the Indian system has yet to recover fully" (p. 306). Malhotra and others have also faulted Mrs. Gandhi for polarizing Indian politics, for believing she was indispensible, and, most important, for destroying the Congress Party. Some commentators expressed admiration for the relationship Mrs. Gandhi developed with the Indian people, but also acknowledged that she lacked the ability to follow through on her commitments. Rajni Kothari (1988) pointed out that she "captured the attention and loyalty of the Indian masses far more than the traditional radical left." He went on to say: "The basic contradiction in Indira Gandhi's brand of populism . . . lay in the fact that whereas her appeal was to the rural masses and the poorer strata, the power structure at the centre on which she relied so much was essentially urban, upper middle class, bureaucratic and to not a small extent capitalist" (p. 2226).

The assessments of her contemporaries seemed basically accurate, but most of them tended to underestimate the constraints facing Mrs. Gandhi—an international environment hostile to the Third World, domestic poverty and inequality, polarized citizens impatient with two decades of unfulfilled promises, as well as party political bosses and, of course, sexism. The class structure in a backward capitalist political economy further constrained Mrs. Gandhi's options. The party structure she inherited was not able to meet the challenges of the 1960s. Destroying the party was hardly a creative solution, but transforming it to represent the subordinate classes was beyond her capability. Male hostility to her independent action from her husband in the 1950s and from the party bosses during her first years as prime minister led her to distrust leaders she did not control. The conventional institutions through which political recruitment occurred and political leadership was exercised—English university life, Parliament, cabinet, Congress Party—did not work very well for a woman and so they were downplayed and disregarded. With limited room to maneuver, Mrs. Gandhi survived politically through populist appeals, centralization of power, and ad hoc improvisations. These, in turn, created policy zigzags and deinstitutionalization, and contributed toward the polarization of politics during her time in office.

The consequences of the survival strategies devised by Mrs. Gandhi appear extremely negative from the vantage point of later years. The Indian government faced violent secessionist movements in the Punjab and Kashmir; the level of violence among religious groups, castes, and classes was extremely high; politics remained corrupt; and the violence-plagued 1991 elections took the life of Rajiv Gandhi and resulted in minority Congress government lacking in leaders of national stature. The contributions of aspects of Mrs. Gandhi's survival strategies could be seen in each of these problems—her political interference in Punjab and Kashmir politics; her frequent use of government repression; her use of communal appeals in the last years of her life; her ridding Congress of strong leaders; and, most important, the deinstitutionalization of the Congress Party and corruption of political life more generally.

It does not seem necessary to focus on childhood insecurity to explain Mrs. Gandhi's urge to dominate the national scene in her sense of indispensability. Her experiences in childhood and as a young adult revolved almost completely around duty to the nation; this cause took her father away for long periods of her childhood, and it destroyed her marriage.

No wonder the boundaries between her and her own interests and those of the nation were so blurred. The phrase coined by party president D.K. Barooah, "Indira is India, India is Indira," resonated in her (Rudolph & Rudolph, 1987, p. 135). In Mrs. Gandhi's will, written shortly before her death, she wrote, "No hate is dark enough to overshadow the extent of my love for my people and my country; no force is strong enough to divert me from my purpose and my endeavor to take this country forward" (quoted in Malhotra, 1989, pp. 307–308). As in her childhood, the public became private, and the private became public. The Indian people were her children; members of her family were the only people capable of leading them.

Author's Note: Thanks to the College of Liberal Arts and Sciences at the University of Colorado at Denver for awarding me a small grant to write this chapter; and to my brother, Jim Matson; and to Sue Ellen Charlton and Betsy Moen, my feminist academic support group, for helpful comments on an earlier draft.

NOTES

1   For overviews of the Indian context, see Bardhan (1984, pp. 548–549), Frankel (1978, pp. 96–97, 548–549), and Hardgrave and Kochanek (1986, pp. 4–11).
2   For a discussion of succession politics, see Brecher (1966) and Frankel (1978, pp. 228–229, 240–245, 288–292).
3   The Lok Sabha (House of the People) is the directly elected lower house of Parliament.
4   The Defence of India Rules were preventive detention regulations authorized by the 1971 external emergency declared during the Bangladesh War, which was still in effect.

REFERENCES

Anderson, W.K. (1982). India in 1981: Stronger political authority and social tension. *Asian Survey*, *22*(2), 119–135.

Anderson, W.K. (1983). India in 1982: Domestic challenges and foreign policy successes. *Asian Survey*, *23*(2), 111–122.

Banerjee, S. (1984). Contradictions with a purpose. *Economic and Political Weekly*, *19*(48), 2028–2031.

Bardhan, P. (1984). *The political economy of development in India*. Oxford: Basil Blackwell.

Bhargava, A. (1988). Indian economy during Mrs. Gandhi's regime. In Y.K. Malik & D.K. Vajpeyi (Eds.), *India: The years of Indira Gandhi*. Leiden, Netherlands: E.J. Brill.

Bhatia, K. (1974). *Indira: A biography of Prime Minister Gandhi*. New York: Praeger.

Bobb, D. (1984, November 30). The Indira enigma. *India Today*, 94–103.

Bobb, D. (1991, June 15). Ordeal of Prince Charming. *India Today*, 30–39.

Brass, P. (1988). The Punjab crisis and the unity of India. In A. Kohli (Ed.), *India's democracy: An analysis of changing state-society relations*. Princeton, NJ: Princeton University Press.

Brecher, M. (1966). *Succession in India: A study in decision making.* London: Oxford University Press.

Bumiller, E. (1990). *May you be the mother of a hundred sons.* New York: Fawcett Columbine.

Carras, M. (1979). *Indira Gandhi in the crucible of leadership: A political biography.* Boston: Beacon.

Chadney, J.C. (1988). Family planning: India's Achilles' heel? In Y.K. Malik & D.K. Vajpeyi (Eds.), *India: The years of Indira Gandhi.* Leiden, Netherlands: E.J. Brill.

Chatwin, B. (1989, Spring). On the road with Mrs. Gandhi. *Granta, 26,* 107–130.

Cohen, S.P. (1988). The military and Indian democracy. In A. Kohli (Ed.), *India's democracy: An analysis of changing state-society relations.* Princeton, NJ: Princeton University Press.

Das Gupta, J. (1988). Ethnicity and development in India: Assam in a general perspective. In A. Kohli (Ed.), *India's democracy: An analysis of changing state-society relations.* Princeton, NJ: Princeton University Press.

Dutt, V.P. (1990). India and the super powers. In A.K. Damodaran & U.S. Bajpai (Eds.), *Indian foreign policy: The Indira Gandhi years.* New Delhi: Radiant.

Fallaci, O. (1976). *Interview with history* (J. Shepley, Trans.). New York: Liverlight.

Frankel, F.R. (1978). *India's political economy, 1947–1977: The gradual revolution.* Princeton, NJ: Princeton University Press.

Fraser, A. (1988). *The warrior queens.* New York: Vintage.

Gandhi, I. (1980). *My truth* (E. Pouchpadass, ed.). New York: Grove.

Gupta, A. (1989). The political economy of post-independent India: A review article. *Journal of Asian Studies, 48*(4), 787–797.

Hardgrave, R.L., Jr. (1984). India in 1983: New challenges, lost opportunities. *Asian Survey, 24*(2), 209–218.

Hardgrave, R.L., Jr. (1985). India in 1984: Confrontation, assassination, and succession. *Asian Survey, 25*(2), 131–144.

Hardgrave, R.L., Jr., & Kochanek, S.A. (1986). *India government and politics in a developing nation* (4th ed.). New York: Harcourt Brace Jovanovich.

Hart, H.C. (1976). Indira Gandhi: Determined not to be hurt. In H.C. Hart (Ed.), *Indira Gandhi's India: A political system reappraised.* Boulder, CO: Westview Press.

Hutheesing, K.N. (1969). *Dear to behold: An intimate portrait of Indira Gandhi.* London: Macmillan.

Indira Gandhi's bequest. (1984). *Economic and Political Weekly, 19*(44), 1849–1850.

Kapur, A. (1988). Indian security and defense policies under Indira Gandhi. In Y.K. Malik & D.K. Vajpeyi (Eds.), *India: The years of Indira Gandhi.* Leiden, Netherlands: E.J. Brill.

Kaviraj, S. (1986). Indira Gandhi and Indian politics. *Economic and Political Weekly, 21,* 1697–1708.

Kissinger, H. (1979). *White House years.* Boston: Little, Brown.

Kochanek, S.A. (1976). Mrs. Gandhi's pyriamid: The new Congress. In. H.C. Hart (Ed.), *Indira Gandhi's India: A political system reappraised.* Boulder, CO: Westview Press.

Kohli, A. (1989). Politics of economic liberalization in India. *World Development, 17*(3), 305–328.

Kothari, R. (1988). Integration and exclusion in Indian politics. *Economic and Political Weekly, 23*(43), 2223–2287.

Malhotra, I. (1989). *Indira Gandhi: A personal and political biography.* Boston: Northeastern University Press.

Malik, Y.K. (1988). Indira Gandhi: Personality, political power and party politics. In Y.K. Malik & D.K. Vajpeyi (Eds.), *India: The years of Indira Gandhi*. Leiden, Netherlands: E.J. Brill.

Manor, J. (1983). Anomie in Indian politics. *Economic and Political Weekly, 28*(19–21), 725–734.

Manor, J. (1988). Parties and the party system. In A. Kohli (Ed.), *Indira's democracy: An analysis of changing state-society relations*. Princeton, NJ: Princeton University Press.

Manushi Collective. (1979–1980, December–February). Our alarming silence: Women, politics and the recent elections. *Manushi, 4*, 2–6, 76.

Masani, Z. (1976). *Indira Gandhi: A biography*. New York: Thomas Y. Crowell.

Moraes, D. (1980). *Indira Gandhi*. Boston: Little, Brown.

Ninan, T.N. (1984, November 30). The zigzag march. *India Today*, 104–107.

Norman, D. (1985). *Indira Gandhi: Letters to an American friend, 1950–1984*. New York: Harcourt Brace Jovanovich.

Puri, B. (1985). Era of Indira Gandhi. *Economic and Political Weekly, 20*(4), 148–150.

Richter, L.K. (1990–1991). Exploring theories of female leadership in South and Southeast Asia. *Pacific Affairs, 63*, 524–540.

Roy, A. (1984). The failure of Indira Gandhi. *Economic and Political Weekly, 19*(45), 1896–1897.

Rudolph, L.I., & Rudolph, S.H. (1987). *In pursuit of Lakshmi: The political economy of the Indian state*. Chicago: University of Chicago Press.

Rushdie, S. (1980). *Midnight's children*. New York: Alfred A. Knopf.

Rushdie, S. (1985). Introduction. In T. Ali, *An Indian dynasty: The story of the Nehru-Gandhi family* (pp. xi–xv). New York: G.P. Putnam's Sons.

Shourie, A. (1983). *Mrs. Gandhi's second reign*. New Delhi: Vikas.

Tharoor, S. (1982). *Reasons of state: Political development and India's foreign policy under Indira Gandhi 1966–1977*. New Delhi: Vikas.

Tully, M., & Jacob, S. (1985). *Amritsar: Mrs. Gandhi's last battle*. London: Jonathan Cape.

Weiner, M. (1978). *India at the polls: The parliamentary elections of 1977*. Washington, DC: American Enterprise Institute.

Wolkowitz, C. (1987). Controlling women's access to political power: A case study in Andhra Pradesh, India. In H. Afshar (Ed.), *Women, state, and ideology: Studies from Africa and Asia*. Albany: State University of New York Press.

7

Golda Meir

A Very Public Life

Seth Thompson

From her birth as Golda Mabovitch in Kiev, Russia, in May 1898 to her death in Jerusalem in December 1978, three themes run through the life of Golda Meir: her sense of Jewish identity, a conscious commitment to a public political life, and gender.

Golda Meir's sense of being Jewish began in early childhood amid poverty, pogroms, and pervasive insecurity; it matured into an unshakable commitment to Zionism and an understanding that the individual Jew's fate and future were inextricably linked to the creation and maintenance of a Jewish state.[1] It led her to leave the relative comfort of the United States in the 1920s for the challenges of pioneering in Palestine, sustained her through hardship, and animated her political career.

The desire to participate actively in public purposes and life was first clearly expressed in Golda Meir's work with the Labor Zionist movement in the United States as organizer, orator, and fund-raiser, and shortly afterward her decision not only to be a pioneer in Palestine but also to join the fledgling kibbutz movement and live in a collective. When events and personal considerations prevented her from remaining on the kibbutz, she found a way to develop a much-needed job into the first step on the ladder to a formal political and governmental career.[2] In fact, some of the most emotionally trying moments in her life were the result of a preference for the public over the private.

While gender is an inescapable fact of social life, its impact and salience varies with time, setting, and a person's position in the life cycle. In Golda Meir's case, as the following analysis will show, while initially of great consequence, gender issues played a decreasing role over time. This is because Golda herself refused to be bound by conventional definitions, even when that refusal carried a heavy emotional price, and because she lived most of her life in a society that was in the midst of defining itself, heavily influenced by an egalitarian ideology, and acutely aware that it had an opportunity to serve as an example.[3]

This chapter offers an understanding of Golda Meir as person and national leader by dividing her life into four relatively distinct phases and commenting on the impact of the three themes outlined above during each stage. The concluding section discusses Golda's own perception and assessment of the relevance of gender to her career and then offers some summary reflections on the impact of gender on Golda Meir, the political leader and the person.

FROM KIEV TO PALESTINE

The first eight years of Golda Mabovitch's life were spent in Kiev and Pinsk at a time when anti-Semitism raged and the Czarist order began to crumble. Her own memories of the period revolved around physical threats, economic insecurity and discrimination, and nascent political activity. "That gay, heart-warming, charming *shtetl* on whose roofs fiddlers eternally play sentimental music, had almost nothing to do with anything I remember" (Meir, 1975, p. 15). What she did remember was potential violence from Gentile neighbors; mounted Cossack patrols; the fact that her father, a skilled carpenter, was barely able to eke out a living and was the victim of overt discrimination when cheated out of a moderately lucrative contract; and the involvement of her older sister in clandestine political discussion groups. When she was 6 years old, her father left the family to seek a new life in the United States; two years later, he sent for his wife and three daughters (Sheyna, four years Golda's senior; Golda; and Golda's younger sister, Clara) to join him in Milwaukee, Wisconsin.

In Milwaukee, the family first survived and then attained a modicum of prosperity through the joint efforts of both parents. Her father continued to ply his trade as a carpenter and her mother provided a steady income by running a small grocery store (with Golda as an unwilling clerk before and after school). Golda quickly established herself as an exceptional student in elementary school, and tagged along with her older sister to informal meetings of a group of young Russian emigrés who vigorously debated politics, revolution, Zionism, and philosophy. (Indeed, Golda titled the second chapter of her autobiography "A Political Adolescence.")

She experienced her first political success as the main organizer and keynote speaker, at age 10, of a benefit show to raise money for her class-mates who could not afford the nominal charge of textbooks. In hindsight, one can see patterns that would be repeated time and again: identification of a wrong that needed to be rectified, a focus on fund-raising, diligent organizing and persuading (including talking the owner of a hall into rent-ing it on the promise of payment after the event), and delivery of a major address ad lib.[4]

The end of Golda's grammar school career also brought to a head un-derlying conflicts with her parents. Her relationship with her parents was rarely easy. She clearly resented having to assist her mother in the shop (Meir, 1975, p. 32), she was strongly influenced by her older sister's politi-cal interests and activities (which had led Sheyna to break with her parents and move out), and (one suspects) success in school and as a leader among her peers had led her to see possibilities beyond the traditional and con-ventional fate of most young women of her generation and circumstances. The battle was joined over education: Golda's passionate desire to attend high school versus her parents' belief that further education was not only unnecessary but also dangerous to a young woman's marriage prospects. Her solution was to enroll in high school anyway and get a part-time job to secure economic independence.

Golda's autonomy was underscored when she accepted an invitation from her older sister to come to Denver, Colorado, where Sheyna was recu-perating from a serious bout of tuberculosis. In Denver, Golda lived with Sheyna and her husband, experienced the difficulties of making a living at unskilled labor, and became an increasingly active member of a group of young Jewish intellectuals. It was at this point that she decided that the Labor Zionist movement, a blend of utopian socialist ideals and commit-ment to a Jewish state in Palestine, was her philosophical and emotional home. She also met Morris Myerson, who was profoundly disinterested in politics but keenly interested in art and music, areas in which Golda felt ignorant.

The sojourn in Denver was followed by a reconciliation with her family and return to Milwaukee, where Golda finished high school (and started training as a teacher), married Morris Myerson in 1917, and became increasingly publicly active in the Zionist movement. Her political role developed; she went from being one of several organizers and sidewalk orators to being the person who was asked to accept responsibility for raising the funds to keep a struggling party newspaper going.

The fact that this meant extensive travel throughout the upper Midwest and into Canada, that only months after her wedding Golda was packing her bags and leaving for weeks or months at a time, seemed to her merely a necessary means to a good end. Her father had a more conventional reaction—fury. Golda's autobiography is unclear about her new husband's feelings in this matter; from the perspective of 50 years later, she first portrayed him as understanding that she could not turn down the movement, then recognized that there must have been some significant pain (Meir, 1975, pp. 66–67). She had also decided to leave for Palestine at the first opportunity (Meir, 1975, pp. 66–67). She would have to wait until the war ended and a tenuous civil order was established by the mandatory authorities in Palestine, but the decision was irrevocable and, she felt, inevitable. The opportunity came in 1921 and, leaving friends and most of her family behind, she joined a small band of American Jews on a difficult voyage to the Middle East.[5]

INTELLECTUAL, POLITICAL, AND SOCIAL FOUNDATIONS

The first 23 years of Golda Meir's life established the themes and directions that would dominate the next 57. Her social and intellectual life revolved around the Jewish communities in Russia, Milwaukee, and Denver. She felt little attachment to the Russia of her childhood and soon came to regard the United States as a way station on the route to Palestine. In her mind, the logic was as simple as it was elegant: to be Jewish is to be a Zionist, and to be Zionist is to participate in the creation of the Jewish state in Palestine. It was that sense of identity and purpose that gave meaning and direction to her life career, and she clung to it even at the cost of physical and emotional distress.

Golda's involvement with the movement honed her political skills and gave her an arena in which to use them. She established a reputation as an effective speaker before medium-sized to large groups, and as a persuasive advocate in more intimate settings. Her success flowed in part from facility with language (initially English and Yiddish, adding Hebrew later in life); in part from a straightforward, powerfully simple logical presentation; in part from the depth and sincerity of her convictions (and their uncomplicated nature); and in part from her ability to speak extemporaneously.[6] She also demonstrated her ability to direct and organize other people. More important, she took for granted that public purposes had priority over private desires, that one's identity and fate as an individual were inseparable from the larger Zionist project of creating a setting where Jews could control their identity and fate as a people. Reflecting on the earliest days of her marriage, when she was traveling extensively, Golda wrote, "Whenever I was out of town, I wrote long letters to him, but they tended to be more about the meeting I had just addressed or the one I was about to address, the situation in Palestine or the movement than about us or our relationship" (Meir, 1975, p. 67).

The fact that she was female also had a significant impact on this first quarter of Golda's life. She grew up in a family where the father was well intentioned but somewhat distant and did not appear able to cope well with the external world. It was her mother who organized things, who opened a store only weeks after arriving in the United States and before she knew any English, let alone anything of the finer points of retailing. Their resistance to Golda attending high school was explicitly based on beliefs about what was necessary and proper to enhance the marriage prospects of a young lady. Inevitably, given the time and place, much of what Golda did conflicted with conventional expectations: sidewalk oratory on behalf of "radical" political movements; the grand project of emigrating to Palestine; the stint as traveling fund-raiser; and this sort is unusual enough to arouse unease and opposition from many parents, regardless of the gender of the offspring. But unquestionably it was far more difficult to accept in a daughter than in a son. The struggle to establish an autonomous self and gain the freedom to do what she felt she must was harder for Golda precisely because she was female.

PIONEERING IN PALESTINE

The 12 years between her arrival in Palestine and Golda's accession to a position in the emerging Zionist political elite can be seen as laying the foundation for the rest of her life. The centrality of Jewish and Zionist identity to Golda's self-definition and self-assessment was the justification for the hardships and trials of the period. After laconically describing some of the difficulties of finding sufficient food and shelter in the first days in Tel Aviv, Golda noted:

> There were all kinds of compensations for these small hardships, like walk-ing down the street on our first Friday in Tel Aviv and feeling that life could hold no greater joy for me than to be where I was—in the only all-Jewish town in the world . . . only here could Jews be masters, not victims of their fate. So it was not surprising . . . I was profoundly happy. (Meir, 1975, p. 81)

It was Golda who insisted on tackling the rigors of life in a collective enter-prise to carve a farming community out of wasteland. She felt compelled to prove herself to other members, not so much because she was a woman but because she was the "American girl," and there were suspicions that she was thus too soft and too pampered to really take it (Meir, 1975, pp. 87–88). But she not only demonstrated her ability to work as hard as anyone, she also eagerly embraced the communal and collective life, living with people "who debated everything so thoroughly and with such intensity and who took social problems so seriously" (Meir, 1975, p. 93). But no matter how much she enjoyed the discussions and debates, Golda evinced an important aspect of her public career: a penchant for seeing that something should be done and doing it, without much regard for the ideological niceties.

The kibbutz movement's emphasis on equality encouraged women to tackle the work of the fields and led many to see work in the commu-nal kitchen as retrograde. Golda had no doubts about equality. But she did not define kitchen work and the quality of the communal meals as an ideological issue. To her, there were only simple practical questions: Why shouldn't even simple food be properly cooked? Why was it more virtuous to drink out of cracked and rusting enamel cups instead of clean glasses? Why shouldn't the communal table be more or less properly set? And so, in the face of objections from some of the other women, she reorganized the kitchen (Meir, 1975, p. 89). That style of leadership—directive, problem oriented, somewhat simple and unreflective—would remain throughout her career.

The kibbutz experience also brought to a head the conflict between the public and private dimensions of Golda's life. The backbreaking labor that she gladly accepted and even savored as her contribution to creating the Jewish homeland was almost unbearably tedious to her husband, who had never shared her Zionist convictions and was frequently ill. While she relished the give and take of collective life, he felt acutely the lack of privacy. And as Golda dreamed of raising children and living her life in a Jewish socialist polity, Morris dreamed of a traditional family, in which the parents, not the entire community, were responsible for the children. After two years of increasing strain between them and serious deterioration in his health, Golda abandoned the struggle, and she and Morris left the kibbutz for Tel Aviv and then Jerusalem.

The period between 1923 and 1928 was extremely difficult. Golda and her husband, like most of the other Jewish immigrants, were poor—jobs were hard to find and tenuous—and they made do in a small, two-room apartment. Life became even more constrained with the birth of a daughter and then a son. For Golda, the physical hardships were compounded by the depressing sense that she was sitting on the sidelines and missing the struggle to create a new society. The hard life of the kibbutz had a larger political meaning; poverty in Jerusalem was strictly private (Meir, 1975, p. 102).

ENTRY LEVEL FOR A POLITICAL CAREER

The physical aspects of Golda's life did not get easier in 1928 when she accepted a position as secretary of the Women's Labor Council of the Histadrut,[7] but the move restored her fundamental sense of participating in the birth of the Jewish state and creation of a new society, and revitalizing her sense that the difficulties of the movement had meaning and purpose. The Histadrut position was pivotal in Golda's public and personal lives. It gave her entrée to the merging political elite; from that point on, she would play a more and more prominent role in the emergence of Israel and the internal politics of the Left. The position also brought the conflict between the private roles of wife and mother and her desires for a public life into stark relief. The job with the Women's Labor Council meant moving from Jerusalem to Tel Aviv, as well as substantial travel throughout Palestine and even abroad. It was difficult for Morris, who had very traditional expectations and values, to accept the fact that his wife was going back to work. It soon proved impossible for him to live with a woman whose first interest was her public life and who would be gone much of the time. The couple separated amicably, Golda and the children moving to Tel Aviv and Morris remaining in Jerusalem. He visited frequently on the weekends, and they remained friends until his death in 1951.

In Golda's mind, the marriage had failed well before she took the job; the separation was simply an admission of the fact. Her explanation is confined to the personal level:

> The tragedy was not that Morris didn't understand me, but, on the contrary, that he understood me only too well and felt he couldn't make me over or change me. I had to be what I was, and what I was made it impossible for him to have the sort of wife he wanted and needed. So he didn't discourage me from going back to work, although he knew what it really meant. (Meir, 1975, p. 112)

Golda did not recognize that their individual differences were problematic precisely because they were contrary to expectations for gender roles. A man who felt a public career was necessary, who could not be happy with purely private pursuits, married to a woman with traditional values, would not be faced with a choice between career and relationship. This is the clearest and most dramatic instance of the impact of gender on Golda Meir's life and career.

Gender was also directly linked to her job. Given the egalitarian strain in Zionist ideology (and perhaps the somewhat lower priority and salience of specifically "women's" work), it was nearly inevitable that the secretary of the Women's Council be female. The Women's Labor Council was involved in a variety of activities, but the major emphasis was on vocational training for the hundreds of young men who were arriving in Palestine without any relevant job or agricultural skills, at a time "when the idea that women should be trained for anything, let alone agriculture, was still considered absurd by most people" (Meir, 1975, p. 113).

Golda succeeded at the job and gained a reputation for effectiveness because the position gave her an opportunity to tackle problems that required her particular skills: concentrating on "practical" rather than theoretical issues, persuasively representing her organization within the emerging elite in Palestine, and traveling abroad as a persuasive representative of Jews in

Palestine. Her sheer physical stamina and capacity for long hours of sustained work were obviously important ingredients in her success.

Throughout her autobiography, Golda Meir portrays herself as someone who simply did what was needed and accepted jobs as they were offered. She does not reflect on her motives deeply and does not even hint at ambition. It is impossible to determine whether she saw this position as a potential first step to something bigger and better. On the face of it, this was not a position of great power or opportunity for national prominence. If someone other than Golda Meir had become responsible for "women's" matters within Histadrut, there is no reason to assume that person would have become a member of the elite, let alone cabinet minister or prime minister. But, consciously or not, Golda made the job into a launching platform.

GOLDA'S FIRST PUBLIC CAREER

Golda Meir's career in national politics can be divided into two logical segments. Her first career ran from 1928 to 1968 and includes her entry into the political elite, role in the struggle for independence, critical contribution as fund-raiser abroad, service as ambassador and then cabinet minister, and nongovernmental role as party elder and coalition builder. The first period ends with her presumptive retirement from public life at age 70 in 1968. It includes the creation of the State of Israel and three wars. Rather than attempt a comprehensive review of the events and achievements of 40 tumultuous years, I will highlight those that illustrate the impact of gender, Jewish identity, and commitment to a political life on Golda Meir's life and career.

Golda had been suspect in the eyes of some members of her kibbutz because she was "the American girl." In her new role in the Histadrut, her years in Milwaukee and command of English were distinct advantages. She spent a substantial amount of time in the 1930s traveling in the United States and Great Britain, building support and raising funds for the Jewish settlers in Palestine in general and Histadrut programs in particular. Golda was, in many ways, an obvious choice for a person to send abroad. She had well-developed speaking skills and considerable experience in persuading groups and public meetings, and had been involved in successful fund-raising even before she came to Palestine. She was quite willing to travel, even when that meant leaving her two youngsters with her sister. Although the language of her early childhood was Yiddish, she had a native speaker's fluency in English as well. At the same time, it may not be completely off the mark to speculate that she was "available" for extensive foreign travel that would take her out of Palestine for months at a time because she was a woman and responsible for "women's issues" within the Histadrut, and hence perceived as more easily spared. The pattern was to be repeated in 1948.

In addition to direct responsibility for the Women's Council and her foreign travels, Golda was active in the formation of the Mapai political party and began to move into the ranks of the political elite. Her work was rewarded with a series of promotions, culminating in a 1946 appointment as head of the Political Bureau of the Jewish agency in Jerusalem.[8] During this period, Golda received national attention as a feisty and defiant witness in a British trial against two men accused of smuggling arms to the Haganah (the official military wing of the Jewish Agency) and as one of the few members of the elite who was neither arrested nor forced into hiding by the British crackdown in June 1946.[9]

By 1947, Golda was responsible for settling the new immigrants arriving from Europe (and deeply involved in the increasingly bitter conflict with British authorities over the entry of Jews, many survivors of Nazi concentration camps). Late in 1947, it was decided that the demands of military security for Jews in the face of violent local opposition to the United Nations partition plan and defense against Arab attacks on the Jewish state when it did emerge required raising a large amount of money rapidly. Previous appeals to foreign Jewish communities had been couched in terms of hundreds of thousands of dollars donated in the course of a year; now the leadership felt that millions were needed immediately.

Golda Meir was sent. (David Ben-Gurion, the overarching and, at times, overbearing figure in the creation of Israel, initially insisted that he was the only person who could carry out the project. But a meeting of the leadership declared it necessary that he stay in Palestine and readily accepted Golda's offer to leave for the United States.) It was a continuation of what she had been doing for several years, but at a much larger order of magnitude. In six weeks of nonstop touring and talking, Golda Meir raised $50 million.[10] After her return, she participated in negotiations surrounding the drafting of the Israeli constitution and the decision on when to declare the state. Clear evidence of her elite status is the fact that she was one of 200 people invited to participate in the signing of the proclamation of the State of Israel.

It was also in 1947 that Golda Meir was the Jewish Agency's secret emissary to King Abdullah of Transjordan (great grandfather of the present King Abdullah II of Jordan). Abdullah, by no means secure on his throne, had little to gain from war with Israel when the British left, and the Israelis were certainly willing to explore any avenue to delete the well-armed and -trained Arab Legion from the military equation. The result was two almost surreal sessions, with Golda and a colleague disguised as an Arab couple slipping into Jordanian territory to meet with the king. In Golda's telling, there was a moment when Abdullah seemed to have agreed to refrain from joining an Egyptian-Syrian-Iraqi assault, but in the end he was unable to resist the call to join the Arab armies besieging Israel, and the midnight meetings were relegated to historical marginalia.

THE AMBASSADOR

No sooner had Golda's signature dried on the declaration of independence than she was leaving the country for a fund-raising tour of the United States. This time she raised $75 million in a matter of weeks. Instead of returning to Israel, Golda was notified that she had just been appointed the first Israeli ambassador to Moscow.

After a year in the Soviet Union, she finally returned to Israel to begin a seven-year tenure as minister of labor. Two major factors underlay Golda's selection for the labor portfolio. Her previous career in the Histadrut meant that she was familiar with both the issues and the key players, and the developing pattern of relations between Israel and the USSR did not require a high-profile ambassador. Her first major challenge was the construction of housing and infrastructure for the hundreds of thousands of Jews from Europe and elsewhere in the Middle East who were flocking to Israel. Golda Meir was ideally suited to the challenge of designing and building cheap, simple housing that would allow the new immigrants rapidly to leave the transit camps, with their primitive facilities and multifamily tents. When the costs quickly grew far too large to be accommodated by the national budget, she had the skill and experience to take to the road and raise the money in the United States from private donations and bond sales.

During this period, Golda was a candidate in a contested election for the first time.[11] She ran for mayor of Jerusalem but was denied election by the votes of two representatives of religious parties on the town council, explicitly because of her gender. Twenty years later, Golda followed a rather matter-of-fact account of the incident in her autobiography (even noting that it was fortunate for her because she could then stay in the Labor Ministry) with sharp denunciation of the two individuals and strong protest at the blatant injustice. She described herself as "engaged" at the time; the hurt was still very deeply felt (Meir, 1975, pp. 281–282).

FROM LABOR TO FOREIGN AFFAIRS

In early 1956, David Ben-Gurion reshuffled his cabinet to remove Moshe Sharet from the foreign ministry and replace him with Golda Meir. In addition to a personal and political dispute between the two men, Sharet was too reluctant to strike back with military force after each guerrilla incursion from Egypt or Jordan and argued vigorously against what he felt was an overly rigid, hard-line policy toward Israel's neighbors. Golda was hardly open to that charge and was an active participant in the planning of the joint Israeli, French, and British attack on Egypt in October 1956. She quickly earned a reputation at the United Nations and elsewhere for taking uncompromising positions and for her resistance to any concessions in the negotiations for a cease-fire and disengagement agreement after Israel had pushed the Egyptians out of the Sinai Peninsula. However, the British and French assault on Cairo and attempt to land at the canal were withdrawn under heavy pressure from the United States, the Soviet Union, and most of the world opinion.

For the next nine years, Foreign Minister Golda Meir would be Israel's most public voice in world politics. She earned a reputation for two things in particular: a confrontational style and staunch line in dealing with the Arab–Israeli conflict, and an active campaign to develop close ties with the emerging nations of the Third World. She traveled extensively, particularly in Africa, and was the spearhead of a series of Israeli initiatives to transfer the lessons learned in nation building in Palestine to Africa and Asia. In addition to offers of technical assistance, she brought her no-nonsense, practical, and unassuming personal style to her hosts. She genuinely enjoyed meeting common people and seemed particularly adept at establishing rapport with the women and children of small villages.

In 1965, Golda could look back on a political career that featured increasingly important leadership positions, important contributions to settling hundreds of thousands of new Israelis, an extensive range of contacts and quiet cooperative efforts between Israel and the nonaligned states of Asia and Africa, a number of memorable confrontations with Arab and other delegations at the United Nations, and an important role in creating and maintaining a political party embodying the Labor Zionist principles she had first embraced as a young adult in Milwaukee. Her active life and frequent travels were taking a toll on her health and stamina, she felt she was missing the joys of quiet reflection and her grandchildren, and she decided the time had come to retire from active cabinet service.

On a speculative note, it may also be that Golda realized that the foreign ministry would be the summit of her political career. Ben-Gurion was clearly nearing the end of his remarkable role as the most dominant force in Israeli political life and had already anointed Levi Eshkol as his successor, and there were several powerful figures waiting in the wings: Dayan, Allon, Gallili, et al. If Golda ever entertained thoughts of the top job, it was not a likely prospect any longer.[12]

Of course, as she put it, she did not intend to retire to a "political nunnery." After less than a year, she returned to public life at the request of Ben-Gurion and others to become head of the Mapai party and to rebuild the labor coalition.[13] Golda was available for the job for three primary reasons. Her absence from day-to-day political life meant she was not tied to any personalized fractions that had formed around several powerful individuals jockeying for position in the cabinet. Her political philosophy was a rather uncomplicated embrace of the basic principles of socialist Zionism and with little concern for the nuances of philosophy and ideological distinctions that exerted a centrifugal force among the parties in the coalition. And, as she had repeatedly demonstrated, she could mount extremely persuasive appeals for cooperation and action.

As party head but without a cabinet portfolio, Golda Meir played a relatively modest role in the discussions and planning during early 1967 and was not directly involved in the central decisions surrounding the Six-Day

War of June 1967 or the protracted negotiations at the United Nations, in Washington, and elsewhere in its aftermath. But she was clearly supportive of the decision to initiate military action once it appeared to Israel that war was inevitable, shared the exultation at the entry of Jews into East Jerusalem, and endorsed the decision to retain control of the West Bank, Gaza Strip, and Golan Heights, pending formal negotiations with Jordan, Syria, and Egypt.

By early 1968, Golda had completed the task of forging a workable coalition and creating the Labor Alignment and had turned 70.[14] This time she retired and meant it—or so she thought.

THE PRIME MINISTER

Golda Meir's retirement lasted slightly more than a year. In February 1970, Levi Eshkol, Israel's prime minister, suffered a fatal heart attack. Israel was in the midst of what had become known as the War of Attrition, with a constant low level of armed clashes between Israeli and Egyptian air and ground forces at the Suez Canal and Syrian forces in the Golan. The Labor Alignment threatened to split along the lines of the personal and political rivalry between Moshe Dayan and Yigal Allon. Levi Eshkol had been forced to include the leadership of several key right-wing parties (including Menachem Begin) in his governing coalition. A number of individuals and factions settled on Golda as an interim prime minister until parliamentary elections could be held, with the potential of realigning the factional balance of power.

Golda became prime minister in March 1970, selected by a party caucus instead of national elections, saddled with the assumption that she was merely a caretaker, facing a cabinet representing an unmanageably diverse political constellation, with the level of violence between Israeli and Egyptian forces at Suez escalating, and the Israeli economy reeling under the strain of enormous defense expenditures and the continued mobilization of a sizable number of reservists. Her response to action: negotiations with the Nixon administration for direct aid, with the purchase of Phantom jets on concessionary terms as a first priority, and a high-profile visit to Washington; attempts to control the inflationary spiral by actively discouraging strikes and wage hikes; and continuing conflict with the Begin forces over the issue of making *any* concession to the United States for the sake of getting aid.

The actions and initiatives did not immediately solve the problems. The trip to Washington yielded private assurances but not public announcement of Phantom jets or other weapons; the economy continued to worsen; the confrontation along the Suez continued to escalate and Russian advisers began to play a larger role.

As national elections approached in October 1970, the only obvious change in the Israeli political landscape was the fact that Golda Meir had become the central figure. She was no longer an interim figure selected by party leaders and slated to return to retirement as soon as the major contenders sorted things out; she was the prime minister and the unquestioned choice to lead her party into the elections. The elections resulted, as usual, in a divided outcome, with Golda's party falling 5 seats short of an absolute majority in the 120-member Knesset. But between her personal popularity and prominence and the size of her parliamentary bloc, it was obvious that she would form the next government. That government included representatives of the right wing, including Begin. A measure of Golda's political strength is the fact that when the Begin forces left the cabinet some months later after a confrontation over strategy in dealing with the Nixon administration, she was easily able to replace them with other parties and strengthen her support in the Knesset.

Israeli foreign policy under Golda Meir was marked by increasingly close ties with Washington;[15] a cease-fire along Suez that silenced the guns temporarily; a consistent demand that Egypt, Jordan, and Syria agree to face-to-face negotiations with Israel and rejection of any other mode of negotiations; and an end to most of Israel's ties to Africa and Asia.[16] In tone and content, it was little different from the policies that earlier governments had adopted and Golda had pursued as foreign minister.

Domestic problems proved no more tractable. The economy did not improve, inflation soared (as it did in much of the world, although more steeply in Israel), and tensions between religious and secular Israelis and between "European" and "Oriental" Jews, and the more general tensions that ultimately were to lead to the replacement of the founding Zionist establishment by a deeply divided elite, continued to grow.[17]

The pivotal event of Golda Meir's career as head of the government was the war that erupted on October 6, 1973.[18] The Soviet Union had rearmed both Egypt and Syria after the Six-Day War, and the Egyptians in particular had embarked on a massive training program to remedy the gross deficiencies of their combat units. Faced with Israeli fortification along the Suez Canal (the Bar-Lev line), the Egyptians developed a plan to outflank the positions by launching an amphibious assault. Israeli intelligence was correct in May when it discounted data suggesting military conflict was imminent. But assessments in September ignored or misinterpreted evidence that political and military preparations for a major offensive were well under way. Egypt attacked across the Suez and drove up the Sinai Peninsula; Syria simultaneously launched an attack from the Golan Heights that nearly broke through the second line of Israeli defenses. There was no triumphant six-day rout; Israeli forces retreated and suffered heavy casualties.[19] The tide of battle did not turn until an American resupply program took effect. The end of fighting led to a period of tense negotiations, brokered by Henry Kissinger and Richard Nixon, leading to the disengagement of the combatants and a partial Israeli withdrawal from Sinai.

The war was traumatic for Israelis. The myth of military invincibility was profoundly shaken. The Egyptian military showed a capacity for battlefield coordination and mastery of modern weaponry that was a sharp contrast to the ineptitude of 1967. The complacent trust that Israeli technological superiority would easily offset the huge difference in human resources was radically undermined. Not since 1948 had there been such a serious threat of military defeat.

There was an immediate search for understanding and responsibility. Attention and accusations focused on Moshe Dayan as minister of defense, the army's chief of staff and senior generals, and the intelligence establishment, who were blamed for allowing Israel to be surprised. Golda was not directly blamed. She was seen as a victim of the military and intelligence officers who failed to foresee the attack. Her decision not to mobilize the reserves and launch a preemptive strike on October 5 was attributed to tragically flawed advice. During the fighting itself, she followed the precedent of other prime ministers in wartime of allowing the military staff and field commanders to run the war.

Parliamentary elections in December produced little change in the Knesset and returned Golda to office, but the fallout from the war was only beginning. The pressure on Dayan to resign as defense minister and on key military and intelligence officers to step down was overwhelming. The public mood was bleak, the domestic dilemmas facing the country were even less tractable than before the war, and there were intense and difficult negotiations with the United States as Kissinger and Nixon became the key players in efforts to construct a postwar settlement that would meet Israeli needs for security and Arab demands for return of territory.

By April 1975, Golda had had enough and announced her irrevocable decision to resign. The disengagement agreement that Kissinger put together was in place and the immediate security problems seemed manageable. It was a good moment to leave. On June 4, as the disengagement agreement was being implemented and Israeli prisoners were coming home from Egypt and Syria, Golda Meir became a private citizen. The last three years of her life were spent in retirement with her grandchildren and family; she died in December 1978 of leukemia.

She was replaced as prime minister by Yitzhak Rabin, whose brief tenure was marked by the continuing demise of the Labor Alignment and the emergence of the right-wing Likud group headed by Menachem Begin, who came to power in 1976, effectively ending some 50 years of dominance by the Zionist Left. The power of the Labor Zionist movement and the founding generation in Israeli politics had been eroding for some time. The original elite was aging and passing from the scene; the national agenda was changing, with new issues replacing the challenges of the first 25 years; and the old ideological consensus was not automatically shared by younger Israelis, particularly the Sephardim.[20] The fact that Israel was caught by surprise by the Arabs and suffered serious initial setbacks in the Yom Kippur War was traumatic for most Israelis and sharply underscored the image of Labor politicians as a tired old elite that had lost the will and ability to lead.[21]

AN EVALUATION

As prime minister, Golda Meir dealt with essentially the same issues with the same approaches that marked her entire career. Her record of achievement in coping with domestic policy during her five years in office is minimal. The economy worsened and continued to decline until a combination of the changes instituted by the Begin government and substantially increased U.S. aid in the late 1970s allowed inflation to ease and growth to resume. With the advantage of historical perspective, it seems clear that there was little Golda or her government could have done to make much difference at the time. The religious/secular cleavage remains a fact of Israeli political life; if anything, it is today a more prominent dimension than in the past. The gap in standards of living, education, and political orientation between Ashekenazim (Jews whose roots are in Europe) and Sephardim remains; the political gap has grown even as the material differences have narrowed.

Conflict with the Arabs and war dominated the agenda during Golda's tenure, just as they had throughout much of her earlier career. Her position on the use of force and her understanding of the Arab–Israeli conflict were not qualitatively different from the perspectives of her peers. Some of the elite were a little more hawkish, some a little more dovish and willing to search for compromise, but Golda fit solidly in the mainstream.

Prime Minister Meir drew her political strength from her ability to maintain a coalition of generally socialist parties in the Knesset. While she was initially chosen as a caretaker prime minister until the next election, Golda was able to use the skills and political relationships developed during her years of public service to build her own political base. She had revitalized the Mapai party during her service as chair, and many Knesset members owed their seats to her. Her long career in government meant that she knew many parliamentarians personally and could call in old debts. And her grandmotherly image and unpretentious personal style proved immensely popular with Israelis (Peretz, 1979, pp. 97–100).

Golda changed more than the traditional ban on smoking in cabinet meetings during her years as prime minister. She reorganized the work of the cabinet by assigning specific issues to subcommittees to work out the details and formulate recommendations. That left the full cabinet free to debate basic policy issues and deal with competing recommendations for action.

More important, she expanded the pattern of informal consultation and decision making that had been a prominent feature of every prior Israeli government. Golda would frequently invite a select group of cabinet members, her closet political allies and trusted advisers, to meet in her home to discuss and work out major issues. These meetings were often held on Saturday, the day before the regularly scheduled Sunday cabinet meeting and, more often than not, when the full cabinet met it was to ratify what had been decided the night before. The participants in the informal meetings were quickly dubbed the "kitchen cabinet," which was often literally true, as they gathered around the kitchen table. Golda would contribute to the informal domesticity by making and pouring the coffee or tea and, perhaps, baking cookies. But the tone and setting did not obscure the fact that this was Golda Meir's meeting. She set the agenda, she invited the participants, she decided when a consensus had emerged, and she announced the decisions.[22]

Golda Meir was a strong, self-confident person with few doubts about her abilities or the correctness of her positions. She had a high tolerance for discussion but a very low tolerance for explicit disagreement (Elizur & Salpeter, 1973, p. 34).

GOLDA MEIR AND GENDER

Golda Meir's career seems to have been shaped primarily by the interaction between her personal attributes—high energy, preference for concrete problem solving over reflection or ideology, skills as speaker and fund-raiser—and the political environment. Aside from the mayoral election lost because of explicit bias on the part of religious parties, gender appears to have played a secondary role in shaping Golda's public career. There are two major considerations supporting this conclusion.

First of all, Golda Meir's public career took place in extraordinary times: the pioneering Zionist period, then the struggle for statehood, followed by life in a political system in which all other concerns were periodically swept aside in the face of a direct military threat. The recurrent crisis periods, when the question of physical survival was overwhelming, led to a powerful sense of shared experience and common purpose that helped override personal differences. In the aftermath of the Six-Day War, the grip of socialist-inspired Zionists on Israeli political life seriously weakened; and the more conservative opposition, led by Menachem Begin, began to close in on power. Several profound divisions emerged, and Israel has not enjoyed sustained periods of consensus since. But by the time the founding generation began to lose its unquestioned authority, Golda was already at the peak of her career. Her membership in the generation of pioneers and heroes and her distinguished public career left her poised (although she did not know it) for accession to the ultimate position.

Second, the situation and experiences of Golda's generation were reinforced by an explicit commitment to equality on the part of the early

Zionist movement. The members of Golda's generation were people who came to a new country from old lands and old societies. They certainly brought a great deal of cultural baggage along, but the shared consciousness of creating a new society and becoming new people reduced the impact of preexisting biases and unexamined assumptions. From the self-conscious discussions and debates of the kibbutz movement to the self-proclaimed principles of government,[23] the normative goal was equality. That by itself was probably not enough to overcome bias, but it likely inhibited overtly biased actions.[24]

As foreign minister, Golda Meir was quite ready to use force against Egypt in 1956, with or without the cooperation of the French and English; she was strongly supportive of Israel's actions in the Six-Day War of June 1967, although she was not then in the government. When she left retirement to become prime minister, she was faced with the challenges of the traumatic Yom Kippur War of October 1973. The decision not to preempt reflected calculations of the reactions from the United States and other sources of support for Israel, as well as intelligence estimates. It was not a generalized reluctance to resort to military means. Golda was an outspoken and assertive defender of Israel's positions in the United Nations, and was consistently unwilling to make the first concession.

As she wrote her autobiography in 1975, Golda tried to understand Arab motives for the 1948 assault on Israel and the subsequent enduring conflict and recurrent wars. She found her enemies unfathomable. This passage is worth quoting at length, not only because it illustrates the conceptual framework she applied to the central foreign policy facing Israel, but because it captures the style and flavor of her approach:

> It has never ceased to astonish me that the Arab states have been so eager to go to war against us. Almost from the very beginning of Zionist settlement until today they have been consumed by hatred for us. The only possible explanation—and it is a ridiculous one—is that they simply cannot bear our presence or forgive us for existing, and I find it hard to believe that the leaders of *all* the Arab states are and always have been so hopelessly primitive in their thinking.
>
> On the other hand, what have we ever done to threaten the Arab states? True, we have not stood in line to return territory we won in wars they started, but territory, after all, has never been what Arab aggression is all about—and in 1948 it was certainly not a need for more land that drove the Egyptians northward in hope of reaching and destroying Tel Aviv and Jewish

Jerusalem. So what was it? An overpowering irrational urge to eliminate us physically? Fear of the progress we might introduce in the Middle East? A distaste for Western Civilization? Who knows? Whatever it was, it has lasted—but then so have we—and the solution will probably not be found for many years, although I have no doubt that the time will come when the Arab states will accept us—as we are and for what we are. In a nutshell, peace is—and always has been—dependent entirely on only one thing: The Arab leaders must acquiesce in our being here. (Meir, 1975, p. 232)

There may be a temptation to attribute "toughness" and "intransigence" to the real or imagined pressure on a woman to overcome suspicions that she is "too soft."[25] It is impossible to rule that hypothesis out completely, but there is compelling evidence for a more straightforward hypothesis that Golda Meir's stance toward Israel's Arab adversaries was born out of her understanding that Jews lived in a dangerous world and must rely on themselves alone for survival, and a rather simplistic cognitive style that saw issues in stark good versus evil terms.[26]

That Golda's account of her childhood in Russia begins with two frightening incidents—a near-miss encounter with Cossacks galloping down an alleyway over the heads of small children, and the fearful preparations her father tried to make against violence from his Gentile neighbors—seems to underline her own sense that Jews are threatened. She returns to the theme at the very end of her memoir, reflecting on the trials of a small state in a "harsh, selfish materialistic" world in which great powers are susceptible to "blackmail" and survival ultimately depends on self-defense (Meir, 1975, p. 460).

Golda's autobiography and published speeches reflect a relatively uncomplicated view of the world. The autobiography has few purely reflective passages and little speculation on alternative explanations. Her writing is devoid of rhetorical flourishes, nuances, or asides; the judgments of people and events are clear and unambiguous. She notes the contrast between her approach to issues with that of the professional diplomats she inherited when she became foreign minister. "Many of the more senior ambassadors and officials had been educated at British universities, and their particular brand of intellectual sophistication . . . was not always my cup of tea" (Meir, 1975, p. 292). The passage seems to reflect both a preference for a less-complex approach to questions and the self-consciousness of a Wisconsin Teachers' College dropout in the presence of graduates of Oxford or Cambridge. In sum, it appears more reasonable to attribute Golda Meir's attitude toward the Arab–Israeli conflict in general, and the use of force in that arena in particular, to her individual history and development than to any major causal impact of her gender.

In her own reflection on her life and career, Golda appears to assign gender a minor role:

> I am not a great admirer of the kind of feminism that gives rise to bra burning, hatred of men or a campaign against motherhood, but I have had very great regard for those energetic hard-working women within the ranks of the labor movement . . . who succeeded in equipping dozens of city-bred girls with the sort of knowledge and training that made it possible for them to do their share . . . in agricultural settlements throughout Palestine. That kind of constructive feminism really does women credit and matters much more than who sweeps the house or sets the table.
>
> About the position of women generally, of course, there is very much to say . . . but I can put my own thoughts on the subject into a nutshell. Naturally women should be treated as the equals of men in all respects, but, as is true also of the Jewish people, they shouldn't have to be better than anyone else . . . or feel that they must accomplish wonders all the time to be accepted by all.
>
> The fact is that I have lived and worked with men all my life, but being a woman has never hindered me in any way at all. It has never caused me unease or given me an inferiority complex or made me think that men are better off than women—or that it is a disaster to give birth to children. Not at all. Nor have men ever given me preferential treatment. But what is true, I think, is that women who want and need a life outside as well as inside the home have a much, much harder time than men because they carry such a heavy double burden . . . and the life of a working mother who lives without the constant presence and support of the father of her children is three times harder than that of any man I have ever met. (Meir, 1975, pp. 113–115)

Three aspects of these reflections on gender, the only point in her autobiography where Golda comments at any length on the question, deserve mention. First, her juxtaposition of "bad" feminism with "good" practical work is quite consistent with Golda's preference for the concrete over the abstract and the immediate problem over the larger question. It also sounds like the reaction of a woman whose perceptions of gender issues were set in the very different time and society of the post-World War I United States, when the issues and expressions of the commitment to equality were quite different.

Second, Golda clearly did not think that gender affected her political career or relationships with colleagues. In keeping with her general aversion to broad issues or social analysis not directly related to the struggle for a Jewish state, she did not ask whether her experience was typical or unique. The question of whether the larger society had lived up to the egalitarian goals of the founders of the state, or whether even in Israel there was bias and discrimination, was simply ignored.

Third, the comments about the double or treble burden of the woman who seeks a public career clearly reflect Golda's life history. They are followed by her comments on the way in which she raised her two children, including her overwhelming guilt at leaving them to travel abroad (Meir, 1975, p. 115). But the discussion is rooted at the personal level and tacitly accepts the social order that necessitates the extra burden on women. There is no comment on the fairness of social arrangements or her own acceptance of some critical assumptions about what women were supposed to do.

Several aspects of Golda Meir's life seem to have mitigated the impact of gender. While she was born into a quite traditional culture, the fact that her father left the family to seek a better life forced and allowed her mother to assume the role of head of the household.[27] Even when the family was reunited in Milwaukee, it was her mother's ability to cope with the practical business of opening and running a store that was the critical factor in moving from poverty to modest wealth. Her older sister's involvement in politics in Russia and among emigré intellectuals in the United States gave her another example of a strong woman in a leadership role.

As a young adult, Golda embraced a highly egalitarian form of Zionism. She was impelled not just to go to Palestine but to join the explicitly utopian communal society of the kibbutz. Her sense of herself as strong and capable was reinforced by her ability to meet the rigorous physical and social demands of the community and to exert her skills in organizing portions of the daily routine.

Thus, by the time she was forced (as she saw it) to make a choice between the demands of her private role as wife and mother and her public role as participant in the creation of a new society, she was accustomed to acting independently and deeply committed to the necessity of life in the public sphere. Gender was hardly irrelevant; Golda's assumptions about what a woman should do and her responsibilities to her husband and children caused her years of personal suffering, but she was sufficiently free of traditional constraints to opt for the public over the private life.

Gender did have an obvious direct effect on the early stages of her political career through her position with the Women's Council of Histadrut. Her personal and political skills enabled her to transcend the potential constraints of "women's issues" and move increasingly into other roles, most critically as representative of Jews in Palestine and fund-raiser in the United States. While gender may have had some impact on Golda's selection for the various fund-raising campaigns, her background in America, flair for blunt and persuasive speech, and linguistic skills were clearly the primary factors.

But her subsequent career, in both foreign and domestic policy arenas, would appear to support her assertion that she did not experience to a great extent the direct effects of whatever gender bias existed. Her positions on issues did not distinguish her from her male colleagues. Her toughness as a negotiator was often noted, but Golda Meir is hardly the only Israeli politician or prime minister to be accused of "intransigence" by opponents. It was her political history and the accident of Levi Eshkol's untimely death that propelled her into the prime ministership.

At the outer edge of relevance are matters of personal style. Other Israeli prime ministers had informal sessions with advisers; Golda's "kitchen cabinet" met in the kitchen, and she would often make coffee or set out something to eat. When it was her turn in the communal kitchen on the kibbutz, she saw to it that coffee and sandwiches were waiting for the sentries as they came off duty at midnight; she would do the same thing for her bodyguards as prime minister when she had a sleepless night. There were occasions on which she cried in public when some, if not all, of her male colleagues were dry eyed. Some observers used "grandmotherly" as a descriptor of her appearance and demeanor. Much of this is gender related. All of it is far more personal than political.

To the extent that a single case will allow generalization, Golda Meir's life suggests that gender is never irrelevant but that it is not necessarily the sole, or even major, determinant of political success. The traditional division of sex roles that assigns almost exclusive responsibility for the private sphere to women and by and large reserves the public sphere for men made it far more difficult for Golda Meir to choose a public life. The sense that she was somehow not meeting her obligations as wife and mother added guilt and anguish to her life; it did not deter her.

The life of a woman in the twentieth century cannot avoid being affected by her own understanding of her gender and the larger society's beliefs about women. But for Golda Meir, that impact of negative aspects of gender stereotypes held by others was mitigated by the combination of a distinctive set of experiences early in life and the fact that her career paralleled the conscious creation of a new society.

Author's Note: Excerpts from *My Life* by Golda Meir, © 1975 by G.P. Putnam. Used with permission of The Putnam Publishing Group.

NOTES

1 Golda Meir was, throughout her life, a person of action rather than contemplation; an organizer, persuader, and mover rather than a reflective thinker. Perhaps the clearest statement of her views is a speech she delivered at Dropsie College, a Jewish institution in Philadelphia (reprinted as "The Zionist Purpose" in Meir, 1973).

2 Despite her repeated protestations that she would have been happiest had she been able to remain a comparatively anonymous member of a small farming collective, it is hard to imagine Golda Meir restricted to such a small arena.

3 Throughout this chapter, Ms. Meir is referenced to as Golda, in keeping with standard usage in both Israeli politics and much of the scholarly literature. Particularly at the height of her popularity, Israelis referred to the prime minister as Golda for many of the same reasons Americans had earlier called President Eisenhower Ike.

4 For the relevance of a political leader's initial success to later political style, see Barber (1972, p. 11).

5 Morris came, reluctantly, and at the last minute Golda convinced her older sister to come with them, leaving her husband behind to raise the money to bring himself and the children later—let no one underestimate Golda's power of persuasion!

6 See the selection in Meir's 1973 book, *Golda Meir Speaks Out*. These are clearly speeches with a purpose, not philosophical or reflective discourses.

7 The Histadrut was the general organization for labor created by the Zionist movement in Palestine. It was (and is) far more than a labor union, serving as both owner of enterprises and representatives of workers' interests. The Histadrut has always attempted to meet the personal and social needs of the labor movement.

8 The Jewish Agency was the quasi-state organization that coordinated the various groups and movements involved in Jewish life in Palestine under the British mandate. It was, and understood itself to be, a government in training. Note that although Golda's job now moved her from Tel Aviv to Jerusalem, where her husband still lived, they did not resume their life together.

9 Golda was clearly disappointed to be ignored by the British. The fact that her name was not on the list of those to be arrested was perhaps related to the fact that her official responsibilities were only indirectly related to the military dimension of the struggle for independence, perhaps a reflection of a belief that women would not be much of a danger.

10 She could not resist quoting, ostensibly for the sake of denying, Ben-Gurion's remark, "Someday when history will be written, it will be said that there was a Jewish woman who got the money which made the state possible."

11 In the Israeli system, members of Parliament, the Knesset, do not run as individuals from districts but as names on party lists. Seats are allocated to parties via proportional representation.

12 As noted earlier, Golda did not present herself as ambitious or even interested in a political career beyond being willing to serve and wanting to get the tasks at hand accomplished.

13 Israel uses a system of strict proportional representation and nationwide constituencies to allocate parliamentary seats. The result is a multiparty system in which there are two broad tendencies: parties whose ideological positions are marked by varying degrees of free-market economics, more traditional nationalism, or commitment to transforming Israel into an explicitly religious state. From the early 1920s through Menachem Begin's election in 1975, the Labor Coalition of the relatively leftist parties dominated Israeli political life. Both the Labor and Likud (rightist) coalitions have been marked by uneasy alliances among relatively independent parties who vigorously preserve their ideological and doctrinal distinctions even as they reach agreement on lines of policy.

14 She commented, "It is not a sin to be seventy but it is also no joke" (Meir, 1975, p. 374).

15 For an account of the evolution of the U.S.–Israeli relationship during Golda's tenure, see Safran (1978, pp. 448–475).

16 The relationships that Golda had been instrumental in developing as foreign minister were causalities of the Six-Day War.

17 For a thorough discussion of the dynamics of domestic problems and their political implications, see Perlmutter (1985, pp. 220–230).

18 Often referred to in Israel as the Yom Kippur War, with the accompanying connotations of a sneak attack launched on a solemn religious holiday, it is consistently labeled the October War by the Arabs. Safran (1978, pp. 278–316) describes the course of the war itself and deals with the controversies surrounding the Meir government's handling of the situation (pp.180–187). See also Perlmutter (1985, pp. 232–237) for a succinct discussion. Heikal (1975) and al Shazly (1975) present insider accounts of the Egyptian war effort.

19 In roughly two weeks of fighting, 2,500 Israelis were killed. As a proportion of the population, this is roughly double the losses the United Sates suffered during the entire Vietnam War.

20 The Sephardim are the so-called Oriental Jews, who are descended from the Jewish communities expelled from Spain in 1492 and who settled in various areas of the Middle East.

21 See, for example, the discussion in Perlmutter (1985, p. 230) or the far more critical assessment in Avishai (1990, pp. 29–41) titled "Golda Meir's Last Hurrah."

22 The kitchen cabinet sessions are discussed in detail in Elizur and Salpeter (1973, chap. 3) and Golda's style as prime minister is described in Shimshoni (1982, pp. 203–204).

23 Note, for example, that the second of the 14 points defining the purpose and policies of the new government of the new State of Israel, issued by David Ben-Gurion in May 1948, was equality of men and women.

24 For a contemporary evaluation of the status of women in Israeli political life, see Swirski and Safir (1991), particularly the chapters in Section 3, "Golda Notwithstanding: Participation and Powerlessness."

25 See the discussion at several points in Fraser (1989, especially chap. 17).

26 See, for example, Amos Perlmutter's (1985, pp. 204–208) characterization of her worldview as "narrow and simple" and his discussion of how broadly shared the basic tenets were among the Israeli elite.
27 In Golda's memory, her father's action was necessitated by his lack of practical business sense and the pervasive anti-Semitism of Czarist Russia.

REFERENCES

Al Shazly, S. (1975). *The crossing of the Suez*. San Francisco: American Mideast Research.
Avishai, B. (1990). *A new Israel*. New York: Ticknor & Fields.
Barber, J.D. (1972). *Presidential character*. Englewood Cliffs, NJ: Prentice-Hall.
Blashfield, J.F. (2010). *Golda Meir*. Salt Lake City, UT: Benchmark Books.
Burkett, S. (2009). *Golda*. New York: Harper Perennial.
Elizur, Y., & Salpeter, E. (1973). *Who rules Israel?* New York: Harper & Row.
Fraser, A. (1989). *The warrior queens*. New York: Alfred E. Knopf.
Heikal, M. (1975). *The road to Ramadan*. New York: Quadrangle.
Meir, G. (1973). *Golda Meir speaks out*. London: Weidenfeld & Nicolson.
Meir, G. (1975). *My life*. New York: G.P. Putnam.
Peretz, D. (1979). *Government and politics of Israel*. Boulder, CO: Westview Press.
Perlmutter, A. (1985). *Israel: The partitioned state*. New York: Charles Scribner's Sons.
Safran, N. (1978). *Israel: The embattled ally*. Cambridge, MA: Harvard University Press.
Shimshoni, D. (1982). *Israeli democracy*. New York: Free Press.
Swirski, B., & Safir, M. (Eds.). (1991). *Calling the bluff*. New York: Macmillan.

8

Ma Ellen—The Iron Lady of Liberia

Evaluating Ellen Johnson Sirleaf's Presidency

Farida Jalalzai

> My Administration shall empower Liberian women in all areas of our national life. We will support and increase the writ of laws that restore their dignity and deal drastically with crimes that dehumanize them. We will enforce without fear or favor the law against rape recently passed by the National Transitional Legislature. We shall encourage families to educate all children, particularly the girl child. We will also try to provide economic programs that enable Liberian women—particularly our market women—to assume their proper place in our economic process.
>
> **Ellen Johnson Sirleaf**
> **Inaugural Address, January 16, 2006**

These sentiments were expressed by Ellen Johnson Sirleaf upon her inauguration as the first popularly elected female president of an African nation. She committed to developing and enforcing women-friendly policies and incorporating and empowering women in all aspects of society. She pledged, therefore, to act on behalf of women's substantive interests. Having completed her first term and just embarking on a second, has Johnson Sirleaf fulfilled these promises?

This chapter examines the circumstances of Ellen Johnson Sirleaf's rise to the Liberian presidency, particularly the structural and institutional dynamics leading to her victory. In constructing the context providing her ascension, important personal background details surface. I evaluate Johnson Sirleaf's accomplishments as well as continued challenges. The chapter concludes with understanding her leadership style and the type of representation she offers women. Of particular concern is whether Johnson

Sirleaf's presidency challenges or reinforces traditional gendered leadership norms.

We can explain Ellen Johnson Sirleaf's ascension as the consequence of an open electoral field, political instability, blending of traditional feminine and masculine traits and expertise, the strong support of a woman's peace movement, and the lack of partisan loyalty among voters. She also boasted experience her challengers lacked. To date, she has improved basic services, the economic picture, and maintained peace. Still, she faces challenges in combating corruption, improving security, and eradicating poverty. Johnson Sirleaf's leadership style is a gendered blend of strength and compassion. Overall, Johnson Sirleaf appears to further women's descriptive, substantive, and symbolic representation and complicates traditional notions of women executive's leadership styles.

CONTEXT

Johnson Sirleaf gained the presidency within a war-torn and unstable political context. Unlike most African countries, Liberia did not endure independence struggles. Established as a country of freed American slaves in West Africa, democratic transition and consolidation proved problematic. Though hardly a democratic success story, Liberia generally enjoyed relative stability until Samuel Doe deposed President Tolbert in the face of economic riots in 1980. Prior to that period, the minority population of American descendants dominated politically, leaving the majority out of power.[1]

Ellen Johnson Sirleaf became president after many years of civil war, following multiple arrests and exiles in the face of her opposition to authoritarianism; her rise was anything but certain and sudden. She arose as a political figure in resistance to the Samuel Doe regime, resulting in her exile to Kenya from 1983 to 1985 (BBC News, 2005). Upon returning to Liberia, she was placed under house arrest. In 1989, Charles Taylor led a military coup against Doe and subsequently executed him, sparking a civil war (BBC News, 2012). Johnson Sirleaf initially supported Taylor, a decision that came back to haunt her presidential bid. Between 1989 and 1996, Liberia experienced complete state failure, characterized by extreme violence claiming 250,000 (mostly civilian) lives (Moran, 2008) and displacing another three million. The Council of State, a six-person collective presidency led by Ruth Perry, governed during a temporary peace agreement (Jackson-Laufer, 1999). Exiled yet again, Johnson Sirleaf returned in 1997 to compete in the presidential elections following Doe's death. She placed second after Taylor, who later charged her with treason because of her opposition. Taylor gained popular election in 1997 (Harris, 2006) in a largely free and fair contest (Moran, 2008).

Among many of the challenges Liberia faced were economic. Liberians enjoyed very limited land and property rights (Ohiorhenuan, 2007). During the civil war, the gross domestic product declined from almost $1,000 per capita in 1980 to below $100 in 1995 (Ohiorhenuan, 2007). Women faced particular poverty. Though active in the economy, they failed to participate in the most profitable sectors (Bekoe & Parajon, 2007). As in most African countries, women's parity with men in various spheres, including the economic, left much to be desired. For example, the United Nations Gender Related Development Index scored Liberia a .430, placing it among the lowest worldwide in gender parity.[2]

Women received the right to vote in 1946, a fairly long period of time. As far as the political pipeline, women faced daunting challenges. Women constituted only about 13% of the lower house prior to Johnson Sirleaf's election.[3] Though quite low, this was an improvement compared to previous years. In 2000, only 7% of legislators were women. Liberia utilizes single member districts elected through first past the post; such electoral designs lead to lower levels of women compared to multimember proportional representation districts (Reynolds, 1999; Salmond, 2006). Unlike many other African countries, Liberia lacks gender quotas, also limiting women's chances (Krook, 2009).[4]

At the same time, women's grassroots organizations gained traction in Africa. According to Adams (2008), women's participation in such groups was most prevalent in Liberia. The Women of Liberia Mass Action played critical roles in initiating peace talks and creating the interim Council of State (Adams, 2008, p. 481). Their involvement facilitated links to more formalized political institutions. Voter registration campaigns aimed at women increased their percentage on the voting rolls from 30% to 50% (National Elections Commission, 2005), and this mobilization is often credited with paving the way for Johnson Sirleaf's victory.

Executive arrangements in Liberia tend not to be favorable to women's chances. Featuring a unified executive system, power is concentrated in a president possessing vast powers. These include playing a major role in governmental formation, making key appointments, chairing cabinet meetings, vetoing legislation, authorizing emergency decrees, foreign policy and defense roles, and the ability to dissolve the legislature (see also Jalalzai, 2010). Further difficulties amass since election to the Liberian presidency is through the popular vote (Jalalzai, 2010). At the same time, we should not overstate the powers of the Liberian presidency, since the position lacks worldwide stature. Women may be more apt to gain power in countries with limited global import. Other women gaining dominant presidencies nearly always possess blood or marital ties to a male executive or opposition leader; this is not the case for Johnson Sirleaf (Jalalzai, 2008). She, therefore, represents a departure from the typical female president.[5] Given this seeming anomaly, Johnson Sirleaf may be even more important to consider. Perhaps examining her personal story will shed some light on key circumstances enabling her rise.

BIOGRAPHICAL SKETCH

Ellen Johnson Sirleaf was born in Liberia in 1938. While she lacks the traditional kinship ties that dominant women presidents worldwide typically possess, her father was a legislator, providing her some political socialization. She was educated in Liberia until she came to the United States to attend the University of Colorado, where she studied economics. She obtained a Masters of Public Administration degree from Harvard University (CBC News Online, 2006). Though she married at the very young age of 17 (BBC News, 2011) and had four children, she divorced her abusive husband before embarking on her political career (Johnson Sirleaf, 2009). While this may depart from the typical expectations placed on women in African societies, some of the newest women executives worldwide also share divorced backgrounds.[6]

Johnson Sirleaf returned to Liberia following her education, immediately entangling in national politics, serving as President Tolbert's finance minister (Adams, 2010). She narrowly escaped death in 1980 when all but four cabinet ministers were executed following Samuel Doe's coup (Kosciejew, 2012). After Tolbert's ousting, Johnson Sirleaf protested Doe's presidency, eventually leading her to flee Liberia. While working for Citibank during her exile in Kenya, she continued agitating for democratic transition. In 1985, she returned to Liberia to run for the Senate. She was arrested and sentenced to 10 years in prison for one of her speeches. She was released to house arrest after several months and once again exiled to Kenya (CBC News Online, 2006).

In addition to serving as vice president for Citibank and HSBC, she worked for the United Nations Development Program's Regional Bureau for Africa, the World Bank, and was president of the Liberia Bank for Development and Investment. She also served on the board of the International Monetary Fund. This, along with political experience gained under the Tolbert government, suggests that Johnson Sirleaf boasted varied and impressive credentials, which proved to be an important asset as she set her sights on the presidency. Recognizing that Charles Taylor did not afford Liberians a democratic alternative, she challenged him in the 1997 presidential elections (BBC News, 2005; CBC News Online, 2006).

PATH TO POWER

Johnson Sirleaf's presidential aspirations would not be realized in 1997. Taylor won in a landslide, attaining over 75% of the vote (Harris, 1999). Running as a Unity Party candidate, Johnson Sirleaf came in second with 10%. Taylor's victory was due in some part to the short preparation time provided to opposition parties and electoral rules advantaging his party (Harris, 1999). Johnson Sirleaf significantly delayed her entry into the race. Her connections to the unpopular Tolbert administration, status as an urban elite, and absence during the war also proved vulnerabilities (Adams, 2010). Above all, Taylor benefited from the public's belief that if he lost, war was imminent. Lastly, many felt Taylor could better handle Liberian security issues (Harris, 1999).

Shortly after Taylor's victory, however, civil unrest and war broke out. Two years later, Taylor faced rebellion from another armed faction, forcing him to flee to Nigeria in 2003. Following the establishment of an interim government in which Johnson Sirleaf played a pivotal role, she again ran for the presidency in 2005 (Bauer, 2011).[7] Noting earlier that women absent family ties failed to secure dominant presidencies worldwide, and no woman ever won a presidential election in Africa, what factors can we credit for Johnson Sirleaf's success? We can explain this by examining the following: the absence of an entrenched incumbent, political instability, her careful utilization of gender stereotypes in the aftermath of civil war, the strong support of a woman's peace movement, the lack of partisan loyalty among voters, and the qualities of Johnson Sirleaf in relation to her main competitor, George Weah.

AN OPEN ELECTORAL ENVIRONMENT

A critical factor facilitating Johnson Sirleaf's victory was the absence of an entrenched incumbent (Harris, 2006). Taylor was out of the running, and rebel forces also failed to present an opposition, quite unusual given Liberia's troubled past (Harris, 2006). Even when Liberia enjoyed relative stability, executive rule existed under settler oligarchies. As such, 2005 offered the most open electoral field in Liberia in at least a century (Sawyer, 2008).

Fifty-nine people attempted candidacies; 22 eventually gained official certification to wage bids (Sawyer, 2008). In contrast to 1997, parties received plenty of preparation time, and Johnson Sirleaf did not delay her candidacy. Her United Party benefited from its relatively long history and membership consisting primarily of educated professionals. Her closest competitor turned out to be George Weah, a candidate from the Congress for Democratic Change (CDC), a party he had newly formed.

The party system in Liberia is weak and based more upon individual personalities; ideological differences do not appear salient (Thomas & Adams, 2010). Parties do divide, however, on the basis of region and member backgrounds (Sawyer, 2008). According to Harris, Liberians tended not to show partisan loyalty in 2005:

> In a continent where ethno-regional issues often play out strongly in party politics, and the electorate in a certain area can, to a large extent, be relied on to vote for one party across the board, Liberians showed little loyalty to any of the parties. The result was a patchwork of party victories in the Senate and House of Representatives across the 15 counties, which, further, did not even follow the nodes of popularity of the presidential candidates. (Harris, 2006, p. 377)

In the 1997 elections, the electorate could not legally vote for different parties for various offices. The 2005 rules allowed them to split their tickets. Therefore, Johnson Sirleaf benefited from the relatively open electoral environment absent an incumbent and rebel force opposition, as well as the more auspicious electoral rules. At the same time, these same conditions could have been used to the advantage of other candidates. Why did circumstances most advantage Johnson Sirleaf?

Political Instability and the Successful Utilization in the Gender Stereotypes

Repeatedly noted, Liberia experienced political instability for decades leading to Johnson Sirleaf's rise to power. This provided avenues for marginalized actors, including women, to enter the political fold, including executive offices (Jalalzai, 2008). Consistent with traditional gender roles such as motherhood, women may be looked to as unifiers in the aftermath of conflict. Though these gender stereotypes generally confine women, women can sometimes exploit these same ideologies for promotions to power (Tripp, Casmiro, Kwesiga, & Mungwa, 2009). Referred to by many in her country as "Ma Ellen," Liberians indeed expected Johnson Sirleaf to rebuild this war-torn nation and unify its people (BBC News, 2005). Her success relied on using a careful combination of gender stereotypes. Her education and experience in high-profile positions in both the private and public sector provided validation that she could exercise traditional masculine traits and revealed expertise on what were viewed as male issues (Adams, 2010, p. 161). Purposely utilizing the label "Iron Lady," she strove to be seen as tough enough to challenge the male leaders responsible for war and corruption (Adams, 2010). Media coverage often reinforced her masculine qualities (Thomas & Adams, 2010). At the same time, she repeatedly suggested that her feminine attributes qualified her for the presidency at that particular time. According to Adams (2010):

> Sirleaf's campaign implicitly argued that as a woman—and a mother—she would bring feminine leadership qualities, such as warmth and compassion, to the presidency. After years of corruption, mismanagement, and violence associated with Liberia's previous male leaders, Sirleaf's commitment to

create a government that was more honest, open, and responsive to constituents resonated with Liberians. (p. 162)

Johnson Sirleaf, like women leaders in Latin America and Asia, capitalized on public views that women held advantages over men in possessing different traits such as honesty and compassion. Devastated by years of mismanagement and brutality, her message gained traction with voters; "Ma Ellen" could be trusted and would bring the Liberian family together. Though she campaigned on a myriad of issues, she paid close attention to ones the public typically consider women's strengths, including education and children's policies, as well as peace (Thomas & Adams, 2010).

WOMEN'S ACTIVISM

Women's activism in Liberia proved to be a very strong force in the removal of Charles Taylor and the subsequent peace reconciliation. According to Jacqui Bauer (2009), women's groups maintained high levels of activity at the same time other organizations significantly diminished their involvement. Women played peace-building roles throughout Liberian history and benefited from the fact that some women accumulated experience in leadership. Perhaps most strikingly, women activists united for the first time *across* class, ethnic, and religious differences. They helped create the opening of space, seizing new opportunities resulting from the destruction of existing social and political institutions (Bauer, 2009), affording them the necessary autonomy to take on women's issues. This freedom previously proved unavailable to women's organizations (Adams, 2008).

Women's organizations influenced the electoral commission to encourage parties to have women comprise 30% of their candidates (Sawyer, 2008). These groups also held women voter registration drives. The sharp rise of the female electorate in 2005 may have contributed directly to Johnson Sirleaf's victory (Adams, 2008, p. 482). Literate women provided the greatest support of her candidacy among all subgroups (National Elections Commission, 2005). Of course, this support could not have existed absent enthusiasm for the strong qualities Johnson Sirleaf possessed.

CANDIDATE STRENGTHS AND WEAKNESSES

While I depicted garnering a majority vote as a difficult proposition for women, one of the possible benefits of Liberia's presidential voting system is the utilization of runoff elections in the absence of a majority winner. Given the multiparty nature of Liberian contests in the lead up to the 2005 election, the likelihood of a plurality winner appeared strong, and almost certain, considering 22 candidates vied for the presidency. Therefore, Johnson Sirleaf did not have need to obtain a majority. In fact, she trailed behind former soccer star George Weah. Weah obtained 28.9% of the vote; Johnson Sirleaf gained 19.8%, enough to reach the next round of voting.

Weah's candidacy obviously resonated with a large portion of the electorate. What were his strengths and weaknesses in comparison to Johnson Sirleaf's, and how do these relate to the particular context? Weah convincingly constructed an outsider image, since he held no prior political positions and did not play a part in any of the previous presidential administrations. Since the public witnessed corrupt and heavy-handed leadership for so long, this could be an important asset, given the public's desire for change (Harris, 2006). His outsider status stood in sharp contrast to Johnson Sirleaf, who gained criticism for her previous support of warlord Charles Taylor. Weah spent most of his time outside the country in his capacity as an international soccer player and was absent during the civil war.[8] As proof of his contrast to the typical political elites, he claimed his lack of education made him more similar to his constituents (Sawyer, 2008). This message appealed especially to younger voters, who generally lacked educational opportunities. Weah, therefore, appeared more relatable.

At the same time, Weah's inexperience provided critical vulnerabilities. How could he be expected to rebuild a war-torn country absent political experience? He also largely ran a disorganized campaign, and reports speculate that he spent funds irresponsibly (Harris, 2006). Given her economic experience, political savvy, and international support, Johnson Sirleaf could still represent enough of a change candidate at the same time she seemed up to the many challenges in rebuilding Liberia. As stated, Johnson Sirleaf carefully crafted an image boasting her experience while being a unifying force at a critical time in Liberia's democratic transition.

2005 SECOND ROUND ELECTION RESULTS

Had the Liberian presidential voting system not required a majority vote winner, Weah would have been installed as president. While she trailed behind Weah in the first round, Johnson Sirleaf performed well enough to inspire others of her electability. In this way, the executive selection processes benefited Johnson Sirleaf in her presidential pursuits. Still, we cannot underestimate the importance of political instability, her successful use of gendered stereotypes carefully balancing feminine and masculine traits and issues, the openness of the field, the support of a woman's movement, and weaknesses of opponents. With this in mind, we may understand why Johnson Sirleaf won with 59% of the second vote to Weah's 41% (National Elections Commission, 2005).

JOHNSON SIRLEAF'S VICTORY IN RELATION TO OTHER AFRICAN WOMEN'S PRESIDENTIAL CANDIDACIES

To truly appreciate the historic nature of Johnson Sirleaf's victory, I must note the difficulties women faced in attaining presidential offices in Africa (see also Adams, 2008). All previous African women executives held prime ministerships—*not* presidencies (Jalalzai, 2010). The presidency appears both ubiquitous and dominant in Africa. Prime ministerial powers do not rival the presidents who often may unilaterally appoint and dismiss them. Did women fail to enter the presidency because they tend not to compete? To date, at least 38 women in 25 African countries have sought the presidency; only Johnson Sirleaf stands victorious.[9] Women's failure to break the executive glass ceiling in Africa stems not from a complete lack of trying. Election results indicate that no women apart from Johnson Sirleaf placed anywhere near the top among presidential candidates. At least 10 candidates run in nearly all African presidential elections. Twenty or 30 people may even face off in the first round. Women do not perform well in these elections, regularly receiving less than 1% of the vote. Not only do African women presidential candidates lose—they do not even come close to victory. It is unclear whether their lack of viability derives from their gender. Still, Johnson Sirleaf's successful presidential bid appears anomalous and unlikely to be repeated anytime soon.

CHALLENGES AND SUCCESSES

Liberia faced multiple obstacles as Johnson Sirleaf embarked on her presidency. Years of war demolished Liberia's already fragile infrastructure. The entire power grid was destroyed. Less than 15% of the population enjoyed access to running water. Roads were in disrepair (Foster & Pushak, 2011). Johnson Sirleaf's advancements appear mixed, but mostly positive on balance. Approximately 60% of the roads appear to be in good condition, though this falls below benchmarks set by the World Bank (Foster & Pushak, 2011). While only small portions have running water, 76% utilize water from wells or boreholes (Foster and Pushak, 2011). Power is still only accessible to about 3% of Liberians through government-restored lines while others utilize generators (Foster & Pushak, 2011). Reestablished lines are prone to outages.

Johnson Sirleaf unveiled Liberia's Poverty Reduction Strategy (PRS) when she took office, outlining the government's vision and plan for spurring economic growth in her first three years. The International Monetary Fund (IMF) assisted Liberia in plan development. The IMF released two of its annual reports assessing the extent to which Liberia met its goals. By the end of the first year, Liberia realized only about 21% of its objectives (IMF, 2010). While certainly leaving room for improvement, given the dismal position of Liberia, results generally seemed encouraging. The successes of the second year far surpassed those of the first. Infrastructure advances including the building of roads and bridges gained accolades. Health facilities and schools also expanded (IMF, 2011). Her administration implemented free and compulsory education. Overall, the goal completion rate increased to 80%. The IMF specifically credited these positive developments to Johnson Sirleaf and her government.

Liberia's economic circumstances appear more promising. Its economy is enjoying modest growth, and the IMF anticipates strong advances in gross domestic product through 2012. Its inflation rate in 2010 was about 7% (U.S. Department of State, 2012). Average real income has increased by 13%. A major victory is the erasing of its $4.6 billion in foreign debt (Nossiter, 2011). The country may now borrow again for much-needed development projects. Service industries are rapidly growing. Implementation of a tax system is beginning to provide the country with revenue (IMF, 2010). When she took power, the annual budget for the country was $80 million; today it is $516 million (Allen, 2011). Although still quite small, it clearly increased dramatically.

Liberia is now benefiting from $13 billion in foreign investment. Projects include the Chinese-funded Bong Mines (China Union) and iron ore exploration (Arcelor Mittal). American-based Chevron also is trying to see if the coast may supply oil. China provides Liberia an estimated 20 million dollars in aid (Tran, 2011). The future of these types of ventures and the extent that the Liberian people profit, of course, appears uncertain.

Though its economy is on the mend, unemployment remains a major problem; a staggering 85% of the population is unemployed (Foster & Pushak, 2011). Life expectancy is only 57. Its ranking in the United Nations Human Development is near the bottom, placed 182 out of 187 countries. Though Johnson Sirleaf's administration has constructed more than 250 schools, on average, Liberians complete only four years of education (UNDP, 2011).[10]

Beyond the economy, issues of security and corruption appear salient. Critics claim that Johnson Sirleaf does not take the issue of corruption very seriously. Upon election, she promised to take a zero tolerance stance on corruption. However, she needed legislative support to undertake some of her antipoverty measures. By pushing more anticorruption legislation during this broader reform, she faced disapproval from some legislators (Mahtani, 2010). After the president established Liberia's Truth and Reconciliation, it listed her as one of the 50 officials that should be barred from holding public office for 30 years. This was in response to her previous support of Charles Taylor (Clarke & Schmall, 2011). Mahtani argues that corruption has plagued Liberia since its inception:

When the families of freed American slaves who returned to the continent to found Liberia in the 19th century failed to establish coherent governance, politics took its cues from other influences: the shady freemasonic lodges of the Americo-Liberian settlers and indigenous secret societies. Patronage and connections took precedence over procedure. And although those elite families saw their hegemony crumble when Samuel Doe seized power in 1980 in the wake of food riots, the old habits persisted and grew. Taylor's rebellion ousted Doe, and in so doing destroyed much of the remaining fabric of Liberia's government institutions. Then, Taylor's presidency became a case study in kleptocracy and warlordism. By political necessity, the transitional government that followed, preceding Sirleaf's administration, was made up by many of those who made money during the Doe and Taylor years. Even some members of Sirleaf's government retains shady figures from the past. (2010, p. 1)

During her first term, Johnson Sirleaf dismissed several members of her cabinet amid allegations that they had embezzled millions of development dollars. Others, like her justice minister, were sacked because of their perceived light stances on corruption cases. While the president has fired some corrupt officials, she retained others. After she removed her public works minister for mishandling government contracts, she appointed him as a presidential advisor (Mahtani, 2010). In contrast, she fired her auditor general, claiming he went too far in trying to crack down on corruption (Clarke & Schmall, 2011). Saying she did not know if she could actually trust *anyone*, she selected several members of her family, including her son, to fill important posts, leading to further criticisms. She appointed many elite Liberian families to a slew of bureaucratic positions. While the operating budget has increased, nearly half of it is spent on salaries rather than critical projects.

The issue of corruption played a major role in her reelection campaign and is generally seen as a potential vulnerability. As she embarked on her second term, she promised to make fighting corruption her priority. She is calling upon the legislature to develop a code of conduct for office holders (Nyenon, 2011). The head of Liberia's anticorruption commission still does not possess direct powers to prosecute public officials misusing governmental funds (Stearns, 2011). Corruption bears directly on Liberia's economy. International investors may be skeptical of funding the country if funds are misused. U.S. Secretary of State Hillary Clinton notified Johnson Sirleaf that unless she begins to better control corruption, the nation's growth prospects remain compromised (AFP News Agency, 2012).

Security also continues to pose a major threat to Liberia. Violent crime remains rampant (Parley, 2011). While Johnson Sirleaf can be credited with maintaining a state of general peace, sexual assault is escalating. Child victims are on the rise, many younger than 5 years old (Clarke & Schmall, 2011). Johnson Sirleaf helped establish the sexual and gender-based violent crimes unit in the Justice Ministry in 2009 to focus exclusively on gendered crimes. Only seven trials were conducted by 2011, with four resulting in convictions (Amnesty International, 2011). Few rapists are brought to justice. Police forces and the judiciary appear ineffective and corrupt. The police may sometimes be complicit in the abuse of women bringing charges forward (Clarke & Schmall, 2011). Finally, instability in Cote d'Ivoire poses security challenges for Liberia's border (Parley, 2011). The United Nations still has 8,000 peacekeeping troops stationed there. Some critics threatened violence if she gained reelection (Clarke & Schmall, 2011). Once again, we

216 • Farida Jalalzai

can link economic ties to security; widespread unemployment presents a security threat.

Johnson Sirleaf must be credited with the positive role she plays in Liberia's economic recovery and maintaining peace. She entered the presidency during a critical period of transition for the country and faced many difficult challenges. She accomplished a great deal, but more work remains. Though Liberia is experiencing economic growth, little of this has actually been passed on to most of the general public who continue to face abject poverty and some of the highest rates of unemployment worldwide. If this does not change, Liberia's prospects for peace remain dubious. Unquestionably, democratic stability remains elusive without greater transparency.

JOHNSON SIRLEAF'S REELECTION

Johnson Sirleaf pledged to be a one-term president, but she claimed she needed more time to finish the job she started (Mahtani, 2010). One of her reelection campaign slogans was "when the plane hasn't landed yet, don't change the pilots" (BBC News, 2011). Some viewed this broken promise as evidence of an abuse of power. She competed against 15 other candidates, including George Weah and Prince Y. Johnson, former rebel leader and head of the Independent National Patriotic Front of Liberia. Her closest competitor, however, turned out to be Winston Tubman, the nephew of William Tubman, the former president who held power for nearly 30 years. Winston Tubman ran in the 2005 election and previously held the justice portfolio under Samuel Doe (Schmall, 2011).

In the midst of the campaign that October, Johnson Sirleaf, along with fellow Liberian activist Leymah Gbowee, won the 2011 Nobel Peace Prize. While this event certainly did not completely suppress criticisms, it made it more difficult to consider her presidency a failure, as her opponents argued. Tubman called the prize undeserved and said it was given to her as a means by outside forces to ensure victory. Most do believe that Johnson Sirleaf's electoral chances increased after the prize announcement (Schmall, 2011). During the first round, Johnson Sirleaf won 44% of the vote, while Tubman amassed 33%, triggering a runoff election to be held in November. Still, it is quite unlikely that it dramatically altered results.

While both Johnson Sirleaf's accomplishments and work remaining were outlined previously, it is worth noting that despite tremendous gains, most Liberians continued to live in poverty. A segment of the population, therefore, was responsive to Tubman's appeals. Many agreed she had not been serious enough about corruption. In response, Johnson Sirleaf repeatedly noted that her first term was about restoring basic services and tackling the fundamentals. The job, however, was not yet done.

Going into the runoff, opposition forces called into question the transparency of the first round of the elections. As a result, Tubman called for an election boycott. International observers including the Carter Center reported that these claims were unsubstantiated, purporting election results as free and fair (Schmall, 2011). Most felt the boycott initiation represented a desperate attempt to call into question Johnson Sirleaf's reelection; it is very unlikely Tubman would have won had he not withdrawn (Schmall, 2011). The day before the runoff, police killed two CDC supporters they clashed with at a Tubman demonstration. Tubman believed this to be a botched assassination attempt against him (Newstime Africa, 2011). While Johnson Sirleaf claimed an overwhelming victory of 91%, voter turnout appeared quite low (Election Watch, 2012). Still, she secured a second term, a necessary condition for her to finish the job she started.

REPRESENTATION OF WOMEN

Having completed her first term, it is possible to evaluate the extent to which Johnson Sirleaf actively promotes women's representation. Scholars consider various types of representation that women may achieve including descriptive, substantive, and symbolic representation (Pitkin, 1967). Descriptive representation relates to the extent to which representatives possess the same physical or social characteristics of their constituencies and have shared experiences (Mansbridge, 1999). Women's descriptive representation is simply a by-product of women executives' ascensions rather than through specific actions taken in their offices. In contrast, substantive representation considers whether women leaders act more on behalf of women's interests. Finally, symbolic representation involves emotional responses, especially when constituencies believe their representatives will credibly represent their interests. Women constituents may sense that female national leaders better account for their interests, increasing women's levels of political participation, trust, interest, and engagement. Examining these three related but distinct modes, to what extent does Johnson Sirleaf represent women?

When she first came to the presidency, Johnson Sirleaf acknowledged a desire to appoint a large number of women to her cabinet. She recognized, however, a paucity of qualified women. She appointed five women to her 21-person cabinet. Women, therefore, comprised 24%, or nearly a quarter of her cabinet. Though this is not gender parity, women did occupy some prestigious portfolios including Finance, Justice, and Commerce.[11] Later during her first term, her female commerce minister became the foreign affairs minister, and she also appointed a woman to the agricultural portfolio. She generally tended to name reform-oriented women to positions.

Upon reelection, she appointed six female cabinet ministers; they hold the following portfolios: Justice, Agriculture, Commerce, Gender and Development, Education, and Labor.[12] Some were holdovers from the latter part of her first term.[13] Women, therefore, comprise 32% of her current cabinet. Rather than concluding that she is even more committed to cabinet gender parity, this increase is due to a slight reduction in ministries between her terms.[14] Also, apart from the justice minister, women tend to hold less prestigious and more feminine positions. Yet, beyond the cabinet, she promoted women to key positions in the military and the police. She set a target of 20% of both institutions to be made up of women, which was met by 2009 (Bauer, 2011, p. 101). She also appointed a female police chief. She selected two female justices for the five-member Supreme Court (Bauer, 2011). Together, these findings suggest that Johnson Sirleaf is indeed committed to advancing women in her cabinet and in other high-profile positions. While some occupy more "feminine" positions, others led what are considered more masculine ones, largely suggesting a positive development for women in Liberia.[15] As such, Johnson Sirleaf furthers women's descriptive representation and possibly aids their substantive and symbolic representation through these appointments.

Another way of assessing Johnson Sirleaf's advancement of women is through particular policies she initiated and supported. As stated, she constructed the sexual and gender-based violent crimes unit in the Justice Ministry in 2009 to focus exclusively on gendered crimes. She established the Market Women's Fund, which promotes literacy and helps women traders obtain micro credit.[16] Many of her educational initiatives focus on girls and women. She continually highlights the need to pay close attention to girls:

> It will be to Liberia's benefit when our women are educated and contribute as equal partners in government and in the private sector. We know that investing in girls and women yields the most dividends in any country's development . . . it benefits the entire community because when you improve a girl's life, she can help her parents, her siblings and especially her own family when she is prepared to have one. (Williams, 2012)

By 2011, Liberia's GDI increased to .671.[17] The Nobel Peace Prize recognized the work she conducted on behalf of women's rights (Cowell, Kasinof, & Nossiter, 2011).

Johnson Sirleaf is also a very outspoken proponent of women's representation through her rhetoric. She does not shy away from questions relating to her concern for women. Moreover, she campaigned specifically on behalf of women's rights and appealed to women voters. As president, she repeatedly gives special consideration to the role of girls and women in the rebuilding of Liberia.

Johnson Sirleaf's example provides a powerful role model for girls and women, directly challenging the notion that politics is a men's only club. According to Johnson Sirleaf: "I have led the way for moving women from traditional roles to strategic positions and inspired girls and women throughout Africa to seek leadership positions" (Harris, 2010). Says Liberian activist and founder of the Liberian Women's Initiative, Etweda "Sugars" Cooper, because of the presidency of Johnson Sirleaf:

> There's a sense of pride among women that, "I can do this!" It's helped build confidence in themselves. And there are many projects and opportunities going on for women. There are more women in government today and more women employed in the private sector. The gender agenda is being pursued. And the mere fact that we have freedom of expression and freedom of movement, that we're not being harassed by security services, that makes it very different from the past. You can talk about rape now and not be stigmatized and justice is being pursued. (Costello, 2011)

━━━━━━━━

LEADERSHIP STYLE

We may also evaluate the extent to which Johnson Sirleaf's leadership style is gendered. Feminine styles of leadership tend to highlight collaboration, negotiation, and generally a consensual approach while hierarchical, top-down leadership characterizes masculine modes. Johnson Sirleaf utilizes a blending of gendered styles. Ayesha Kajee, former researcher at the South African Institute of International Affairs, noted that Johnson Sirleaf combined traditional feminine and masculine leadership styles encompassing:

> the traditional strength of will, ambition and determination associated with African leaders, which will prevent her being abused by the old boys' club because she can fight most battles on equal terms with them, and also the nurturing, reconciliatory and healing qualities that her shattered nation requires to rebuild the national spirit and collective human dignity. (in Gutiérrez, 2008)

Many of Johnson Sirleaf's remarks confirm this leadership strategy: "I'm a mother, so there's a certain sensitivity that I bring to the job, a certain caring and sharing that I'm able to balance with the need for hard decisions and courage. . . . Where we have seen women leaders, they have been strong, honest and effective. They have all left something behind that they and their people can be proud of" (McClanahan, 2011).

She is regularly referred to as having nerves of steel and as being Liberia's "Iron Lady" (ANP/AFP, 2012). This is all at the same time she is affectionately known as "Ma Ellen." While women often are depicted as weak, they routinely play strong roles within the family as mothers. Johnson Sirleaf's presidency suggests that a woman can successfully blend traditional feminine expectations for caring, compassion, and honesty with strength of leadership. In this way, she broadens understanding of gendered performance, complicating the simple binaries between the feminine and masculine. Given the needs of the Liberian people, it makes sense that Johnson Sirleaf could bring strength, understanding, and build peace. While it is still too early to offer any definitive conclusions about her performance, given the monumental tasks she confronted, her presidency appears to largely be a success.

CONCLUSIONS

Ellen Johnson Sirleaf remains the only female elected president of an African nation to date. Unlike many female presidents around the world, she lacks family ties to a former president or opposition leader. We can explain her victory by the absence of an entrenched incumbent, political instability; her blending of both traditional feminine and masculine traits and expertise in the aftermath of civil war; the strong support of a women's peace movement; and the lack of partisan loyalty among voters. She also boasted experience in both the political and financial sectors. To gain re-election, she successfully argued that she faced monumental tasks during her first term, and while she instituted a number of improvements, she needed more time to finish the job. As such, she convincingly highlighted the riskiness of changing direction.

Johnson Sirleaf's leadership style is a blend of strength and compassion. She has strong will as well as a commitment to furthering the betterment of the Liberian people. She is especially dedicated to increasing the status of women and girls, and this is evident in her rhetoric, governmental appointments, and policy initiatives. To date, she has improved various services, the economic picture, and maintained peace. Still, she faces challenges in combating corruption, promoting security, and eradicating poverty. Her full impact remains to be seen, but it is conceivable that her presidency sends important cues to the country and the world that politics is not just a man's game. Overall, Johnson Sirleaf appears to further women's descriptive, substantive, and symbolic representation.

NOTES

1 Less than 5% of Liberians descend from America (BBC News, 2012).
2 This measure is from the United Nations Development Index from the 2009 Human Development Report that assesses women's levels of poverty, education, and life expectancy rates in relation to men's (coded from 0 to 1, 1 indicating perfect parity); http://hdr.undp.org/en/media/HDR_2009_EN_Table_J.pdf. The ability of Johnson Sirleaf to gain the presidency confirms other research failing to establish a positive connection between women's general socioeconomic status and political representation (Matland, 1998; Moore & Shackman, 1996).
3 Data is from October 2005, InterParliamentary Union. http://www.ipu.org/wmn-e/arc/classif311005.htm

4   Women's cabinet presence is difficult to assess, given the lack of historical data available for Liberia. The Electoral Commission tried to persuade parties to have at least 30% of their candidates comprised of women but met little success (Thomas & Adams, 2010).

5   Women are beginning to gain ground absent family ties in Latin America as of late. Two examples include Laura Chinchilla of Costa Rica and Dilma Rousseff of Brazil.

6   For example, Michelle Bachelet (Chile), Tarja Halonen (Finland), and Angela Merkel (Germany) are divorced.

7   Johnson Sirleaf resigned from the interim government in 2004, since members could not be presidential candidates.

8   He played for different teams over his career, including Manchester United.

9   Author analysis of a variety of websites, including African Elections and The International Foundation for Electoral Systems Election Guide, AfricanElections, http://africanelections.tripod.com/cf.html#1993_Presidential_Election; The International Foundation for Electoral Systems, http://www.electionguide.org/results.php?ID=870 Election Guide. I exclude Jacqueline Lohouès-Oblé's 2010 candidacy in Cote d'Ivoire because elections were repeatedly pushed back. Countries featuring women presidential candidates include Algeria, Angola, Benin (two), Burkina Faso, Central African Republic, Congo-Brazzaville, Cote d'Ivoire Democratic Republic of the Congo (five), Gabon (three), Guinea-Bissau (two), Kenya (two), Liberia (two including Johnson-Sirleaf), Madagascar, Malawi, Mauritania, Nigeria (three), Rwanda, Sao Tome and Principe, Senegal, Sierra Leone (two), Sudan, Tanzania, Togo, Uganda, Yemen, Zambia. Other women were scheduled to run in presidential elections after I conducted this count. All women candidates running in Burundi and Rwanda, however, lost their bids, and presidential elections in Angola were postponed.

10 UNDP, "Liberia: Country Profile-Human Development Indicators," United Nations Development Programme, 2011, http://hdrstats.undp.org/en/countries/profiles/LBR.html.

11 Other female appointments included Minister of Gender and Development and Youth and Sports.

12 Cabinet data is from Carter 2012 and Executive Mansion of Liberia website: http://www.emansion.gov.lr/index.php.

13 Some head the same ministries, and others shuffled to other cabinet positions.

14 The rural development ministry is currently defunct, and there is no information on the new appointee to the Ministry of Planning and Economic Affairs; the previous minister, Amara M. Konneh, moved to Finance though he is still listed as the current minister of this department on the President of Liberia website (last updated April 5, 2012). This reduces the total number of cabinet appointees at the start of Johnson Sirleaf's first and second terms from 21 to 19, respectively.

15 While it is difficult to obtain older data on Liberian cabinets, the few lists of cabinets suggested that women rarely held cabinet appointments.

16 Ellen Johnson Sirleaf Women's Micro Credit Fund Website: http://www.smwf.org/#

17 United National Human Development Report 2012; http://hdrstats.undp.org/en/countries/profiles/LBR.html.

REFERENCES

Adams, M. (2008). Women's executive leadership in Africa: Ellen Johnson Sirleaf and broader patterns of change. *Politics & Gender*, 4(3), 475–485.

Adams, M. (2010). Ma Ellen: Liberia's Iron Lady? In R. Murray (Ed.), *Cracking the highest glass ceiling: A global comparison of women's campaigns for executive office*. Santa Barbara, CA: Praeger.

AFP News Agency. (2012, January 16). Clinton says Liberian corruption a stumbling block. http://www.google.com/hostednews/afp/article/ALeqM5jtYKEuIgqyU5exL0MAtQ MFZFtFOw?docId=CNG.f4017fd8fc0fc29b1e449bac606e4e13.211.

Allen, B. (2011, September 30). Ellen Johnson Sirleaf—"Ma Ellen"—and her Liberian presidential re-election bid. *PRI the World*. http://www.theworld.org/2011/09/ ellen-johnson-sirleaf-ma-ellen-liberian-presidential-re-election.

Amnesty International. (2011). Liberia. *Amnesty International Report 2011: The state of the world's human rights*. London: Amnesty International. http://www.amnesty.org/en/ region/liberia/report-2011.

ANP/AFP. (2012, January 16). Liberia: Sirleaf—Women's icon with nerves of steel. *Radio Netherlands Worldwide*. http://allafrica.com/stories/201201162179.html.

Bauer, G. (2011). Sub-Saharan Africa. In G. Bauer and M. Tremblay (Eds.), *Women in executive power*. London: Routledge.

Bauer, J. (2009). Women and the 2005 election in Liberia. *Journal of Modern African Studies, 47*(2), 193–211.

BBC News. (2005, November 23). Profile: Liberia's "Iron Lady." http://news.bbc.co.uk/2/hi/ africa/4395978.stm.

BBC News. (2011, October 7). Profile: Liberia's Ellen Johnson Sirleaf. http://www.bbc.co.uk/ news/world-africa-15212382.

BBC News. (2012, January 12). Liberia Profile. http://www.bbc.co.uk/news/world-africa-13729504.

Bekoe, D., & C. Parajon. (2007, May). *Women's role in Liberia's reconstruction*. United States Institute of Peace. http://www.usip.org/publications/women-s-role-liberia-s-reconstruction.

Carter, J. B. (2012, February 11). Blamo Nelson, Lewis Brown, 12 others confirmed. *Daily Observer*. http://www.liberianobserver.com/index.php/news/item/441-blamo-nelson-lewis-brown-12-others-confirmed.

CBC News Online. (2006, March 28). Ellen Johnson Sirleaf: Liberia's "Iron Lady." http:// www.cbc.ca/news/background/liberia/sirleaf.html.

Clarke, P., & E. Schmall. (2011, October 2). Fighting for survival. *Newsweek*. http://www. thedailybeast.com/newsweek/2011/10/02/liberia-s-election-hard-times-for-ellen-johnson-sirleaf.html.

Costello, A. (2011, October 18). What has Ellen Johnson Sirleaf done for Liberian women? *PBS*. http://www.pbs.org/wnet/women-war-and-peace/features/what-has-ellen-johnson-sirleaf-done-for-liberian-women.

Cowell, A., L. Kasinof, & A. Nossiter. (2011, October 7). Nobel Peace Prize awarded to three activist women. *New York Times*. http://www.nytimes.com/2011/10/08/world/nobel-peace-prize-johnson-sirleaf-gbowee-karman.html?pagewanted=all.

Election Watch. (2012). Election results (September–December 2011). *Journal of Democracy, 23*(1), 176–181. doi: 10.1353/jod.2012.0012.

Executive Mansion of Liberia. http://www.emansion.gov.lr/index.php.

Foster, V., & N. Pushak. (2011). Liberia's infrastructure: A continental perspective. *Policy Research Working Paper 5597*. The World Bank.

Gutiérrez, M. (2008, January 9). Is there a gender-specific leadership style? *Inter Press Service News Agency*. http://ipsnews.net/news.asp?idnews=40726.

Harris, D. (1999). From "warlord" to "democratic" president: How Charles Taylor won the 1997 Liberian elections. *Journal of Modern African Studies, 37*(3), 431–455.

Harris, D. (2006). Liberia 2005: An unusual African post-conflict election. *Journal of Modern African Studies, 44*(3), 375–395.

Harris, L. (2010, November 1). Female heads of state: The chosen ones. *Glamour.* http://www.glamour.com/women-of-the-year/2010/female-heads-of-state.

International Foundation for Electoral Systems. Election guide. http://www.electionguide.org/results.php?ID=870.

International Monetary Fund. (2010, October). Liberia: Poverty reduction strategy—progress report. http://www.imf.org/external/pubs/ft/scr/2010/cr10194.pdf.

International Monetary Fund. (2011, July). Liberia: Poverty reduction strategy paper—second annual progress report, 2009–10. http://www.imf.org/external/pubs/ft/scr/2011/cr11214.pdf.

InterParliamentary Union. http://www.ipu.org/wmn-e/arc/classif311005.htm.

Jackson-Laufer, G.M. (1999). *Women rulers throughout the ages: An illustrated guide.* Santa Barbara, CA: ABC-CLIO.

Jalalzai, F. (2008). Women rule: Shattering the executive glass ceiling. *Politics & Gender, 4*(2), 1–27.

Jalalzai, F. (2010). Madam President: Gender, power, and the comparative presidency. *Journal of Women, Politics & Policy, 31*, 132–165.

Johnson Sirleaf, E. (2009). *This child will be great: Memoir of a remarkable life by Africa's first woman president.* New York: Harper Collins.

Kosciejew, M. (2012, January 26). Becoming Ellen Johnson-Sirleaf: The controversial political career of Africa's "Iron Lady." *Conflict, Economy, Governance, Politics, Women's Rights.* http://www.caaglop.com/robbenisland-blog/tag/ellen-johnson-sirleaf/.

Krook, M.L. (2009). *Quotas for women in politics: Gender and candidate selection reform worldwide.* New York: Oxford University Press.

Mahtani, D. (2010 May 28). Tarnishing the Iron Lady of Liberia. *Foreign Policy.* http://www.foreignpolicy.com/articles/2010/05/28/tarnishing_the_iron_lady_of_africa.

Mansbridge, J. (1999). Should blacks represent blacks and women represent women? A contingent "Yes." *Journal of Politics, 61*(3), 628–657.

Matland, R.E. (1998). Women's representation in national legislatures: Developed and developing countries. *Legislative Studies Quarterly, 23*(1), 109–125.

McClanahan, P. (2011, March 10). The NS interview: Ellen Johnson Sirleaf, president of Liberia. *The New Statesman.* http://www.newstatesman.com/africa/2011/03/interview-liberia-president.

Moore, G., & G. Shackman. (1996). Gender and authority: A cross national study. *Social Science Quarterly, 77*(2), 273–288.

Moran, M. (2008). *Liberia: The voices of democracy.* Philadelphia: University of Pennsylvania Press.

National Elections Commission. (2005, September 10). *2005 voter registration statistics.* http://www.necliberia.org/statistics-maps/dstatistics10september2005.pdf.

Newstime Africa. (2011, November 14). Despite the controversies, Ellen Johnson Sirleaf's re-election as president of Liberia is seen as a boon for women. *Newstime Africa.* http://www.newstimeafrica.com/archives/23290.

Nossiter, A. (2011, October 7). Prize or not: Liberian faces tough race to keep office. *New York Times.* http://www.nytimes.com/2011/10/08/world/africa/prize-or-not-liberian-faces-tough-race-to-keep-office.html?pagewanted=all.

Nyenon, T. (2011, December 14). Sirleaf blames corruption on legislature? *Independent Eye News.* http://indeye.org/?p=938.

Ohiorhenuan, J. (2007). The challenge of economic reform in post-conflict Liberia: The insider's perspective. *United Nations Development Report.* United Nations Development Programme. http://www.undp.org/cpr/content/economic_recovery/Background_5.pdf.

Parley, W.W. (2011, September 20). Liberia: Security tensions mount. *The New Dawn.* http://allafrica.com/stories/201109200826.html.

Pitkin, H. (1967). *The concept of representation.* Berkeley: University of California Press.

Reynolds, A. (1999). Women in the legislatures and executives of the world: Knocking at the highest glass ceiling. *World Politics, 51,* 547–572.

Salmond, Rob. (2006). Proportional representation and female parliamentarians. *Legislative Studies Quarterly, 31*(2), 175–204.

Sawyer, A. (2008). Emerging patterns in Liberia's post-conflict politics: Observations from the 2005 elections. *African Affairs, 107*(427), 177–199.

Schmall, E. (2011, November 10). Liberia's president wins boycotted runoff vote. *New York Times.* http://www.nytimes.com/2011/11/11/world/africa/liberias-president-ellen-johnson-sirleaf-wins-election.html.

Stearns, S. (2011, August 3). Corruption crackdown dominates Liberian presidential campaign. *Voice of America.* http://www.voanews.com/english/news/africa/west/Corruption-Crackdown-Dominates-Liberian-Presidential-Campaign-126668053.html.

Thomas, G., & M. Adams. (2010). Breaking the final glass ceiling: The influence of gender in the elections of Ellen Johnson Sirleaf and Michelle Bachelet. *Journal of Women, Politics & Policy, 31*(2), 105–131.

Tran, M. (2011, August 23). Poverty matters blog: Sirleaf on course to win a second term as president of renascent Liberia. *The Guardian.* http://www.guardian.co.uk/global-development/poverty-matters/2011/aug/23/sirleaf-second-term-president-liberia.

Tripp, A.M. (2001). The new political activism in Africa. *Journal of Democracy, 12*(3), 141–155.

Tripp, A.M., I. Casimiro, J. Kwesiga, & A. Mungwa. (2009). *African women's movements: Transforming political landscapes.* New York: Cambridge University Press.

United Nations Development Project. 2011. *Liberia: Country profile—human development indicators.* United Nations Development Programme. http://hdrstats.undp.org/en/countries/profiles/LBR.html.

United Nations Human Development Report. (2009). http://hdr.undp.org/en/media/HDR_2009_EN_Table_J.pdf.

United National Human Development Report. (2012). http://hdrstats.undp.org/en/countries/profiles/LBR.html.

U.S. Department of State. (2012, February 17). Background notes: Liberia. http://www.state.gov/r/pa/ei/bgn/6618.htm

Williams, W. (2012, February 13). Invest in girls education—says President Sirleaf, U.S. Ambassador Greenfield. *Front Page Africa.* http://frontpageafricaonline.com/index.php?option=com_content&view=article&id=2475:invest-in-girls-education-says-president-sirleaf-greenfield&catid=67:news&Itemid=14.

Women's Micro Credit Fund Website: http://www.smwf.org/#.

9

Angela Merkel

From Serendipity to Global Success

Janie S. Steckenrider

The chance of a Protestant, East German, divorced woman without children becoming chancellor of Germany in a political career of only 15 years by way of the political party billed as the party of the family and dominated by West German Catholic men falls into the "flying pigs" category. Yet this is exactly what Angela Merkel accomplished. Hers is a remarkable story of national leadership launched by serendipity but repeatedly advanced by her quick political learning, pragmatic negotiating skills, and an ability to capitalize on the missteps of others. Since her against-all-odds rise to be elected chancellor in 2005, Angela Merkel has successfully guided Germany into a thriving economic powerhouse and propelled herself into a leader on the world stage. Merkel is the *most powerful woman* in the world and, more important, is one of a handful of the *most powerful world leaders,* male or female.

When Merkel was elected chancellor of Germany, female heads of state were not unusual in Scandinavia or in Asia, where a number of women had been president or prime minister. But a woman leader was hardly common in the male-dominated political culture of Germany, where women had long been underrepresented in major political offices. How a dowdy female Ossi (a term characterizing the unsophisticated East Germans) whom many considered boring and provincial broke into the upper echelons of united Germany clearly raises the classic political question of who achieves power and under what conditions? Thompson and Lennartz (2007) attribute Merkel's political ascent to her ability to skillfully turn her "handicaps" of gender and origin into a political advantage. Given her early life and subsequent accomplishments, leadership scholars

Cronin and Genovese (2012) would characterize Merkel as a leader who was made, not born.

Angela Merkel was an apolitical physicist who became politically active in the dying days of East Germany, largely by happenstance. Shortly into her political career, Helmut Kohl, the first chancellor of a unified Germany, wanted a balance in his political appointments and was specifically searching for suitable former East Germans, for Protestants, and for women. This made Merkel especially desirable as a "three-fer" (Wiliarty, 2010). Merkel was additionally lucky because she possessed the political asset of not being tainted by any link to the Ministry of State Security (Stasi, the most feared and hated institution of the East German government). This was a problem for many East Germans, since more than 400,000 (1 in 25 adults) had worked for the heavy-handed security police (Wiliarty, 2010). Thus, Merkel began her political ascent as Kohl's youngest cabinet member, albeit in a position with virtually no independent standing, and was publicly referred to as "Mein Madchen" (my girl) by Kohl.

Merkel's rise to power and her exercise of leadership fit the model described by Cronin and Genovese (2012) in *Leadership Matters: Understanding the Power of Paradox*:

> We believe that the most effective leaders are synthesizing and integrative thinkers who resiliently adapt to the opportunities, luck and paradoxes that confront every venture. (p. ix)

While Merkel may have been nothing more than a weak minister under Kohl, she had a front row seat to the leadership and political skills adroitly exercised by the chancellor. Even today she is often described as taking the "Kohl wait and see" approach on political issues by letting all the political players line up before she takes a position. Ironically, it was her mentor Kohl's involvement in a major slush fund scandal that led Merkel to take charge of her own political fate by turning her back on Kohl and strategically maneuvering herself up the political ladder. In this pivotal career moment, Merkel demonstrated the criteria of effective leadership outlined by Cronin and Genovese, as she adapted to the opportunities and luck presented in her mentor's scandal.

The life story and political career of Angela Merkel is a tale of the ability to turn serendipity into a seat at the very small table of world leaders.

Merkel epitomizes what the first chancellor of Germany Otto Bismarck meant when he said, "Politics is the art of the possible."

THE PASTOR'S DAUGHTER

The most striking aspect of Angela Merkel's uneventful youth occurred in her first few weeks (Thompson & Lennartz, 2007). Angela Dorothea Kasner was born July 17, 1954, in Hamburg, West Germany, and moved with her family to East Germany when she was three months old. Her father, Horst Kasner, born in Berlin and a Lutheran pastor, moved to East Germany to take over a country church in Quitzow near his native Brandenburg. Her mother Herlind, unlike most East German women of the time, was a housewife who postponed working as an English and Latin teacher until her children were older. Angela has two younger siblings: brother Marcus and sister Irene.

Angela grew up in Templin, a rural area about 80 km north of Berlin, where her father was head of a seminary for the higher education of pastors. During her youth, the family freely traveled from East to West Germany and owned two cars. Both of these facts suggest that her father had a "sympathetic" relationship with the communist regime because such freedom and luxuries would have been impossible for a pastor and his family (Bond, 2011). Her father, a socialist idealist, was known as "the red Kasner" who left the West to take up a pastorate in East Germany out of a conviction he was more needed there. At one point, Horst was blackmailed to cooperate with the Stasi when it was discovered he possessed an article by Soviet dissident Andrei Sakharov. Angela's father refused and spared his family any involvement in this chapter of East German history. This prophetic decision by her father later became a political asset to Angela's political advancement (Thompson & Lennartz, 2007).

Merkel's apolitical childhood yields no indication she aspired to someday be chancellor of Germany. Identified early as a gifted student in math, science, and language, Angela got top marks in school and had no run-ins with school authorities. She was not active in East German government or in opposition to it. Like most students, Angela was a member of the official Socialist-led youth movement, Freie Deutsche Jugend (Free German Youth), but did not take part in the secular coming-of-age ceremony

Jugendwiehe that was common in East Germany. Interestingly, growing up as the daughter of a Protestant pastor did not lead Angela to become active in church-linked "peace prayers" or other religious-based activities.

Angela's father Horst was a pivotal influence in her life in numerous ways. His religious profession overshadowed her youth since it was not easy being the daughter of a pastor in the religion adverse Communist school system of the 1960s. In fact, having a pastor father in officially atheist East Germany made Angela feel that she had to be better than her peers just to have the opportunity to study at the university (Thompson & Lennartz, 2007). Even though she was close to her mother Herlind, Angela's relationship with her father was difficult, yet Horst was a strong influence and the moral authority in molding Angela. Horst was an outwardly cold father who seemed to prefer his parishioners to his family, prompting Angela to constantly struggle for his approval. She has publicly stated that the process of "cutting the umbilical cord" to Horst was particularly protracted and has argued it was her father's high expectations that fueled her later political ambitions (Thompson & Lennartz, 2007).

Angela began her studies in physics at University of Leipzig in 1973 and received her doctorate in 1978. Her dissertation, "The Calculation of Speed Constants of Elementary Reactions in Simple Carbohydrates," is certainly not the sort of expertise one would expect of a future chancellor. By her own admission, the choice of theoretical physics in itself was an indication of Merkel's apolitical orientation at the time. Angela claims she wanted to avoid a university subject involving state indoctrination and saw the natural sciences as a prestigious, nonideological subject with the greatest possible academic freedom. In fact, the only indication of any political activity during her university years was her weekly visit to a student group where politically sensitive subjects were often discussed. Angela, the student, was described by her colleague Michael Schindhilm as a young scientist without any illusions and in no hurry to complete her doctorate (Rueschemeyer, 2009; Thompson & Lennartz, 2007).

She went on to work at the Central Institute for Physical Chemistry at the Academy of Sciences in Berlin from 1978 to 1990. She learned to speak fluent Russian and published a number of research papers on chemistry and physics. Hinting at a budding political career, Angela became a member of the Freie Deutsche Jugend district board and secretary for Agitprop (Agitation and Propaganda) while at the Academy of Sciences.

Almost a footnote in Angela's life is her marriage, divorce, and re-marriage during her university and Academy of Sciences years. In 1977, Angela married physics student Ulrich Merkel, whom she divorced four years later. His description of the end of their marriage is quite telling of Angela's personality: "she seemed to have the conversation about leaving me only with herself" (Boyes, 2005). At the time of her divorce, Angela was completing her doctorate in physics and under the influence of scientist Joachim Sauer, a quantum chemist, whom she met in 1981 and privately married on December 30, 1998. Not a visible first husband, Sauer remains out of the media spotlight and has been compared to Denis Thatcher, but without the gin and charm (Thompson & Lennartz, 2007). Sauer has two adult sons, but Angela never had any children with either husband. Her lack of motherhood is a personal factor that had later political ramifications and was brought up as a campaign issue.

The key to the riddle of Frau Merkel is growing up in the former East German Communist state. The experiences of those years strongly imprint her current political leadership. Merkel has never publicly criticized her family's move to East Germany that so profoundly shaped her youth, yet she claims she inwardly rejected the East German system. Angela considered communist rule as inhumane and lacking in a future. Without showing it outwardly, she said she engaged in "inner immigration." Merkel has even gone so far as to say she was prepared to leave her parents and flee to the West, if it became necessary (Thompson & Lennartz, 2007).

Much of Merkel's approach to governing and her guiding political principles stem from her East German youth. For example, Merkel sees the individual, not the state, as the central actor in political and economic life. She openly states her experiences under totalitarianism made her value freedom and the responsibilities it entails. This impacts how she views the role of the state in the economy in relation to the people: "It is individuals who generate goods and ideologies and come into competition with one another. The role of politics is to manage competition to make it as efficient as possible while ensuring that the state is able to support the weakest" (Benoit, 2005). Merkel is conscious of the continuing East/West differences and notes that Western Europe "is too used to freedom and cannot imagine that it could ever be lost" (Dejevsky, 2005). She is generally laconic about her previous life in East Germany and tends only to hint at the complexities, but did say, "In the GDR, I was always a political animal. The system and state were perpetually at odds with themselves and common sense. The question was always how you could reconcile the two. There was this constant personal argument going on" (Dejevsky, 2005). Clearly, even though Merkel took an apolitical path to adulthood, there are significant political tenets and behaviors she learned in her East German childhood that guide how she carries out her leadership and how she governs today.

Almost every leader has a defining moment in her life that she recalls as forever impacting who she is, her philosophy, her values, and what she stands for. Merkel's career and life-changing event occurred in November 1989 when the Berlin Wall fell (Rueschemeyer, 2009). She was 35 years old and working as a research physicist in Berlin. It was the fall of the Wall that first prompted Merkel to become politically active, and within a month she joined Demokratischer Aufbruch (Democratic Awakening), one of the new pro-democratic political parties in East Germany (Wiliarty, 2010a.) The cataclysmic importance to Merkel of the fall of the Berlin Wall cannot be overstated. Years later as chancellor at a ceremony recognizing a Dane whose cartoon about Mohammad provoked Muslim protests and the presentation of an award for which Merkel received considerable criticism, Merkel said, "Freedom for me personally is the happiest experience of my life. Even 21 years after the Berlin Wall fell, the force of freedom stirs me more than anything else" (Engleman, 2010).

THE POLITICAL CONTEXT: THE WALL CAME DOWN BUT THE DIVIDE REMAINED

Angela Merkel rose to power in a political environment defined by the fall of the Berlin Wall and the ensuing conflict in unifying two very different German societies. The Wall that divided East and West Germany may have come down in November 1989, but the fundamentally different world approaches and the significant economic gap between the two regions remained. This created steep challenges for the new unified government and provided rare opportunities for Merkel to be in the right place at the right time with the right credentials as the new unified government was formed.

The differences between the West and East Germans were deeply entrenched. The Wessi (former citizens of West Germany) worldview was competitive, aggressive, and a product of the capitalistic society of West Germany. In direct contrast was the Ossi approach, described as passive, indolent, and the expected product of the security of living in a Communist regime. The Easterners resented the Westerners' arrogance and insensitivity, while the Westerners thought the Easterners were unsophisticated and unmotivated to actively address their major problems. The euphoria of the fall of the Berlin Wall and of the end of the 40-year communist system was tempered with an underlying resentment and a disillusionment toward re-unification by those on both sides of the Wall.

The political context of that time is key to setting things in motion for Merkel's political future. Helmut Kohl, the longest-serving German Chancellor since Bismarck, oversaw the unification efforts and was widely popular, but in 1998 things in Germany started to go amok and forced changes to the political landscape that ultimately benefited Merkel. The economy was faltering and unemployment was over 10% nationally and above 20% in former East Germany. In reaction, a number in the Christian Democratic Union party (CDU) wanted Kohl to step down, but he ran for reelection and his coalition was defeated. Kohl was replaced by Gerhard Schroder, the pragmatic leader of the Social Democratic Party (SPD), in a coalition with the Green Party. However, Schroder's government got off to a rocky start due to his indecisiveness, internal dissent within his party's left wing, and conflict in the coalition with the Green Party. The CDU, now out of government for the first time since 1982, also faced troubles within its inner structure. Party upheaval occurred in 1999 when a number of revelations about illegal campaign contributions to the CDU emerged and forced Kohl to resign his leadership post as head of the party. The following year in a reorganization effort, the Christian Democratic Union selected Angela Merkel as their Chair, making her the first East German and the first woman to lead a major political party in Germany.

The Schroder SPD-Green Party coalition government focused its efforts on reforming the German welfare system and on improving the economy. Their goals were to decrease welfare costs despite the increasing number of beneficiaries; to relieve businesses of high taxes and labor costs by encouraging them to move their plants overseas; and to decrease German reliance on nuclear power. By the 2002 election, the government's efforts to improve the economy had not succeeded. Economic growth was sluggish and high unemployment continued, especially in East Germany. Nonetheless, despite the German economic problems, Schroder won with a campaign focused on opposing U.S. policy toward Iraq. In his new term, Schroder attempted to build a consensus on his economic reforms, but the required sacrifices were not popular among the German people. The economy continued to worsen and Schroder called an early election for 2005. Merkel emerged from that election as the new Chancellor, making her the first woman and the first East German to be the leader of Germany. Her challenges ahead were immense. Merkel was elected at a time of the highest German unemployment since the Weimar Republic, the German economy was stagnant, and the country was on the verge of a recession (Dejevsky, 2005).

The political context surrounding Angela Merkel was also defined by the East/West differences that extended to gender roles. Women in East Germany were typically employed full-time and were mothers, accustomed to an extensive day care system (Wiliarty, 2010a). In many ways, they were far more feminist and egalitarian than the women in the West. Still, the women of the West were scornful of the "Muttis" (Mommies) of the East and considered them culturally backward (Ferree, 2006). Western women were more likely to delay childbirth longer than Eastern women and to be stay-at-home moms. Unification was not only about merging two governmental systems; the political parties had to bring together a large number of members and politicians with very different backgrounds and ideas on the role of women in society (Wiliarty, 2010a).

At the time Merkel's career rapidly advanced in unified Germany, women comprised a small segment of political leaders. In 1990 when she was elected to the first parliament of reunited Germany, women held 27% of the Social Democratic Party seats and 14% of the Christian Democratic Union seats. (Ironically, women made up 37% of the parliament in the former East Germany.) By the 2002 to 2005 legislative period, 38% of the SPD seats were female, and 23% of the CDU seats. Part of the improvement can be attributed to the introduction of the "zipper list" of alternating the list of male and female names on the party ticket (Ferree, 2010). When Merkel was elected Chancellor in 2005, women comprised a total of 32% of the Bundestag (the lower house of Parliament) and held 20% of the CDU seats and 36% of the SPD seats. Women also headed five of the 15 federal ministries, mostly in departments generally identified as dealing with "women's issues": Family, Senior Citizens, Women and Youth; Education and Research; Justice; Health; Economic Cooperation and Development (Rueschemeyer, 2009).

Angela Merkel entered a political environment newly focused on unifying the two very different cultures, world approaches, economies, and political systems of East and West Germany. The combination of her background and experience was a strong asset she brought to the transition and to face the economic and social challenges of a unified Germany. Merkel, the East German and pragmatic physicist, considered the initial euphoria surrounding unification as adverse to Germany's overall development and believed Germans were being too self-absorbed and myopic. Already politically visionary, Merkel thought time was being lost, as Germans were so carried away with the joy of unification that they lost sight of the need to compete beyond Germany (Dejevsky, 2005). Unlike most West Germans, Merkel had no romantic attachment to the German welfare state, the market economy, or its brand of capitalism. At the same time, from her East German roots Merkel knew what could happen if the transfer of power from the state to the individual is not achieved. She privately recounted how she watched the East German unsustainable economy and political system built over five decades collapse in months, and she vowed nothing similar would happen in unified Germany (Benoit, 2005). It is clear to see how her economic commitment and this political perspective continue to be the guiding principles of her leadership. Ultimately, the unlikely East German woman with the sensible hairdo and no-nonsense clothes was able to merge the differences of the East and West Germans and to strategically position a strong unified Germany as a global powerhouse.

THE PATH TO POWER: SERENDIPITY, PROVEN LEADERSHIP, AND BEING UNDERESTIMATED

Angela Merkel's remarkably rapid 15-year political advancement from working as a research scientist to becoming the first female Chancellor of Germany is explained by the confluence of three factors. First is the role of serendipity and fortuitous circumstances in her life. In this sense, Merkel's career is aligned with Machiavelli's discussion in Chapter XXV of *The Prince*, describing the role of Fortuna in assisting several great conquerors by creating the opportunity for success, but yet requiring the leader to take advantage of it. Repeatedly when a higher political position opened up,

Merkel uniquely possessed the rare combination of the sought-after set of credentials to make her the perfect, and often the only, political choice. In politics, however, merely obtaining a position is never enough to further one's political career. The politician has to possess the ability to carry out that job, not in just an adequate manner, but in extraordinary fashion. Merkel demonstrates this second significant factor of having outstanding leadership skills that she has consistently proven. She has made a success of every position along her path, starting as government spokesperson after the Berlin Wall fell to chairing the European Council and the G8. A colleague when she was Minister of Women and Youth said, "Angela could have been assigned to the Bat Ministry of the United Nations and she would have made something out of it" (Wiliarty, 2010a, p. 168). The third factor explaining Merkel's meteoric rise is the tendency of her political colleagues, mentors, and opponents to underestimate the talent and driven ambition of this reserved woman. Broad siding may be too strong a term, but Merkel definitely capitalized on the tendency of others to underestimate her, much to their eventual chagrin.

The first explanatory factor of serendipity was set in motion by the sudden and unexpected changes brought about by German reunification. Looking back, this is when, as Shakespeare put it, Merkel began to have "greatness thrust upon" her. In the wake of the fall of the Berlin Wall, Merkel joined the Demokratischer Aufbruch in what seems to be no more than a coincidental choice since Merkel claims her decision was largely intuitive and not based on any clearly defined political preference (Thompson & Lennartz, 2007). Merkel became more politicized during Wendezeit (the transition period leading to unification) as she took a leave of absence from her job at the Academy of Sciences to work full-time as the administrator for Demokrastischer Aufbruch, where her low-key style and modest manner often led her to be mistaken for a secretary. Merkel got her first high-ranking political position purely by coincidence when she next became Deputy Spokesperson of the new pre-unification government under Lothar de Maiziere (Wiliarty, 2010a). The party chair Wolfgang Schnur was kept from an appointment due to a double-booking mistake, so he spontaneously appointed Angela as vice spokesperson of the political party, to avoid aggravating the important waiting visitor likely to be disappointed with having to speak to a mere party administrator. However, despite holding a visible position, Merkel was not a powerful figure in the de Maiziere government. But serendipity stepped into her life again. This time it was only because Chief Government Spokesman

Matthias Gehler did not like flying and he sent Angela on the important foreign diplomatic trips that she developed a close relationship with de Maiziere, who called her "my Angela," foreshadowing her similar role with Kohl (Thompson & Lennartz, 2007).

Merkel joined the conservative Christian Democratic Union in 1990 and was elected to the Bundestag from the constituency that remains her electoral district today. A few months prior to being elected, Angela had met Chancellor Kohl at a CDU Conference in Hamburg, and after the federal election when he was looking for a young East German woman to be his Minister for Women and Youth to balance his new post-unification cabinet, he appointed Angela. There were other women who had a better chance to be appointed to the position, but again Merkel advanced due to serendipity and fortuitous circumstances. Cordula Schubert, who headed this same ministry in the de Maiziere government, did not win her seat in the Bundestag, and former Volkshammer President Sabine Bergmann-Pohl lost out when de Maiziere told Chancellor Kohl not to choose her (Wiliarty, 2010a).

Now appointed a minister, Merkel became known as Chancellor Kohl's Madchen, a nickname Angela later admitted gave her mixed feelings. Merkel did not like being so dependent on the paternalistic Kohl, but she recognized the political protection the status gave her (Wiliarty, 2010a). The Ministry of Women and Youth was small with little authority, yet Merkel saw this as an opportunity not a hindrance, because she gained a political apprenticeship under Chancellor Kohl without managing a huge administration. While she was Minister of Women and Youth, Merkel also became deputy leader of the CDU, again by coincidence. The deputy leader position had been created especially for Lothar de Maiziere, but he was forced to resign after revelations that he cooperated with the Stasi. However, shortly after Merkel's party appointment, the number of deputy leaders was increased to four and her formal powers were significantly reduced. This was a public slap in the face to Merkel and a more general statement of German attitudes toward women in political positions. Merkel was next appointed Minister of Environment, Conservation and Reactor Safety after Kohl's 1994 re-election. This gave Merkel a more difficult and controversial policy area (Thompson & Lennartz, 2007). Overall, her status as Chancellor Kohl's protégé and her two ministry positions gave Merkel the visibility and platform to continue to build her political career.

Merkel's political ascent up to this point demonstrates the role of all three factors of serendipity and fortuitous circumstances, proven leadership ability, and being underestimated. Even Merkel acknowledges she became spokeswoman for Demokratischer Aufbruch "by chance" (Dejevsky, 2005). Also by providence, Chancellor Kohl wanted to balance his appointments, and Angela, as a woman, an Easterner, and a Protestant possessed the criteria of these under-represented groups in the CDU. At the time of her advancement to the cabinet, much was made of Merkel's triple quota status (Wiliarty, 2010a). Equally, Merkel's lack of early political engagement in former East Germany and having no tie to the Stasi luckily gave her a "white vest" not possessed by most East German politicians (Thompson & Lennartz, 2007). While the internal structure of the CDU may have generated the need for women and Easterners to fill cabinet positions, not all individuals with these criteria had the leadership skills to stay in office. Cognizant that her political future depended on demonstrating her leadership abilities, Merkel was able to transform herself from a political novice into a respected cabinet minister. It is crucial to note that this political learning is definitely not inevitable, and is indicative of a gifted leader. Merkel was the only one of the three appointed Easterners who was able to last the entire legislative period (Wiliarty, 2010a).

Merkel, as have many female leaders, came to prominence through a connection with a male politician and then faced the double bind of being dependent on him since she was widely regarded as a protégé of Chancellor Kohl and viewed under his shadow (Wiliarty, 2008a). Chancellor Kohl plucked Merkel from relative obscurity, became her patron in the CDU, allowed his soaring power and popularity to also shine on her and, therefore, assumed he could expect Merkel to be loyal to him. This type of underestimation of Merkel was consistent among her mentors, colleagues, and her rivals. Given her unassuming political style and her seeming acquiescence to being dismissed as Mein Madchen, Chancellor Kohl and other politicians felt, quite wrongly it turns out, that a woman from the East would hardly pose a threat to their ambitions (Dejevsky, 2005). This underestimation of Merkel created the opportunity for her next political move and ultimately led to Kohl's downfall when he became embroiled in a corruption scandal.

In the election of 1998, Kohl and the CDU lost to Gerhard Schroder and the Social Democratic Party (SPD). This was a turning point for the CDU and created a great deal of internal party position shuffling and turmoil.

Helmut Kohl, elected party chairman in 1973, resigned and in his resignation speech anointed Wolfgang Schauble to become the party chairman (Wiliarty, 2010a). Schauble, the leader of the Christian Democratic Union/ Christian Social Union (CSU, the Bavarian sister party) caucus in the Bundestag, was highly respected and the obvious choice, with no one else of the same stature in the party. As party chair, one of Schauble's powers was to nominate the General Secretary and he selected Merkel. Again, serendipity and internal party forces worked in Merkel's favor and to the detriment of Schauble's preferred choices: Hans-Peter Repnik, Schauble's confident and also from South Baden, would give their area too much representation in leadership; Friedrich Merz, an experienced financial expert, wanted to remain in parliament; Volker Ruhe, General Secretary under Kohl from 1990 to 1992, thought it would be a step back in his career. Equally fortuitous for Merkel, there were calls to appoint an East German and/or a woman, because the party had done poorly in eastern *Lander* (German states), and women in the party saw it as an opportunity to increase their leadership. They pointed to how the party's electoral losses had been particularly severe among women (Wiliarty, 2010a). Of course, merely being from the East and being a woman were insufficient by themselves to be named General Secretary. The selected individual had to possess considerable credentials and political experience. There alone stood Angela Merkel as the potential candidate, and Schauble appointed Merkel as General Secretary of the CDU (Wiliarty, 2010a).

Merkel's next political step up was to become party Chair and this began when a finance scandal hit the CDU and Kohl refused to reveal the donor of DM 2,000,000, claiming he had given his word of honor. In a courageous move, Merkel distanced herself from Kohl by publicly criticizing her former mentor in a leading German newspaper and called for an investigation into the scandal. Merkel's actions increased her visibility and popularity among the German public, but upset Kohl's loyalists, who criticized Merkel for sticking the knife in Kohl's back. When the scandal widened to also force the resignation of the new CDU Chair Schauble, Merkel used the political party manager approach to shore up her relationships with the various segments of the party and used her powers as General Secretary to orchestrate an increased chance of becoming Chair. In 2000, Merkel was elected the first female and the first East German to head a major political party. She was also the first Protestant to lead the CDU, a party with deep Catholic roots.

To achieve this major achievement in political leadership, being a woman worked in Merkel's favor. The CDU was in crisis and needed a new leader to rescue the party. In times of political strife, the traditional stereotypes of female leaders make them seem less Machiavellian. As Thompson and Lennartz (2007) point out, in extraordinary situations where male political leaders are tainted by scandal, the cleaner and softer style of a woman is especially appealing. In these circumstances, the traditional gender attitudes do not block women's advancement, but rather assist them politically. Across the globe, it is women who repeatedly have been seen as those best suited "to clean house" after political scandal. Specific to Merkel's case, she evoked the image of the Trummerfrau, the icon of the postwar period, the German women who uncomplainingly cleared the ruins of the bombed cities to help rebuild the country. Viewed as the party savior, Merkel was elected Chair of the party at the CDU conference, with an overwhelming 96% of the vote. Acknowledging that her rise to political leadership was in the midst of crisis, Merkel told female managers at IBM who were complaining that it is common for women to be appointed to secondary positions but not get the top job, "Perhaps IBM must first go through a real crisis before a woman is allowed to take over the company leadership" (Thompson & Lennartz, 2007, p. 106).

As CDU Chair, Merkel was popular among the German people and was favored to challenge Chancellor Schroder in the 2002 election. This attempted move up the political ranks is the only time Merkel failed to achieve the higher position she desired and the rare occurrence she was outmaneuvered by a political rival. Both Edmund Stoiber, Chair of the CSU, and Angela Merkel, Chair of the CDU, signaled their interest to be the party's candidate. Merkel's advantages were the CDU was the larger party, she had a "clean hands" image because of her willingness to condemn Kohl's behavior regarding campaign contributions, and as General Secretary she had overseen a number of electoral victories, showing she could organize an effective campaign. Stoiber's major advantages were serving as Minister President of Bavaria that had been the stepping stone position for a number of previous CDU Chancellors and he was well respected for his competence on security and economic policy.

Despite the majority of CDU regional elites backing Stoiber and the polls showing Stoiber was more likely to beat sitting Chancellor Schroder, Merkel relentlessly continued to openly campaign, even though doing so by any candidate was considered political suicide. The political cards were stacked against her, yet Merkel stubbornly refused to give up, a trait of unabashed perseverance she continues to exhibit in political situations beyond her complete control. Finally, when a significant majority of the CDU Minister Presidents clearly opposed Merkel, she arranged a secret breakfast with Stoiber to decide who would be the candidate. The meeting itself was a strategically political move by Merkel, since the writing was already on the wall that she had no chance. Afterward, Merkel announced Stoiber would run as the CDU candidate for Chancellor. In the end, Stoiber squandered a large lead in the polls to lose to Chancellor Schroder, and Merkel then took over the parliamentary party leadership from Friedrich Merz, a deal rumored to be what Stoiber was forced to support as a condition for Merkel to withdraw her Chancellor candidacy. Ironically, this losing political episode improved Merkel's long-term credibility, because her new position implied leadership of both the CDU and CSU (Wiliarty, 2010a).

The three factors of serendipity and fortuitous circumstances, proven leadership skills, and being underestimated all came together for Angela Merkel to make her next political move and ascend to the Chancellorship of Germany. In 2005, the Hartz IV reforms of the labor market had not met expectations, unemployment remained high, employers were frustrated by their lack of flexibility, and Schroder's left wing colleagues opposed continuing his reform agenda (Rueschemeyer, 2009). In response, Chancellor Schroder, in a move to discipline his party and gain support for his reform proposals, unexpectedly called for an early election in the middle of his second term (Wiliarty, 2010a). Schroder was gambling that the early election would terminate the damaging debate in the Social Democratic Party and that, given his personal popularity, he could take advantage of his inexperienced opponent Angela Merkel (Chandler, 2010).

The election outcome was definitely not a foregone conclusion for Merkel, whose economic competence was in question when she twice confused gross and net income during political debates. She regained her campaign momentum when she promised to appoint Paul Kirchhof, a former judge at the German Constitutional Court, as her Minister of Finance, only to lose ground when he proposed introducing a flat tax that was generally unpopular with voters. The election results were close and there was no clear victory for Merkel or Schroder. The SPD had experienced an extensive defeat, losing votes to the new left party Die Linke and ending with 222 seats, slightly behind the CDU with 226 seats (Chandler, 2010). Since neither the SPD-Green Coalition nor the CDU/CSU had enough seats for a majority in the Bundestag, both Merkel and Schroder claimed victory. A political standoff ensued.

The SPD was unable to form a coalition with only the Green Party and was unwilling to join with the left party Die Linke, while the CDU/CSU was not able to form a majority government with their preferred coalition partner, the centrist Free Democratic Party (FDP). After exhaustive negotiations led by Merkel, the SPD was forced to join into a Grand Coalition with the CDU/CSU. The only problem was that both parties demanded the Chancellorship. After three more weeks of continuing negotiations, a deal was struck making Merkel the Chancellor, and the SPD got eight of the 16 cabinet seats (Rueschemeyer, 2009). On November 22, 2005, Angela Merkel became the first woman, the first East German, and the youngest person to take the office as leader of Germany. For Merkel, becoming Chancellor reflects the perfect storm of serendipity, leadership ability, and repeatedly being underestimated.

Merkel was re-elected Chancellor in 2009 with a large majority, and this time she formed a coalition government with the CSU and the FDP to carry on her mandate.

THE SCIENTIST MUTTI LEADERSHIP STYLE

Like most leaders, Angela Merkel takes a varying approach to leadership, depending upon what the situation warrants and whether she is wearing her Chancellor domestic bonnet or her Chairwoman of the European Council or Chairwoman of the G8 international bonnet, where the constraints on leadership are more defined. She is adept at hardball tactics, as shown in her dealings with the European financial crises of Greece, Spain, and Italy teetering on bankruptcy, but often her fighting skills are underestimated, since she hides them under her placid exterior. She has a toughness that parallels Margaret Thatcher, to whom she is often compared, but unlike Thatcher, who led from a firmly held economic agenda, Merkel is relatively non-ideological in her leadership approach. Merkel is best described as a consensus builder who is guided first and foremost by pragmatism. Her leadership style is highly influenced by having grown up in a communist regime, by her analytical training as a research scientist, by her tutelage

under Chancellor Kohl, and by her inherent tendency to mother her colleagues to such an extent that she is nicknamed Mutti (Mommy).

Aimed toward consensus building, deliberations under Merkel's leadership are fairly unstructured, with most everyone getting a chance to voice
their opinion to the Chancellor (Bannas, 2006). She is praised for fostering
broad discussions and for her collegial style (Clemens, 2010; Ferree, 2010).
There are no brow beatings in front of colleagues as occurred with previous Chancellors, and Merkel does not speak arrogantly or badly of others.
In fact, she often wraps her criticism in well-meaning advice. As part of her
consensus building strategy, Merkel consistently cultivates and maintains
a broad network of relationships through thousands of phone calls per
month (Clemens, 2010) and casual meetings, often with her loudest and
most public critics, such as having a beer with SPD parliamentary faction
chair Peter Struck (Bannas, 2006). Merkel is instinctively cognizant of the
benefits of a soft hands approach to politics and of keeping her hardball
power tactics hidden. Her traits of a below-the-radar leadership and hidden
control are remnants of growing up in East Germany.

Throughout her career, Merkel has been described as sensible, dowdy,
provincial, effective, direct, and even boring (Bannas, 2006). These are not
adjectives one would expect to describe the most powerful woman in the
world, but rather a middle-aged East German woman. The deeply en-
grained behaviors formulated during her years under communist rule cannot be overlooked in their overwhelming influence on her leadership style
(Dejevsky, 2005). Mushaben (2009) points out the consummate lesson of
East German life was always to try hard but never attract attention to one-
self. The assumption was of always being surrounded by Stasi informants
and any disclosure of private thoughts or political position could become
a subject for Stasi persecution (Van Zoonen, 2006). Remaining uncommit-
ted and out of the spotlight were a matter of survival, and a lesson Merkel
now brings to governing. She lets everyone speak and state his or her position on an issue before she gives any indication of her position. On the
one hand, this is a strategic maneuver for consensus building to imply the
leader can be swayed by the arguments of others, but on the other hand it
has led to doubts whether Merkel stands for anything and to criticisms in
the German newspapers that she does not lead (Thompson & Lennartz,
2007). An example of this consensus-building approach and/or her staying
under the radar instinct was evident over the reforms to the parental leave
plan, when Merkel delayed stating her preference on the length of fathers

leave, the most controversial section, until months into the debate and not until a compromise was reached (Wiliarty, 2010a).

Another major factor reflected in Merkel's leadership style is her academic background and training. Merkel typically comes across as a rational, cold, and non-compromising politician (Van Zoonen, 2006). This in much part reflects her training as a research scientist. Mushaben (2009) describes how this influences her governing:

> As a physicist, Merkel thinks inductively, recognizes the heuristic value of plans, assesses probabilities, and advances through trial and error. She does not make the same mistake twice. She approaches politics as a one-step-at-a-time experiment requiring rational deliberation, making it hard for male counterparts to see through her decisions early on. Merkel's natural world follows observable rules; every decision involves "energy mass" with a particular direction, strength, tempo and significance. Her job is to scan the environment for new configurations, study the longer term "waves," and then ask the right questions in order to derive a correct answer. Her ability to lead a party dominated by conservative male hardliners rests on a "strategy of small steps." She observes their weaknesses and strengths, treating them as constants. (pp. 29–30)

As the former scientist who excelled at indepth research, Merkel always has a good grasp of the nuances of the details of every policy. She brings a scientist's efficiency to everything she does, including politics. This caused an observer to note that one could image Merkel rewiring a plug or rustling up a meal for 12 with the same efficiency as she makes a political speech and answers questions (Dejevsky, 2005). Although long faulted for seeming to lack convictions, much of Merkel's pragmatism and interest in hearing different solutions can be traced back to her training as a physicist (Chandler, 2010).

Frequently compared in leadership style to the Iron Maiden Margaret Thatcher, also a scientist, Merkel is known as the Iron Frau. The two female leaders share the similarities of a scientific businesslike manner, an encyclopedic range of information, an instant grasp of issues and their political implications, an emphasis on practicality, and a refreshing absence of jargon and spin. Yet there are key differences between the two leaders as Eberlein of York University points out, "Traditionally she [Merkel] is very much consensus-oriented. For her, leadership is very much keeping people bored. It is not about saying 'This is what I want; it is the opposite of a Thatcherite leadership'" (Milner & Pitts, 2010). Merkel's take on the comparison when asked if she is the German Thatcher was, "Well, there is one important difference . . . She was a chemist, I am a physicist" (Dejevsky, 2005).

Merkel has a different leadership style than her mentor Helmut Kohl, but her eight years as his Madchen were highly instructive and put a stamp on her current leadership approach. From Kohl, she learned how to organize political majorities, to win debates, to sit out political controversies until they fade away (a specialty of Kohl), to deal with political rivals and former friends, and to set up media contacts (Thompson & Lennartz, 2007). However, Merkel lacks Kohl's room-filling presence and brings consensus almost by the opposite tactic of not putting on a show, as if she wants no one to notice (Bannas, 2006). Merkel owes much of her current leadership style to Kohl's political party manager model that she observed first hand. Like Kohl, she waits for the situation to develop before committing herself to a particular policy until the last moment. Sometimes this looks indecisive, but it allows her to remain connected to various political groups as long as possible. Also like Kohl, Merkel is skilled at negotiation, in appealing to internal party groups and in building coalitions. Even if these attributes were instinctual for her, they certainly were honed during her tutelage under Kohl.

Any head of state who utilizes consensus building as her primary leadership approach focuses her efforts on trying to get everyone behind a policy and in creating an environment where everyone can get along. In much part, this is exactly what a mother does everyday in getting her family to agree to visit dreadful Aunt Mabel or to clean out the garage or in coaxing her children with candy to stop fighting. Merkel is that same mother in how she nurtures her colleagues and also in her image as the metaphysical mother to Germany, as noted by her public nickname, Mutti. Her cabinet meetings are friendly gatherings, where Merkel personally makes sure each minister gets their preferred variety of tea as well as bouquets on their birthday (Wiliarty, 2010b). And just like a mother, Merkel can show her concern for a colleague in a scolding and condescending manner, as occurred in an encounter recalled by Michael Glos, her former economic minister, who resigned early because he felt poorly treated by the Chancellor. Only minutes after her re-election as Chancellor by the German Parliament and when she was walking to her waiting limousine, Merkel ran into Glos. She took the time at this important moment to notice Glos was not wearing a coat and suggested he dress more warmly to protect himself from the cold. Merkel was so perfectly serious and slightly stern that it prompted Glos to reply that she always had his best interest at heart. Even though he is 10 years older than Merkel, Glos said he suddenly felt like a little boy being scolded for foolishly ignoring the risks of catching a cold (Kurbjuweit, 2009).

Merkel's mothering image has now extended more fully to be the Mother of Germany, as found in an analysis of her press coverage in *Der Spiegel* by Sarah Wiliarty (2010b). Merkel is consistently presented as the caring, compassionate mother, which feminizes her scientist-laden image but not at a sacrifice of her attributes of competence, rationality, and seriousness. The press increasingly portrays her in the roles of hostess and mother by describing her shopping lists and her discussions of food for state banquets. This motherly image is useful for Merkel, since she has no children and being identified as the metaphysical mother of Germany subtly implies she has more in common with most Germans. From the perspective of female leadership studies, this portrayal of Merkel as a mother and a hostess may be the development of a new positive stereotype for powerful women leaders. This reframing of the traditional roles of mother and hostess allows female politicians to be gracious, generous, and powerful at the same time they are controlling both the agenda and the decision-making process (Wiliarty, 2010b).

SUCCESS IN POLICIES OF AUSTERITY

Never have expectations for a Chancellor's success been so low as when Angela Merkel came to office. She faced a dismal policy environment of an impending German recession, deep deficits requiring fiscal restraint, sluggish economic growth, high unemployment, and inevitable cuts in welfare to ease the burden on business and taxpayers. The support behind Merkel from the Grand Coalition, an awkward alliance between traditional rivals, was tenuous at best, as the parties held vastly different issue positions and divided right and left on policy solutions (Clemens, 2010). Domestically, Merkel was constrained by strong personalities in a "prickly team" that caught her between her own program preferences of economic liberalism and the necessity to share power pulling her to the centre (Chandler, 2010). Internationally, there were also a host of challenges. Pressures came from the European Zone, as members' economies were crumbling and they looked to Germany to be the major provider of a bailout. Although front and center in world politics as president of the EU and the G8, Merkel faced the constraint of inheriting an already established policy agenda and an institutional procedural structure of equal members that made her job much like "herding cats."

Instead of focusing on the constraints and obstacles confronting her, Merkel prioritized consensus, made accommodations to her coalition partners, and settled for small steps far short of her campaign promises. The *Augsburger Allgemeine*, a major German regional daily newspaper, noted, "peace in the coalition is more dear to [her] than the CDU's profile," while her colleagues accused her of caving in and lacking a clear compass (Clemens, 2010). Nonetheless, Merkel did have a guiding principle: to make Germany globally competitive, which required first and foremost getting Germany's economic house in order (Dejevsky, 2005). She steadfastly held to the overarching importance of austerity to balance the government's finances (Thompson & Lennartz, 2007).

However, Merkel had limited ability to set her own issue agenda. She accepted an SPD-sponsored minimum wage, and went along with increasing the pensions of 20 million seniors. She supported greater labor market flexibility and the right of business firms to opt out of industry-wide bargaining. Merkel faced a SPD veto on any drastic reforms, including the easing of job security and corporatist collective bargaining (Chandler, 2010). Merkel agreed to a comprehensive tax cut plan, increases in state insurance for dementia patients, a child care subsidy for keeping children under age 3 at home, reducing red tape for skilled immigrants, and investing in German infrastructure. While the tax cuts and spending increases could be viewed as merely political maneuvers aimed at enhancing her electoral success, Merkel viewed them as strengthening growth in Germany by relieving the tax burden on those with low and middle income and making the system fairer.

In a number of policy areas, Merkel faced significant conflict yet took decisive action. With a health care system overwhelmed by rising costs and an aging population, Merkel promoted wide reaching reforms and fought with the coalition to successfully negotiate a compromise. Her popularity ratings decreased as a result, and health care experts, business leaders, and regional party ministers criticized the reforms (Williamson, 2006). Immigration also has been a hot button issue for Merkel, especially when she stated the "multikulti" concept of people happily living side by side does not work and immigrants need to do more to integrate themselves into German life, including to learn the language. Coming across as anti-immigration, Merkel later made it clear that Germany welcomed immigrants, and she pledged in a meeting with the Turkish prime minister to improve integration efforts. Another area where Merkel took decisive action was after the Japanese Tsunami, when she drew upon her scientific background and closed seven nuclear reactors. She further announced plans to radically reorder German nuclear energy policy and to shut down some or all of Germany's reactors by 2022 (Czuczka & Donahue, 2011).

Merkel is not afraid to use her military muscle, and parallels the findings in Koch and Fulton's study of national security behavior of 22 democratic nations that female leaders are now more hawkish than their male counterparts (Koch & Fulton, 2011). For example, Merkel vigorously defended Germany's involvement in Afghanistan, despite increased opposition among the German people. She continued her strong military stance even after the public's outrage and demands to withdraw German troops when 59 Afghan civilians were killed in a bombing of two Taliban-hijacked fuel trucks ordered by a German commander who feared they would be used as bombs on wheels near a German base. Ultimately, Merkel stated her regret for the innocent victims and called for an investigation, but made it clear she was furious about the criticisms and that the troops would remain (Boyes, 2009). On other international fronts, Merkel said Gaddafi must go, she refused to respond to Iranian President Ahmadinejad's letter criticizing Israel and questioning the right of the Jewish state to exist, and she opposed the Palestinian bid for membership in the United Nations. Yet, committed to rational leadership, Merkel felt personally betrayed by the Israeli government when settlement building continued beyond the Green Line.

One of the biggest issues thrust upon Merkel has been the worsening European debt crisis that began in insolvent Greece and continues to spread across the Eurozone. The situation needed a decisive crisis manager, and the job fell onto Merkel's shoulders, and is described as forcing her to put some iron into her velvet glove (Milner & Pitts, 2010). Merkel imposed a unilateral ban on some forms of short selling, warned the currency world that a single European currency was in grave peril, and imposed tougher oversight of Eurozone members' fiscal affairs. Merkel brought German austerity as the answer and opposed providing a large stimulus package to rescue nations from what she believed was their own frivolous behavior (Chandler, 2010). The fear of the German people and of Merkel was that Germany, as the most economically prosperous EU member, would be the paymaster in the bailouts for the economic and fiscal mistakes of the other countries. The Germans opposed setting aside billions of Euros to rescue Greece and other countries who lived for years beyond their means while Germans had taken measures of austerity and had continually been told there was no money for tax cuts. Merkel was steadfast in requiring that countries implement measures of austerity as a condition for a bailout from the EU and the IMF. At times, Merkel appeared domineering, dogmatic, and to be bossing Europe around in her opposition, and became lampooned as a Nazi and a dominatrix in newspaper cartoons and protests throughout Europe. Merkel's response was to outline Germany's progress with their austerity measures and how their structured reforms led to more jobs and a robust economy. She asked the world business leaders to be patient, because improving growth and economic stability would be a long drawn-out process (Ewing & Alderman, 2012).

Responding to their own country's frustrations, a number of European political leaders began pushing back against Merkel and her calls for austerity. They contend tax increases and spending cuts would only heighten the recession and deepen the indebtedness of the faltering nations (Erlanger & Castle, 2011; Ewing & Alderman, 2012). They increasingly criticized Merkel for misdiagnosing the Eurozone's economic woes and for insisting on a debilitating program of austerity that many feared would continue the stagnation for another decade (Kirschbaum, 2012). As a consequence, the 2012 elections in Greece and the defeat of President Sarkozy in France were a direct rejection of Merkel and her austerity program that the countries felt was forced upon them.

A NATIONAL LEADER OR A WOMAN LEADER?

Whenever a woman becomes the leader of a country, the question always is raised whether her gender matters in how she governs and in how she carries out her leadership. Ironically, that question is never asked when a man heads a country, because the assumption is his leadership is genderless. Angela Merkel has never had a choice but to "lead as a woman;" however, her reality is a gendered political system where power is very much associated with manhood. She has run for office as a woman, governed as a woman, and negotiated with foreign leaders as a woman, yet Merkel herself has never made a political issue of her gender. Despite being one of the most powerful world leaders, Merkel has never had the privilege of having her gender taken for granted or made invisible.

The literature on gender and leadership finds that the public attributes male and female leaders with a different set of personality characteristics and tends to associate the stereotypical male personality traits as those more compatible with executive office, such as assertiveness, ambition, vision, decisiveness, rationality, and strength. In many ways, Merkel's combination of her East German roots and her scientific background leads to an image that is markedly less feminine and disrupts how the male/female stereotypes are applied to her. Trained as a natural scientist, she instinctively demonstrates a strong emphasis on rationality, competence, and knowledge, all considered male traits. She is described as goal oriented, strong, ambitious, and diligent. Merkel's image is equated with rationality to such a degree that she is never regarded as emotional, but is often considered cold, reserved, and aloof. These characteristics are consistent with her Eastern background that makes it difficult for her to share private emotions. All this adds to the increased association of Merkel with the typical set of masculine traits, since she comes across as distant and unemotional, instead of in the more typically feminine manner of warm and compassionate. Merkel's non-feminine image is so pervasive that the press sometimes uses the neuter form "das Merkel." While scholars have argued that Merkel had to become an "honorary man" in order to succeed, a more positive interpretation from a perspective of female leadership is that Merkel may be forging a new association between femininity and competence (Wiliarty, 2010b).

The roles of wife and mother that typically create a double bind for female leaders have not been significant factors for Merkel. She is fiercely guarded about her private life, and her husband rarely appears with her in public. Merkel benefits by not being publicly displayed in her wife role, because she does not attract attention to her nonstandard gender choice of a public mission instead of private fulfillment (Van Zoonen, 2006). Her lack of children equally removes the double bind of the Mommy Problem that most female leaders face as they struggle to reconcile running a country with raising children. Ironically, there once was an attempt to turn Merkel's lack of children into a Mommy Problem by questioning whether she could relate to German women. In the 2005 campaign, Doris Schroder Kopf, wife of Chancellor Schroder, said of Merkel, "With her biography, she does not embody the experiences of most women. German women are trying to combine children, family and career. That isn't Merkel's world" (Wiliarty, 2010b). Ultimately, the attempt fell flat as Merkel defeated Schroder.

Since becoming Chancellor, Merkel has faced unrelenting scrutiny of her appearance that is de rigueur for female leaders but virtually nonexistent for male heads of state. In today's world of celebrity politics where dress and looks equate to measures of success, all female heads of state have non-stop attention to their appearance and a heightened challenge to convey an image of femininity along with competence, strength, and power. Merkel's marked change in appearance over her career may seem frivolous to note, but her complete make-over also reflects her evolution from an Easterner to encompassing Western German leadership and culture, and her rise as a leader on the world stage. In her early years, Merkel projected a less conventionally feminine image, in black suits and a pudding basin haircut, both attributed to her East German background. There even was a special gesture for Merkel in German deaf sign language of a rectangle in reference to her hairstyle. She generally does not care much about her appearance, but once did snap at a comment about her dull looks, saying that a person was fortunate if one had so few worries (Van Zoonen, 2006). In a way, however, her early unstylish Eastern appearance served her well, since female politicians constantly fight the stereotype of appearance as a signal of office worthiness. Merkel's lack of femininity portrayed an image of being reliable and not flashy that translated into a guide as to how she would govern (Ferree, 2006). With time in office, Merkel got a more fashionable hairstyle and began wearing softer pastel shaded jackets, complete with matching makeup and jewelry. For her, the standard double bind facing many female leaders of becoming more feminine in appearance and thus less competent was disrupted, due to Merkel's Eastern background. She became redefined as more Western and more professional (Wiliarty, 2010b).

Although Merkel has never called herself a feminist, her behavior slants toward feminist sympathies in her policies, her appointments, and in her closest allies. As Chair of the CDU and as Chancellor, Merkel created a significantly different kind of access to the informal channels of political power for women. She has built a "Girls Club" of talented and experienced women whom she draws upon for trusted advice. She has appointed women as ministers and routinely visits women serving in the Bundestag. Her three closest advisors are her female office manager, her female press secretary, and her confidante, Beate Bauman. This female threesome determines who gets access to the Chancellor, assesses every political situation, and even goes shopping together to decide what Merkel will wear (Wiliarty, 2010a). Merkel's heavily female kitchen cabinet has been called the Power Frauen and even the Power Muttis, because the women have had children while working for Merkel. It is not clear whether her female-centered network is a clue to her feminist politics, or is more an indication of how untrustworthy Merkel finds her male colleagues as allies and confidants.

Merkel is a good example of how a female leader can have a feminist effect on gender norms without actually espousing feminist policies (Ferree, 2006). In terms of gender-related issues, Merkel has quietly advocated gender equality and promoted policies favorable to women. In her early career as Minister of Women and Youth, she preserved funding for the extensive East German child-care network, found interim funding to keep East German kindergartens going, and guided a new law on equal rights (Wiliarty, 2010a). She pushed to renew and indefinitely extend a gender quorum in the CDU, believing that it increased female leadership even if it did not reach the goal of one-third women. As Chancellor, Merkel made family leave reform a priority and attempted to modernize the welfare state in terms of family policies. Overall, Merkel has contributed concrete policies to promoting women as workers, advancing gender equality, and serving as a role model for women.

It should be pointed out that there are inherent inconsistencies at work for Merkel in terms of gender and leadership, and they may help explain her political success. On the one hand, Merkel is perceived as the rational technocrat, stemming from her scientific training and East German background. This aligns her with the typically masculine leadership skill set and creates a public mindset that Merkel is suitable and capable to lead the country. On the other hand, and seemingly at odds, is her public designation as the nurturing Mutti to all of Germany, lending her the most feminine of skill sets. These gender role discrepancies are further compounded since Merkel is childless and rarely seen in public in the role of a wife. Yet, she still imparts a mothering image to an entire country. The combination of these two disparate leadership skill sets explains part of her political success and acumen. Merkel is the ultimate nurturing, non-emotional, rational, stern, compassionate leader who, because of this dichotomy, has been able to break traditional gender norms as she projects a "twofer" image across the spectrum of possessing both masculine and feminine leadership attributes.

Yet, Merkel's leadership style of consensus building suggests her gender impacts how she governs. The leadership literature concludes that women tend to lead in a relational manner. Barsh and Cranston conducted a five-year study on leadership and in *How Remarkable Women Lead* (2011) describe women leaders as more collaborative and consensus building in approach. They found that it tends to be women in society who make groups work and, thus, they constantly bring team building to their leadership style. Women leaders excel at listening, which signals empathy and nurturing, each powerful motivators. Merkel clearly brings this type of gendered approach to her leadership style as she builds and tends her relationships, gives a voice to all in a meeting, and prolongs decisions to keep everyone on the team as long as possible. Merkel's consensus building, relationship style contrasts with the typically more assertive, decisive approach of male heads of state. Her male colleagues of Bush, Obama, Sarkozy, and Cameron have all demonstrated the more masculine singular decision-making approach to leadership. In fact, Russia's Vladamir Putin is the Alpha Man example of the diametrical opposite of Merkel's consensus building leadership style.

But just as she has not made her gender the cornerstone in how she leads, Merkel has not made women's issues the center of her public policies. In her political actions and policy agenda, Merkel has approached her role as national leader in a genderless manner. Her leadership style reflects a combination of typically masculine and feminine traits, reflecting her East German background and her training as a scientist. Merkel's policy focus also has not been gendered, but based on what she perceives to be the best for all Germans. Merkel's leadership epitomizes her nickname of Mutti, mother to all Germans. Merkel is a pioneer for women and has broken the glass ceiling in Germany and in global politics. Her greatest achievement is not being a woman national leader, nor is it becoming a national leader in spite of being a woman. Merkel's greatest achievement is proving that a woman can become a head of state and can govern in such a way that gender does not matter. This is ultimately the goal for all women political leaders.

CONCLUSION

While Angela Merkel's meteoric rise to become the first female Chancellor of Germany was in part due to serendipity and to her sheer luck of possessing the desired set of qualifications at key political junctures, her success is not a fluke. Like all extraordinary leaders, Merkel saw opportunity and open pathways in the positions and in the circumstances lying before her. And, like most female politicians, she worked harder, longer, quieter, and unrecognized to seize upon every potential resource and relationship. Without question, Merkel benefited from the increased pressure for gender equity in German politics, from the political disruptions caused by unification, from the campaign finance scandal, and from the organizational structure of the CDU needing women and East Germans. But none of these factors diminish the exceptional set of political skills that Merkel brings to governing and has sharpened over her career. Her political approach and leadership perspective have been influenced as much by her background as an East German and by her scientific training as by her gender. It is Merkel's unique combination of being a woman, an Easterner, and a scientist that best explain her path to power and how she defines being a leader.

REFERENCES

Bannas, G. (2006, November 22). She doesn't put on a show: Angela Merkel's style. *Frankfurter Allegmeine Zeitung*, 3.

Barsh, J., S. Cranston, & G. Lewis. (2011). *How remarkable women lead*. New York: Crown Business.

Benoit, B. (2005, July 2). The pastor's daughter who raises hope of healing Germany. *Financial Times*, 1.

Bond, P. (2001, October 23). *The rise to political power of Chancellor Angela Merkel*. www.examiner.com/article/the-rise-to-power-of-chancellor-angela-merkel.

Boyes, R. (2005, November 9). Defying all the odds. *The Times* (*London*).

Boyes, R. (2009, September 14). Plan to withdraw German troops from Afghanistan becomes election issue. *The Times* (*London*).

Chandler, W.M. (2010). European leadership in transition: Angela Merkel and Nicolas Sarkozy. In S. Bulmer, C. Jeffery, & S. Padgett (Eds.), *Rethinking Germany and Europe*. Hampshire, England: Palgrave Macmillan, 154–170.

Clemens, C. (2010). The Chancellor and her party. In S. Bulmer, C. Jeffery, & S. Padgett (Eds.), *Rethinking Germany and Europe*. Hampshire, England: Palgrave Macmillan, 25–41.

Cronin, T.E., & M.A. Genovese. (2012). *Leadership matters: Unleashing the power of paradox*. Boulder, CO: Paradigm Press.

Czuczka, T., & P. Donahue. (2011, March 28). Merkel's CDU hints at German nuclear-policy shift after state vote defeat. www.bloomberg.com/news.2011-03-28/merkel-party-hints-at-german-nuclear-policy-shift-after-state-vote-defeat.html.

Dejevsky, M. (2005, February 14). Angela Merkel: The Iron Lady of German politics hoping to emulate Thatcher's unlikely rise to power. *The Independent*.

Englemann, K. (2010, September 9). Merkel honors Mohammad cartoonist at press award. Blogs.reuters.com/faithworld/2010/09/09/german-chancellor-merkel-honors-mohammad-cartoonist-at-press-award/

Erlanger, S., & S. Castle. (2011, December 9). German vision prevails as leaders agree on fiscal pact. *New York Times*, A1.

Ewing, J., & L. Alderman. (2012, January 25). Citing Europe's progress, Merkel urges patience. *New York Times*, B8.

Ferree, M.M. (2006). Angela Merkel: What does it mean to run as a woman? *German Politics and Society*, 78(24), 93–107.

Ferree, M.M. (2010). Gender politics in the Berlin republic: Four issues of identity and institutional change. *German Politics and Society*, 94(28), 189–214.

Florin, F. (2011, September 29). Angela Merkel. *New York Times*.

Jalalzai, F., & M.L. Krook. (2010). Hillary and Benazir: Women's political leadership worldwide. *International Political Science Review*, 31(1), 5–23.

Kirschbaum, E. (2012, January 29). Merkel deflects pressure to boost Euro bailout funds. Uk.reuters.com/article/2012/01/29/uk-eurozone-idUKTRE80SOCG20120129.

Kurbjuweit, D. (2009, November 3). Angela the great or just "Mom"? www.spiegel.de/international/germany/angela-the-great-or-just-mom-merkel-s-dream-of-a-place-in-the-history-books-a-659018.html.

Milner, B., & G. Pitts. (2010, May 21). Velvet Chancellor shows some iron. *The Globe and Mail*.

Mushaben, J. (2009). Madam Chancellor: Angela Merkel and the triangulation of German foreign policy. *Georgetown Journal of International Affairs*, Winter/Spring, 27–35.

Rueschemeyer, M. (2009). East German women in the Parliament of Unified Germany. In M. Rueschemeyer & S.L. Wolchik (Eds.), *Women in post-communist parliaments*. Bloomington: Indiana University Press, 131–160.

Thompson, M.R., & L. Lennartz. (2007). The making of Chancellor Merkel. *German Politics*, 15(1), 99–110.

Van Zoonen, L. (2006). The personal, the political and the popular: A woman's guide to celebrity politics. *European Journal of Cultural Studies*, 9, 287–301.

Walter, N. (2012, February 8). Germany's hidden weaknesses. *New York Times*, A23.

Wiliarty, S. E. (2010a). *The CDU and the politics of gender in Germany.* New York: Cambridge University Press, 137–157.

Wiliarty, S. E. (2010b). How the Iron Curtain helped break through the glass ceiling. In R. Murray (Ed.), *Cracking the highest glass ceiling.* Santa Barbara, CA: ABC-CLIO.

Wiliarty, S. E. (2008a). Chancellor Angela Merkel—A sign of hope or the exception that proves the rule? *Politics & Gender, 4*(3), 485–496.

Wiliarty, S. E. (2008b). Angela Merkel's path to power: The role of internal party dynamics and leadership. *German Politics, 17*(1), 81–96.

Williamson, H. (2006, October 6). Healthcare reform deal gives boost to Merkel's coalition. *Financial Times,* 9.

10

"Perónisma"

Isabel Perón and the Politics of Argentina

Sara J. Weir

> I cannot offer you great things—I am only a disciple of Perón.
> **Isabel Martinez de Perón, 1973**

It has been 30 years since Isabel Martinez de Perón served as president of Argentina, and her historical value as the first woman chief executive of an American republic not withstanding, she is remembered primarily for an 18-month presidency that was, in the eyes of many, an unmitigated disaster.

As this book goes to press, however, we find that Mrs. Perón remains a person of interest in global politics: an influential political exile whose complicated relationship with the country she once governed continues to create controversy, intrigue, and, most recently, legal maneuvering involving human rights violations allegedly committed during her administration.

While the presidency of Isabel Perón remains the central focus of this chapter, attention has also been given to the role of women in Argentine politics in the 21st century (most notably the current president of Argentina, Cristina Fernández de Kirchner) and the often-complicated roles of women in the Justicialist Party (PJ) and the Perónist movement in Argentina.

CONTEXT

The last three decades have seen many changes in the politics of Argentina, Latin America, and the world with regard to the role of women in public life. Women have increasingly exercised political power and held positions of leadership that—in the past—would automatically have been populated by men.

According to the 2011 Global Gender Gap Report, Argentina ranks 28th among the 134 countries studied. The World Economic Forum, publisher of the report, ranks countries according to their gender gaps, and their scores can be interpreted as the percentage of the inequality between women and men.[1]

The women of Argentina have attained a relatively high level of equality, especially when judged by Latin American standards. Women have emerged as both candidates and officeholders at every level of Argentine government.

In 2012, Argentina has a number of women in high-ranking government positions (including President Fernandez de Kircher and two Supreme Court Justices: Supreme Court Vice President Elena Highton de Nolasco and Supreme Court Justice Carmen Argibay).

BIOGRAPHICAL SKETCH

First, it must be noted that the factual information available regarding Isabel Martinez de Perón's childhood and adolescence is, at best, both unreliable and incomplete. There are specific elements of Isabel's life that appear in several different biographical sources, but official and unofficial accounts of her early life differ greatly.[2] The available narratives are especially polarized regarding Isabel's career as a dancer before she met Juan Perón.

As a child she was called "Estelita," but she was born Maria Estela Martinez Cartas on February 4, 1931, in La Rioja, a provincial capital in northwestern Argentina. Her family moved to Buenos Aires when she was 2 years old and her father, who was an official of the National Mortgage Bank, died four years later.

Very little is known about her relationship with her mother and her siblings, except that she was the middle child, with two older sisters and two younger brothers. According to *Current Biography Yearbook* (1975),

Isabel showed little aptitude for academic studies, leaving school after the sixth grade:

> She reportedly studied ballet and Spanish dancing, acquiring some proficiency in French, developed a taste for romantic Spanish poetry, and qualified as a piano teacher. (p. 313)

Estelita adopted her confirmation name, Isabel, as her stage name around the time she began her career as a professional dancer. She joined the Cervantes Theatre's dance troupe in 1955, but she was dancing with Joe Herald's Ballet in Panama when she met Juan Perón in 1956 (*Current Biography Yearbook*, 1975).

Thirty-five years Isabel's senior, Perón had been married twice before. His first wife, Aurelia Tizón de Perón, died in 1938, and his second wife, María Eva Duarte de Perón (known as "Evita"), died in 1952.

According to several accounts, Isabel—who was ill, unable to perform, and living far away from her native country—met the exiled Perón when he visited her in her backstage dressing room. Soon after their meeting, Juan hired Isabel as his personal secretary.

This seems to be the beginning of Isabel's political education. There is no evidence from her childhood of an interest in politics on Isabel's part, and she is quoted as saying of her early relationship with Juan: "We talked about politics the day we first met and afterwards he trained me to be his political representative" (*Current Biography Yearbook*, 1975, p. 313).

Five years later, in 1961, Isabel and Juan were married in a secret ceremony in Madrid. Juan Perón continued to be the head of the Perónist movement during this time, and it was feared that knowledge of his marriage to Isabel might anger supporters at home in Argentina, who continued to revere his second wife, Evita.

Despite her best efforts, Isabel was never able to truly emerge from behind the shadow cast by Evita. Unlike Evita, Isabel seemed to lack political ambition. While Isabel dyed her hair blonde and adopted the emotional style of speaking that Evita was so famous for, the parallels between the two women went only so far. While it was true that, like Isabel, before becoming Juan's wife, Evita had been an actress, intelligent, and ambitious, "she was also an extremely adroit politician . . . Isabelita, the understudy, lacked Evita's brains, charisma and raw, driving energy" (*The London Times*, 1980).

PATH TO POWER

The path to power for Isabel Perón in Argentine politics can be understood only in the context of the political culture and economic development of twentieth-century Argentina and the role of Perónism in the post–World War II era.

Argentina was a Spanish colony before gaining its independence in the 1920s, and while much of its early political culture can be traced to the conquistadores, later waves of immigration from southern Europe (especially Italy) shaped contemporary Argentine culture and contributed to continuing tensions over national identity. During the period 1857–1930, Argentina experienced a net immigration of 3.5 million people (net immigration equals immigrants minus emigrants). By 1914, 30% of the population was foreign born (Smith & Skidmore, 1984).

A rural peasantry—as seen in many Latin American countries colonized by the Spanish—did not develop in Argentina. Instead, an urban proletariat emerged, made up of immigrants working in agro-export-related industries. It was these workers, along with powerful sectors of the military, who brought Juan Perón to power in 1946 and again in 1973 (after 18 years in exile).

Juan Perón used a combination of personal charisma, collective political ritual, and economic policies that redistributed income in favor of the workers to forge a social movement. Its "extreme dependence on one man" *(verticalismo)* made Perón indispensable to Perónism.

It must be remembered that Juan Perón was never formally overthrown—in 1955, after two serious challenges to his power from the military, he was forced into exile. During his years in exile, Perón continued to head the Perónist movement. In 1960, after several nomadic years, Juan and Isabel finally settled in Spain (with the support of Juan's friend, Spanish dictator General Francisco "el Caudillo" Franco).

Events leading to the presidency of Isabel Perón began when she was called upon to represent her exiled husband in Argentine politics. Isabel traveled to Argentina several times to serve "as Perón's stand-in, successfully promoting his chosen candidates in provincial elections" (*Current Biography Yearbook*, 1975, p. 314) and to keep attention on Juan rather than those who called for Perónist policies under other leadership. Perónism was far from dead, but clear divisions in the movement were emerging as a new generation of labor leaders (the traditional base of Juan Perón's support) were calling for "Perónism without Perón" (Smith, 1983).

By 1971, the military dictatorship of General Alejandro Lanusse agreed to Argentina's return to civilian rule. Isabel again represented her husband in discussions with the government concerning his possible participation in the elections scheduled for 1973.

On March 11, 1973, Hector Campora, Perón's handpicked candidate, won the presidential election with 49.6% of the vote (Smith, 1983).

Campora was unable to reunite the factions of the Perónist movement. The breakdown was apparent when Juan and Isabel formally returned to Argentina in 1973 and were greeted at the airport by some 400,000 followers:

> Left-wing and right-wing Perónists were determined to control the event and to plant their respective banners in the area around the platform . . . A full-scale battle broke . . . with automatic weapons being fired at close range in a packed crowd. ("Thousands Cheer," 1973)

It has been estimated that up to 200 people were killed and thousands were injured. Whether it was part of a plan or a response to events is unclear, but in the months that followed Campora resigned, paving the way for Juan Perón to run for president once again.

The choice of Perón's running mate was very important. Juan Perón had been in poor health, and those closest to him guarded this fact throughout the campaign. He performed the public duties required to keep his image alive, but, increasingly, Isabel represented him outside of the capitol.

Ricardo Balbin, leader of the Radical Civic Union (UCR), was considered as a possible vice-presidential candidate, but in the end Isabel was nominated, in part because she was able to demonstrate political power when acting as a representative for her husband. Many reasons for Juan's selection of Isabel have been given, but it is clear her success as his surrogate and her ability to campaign on his behalf may at least in part explain why he selected her as his running mate in 1973.

The decision to create an "all-Perón" ticket fostered the continuation of Isabel's political education and growth. But while it was Isabel who did most of the campaigning (and she was successful in winning the support of the left-wing Perónists), there were few who considered her qualified to serve as president. The Argentine voters approved of the all-Perón ticket, and Juan and Isabel Perón received 61.85% of the votes cast in the election.

On October 12, 1973, Juan Perón began his third term as president, and Isabel Martinez de Perón became the first woman vice president in Latin America. Isabel had evolved from wife to spokesperson and political representative to elected official—a position the politically ambitious Evita wanted, but was denied.

Historically, the vice presidency in Argentina has not been a powerful position, but given Juan Perón's health, it was clear to some that Isabel would very likely ascend to the presidency. Following the official announcement of the all-Perón ticket, Isabel told the delegates, "I cannot offer you great things—I am only a disciple of Perón" (*Current Biography Yearbook*, 1975, p. 314).

While she may have identified herself as "only a disciple of Perón," Isabel Perón's vice presidency and presidency were also greatly impacted by the legacy of Juan Perón's second wife, Eva Duarte de Perón. While Evita never held political office, her popularity and broad, informal authority made Isabel's ability to govern far more challenging. As Isabel found herself in the position to exercise formal political power, she had fewer resources available to her and was far less charismatic than Evita.

Isabel entered her vice presidency with little formal political experience and without the natural leadership skills of Evita. She took office in a country where women had only been granted the right to vote in 1947. Even with the franchise, much of Argentina remained strongly antifeminist and opposed women's exercising power in public life.

During her vice presidency, Isabel "worked long hours, behaved with quiet dignity and won the country's grudging respect" (*Current Biography Yearbook*, 1975). She served as vice president for less than a year before Juan Perón's death on July 1, 1974. Isabel's announcement of her husband's death was poignant: "With great pain I must transmit to the people the death of a true apostle of peace and non-violence."

During his final term in office, Juan Perón was unable to provide the economic rewards that had successfully united the proletariat during his earlier terms of office. Major divisions within the movement emerged, and upon Perón's death this turmoil surfaced.

Isabel Perón inherited the leadership of a country with deep economic problems, where terrorism and violence were increasingly commonplace, and the Perónist movement was at war with itself. According to Donald

Hodges, "The economic crisis compounded the political crisis, thus result-ing in Isabelita's inability to rule" (Hodges, 1976, p. 167).

Conflict grew, not only with the General Labor Federation (CT), the traditional base of support for Perónism, but also with the more moderate factions of the military, who feared the effects of continuing violence and political repression. For some in the military, the problem was not with repressive policies, but that these policies were directed by the government rather than the military. The political crisis led to a military crisis that was aggravated by economic mismanagement (Hodges, 1976).

The crisis came to a head on March 25, 1976:

> A helicopter that was taking Isabel from the Casa Rosada to the Olivos resi-dence developed "engine trouble" and diverted to the military section of the downtown airport. When it landed, armed soldiers stepped aboard, took her into custody and put her on an air force plane bound for the Andean lake country, where she was placed under house arrest. (Hodges, 1976, p. 499)

Isabel Perón was charged with fraud and corruption and held under house arrest, without trial or conviction, until 1981. In 1981, she was convicted of two charges of corruption but acquitted on several counts of misuse of executive funds. On July 6, Isabel was ordered freed on parole by a federal court. Three days later, she boarded a plane bound for Spain, where she remains in exile to this day (Schumacher, 1981a).

LEADERSHIP STYLE

Following Juan Perón's death, there was some question of whether Isabel would step aside and call for new elections, but she assumed the presidency.

Isabel set out to continue the policies of Juan Perón, but her inner cir-cle of advisers was much narrower than his, drawn increasingly from the ultra-Right sectors of the Perónist movement.

What does this tell us about Isabel Martinez de Perón as chief executive? The short answer is: not much.

Isabel Perón served as president for only 18 months. She faced politi-cal, economic, and military instability—much of which was inherited from

Juan Perón's third administration. The broad-based populist coalition that Perón forged in the 1940s and in 1952 was dissolving, and the urban proletariat, which had been the social base of Perónism, could no longer be counted on to give unqualified support—especially to the government of Isabel Perón.

KEY ISSUES

The problems facing Argentina began before Juan Perón's death, but they grew more serious during Isabel Perón's presidency. It is impossible to know how much of the resistance to her rule among certain sectors of the Perónist movement was because of her gender, but there is certainly evidence that her abilities were questioned even by those who were ready to accept a woman in a leadership position.

The conflict within Perónism had three important elements. The Left was virtually eliminated from the broader movement. The ultra-Left People's Revolutionary Army (ERP) had already split with the rest of the movement and was engaged in armed conflict with the military. The economic benefits of Perón's earlier presidency were no longer available to leftist groups, and the military was increasingly free to engage in government-sanctioned acts of violence and repression against popular movements.

Politically, Juan Perón had made the split certain when he tried to "compel the governor of Buenos Aires to resign because of alleged sympathies for the guerrillas" (Hodges, 1976, p. 168). This chasm deepened after Juan's death when the moderate Left, led by the Montoneros, followed in the footsteps of the ultra-Left by denouncing Isabel's administration. Guerrilla warfare raged in the provinces and was increasingly directed at military targets. As the legitimacy of Isabel Perón's government declined, the Left became popular among traditional Perón loyalists.

The elimination of the Left from the Perónist movement led to a second area of conflict. With the Left now working against the Perónists, the relationship between the remaining factions was destabilized. The new split centered on differences between the major trade union, CGT, which was controlled by the moderate Right, and the government, which was controlled by the ultra-Right (Hodges, 1976).

Finally, the Perónist movement was divided between verticalists and anti-verticalists. The verticalists viewed the Perónist movement as focusing largely on Juan Perón personally. Isabel was Juan's choice to succeed him as the leader of the movement—to question this choice was to be disloyal to Perón. Anti-verticalists, on the other hand, saw the possibility of "Perónism without Perón."

Ripples from the split were felt in Congress and within the governing bodies of the Perónist party.[3] In the end, elements of the Justicialist Party formed a coalition in support of Isabel at the National Party Congress. This brought an end to any chance of removing her from office constitutionally.

The economic problems Isabel Perón inherited were aggravated by her government's mismanagement of the economy. In 1975, the rate of inflation was as high as 350%. Isabel continued the policies of her husband with few exceptions—this meant keeping wages and subsidies high. The combination of high wages, which encourage domestic consumption, declining agricultural exports, and capital flight in search of more stable investment opportunities led to a deteriorating balance of trade and an intractable economic crisis.

PERFORMANCE EVALUATION

Evaluations of Isabel Perón's performance as president are universally poor. Some accounts are sympathetic, arguing that she was a victim of circumstances. Others hold Isabel Perón responsible, at least in part, for the political violence that eventually led to the death or "disappearance" of more than 6,000 Argentine citizens.

It is commonly understood that Isabel Perón was not qualified to serve as president of Argentina. It could be argued that under less difficult circumstances she might have completed her term of office and perhaps gained the political skills to remain an active force in Argentine politics, but given the economic and political crises she faced, there was no time for "on-the-job" training.

Isabel Perón remained leader of the Perónist party until 1985, but she was not a unifying force: she spent most of those years in exile, returning to Argentina only for very brief stays. The verticalist wing of the party continued to support Isabel as the rightful heir to Juan Perón, but this support was never based on judgments about her ability to govern. More democratic elements within the movement wished to see reforms that would lead to a social democratic style of party.[4]

In the mid-1980s, she considered running for office, and pressure was put on the military government to restore Mrs. Perón's full political rights. The question of Isabel's candidacy halted the Perónist party convention in 1983. Dissident factions in the party "demanded that the convention make no decisions until former President Isabel Martinez de Perón returns from exile in Spain" ("Peronists Ask Argentina to Let Mrs. Perón Run," 1983). It was not until Isabel removed herself as head of the party that the Perónist movement began to unify, electing the Perónist candidate, Carlos Menem, to the presidency in 1989.

Isabel Perón inherited the presidency at a very difficult time, but there is no evidence to suggest that she struggled against the repressive forces of the ultra-Right: she seems, instead, to have supported them. A period of extreme repression and state-sponsored terror followed her overthrow.

Although the evidence is inconclusive, she must bear some responsibility for the collapse of civil authority in Argentina.

GENDER

It is impossible to know the degree to which gender and class discrimination so common in this historical period impacted the presidency of Isabel Perón.

It must be remembered that, as undemocratic as Perónism may have been, it was Juan and Eva Perón who gave Argentine women the right to vote in 1947 and who founded the Feminist Perónist party in 1949.

Throughout the twentieth century, especially during the periods of military dictatorship, the modest gains of Argentine women were curtailed. There were, however, men and women who challenged discrimination against women in Argentine society.

During the period 1976–1983 (a time referred to as the "Dirty War"), it was the moral authority of motherhood—as expressed by members of the human rights group Mothers of the Plaza de Mayo—that truly challenged the military government and its policies.

After the period of dictatorship and with the return of democracy to Argentina, a gender-based quota system has facilitated the participation of women in public life.

Isabel Perón governed before these empowering movements and reform. Still, Latin American feminists of this period critically evaluated Isabel Perón's presidency.

A range of feminist scholars commented, assessing her presidency. Two examples include Margo de Bottome and Ana Avalos de Rangle.

Noting that if women are qualified, they should be allowed to hold any office, women's rights activist Margo de Bottome of Caracas, Venezuela, criticized the selection of Isabel Perón:

> because she is not qualified for the post . . . of course, there must be a first
> in history, but this is not a happy cause. ("Thousands Cheer," 1973, pp. 4–6)

Other feminists, such as Ana Avalos de Rangle, took a more positive view of Isabel Perón's vice-presidential candidacy:

> Obviously it demonstrates the importance of a woman's role in society and
> particularly in Latin America. ("Thousands Cheer," 1973, pp. 4–6)

As Marifran Carlson observes, Perónism was antifeminist—the franchise came without the support of Argentine feminists (Carlson, 1988). Yet, as Navarro observes, Perónism opened the door to women politically (Navarro, 1977, 1983). The organizing skills women learned working with the Feminist Perónist party were later used by women activists (most notably Mothers of the Plaza de Mayo) against the brutality and violence of the military government that followed Isabel Perón's overthrow.

Isabel was not a leader of women—she was not a feminist, nor was she successful at mobilizing women through appeals to traditional family (women's) values, such as nurturance and submissiveness to male authority figures. The other avenue that might have been open to her—to exercise political power as a public figure, using power and authority in more traditional (male) ways—was closed to women in Argentine society. Under these circumstances, no woman could have succeeded as president—but it is unlikely that Isabel Perón would have been successful in the presidency even if the political system had been more open to women.

Unlike experienced political leaders such as Golda Meir, Margaret Thatcher, Cristina Fernández de Kirchner, and many other women who have held elected positions, Isabel Perón lacked the political skills and popular support necessary to govern effectively.

Whether Isabel (or Eva) could have been successful as president of Argentina in the twentieth century cannot be known, because the depth of discrimination against women in this period makes it impossible to speculate . . . we can't truly assess their power without examining gender, class and cultural biases in Argentine society. Their political careers cannot be analyzed by twenty-first-century standards.

CONCLUSION

Even in the second decade of the twenty-first century, the controversy surrounding Isabel Perón has not been resolved.

In today's much more democratic Argentina, many still seek answers about the tyranny of their country's past and the role that Isabel Perón played in that past. Her 2007 arrest on charges of human rights violations alleged to have occurred during her presidency made headlines around the world, but on March 28, 2008, a Spanish court ruled to deny Argentina's request for her extradition ("Isabel Perón Arrested," 2007). As of the update to this chapter, the now 82-year-old Isabel Perón remains in exile in Spain ("Spain: Extradition of Isabel Perón," 2008).

In sum, Isabel Perón played three critical roles in the politics of Argentina: chief executive, party leader, and political representative. In the private, informal negotiations that paved the way for Juan Perón's return to power in 1973, she played her most important and successful political role.

The evaluation of her role as president is not nearly so positive. While she inherited the presidency at a very difficult time in her nation's history, there is no evidence to suggest that she attempted to prevent the extreme repression and state-sponsored terror and violence that followed the overthrow of her government.

More recent scholarship documents the changing role of women as political leaders in Argentina and around the world.[5] The 2011 reelection of Cristina Fernández de Kirchner is evidence of this change. Still, Isabel Perón remains an important political figure in the history of Argentina and culturally relevant even in this new era of Argentine democracy.

Author's Note: I would like to extend my gratitude to Stephen Trinkaus for his research support and translation of materials from original Spanish text. In addition, I would like to express my appreciation to Tracey Finch and Western Washington University's Office of Research and Sponsored Programs for their ongoing support of faculty research, and special thanks go out to my editor, Suzanne Scally of Little Wing Desktop Publishing.

NOTES

1   The Word Economic Gender Gap 2011 Report is available online in pdf form: http://www.members.webforum.org/pdf/gendergap/report2011.pdf.
2   Gender and class bias are common in many accounts of the lives of Eva Duarte Peron and Isabel Martinez Peron. For alternative views of the life and work of Eva Peron, see Fraser and Navarro (1985) and Flores (1952). Less scholarly discussion exists about Isabel Peron.
3   This is the formal name of the Perónist party, given to it by Juan Perón when the Constitution of 1853 was amended in 1949, allowing him to serve a second term as president.
4   Carlos Sadi Menem, the former president of Argentina, was the first Perónist party candidate to be selected through a more democratic process.
5   New research has been recently been published by a number of different sources, including the following: "Argentina: From Kirchner to Kirchner," by S.L. Levitsky & M.V. Murillo (2008), *Journal of Democracy, 19*(2) 16–30; "Argentina: The Persistence of Peronism," by E.C. and M.V. Murillo, (2012), *Journal of Democracy, 23*(2), 148–161; "Argentina's Women: Don't Cry for Us," by M. Hinojosa, *Volume Two Country Profiles*, (2009), 210–220; "The Power Behind Peronism," by D. Sax (2004), *Foreign Policy, 144*, 86–87, and many others.

REFERENCES AND SELECTED BIBLIOGRAPHY

Carlson, M. (1988). *Feminismo! The women's movement in Argentina from its beginning to Eva Perón*. Chicago: Academy.
Chaffee, L. (1976). Coup finishes Perónismo era. *Latin American Digest, 10*(3), 1–6.
Current Biography Yearbook. (1975). New York: H.W. Wilson.
Dominguez, J.I. (1987). Political change: Central America, South America and the Caribbean. In M. Weiner & S.P. Huntington (Eds.), *Understanding political development*. Boston: Little, Brown.
Flores, M. (1952). *The woman with the whip: Eva Perón*. Garden City, NY: Doubleday.
Fraser, N., & Navarro, M. (1985). *Eva Perón*. New York: W.W. Norton.
Hodges, D.C. (1976). *Argentina, 1943–1976: The national revolution and resistance*. Albuquerque: University of New Mexico Press.
Isabel Perón arrested over accusations of human rights abuses. (2007, January 12). *The Guardian UK*.
Navarro, M. (1977). The case of Eva Perón. *Journal of Women in Culture and Society, 3*, 229–140.
Navarro, M. (1983). Evita and Perónism. In F.C. Turner & J.E. Miguens (Eds.), *Juan Perón and the reshaping of Argentina*. Pittsburgh, PA: University of Pittsburgh Press.

Page, J.A. (1983). *Perón: A biography*. New York: Random House.

Perón, E.D. (1953). *Evita by Evita*. New York: Proteus.

Perónists ask Argentina to let Mrs. Perón run. (1983, July 26). *New York Times*, 3.

Ratliff, W. (1988). Introduction. In L. Horvath (Ed.), *Perónism and the three Peróns*. Stanford, CA: Hoover Institution.

Schumacher, E. (1981a, July 7). Argentine court frees Mrs. Perón after five years. *New York Times*, 2.

Schumacher, E. (1981b, July 11). Freedom for Mrs. Perón reflects Perónist power. *New York Times*, 2.

Smith, W.S. (1983). The return of Perónism. In F.C. Turner & J.E. Miguens (Eds.), *Juan Perón and the reshaping of Argentina*. Pittsburgh, PA: University of Pittsburgh Press.

Smith, P.H., & Skidmore, T.E. (1984). *Modern Latin America*. New York: Oxford University Press.

Sobel, L.A. (Ed.). (1975). *Argentina and Perón 1970–75*. New York: Facts on File.

Spain: Extradition of Isabel Perón to Argentina is rejected by court. (2008, April 29). *New York Times, World Briefing*, A6.

Thousands cheer triumphant return of Perón. *Latin American Digest, 8*(1), 4–6.

Turner, F.C., & Miguens, J.E. (Eds.). (1983). *Juan Perón and the reshaping of Argentina*. Pittsburgh, PA: University of Pittsburgh Press.

11

Margaret Thatcher and the Politics of Conviction Leadership

Michael A. Genovese

The reaction was deeply polarizing like the woman herself. The 2011 release of the movie *Iron Lady*, starring Meryl Streep as Margaret Thatcher, "Mrs. T." to some, "TBW" ("That Bloody Woman") to others, revealed that the passions associated with her years as prime minister had, if anything, intensified over the years. Twenty years after leaving office, Margaret Thatcher remains a deeply controversial and divisive figure in Great Britain.

In the case of Thatcher, hindsight is not 20–20, but 180. And the release of *Iron Lady* gave Brits a chance to reexamine their past at a time when the British government appears to be repeating it with the David Cameron conservative government of today. The film reopened a wound that in 20 years has not healed. One only has to say her name, and emotions peak, and passions—for or against—boil. For better or for worse, Margaret Thatcher mattered.

In many ways, Margaret Thatcher is a political phenomenon. Not only was she England's first woman prime minister, but she served in that capacity longer than anyone in the twentieth century, won three consecutive elections, reshaped much of the British political landscape, ranks as one of the most important prime ministers in British political landscape, has been compared to Clement Attlee and Winston Churchill, *and* is the only British prime minister with an "ism" named after her: Thatcherism! There can be no doubt that Margaret Thatcher has stamped her imprint on British politics and life.

How did she do it? How did so seemingly unlikely a character rise to the top of a male world in the most suffocatingly traditional bastion of male supremacy, the British Conservative Party? And how did she so thoroughly dominate her party and political scene as to transform British politics from the old Churchill/Attlee postwar consensus to a new, different political and economic orientation? It is indeed no exaggeration to say that Margaret Thatcher transformed British politics, making *her* mark on government and society. The unlikelihood of achieving such a transformation is matched only by the even greater surface unlikelihood that this would be achieved by a woman, and one such as Margaret Thatcher. What did she do, and how did she do it?

THE CONTEXT

Before Thatcher's rise to power, events of the twentieth century had been unkind to the British Empire. At the turn of the century, Britain ruled one-fifth of the globe; was widely recognized as the hegemon of the West; exerted vast economic, political, and diplomatic leverage throughout the world; possessed a mighty military machine; and basked in the glory and rewards of empire. But in less than a generation, Britain was stripped of empire, might, and glory. Starting with World War I, extending to the depression of the 1930s, and culminating in World War II, Great Britain's rapid decline in economic, military, and geopolitical power was transformed from *Pax Britannica* to *Pax Americana*.

In the period immediately following World War II, Britain was forced to accept a world role dramatically reduced from the days of empire, as the nation became a peripheral power to the American core. "British decline" became a phrase of common usage. Recovering from the devastation of the war proved a formidable task, but Britain and Europe began the slow climb back. Living standards improved; growth and development proceeded apace; and, as a result of the military and economic alliance with the United States and the development of a postwar consensus at home, Great Britain slowly regained a sense of economic security and social advancement.

The postwar "consensus" (or settlement) that came to so utterly dominate British politics emerged out of Winston Churchill's wartime consensus government and postwar recovery plans, but came to full fruition under the prime ministership of Clement Attlee. The consensus consisted of an agreement on the part of both Labour and the Conservatives over how postwar Britain should be governed. Its elements included agreement on both the foreign policy and domestic/economic components of British politics. The foreign policy elements included a bipartisan approach to problem solving, support for NATO, decolonization (in the 30 years after World War II, more than 30 nations achieved independence from British rule), and Britain as a nuclear power. The domestic/economic elements of the consensus consisted of a bipartisan commitment to full employment, greater acceptance of trade unions in the political arena, more public ownership of industry, the pursuit of a mixed economy of public and market orientation, active economic management of the economy by the government, and the rise of the social welfare state. This required an active government, significant public expenditures, and high taxation.

This consensus proved remarkably durable. It resulted in a striking continuity between governments and parties, and resulted in a marriage of sorts between modern capitalism and social democracy (Kavanaugh, 1990, pp. 26–62). But the great successes of the consensus, and the economic and political recovery it engendered, did not last forever. As economic and political problems rose in the 1970s, cracks in the consensus began to emerge.

The solidity of the postwar consensus was jeopardized by a combination of factors, none more menacing than the economic and trade union problems that beset England in the early 1970s. The promise of the postwar consensus—full employment, economic growth, security—was undermined as OPEC oil embargoes, strikes by trade unions, rising joblessness, inflation, and overall economic malaise challenged the legitimacy of the consensus. The center could not hold. As Peter Jenkins (1988) notes, "Economic failure had gradually taken its toll on the social cohesion and stability which had made Britain for so long one of the political wonders of the world" (p. 30). England's postwar recovery, sluggish by European standards, went into a tailspin, and the consensus began to unravel. Britain began to be seen, and to see itself, as being in a state of decline and deindustrialization. The British governing class was being challenged. Decline threatened to continue beyond the nation's ability to arrest its extension.

It was not until the mid-1970s that the consensus came to be seen as the enemy of economic growth. Britain came to be seen as "ungovernable" and an "overloaded" state. The government seemed on the verge of economic bankruptcy and political insolvency. Britain was seen as "the sick man of

Europe"; trade union strikes increased in number and severity and came to be seen as "the British disease." Big government was not working. High inflation, low economic growth, high unemployment, strikes, and weak government conspired against the consensus.

By the mid- to late 1970s, a window of political opportunity opened for those wishing to challenge the consensus. The economic downturn exposed a weakness in the consensus as the government's performance could not match public expectations. All that was missing was a viable challenger with a salable alternative. At first, that person *did not* appear to be Margaret Thatcher, for, up until her prime ministership, Thatcher was an unlikely rebel: a woman, a traditional Tory conservative, a team player.

THATCHER'S EARLY LIFE OR "WHY CAN'T YOU BE MORE LIKE MARGARET ROBERTS?"[1]

If Margaret (Roberts) Thatcher had been a man, biographers would have insisted that she was "born to be politician."[2] But if anyone in her day had seriously thought that a girl born to middle-class British parents in Lincolnshire in 1925 could one day become leader of the Conservative Party and prime minister, he or she would have been thought mad. With all the political schooling Margaret Roberts received at the feet of her father, the England of 1925 and beyond was distinctly a "man's world." The social expectations of middle-class women when Margaret was growing up were centered almost exclusively on home and family. Thus, Margaret Thatcher's political career looms all the more remarkable, given the odds against her.

Margaret Roberts, second daughter of Alfred and Beatrice Roberts, grew up in the small town of Grantham, Lincolnshire. The daughter of a grocer, she lived with her family above their shop. Alfred Roberts was a successful small businessman and was very active in civic affairs. He was, beyond question, the biggest influence on Margaret's life (Campbell, 2009).

Alfred Roberts, who had only minimal formal education but was a voracious reader, instilled in his youngest daughter a need to win, an ethic of work, a drive to succeed. Alfred Roberts dominates Margaret Thatcher's recollections of childhood. He is seen by his daughter as teacher, mentor, guru, and guide. No other figure in her life comes close to the influence of

Alf. When she became Britain's first woman prime minister, she spoke of her father:

> He brought me up to believe all the things I do believe and they are the values on which I have fought the election. It is passionately interesting to me that the things I learned in a small town, in a very modest home, are just the things that I believe have won the election. I owe almost everything to my father. (quoted in Webster, 1990, p. 3)

Such tributes to her father were not unusual. He overwhelms her memory and is seen as the force that shaped her and moves her.

To Alf, Margaret was more than a daughter; she was "pupil, protégée, and potential *alter ego*, the offspring who could and would achieve the greater, wider life which circumstances and the accident of birth had denied him" (Harris, 1989, p. 59). Alf was very active in the affairs of his community, serving as lay preacher in the local Methodist church and as a school governor; borough councilor; alderman; and, finally, mayor of Grantham. Margaret was thus reared on a life of public affairs and learned about politics at her father's knee.

As for shaping her character, Margaret recalls two lessons she learned from her father that stand out: First, "You must make your own decisions. You don't do something because your friends are doing it. You do it because you think it's the best thing to do"; and second, "Don't follow the crowd; don't be afraid of being different. You decide what you ought to do, and if necessary you lead the crowd. But you never just follow" (quoted in Harris, 1989, p. 66). During her prime ministership, these two traits would be borne out time after time. Biographer Kenneth Harris (1989) asked the prime minister what she had learned from her father, and she responded:

> His simple conviction that some things are right, and some are wrong. His belief that life is ultimately about character, that character comes from what you make of yourself. You must work hard to earn money to support yourself, but hard work was even more important in the formation of character. You must learn to stand on your own feet. There was a great emphasis on learning to stand on your own feet. There are many things which ought never to be done for money—marriage, for instance. Money was only a means to an end. Ends never justified means.

The contrast between Margaret's relationship with her father—so close, so influential—and her relationship to her mother is absolutely striking. Where she identified with and tried to emulate her father, she seems intent on erasing the memory of her mother from her life. Hugo Young (1989) notes that in Thatcher's "adult mind, Alfred was as prominent as her mother was obscure" (p. 4). Thatcher mentions Beatrice rarely, and whenever an interviewer attempts to draw her out on the subject of her mother, she almost always turns the answer into a reference to her father. This obsessive avoidance of discussion of her mother relegates Beatrice to a mere footnote in Margaret Thatcher's life. In fact, there is no mention of her mother in Thatcher's *Who's Who* entry, where Thatcher is listed simply as her father's daughter.

Beatrice Roberts was a quiet, house-centered wife, a subordinate figure within the family dominated by Alfred. In a 1975 interview, Thatcher said of her mother, "I loved my mother dearly, but after I was fifteen we had nothing more to say to each other. It wasn't her fault. She was weighed down by the home, always being in the home" (*Daily Telegraph*, February 5, 1975). Margaret Thatcher seems to feel she owes almost everything to her father, and practically nothing to her mother. As Young (1990) notes, "There is scarcely an aspect of Alfred that has failed to find its way into the politics of his daughter. Rarely in the history of political leadership could one find an example of such extravagant filial tribute" (p. 4). As an interesting note, many strong male leaders had strong or dominant mothers. In Thatcher's case, she had a strong father to guide her.

If the impact of Alfred overwhelms, the impact of religion on Margaret Thatcher seems negligible. She was raised as a strict Methodist and regularly attended Sunday services, but one finds very few clues that this had anything but a peripheral impact. One is also hard-pressed to find many clues into the makeup of Margaret Thatcher from her school days. She had few close friends and (at her father's insistence) spurned almost all social activities. She was in school, as in all other things, very serious, officious, and hardworking. Even in her days at Oxford, where she began to emerge as a social being, she remained aloof and withdrawn from most of her contemporaries. Home, not school, not church, not community, shaped Margaret Thatcher. And in the home, Alfred dominated (Webster, 1990, p. 6).

Margaret entered Somerville College, Oxford, in 1943 to study chemistry. In college she became active in the Oxford University Conservative Association, eventually becoming its president. She was, according to her tutors, "able but not noticeably imaginative, studious but not creative" (Little, 1988, p. 94). She completed her degree with upper second-class honors.

What are we to make of this childhood and upbringing? Several characteristics stand out as shaping the development of Margaret Roberts (Thatcher). She was driven to achieve by a father who seemed to be all things to young Margaret. She absorbed as her own the goals, ideas, and aspirations of the father. Hard work, individualism, Victorian values, discipline, combativeness, single-mindedness, frugality, and duty were stressed. Her mother is a mere footnote in all of this, a memory to be overcome, not an influence to be admired. It was Alfred Roberts whom young Margaret aspired to emulate.

After college, Margaret's first job was with British Xylonite as a research chemist at their Manningtree, Essex, plant. The work was mundane, and Margaret's real interest—politics—always came first. But how to pursue a career in politics while working for a living? At this point in life, Margaret began her search for a safe parliamentary seat. Margaret Roberts, young, a woman, of limited means, did not find her early efforts at breaking into politics very easy. In 1949, at the age of 24, she was selected as conservative candidate in Dartford. She changed jobs, joining the research department at J. Lyons and Co., moved into the district, and began to campaign feverishly. But in the 1950 election, while the Conservative Party trimmed Labour's House of Commons majority from 150 to 5, Margaret Roberts lost her election.

During the campaign, Margaret met Denis Thatcher. He was then the managing director of his family's paint and chemical business and, at 36, was 10 years older than Margaret. Denis had been married several years earlier (a fact that, to this day, Margaret Thatcher seems unable to accept or even admit), but was divorced at the time he met Margaret. They were married in 1951. In the same year, another general election took place, and while once again Margaret lost, she cut into the lead of her opponent's majority. But Margaret Thatcher, at the ripe young age of 26, was a two-time loser, newly married, and groping for a political future.

For Thatcher, marriage meant financial freedom. She was free to pursue a political career unencumbered by the demands of job or paycheck. It freed her time and freed her from worry. It also freed her from the traditional demands of housekeeping. Margaret Thatcher did not have to choose between career and marriage; her marriage freed her to pursue her career.

She began to study for the bar, and specialized in tax law. Her studies were interrupted in 1953—but only temporarily—by the birth of twins, Carol and Mark. How could Margaret have children, a home life, *and* a career? Hire a nanny/housekeeper, educate the children in private and boarding schools, and continue the pursuit of power. She would not be a traditional homemaker, like her mother. Denis's financial position allowed Margaret to return to the study of law, and in 1954 she was called to the bar. The children were not a great burden on Margaret Thatcher, and she managed to soothe whatever guilty feelings may have emerged by assuring everyone that no matter what, she was only 20 minutes away from the children, "if I was needed" (Little, 1988, p. 106). As Wendy Webster (1990) writes about the tug between home/children and career for Thatcher, "She made few, if any, concessions to the dual role model then, and its requirement that family needs were women's first responsibility and working life subordinate to this" (p. 38).

In the space of a few short years, Margaret Roberts had married into wealth and security, passed the bar, had twins, and *finally* found a safe parliamentary seat. Jenkins (1988) writes of this meteoric rise: "The idea that the family is the true centre of her moral universe, that she was a paragon of motherhood and wifely virtue, does not fit easily with the speed and determination with which the Grantham girl made good" (p. 85).

If Margaret Thatcher appeared to be overly ambitious, it is because she was. There is a compulsive, driven quality about her determination to succeed. She seemed unfulfilled by home and family and, with an almost desperate determination, sought a safe seat in Parliament. As her past efforts prove, this was not an easy task. A safe seat in prime political real estate, and the battle to be accepted by the party leaders as a candidate for such a seat is a competitive, often bloody, venture. Finally, in 1957, she was accepted by Finchley, a safe conservative district near London. In the next election, in October of 1959, Margaret Thatcher, at the age of 34, was elected to Parliament (Thatcher, 1995).

The 1959 Parliament would last five years, and it was not long before Margaret Thatcher, one of the few women in the conservative cadre, began to rise in the party leadership. In 1961, she received her first ministerial assignment as joint parliamentary secretary to the Ministry of Pensions and National Insurance.

The Conservatives lost the 1964 general election, and Thatcher began a string of shadow offices. In 1965, when Edward Heath took over leadership of the Conservative Party, Thatcher moved to Housing and Land, and after the conservative 1966 defeat, she was promoted to the number-two spokesperson on Treasury matters under shadow chancellor Ian MacLeod. Later she became shadow minister for fuel and power, then shadow minister for transport. In 1969, Heath appointed her shadow minister of education.

When the Conservatives won the general election of 1970, Heath made Thatcher minister of education and science. It was in this capacity she received the appellation "Thatcher the Milk Snatcher" for her cuts in a school milk program (Young, 1990, chap. 6). Her tenure in this office was controversial, and earned her the dubious distinction of being dubbed by the *Sun* "the most unpopular woman in Britain" (Ogden, 1990, chap. 5).

At this stage in her career, Margaret Thatcher was greatly aided by the fact of her gender. The Conservative Party was overwhelmingly male, and in these early days of the women's liberation movement, Heath felt compelled to appoint women to shadow roles. But if gender opened doors for Thatcher, there can be no mistake that, once in office, she performed tirelessly and credibly. If gender got her the job, hard work, determination, and skill kept her there.

The early 1970s were a time of trouble and turmoil for the Heath government. Economic downturns, union problems, and general malaise plagued Britain. Strikes became known as "the British disease," and Britain became known as "the sick man of Europe." As is usually the case in politics, the "in" party was blamed for the problems, and in the general election of 1974, the Conservatives, unable to form a government, fell from power, and Labour took control of the government. Once again, Margaret Thatcher was in opposition. But she would not sit idly by. Thatcher quickly began a move to capture control of the Conservative Party.

Margaret Thatcher was one step away from the pinnacle. But who was Margaret Thatcher? Clearly the small-town virtues and Victorian values she absorbed from her father guided her. As John Vincent (1987) has written:

> Yet this is perhaps the essential Thatcher, the suburban professional woman of the 1950s living in a period of naively moral anti-totalitarianism, of declining taxes, in a state whose frontiers could, it seemed, be rolled back. Putting aside the symbolism (later to be electorally useful) of Grantham, the fifties were her real formative decade; and what her efforts in the eighties proved was that the fifties could not be brought back. (p. 276)

But she was more than this, for Margaret Thatcher was equally determined to rid Britain of the evils of the 1960s and 1970s: socialism, state power, centralization of authority, welfarism. If Thatcher wanted to restore small-town virtues, this meant the destruction of socialism. It was a return to small-town Britain and a return to a vision of nineteenth-century economic liberalism, a free-market economy, which Thatcher sought.

Her character was shaped by life with father, but her public life and her views on politics and policy were also shaped by her times. As Jenkins (1988) has written, "Her crucial political experiences were gained under socialism at home and communism abroad; she was a daughter of the age of austerity, a child of the Cold War" (p. 82). She wanted change, radical change, social transformation—a revolution.

As Margaret Thatcher prepared herself for the exercise of power, she seemed quite ready to lead. She benefited from the aid of mentors such as her father and, later, such figures as Sir Keith Joseph, Airey Neave, William Whitelaw, and Gordon Reece. Thatcher was willing to sit at the foot of a wise man from time to time. She was a good student of the art and science of politics, but when the lesson was over, she resumed control. Was she, as Young claims, "born to be a politician"? Perhaps so, but one would be hard-pressed to say that one such as Margaret Thatcher was born to be prime minister, because she was born before women were given the vote (Webster, 1990, p. 8). Clearly, the tectonic plates of gender politics were shifting. If Margaret Thatcher was reared to be a politician, she certainly was not born to be one. For that to take place, the social changes inspired (insisted upon) by the nascent women's movement created the opportunity for Margaret Thatcher to be a politician. It was a debt that she would not repay.

PATH TO POWER

After the Conservatives' defeats in two general elections of 1974, the party was prepared to jettison Ted Heath and embrace a new leader. But Heath did not give up power easily. After a good deal of political maneuvering, after several of Heath's most likely challengers withdrew from the contest, Thatcher entered the leadership battle. While Thatcher charted a course to the political Right of Ted Heath, it was not yet clear just how far Right or how much of a conviction, or ideological, leader Thatcher was to become (Thatcher, 1995).

After losing three of four elections in a 10-year period, the Conservatives were ready for a change of leadership. In the party's first ballot for leader, held on February 4, 1975, Thatcher outpolled Heath 130 to 119. While this was not enough for her to be elected on the first ballot, it was clear that Heath was out. In the scramble to fill the second-ballot void left by Heath's withdrawal, several people offered themselves, but it was too little, too late. On the second ballot, held on February 11, Thatcher got 146 votes. The next-closest candidate, Willie Whitelaw, got only 79 votes. In what was essentially an anti-Heath leadership battle, Margaret Thatcher emerged as head of the Conservative Party. The party had chosen an outsider, a dissident, and a woman as its new leader.

Thatcher was, as Chris Ogden (1990) notes, "no one's first choice" (p. 119), but she was the only truly conservative challenger to emerge, and in a time when the centrist consensus politics of Ted Heath were held up to ridicule, even as unlikely a candidate as Margaret Thatcher became viable. Harris (1989) argues that Thatcher became head of the party "as the result of a series of accidents" (p. 48), and Ogden (1990) suggests that she led a "coup" against the party regulars (p. 115). Young (1990) says she was "a mistake that should never have happened" (p. 100). Thatcher herself told a newspaper reporter six months earlier, "It will be years before a woman either leads the party or becomes prime minister. I don't see it happening in my time" (Ogden, 1990, p. 119).

While there were some early indications that Thatcher was a radical conservative, her years as leader in opposition belied this. Her shadow cabinet was dominated by unreconstructed Heathlites, and her policy advocacy seemed moderate and cautious. Thatcher's caution reflected the precariously fragile perch upon which her leadership rested. But public appearances aside, Thatcher was determined to chart a new, more radical brand of conservatism for Britain.

In the late 1970s, the new Right, or the more radical Right, gained ground within the Conservative Party. Rejecting the policies and politics of the old consensus-oriented wing of the party, the intellectual center of the Conservative Party began to drift slowly to the right. Thatcher, always skating on political thin ice as party leader, slowly and cautiously moved the party right. She knew her hold on the party was precarious, and a major blunder could cause her demise. She repeatedly said, "I shall have only one chance" (Vincent, 1987, p. 278), for there were always political sharks waiting to depose her.

While in opposition, Thatcher witnessed the collapse of yet another government, as Labour was unable to solve the economic and trade union problems that plagued Britain. Thatcher began to develop economic policies in sharp contrast to the consensus model, and, as economic conditions worsened, this new economic philosophy gained adherents—not so much because it was convincing, but because it was an alternative to the status quo. Margaret Thatcher was again winning by default.

In the general election of 1979, the in party was thrown out, and the out party was put in. Owing her election more to the failure of the Callaghan Labour government than to the attractiveness of her policies or her personality, Thatcher was once again a leader on shaky ground. But she was the leader. She was the prime minister.

In the 1979 election, the Conservatives won a majority of 43 seats. This marked the largest shift from one party to another since 1945. At the time, however, the 1979 election appeared to be anything but a watershed election. While the Conservatives outpolled Labour, Thatcher always ran behind Callaghan in personal popularity and was consistently less popular than her party. While her proposals of tight control of the money supply, lower taxes, trade union bashing, anti-immigration, and racial divisiveness had some appeal, Thatcher's goal of a consensus-shattering social revolution would have to wait. At age 53, she was a prime minister who headed her party but did not yet control or dominate it. Nor did she capture the imagination of the British public.

How did Thatcher win? First and foremost, Labour lost. The 1979 election was a "throw 'em out" election. Second, the ideas that animated Thatcher's drastic social revolution were not yet fully formed, and thus the election was about change, but it was always unclear just how much change was involved. Third, the 1970s were a time of international economic malaise, and Britain suffered more from this than most. Worldwide, ruling parties were thrown out, and Thatcher benefited from this trend. Fourth, while gender mattered, other factors dominated the election, and gender—while important—was overshadowed by the failure of Labour and the desperation of Britain's economic condition. All these factors, and many more, coalesced to bring an unlikely person to power. As Young (1990) points out, Thatcher was "a cluster of paradoxes" (p. 140).

After the results of the 1979 election were announced, Thatcher went straight to her new home at Number 10 Downing Street. The new prime minister stood in front of the black door of Number 10 and said to the crowd of gathered reporters, "I just owe everything to my own father, I really do" (Ogden, 1990, p. 152). While Alfred Roberts had been dead for nine years, it was still to him that she turned at her moment of triumph.

THE THATCHER AGENDA

Margaret Thatcher seemed an unlikely rebel. How could this small-town girl grow up to be a radical, anti-consensus revolutionary? How did she change Britain? Margaret Thatcher's policies—if not her politics—were conservative, perhaps radically so. She attributed her policy formation not to any abstract philosophical principles, but to the everyday lessons she learned from her father.

Thatcher's goal was to break down the postwar consensus and revitalize Britain with a free-market, entrepreneurial public philosophy. The fact that the old consensus was seen as a failure created a window of opportunity through which Thatcher was determined to take Britain. In economic policy primarily, but also in defense, domestic, and social policy, Great Britain would be recast from top to bottom (Thatcher, 1993).

Economic Policy

At the center of the Thatcher revolution was her determination to change economic relations and attitudes radically. As Thatcher often said, "economics are the method. The object is to change the soul" (Ogden, 1990, p. 173). Thatcher's goal was to reverse Britain's economic decline, overthrow the postwar consensus, bury socialism, and change the way the British people thought about politics and economics. In short, she sought a revolution.

In economic terms, the revolution was to be accomplished by curbing public spending, lowering taxes, liberating the entrepreneurial spirit, tightly controlling money, lowering inflation, reducing government regulations, moving toward privatization of publicly owned industries, and busting the unions.³ It was, of course, an amazingly ambitious plan, but one that Thatcher was driven to put into place.

How successful was the Thatcher government in accomplishing its myriad goals in economic policy? On inflation, the government had some early success. Aided by an international recession in the early 1980s, the inflation rate fell dramatically. But by the late 1980s and early 1990s, Britain's price index increased to the point that by 1990, the nation's double-digit inflation was one of the highest in the European Community. Inflation was linked to the control of money supply, a vital strategy for Thatcher. While there was a fairly rigid control of the money supply in the first Thatcher term, as time went by, strict money control was jettisoned in favor of growth policies.

In the area of public spending, Thatcher sought to control growth but was only marginally successful. The rate of growth was reduced, but total spending did increase, albeit at a slightly lower rate. What has been clear is that there has been a marked shift in spending between government programs: defense and law-and-order spending increased, housing and industry money was cut, and education and transportation remained about the same.

Thatcher also sought to rid the public sector of the nationalized industries. The effort at privatization continued apace in the 1980s as the assets of several key industries were sold. Many industries, including British Petroleum, British Aerospace, Rolls Royce, British Steel, British Telecom, Jaguar, British Airways, and British Gas, were privatized under Thatcher.

There was, as promised, a cut in the top tax rate (from 83% to 60%) as well as in the standard rate of income tax (from 33% to 30%). But the value added tax (VAT) rose from 8% to 15%, and employers' national insurance contributions also rose. In 1988, taxes were cut even further, with the top rate dropping to 40% and the standard rate going down to 25%. Overall, however, taxes did not go down. There was a shift from direct to indirect taxes, but not a cut.

As the 1980s drew to a close, Thatcher proposed, and passed into law, a poll tax aimed at shifting the burden of taxes away from the wealthy and onto the middle and lower classes. This tax, the level at which was determined in large part by local authorities, and in which almost everyone had to pay an equal tax total, was presented as a tax reform, but was really a way to try to dump the tax blame on the local (or liberal) governments. The poll tax was highly unpopular and proved to be short lived.

Due in part to increased revenues from North Sea oil that offset declines in manufacturing, Britain experienced economic growth during the 1980s. While this growth was not dramatic, approximately 2%, it did mark an increase over the very sluggish (less than 2%) growth of the 1970s; however, it was lower than the growth of the 1960s.

Union-busting efforts were designed to eliminate what Thatcher saw as the stranglehold that trade unions had over the government. Thatcher was determined to bring the trade unions down, and proved to be unrelenting in this goal. She was very successful. As Dennis Kavanaugh (1990) writes:

> In many respects the Thatcher years have been depressing for the trade unions. The setbacks include mass unemployment, decline of Labour, loss of members, privatization of parts of the public sector, cash limits in much of the public sector, which limited opportunities for bargaining, government initiated incursions into their internal affairs, and minimal access to Whitehall. (p. 237)

Strikes, which had so often crippled Britain, were met with firm resolution and eventually became politically insignificant. Thatcher succeeded in busting union power in Britain.

Linked to the decline in union power was a dramatic rise in unemployment. Upon taking office, Thatcher faced an unemployment rate of 5.4%. This doubled under Thatcher. High unemployment, which may have been a policy goal linked to lowering wages, lowering inflation, *and* busting unions, did have the effect of weakening labor's bargaining power, and, as long as high unemployment did not create significant social repercussions, could be tolerated by the Thatcher government.

Thatcher's policies raise questions about winners and losers. Clearly, labor and the underclass were losers. Under Thatcher, the tax system became less progressive, social services were cut, and unemployment rose. The number of homeless skyrocketed, and government support for housing dropped. The disabled, the weak, the poor, and the elderly all suffered under Thatcher's policies. Under Thatcher, inequality and poverty rose, adding to what Neil Kinnock has called the "archipelago of poverty" in Britain. There was no measurable "trickle down." The big winners were those in the upper class. In short, under Thatcher, the rich got richer and the poor got poorer, and, according to Ogden (1990), "a meaner and greedier society" was created (p. 335).

Thatcher's goal of freeing the economy came at a high cost in human terms. It also required a strong state to implement these goals. That a free economy would go along with a strong, centralized, more intrusive state runs counter to traditional conservative goals. But that is precisely what took place in Britain. Thatcher, more an authoritarian conservative than a libertarian conservative, gave lip service to the rhetoric of the minimalist state, but her activist government expanded the power of the central state and pursued what one of her ministers called "the smack of firm government" (Kavanaugh, 1990, pp. 284, 294). Thatcher attempted to enforce a "moral" code of competitive capitalism. This required government rule making, as well as a good deal of persuasion. The government's education policy serves as an excellent example of the contradictions in a system of heightened government control in a less-controlled economy. The state intruded more often as guide and rule enforcer as Thatcher divested the government of nationalized industries and attempted to create a new model of economic man for Britain.

Military and Defense Policy

When Margaret Thatcher took office in 1979, Britain's international standing was quite low. The heady days of empire had ended, and the "sick man of Europe" had limited power and little prestige. On top of that, Thatcher herself had no prior experience in foreign affairs.

Thatcher's early foreign policy goals were clear: increase defense spending, maintain a nuclear arms deterrent, support the United States, oppose the Soviet Union and communism, support NATO, but maintain cool relations regarding Britain's membership in the European Economic Community (EEC). But Thatcher's policy goals were very quickly overshadowed by her style in foreign affairs: resolute, unyielding, nationalistic, rigid. It was not long before the sobriquet "the Iron Lady," given to Thatcher by the Soviet news agency, TASS, became both a fitting appellation and a description of her style of governing.

After 11 years in office, Thatcher faced several seemingly intractable foreign policy problems. She was unable to make headway with the problems of Northern Ireland (Ogden, 1990, chap. 13), faced severe criticism for her support of the white minority government in South Africa, and stubbornly fought the move to a more truly united European Community, leaving Britain outside the inner circle as Europe moved toward unity in 1992.

On the more positive side of the foreign policy ledger, Thatcher was successful at strengthening the already strong ties between Britain and the United States. In fact, so close was Margaret Thatcher to Ronald Reagan that the mutual fawning society between the two leaders, while it helped both leaders in their respective countries, actually masked a deeper unease that Thatcher felt toward Reagan (Wapshott, 2008). While Thatcher and Reagan competed in public to see who could heap higher praise on the other, in private Thatcher had grave doubts about Reagan's ability. "Poor dear," she once said, "there's nothing between his ears." After a meeting with Reagan, Thatcher remarked, "Not much gray matter, is there?" (Ogden, 1990, chap. 14).

Thatcher's relationship with Mikhail Gorbachev and the Soviet Union represents one of the few cases in which she actually changed her mind. Beginning her term as a rabid anti-Communist, Thatcher was captivated by Gorbachev, concluding, "We can do business together," and indeed Thatcher helped persuade Ronald Reagan that he too could do business with Gorbachev (Ogden, 1990, chap. 18).

On other foreign policy issues, Thatcher faced significant problems, especially in her handling of the transition to black rule in Rhodesia/ Zimbabwe, for which she was given high marks (Young, 1990, pp. 181–183), and her handling of transition of British control of Hong Kong to China (pp. 291–292). But no foreign policy issue loomed larger, or had a greater impact on Thatcher's power, than the 1982 Falkland Islands War. This war, more than any other event, "created" and cemented Thatcher and Thatcherism in the hearts, minds, and politics, of Great Britain.

On March 19, 1982, a small group of Argentineans landed on the Falkland Islands. These islands, just off the coast of Argentina (which the Argentineans called the Malvinas), were claimed by Argentina but had been controlled by Britain since 1833. The Thatcher government responded swiftly and forcefully, sending British forces to the islands to recapture them.

The war itself was in part the result of gross errors of judgment and policy by the Thatcher government. Several steps were taken just prior to the Argentinean invasion that served as indications that Britain was unwilling to fight for or defend the Falklands. This led Young (1990) to conclude that "the war to reclaim the Falkland Islands from Argentinean occupation was the result of a great failure in the conduct of government: arguably the most disastrous lapse by any British government since 1945" (p. 258).

But the errors in judgment ended up being the best thing that ever happened for Margaret Thatcher's leadership. In the aftermath of Britain's Falkland victory, Thatcher emerged in a stronger position than she had ever had before. After victory was assured, Thatcher emerged from seclusion and announced, "Today has put the Great back in Britain," and indeed, that is the way many in England saw it. The Falkland victory proved to be the seminal event in Thatcher's years in power. She was now seen as *the* leader of Britain, with virtually no challengers. And from that point on, Thatcher acted with a bolder, more self-confident style. She was virtually unstoppable. Almost overnight, her hold on power was solidified. Thatcher was now a world figure who halted Britain's retreat and brought victory. Her popularity skyrocketed. Her style, seen as abrasive and strident before the war, was now applauded as firm and resolute. The Falkland victory dramatically transformed Thatcher's leadership and power, and from that point on she dominated, even overwhelmed, the political scene.

Domestic and Social Policy

While Margaret Thatcher was determined to transform Britain through a new economic policy, the domestic and social policy agenda was to contribute to and complement the "Thatcher revolution" (Clayton & Thompson, 1989). Thatcher opposed increases in welfare, hoping instead to shrink the welfare state, reduce its costs, and break the chain of dependency that she felt it created. The problem, however, was not merely economic, but also political, for the social welfare programs were extremely popular, and therefore Thatcher was able to make only marginal changes in funding the policy.

In education, while no drastic cuts took place, Thatcher so politicized the issue that morale plummeted, resulting in a crisis in the educational system. As part of her effort to discredit the leftist-leaning Greater London Council (which eventually she disbanded), which controlled local policy, Thatcher also disbanded the Inner London Education Authority, which controlled local schools. Thatcher was upset that too much social engineering was taking place in the London school system (e.g., each school is required to implement an antiracism program) and was determined to purge the schools of liberal content, regardless of the cost in educational quality. This led Thatcher—in spite of her public statements honoring local control—to centralize education policy further by establishing a national curriculum and national assessment program. Public pronouncements about local control aside, this was centralization of a massive scale. Thatcher thus displayed her willingness to violate her own philosophy (conservative, local control) in an effort to gain her desired political ends (control of the schools).

Thatcher's policy toward British higher education was even more devastating. In both rhetoric and action, Thatcher made it clear that the university system was a political enemy, and her harsh rhetoric and frugal policies created a crisis in higher education. The result has been a "brain drain" (especially in the sciences, but in other academic areas as well), with the very best British scholars leaving England for greener and more welcoming academic pastures abroad.

On the environment, Thatcher's record began with benign neglect, but by the end of the 1980s she discovered environmental protection as an issue and began to increase government activity modestly. Britain, however, long considered the dumping ground for European refuse (toxic and otherwise), has serious environmental problems that were addressed in only the most peripheral manner (Robenson, 1989, p. 38).

Thatcher's efforts at union busting, mentioned earlier, led to some severe domestic repercussions, but ultimately Thatcher outlasted and won out over the unions. In confrontations with Arthur Scargill (who headed the National Union of Mineworkers), the most radical of the union leaders, Thatcher outlasted a union strike and forced the unions to back down. By remaining tough, Thatcher won another victory over her "enemies." But other strikes plagued Britain, and as Thatcher dug in, with her "never surrender" approach, violence erupted. In 1981, in the South London Brixton area, a racially mixed community, riots broke out in which 279 police and an estimated 200 members of the community were injured. Nearly 30 buildings were damaged. No one was killed. How did the prime minister respond? Young (1990) writes:

> From Margaret Thatcher . . . this epochal event elicited a response that hardly did justice to its complexity, still less to the hazards it apparently portended as a consequence of her economic policy. It touched her on one of her least sensitive nerves. As she had sometimes shown before, she possessed no delicacy, such as other politicians of all parties had learned to cultivate, when dealing with black or brown people. Rather the reverse. Permanently on her record, and permanently lodged in the memories of leaders of the ethnic minorities, was the remark she had made on television in January

1978 about the legitimate fears of the white community that it was being "swamped" by non-whites. On immigration she had always belonged instinctively, without effort or much apparent thought, on the hard right of the party. (pp. 233–234)

On seeing pictures of the violence and rioting, Thatcher responded, "Oh, those poor shopkeepers" (Young, 1990, p. 239). Such callousness and insensitivity cemented the minds of the left and underclass an image of Margaret Thatcher as cold, uncaring, and cruel. This conception was not completely off the mark, for Thatcher could be a blind ideologue, more concerned with property than human suffering.

The Thatcher revolution had only marginal impact on healthy policy. In the late 1980s, the Thatcher government began an attempt to place a conservative hue onto the health services system, but the health system was highly popular and nearly immune to deep budget cuts. On crime, the government's policy had little impact; crime and violence remained major problems.

A government in office for a dozen years is bound to face ethical problems from time to time. How did Margaret Thatcher handle such crises? Her first significant ethical challenge came in 1983, when a *Daily Mirror* headline blared "Tory Chief's Love Child." Thatcher's valued cabinet minister and campaign manager, Cecil Parkinson, had been having an affair with his secretary, Sara Keays, who was pregnant. How did Thatcher, the strident advocate and protector of Victorian values, respond? She supported Parkinson. But as events unfolded, and as the political heat was turned up, it became clear that Parkinson had to go. The messy scandal, however, revealed that the prime minister was willing to overlook scandal when it suited her; however, when self-interest dictated, she would jettison even her most trusted aides.

In early 1986, the Thatcher government faced a more serious political scandal: the Westland affair. This scandal was to reflect very poorly on Margaret Thatcher's credibility and her character. Due to carelessness, poor management, and the desire to cover up wrongdoing, Thatcher engaged in what Young (1990) calls "the darker political arts" (p. 427).

Westland p/c was a small helicopter company, the only British company, in fact, that made helicopters. It was facing bankruptcy and went to the government for assistance. Thatcher was a devout opponent of public money going to save businesses, but since Westland was defense related, it merited a second look. Michael Heseltine, a member of Thatcher's cabinet, but seen as a rival for power, was at the time minister of defense. He opposed a buyout deal by the Sikorsky Company, a U.S. firm, and instead favored purchase by a European consortium.

From this point on, the affair took a variety of twists, turns, and back stabs. Thatcher, in part to take a slap at rival Heseltine, sided with Trade and Industry Minister Leon Brittan in favor of the Sikorsky sale. What followed were a series of behind-the-scenes promises and deals, press leaks and lies, accusations and deceits. Thatcher claimed ignorance of all wrongdoing, a claim unconvincing to even the staunchest Thatcherites. At the height of the scandal, Thatcher told one associate, "I may not be prime minister by six o'clock tonight."[4] But amazingly, the opposition could not strike the fatal blow—Thatcher was blessed from the beginning with a weak, divided opposition—and the prime minister weathered yet another political storm. While Thatcher's reputation suffered, she hung on to power, and soon the Westland scandal was forgotten.

Margaret Thatcher always had as her stated goal domestic and social policy to provide less government and promote more individual responsibility. The individual and the entrepreneur were her heroes; the group, the society, the community were secondary. She told an interviewer in 1987, "There is no such thing as society. There are individual men and women and there are families" (Webster, 1990, p. 57). Hardly the comment of a Burkean conservative! As was the case with education and local government control, the goal of less government was often superseded by a narrower, more partisan question of whose ox was being gored. Thatcher was not immune to violating principle when that meant hurting political opponents.

But Thatcher made only very limited headway in these policy areas. By overpoliticizing many of these issues, she ended up having limited impact and few successes. Most social and domestic problems worsened under Thatcher, and after her nearly 12 years in power, the intellectual cupboard on conservative social policy seemed bare.

THATCHER'S LEADERSHIP STYLE

How did Margaret Thatcher exercise power? What was her style of political leadership? In many ways—not solely because she is a woman—Thatcher was a different type of British political leader. Margaret Thatcher was a bold, innovative, ideological leader, a populist radical who relied on a strong sense of self, a warrior image, self-confidence, determination, and "conviction." In fact, she called herself a conviction leader. "I am not a consensus politician," she once said, "I'm a conviction politician" (Jenkins, 1988, p. 3). At another time she said, "The Old Testament prophets did not say 'Brothers, I want a consensus.' They said: 'This is my faith. This is what I passionately believe. If you believe it too, then come with me'" (Rose, 1984, p. 4).

Thatcher came to power determined to end the era of consensus politics that had characterized British politics for more than 30 years. Consensus was, to her, the problem (Harris, 1989, chap. 3). Thatcher was an outsider bent on breaking the consensus. There was thus a crusading zeal about her, a strong sense of belief or conviction that harbored few doubts and allowed little dissent. On taking office, she said, "It must be a conviction government. As Prime Minister I could not waste time with any internal arguments" (quoted in the *Observer*, February 25, 1979).

The sense of moral rigidity and mission led Thatcher continually to ask of subordinates, "Is he one of us?" meaning, Is he ideologically pure and temperamentally strong enough? This question was the test that, after two or three years, all would-be ministers had to answer before being allowed into the corridors of power. This led Thatcher to develop a highly (perhaps overly) personalized, somewhat imperious style of leadership. Inside the executive office, one had to either submit to the cult of her leadership or be dismissed. Few felt free to tell the emperor she had no clothes.

Thatcher's leadership traits demonstrate a paradoxical quality and could be seen as a series of dichotomies: Her single-mindedness was often dogmatic; conviction was often rigidity; strength was often an aggressive drive for control; her determination was often contentiousness; her forcefulness was combative; her moralism was often quarrelsome.

Thatcher was a true believer determined to lead a moral crusade. Her messianic spirit was captured in her pre-prime ministerial comment, "You can only get other people to tune with you by being a little evangelical about it" (Harris, 1989, p. 126). Her messianism fit comfortably with her warrior style, in which she set policy by full frontal assaults on her cabinet, party, and political system. She saw governing as an adversarial, not a collegial, process. Getting her way was everything, and she used fear, threat, intimidation, and all other means of persuasion to win. There may have been a type of method to this madness, in that sense Thatcher had not won the hearts of the British people (public opinion polls reflected only lukewarm support for Thatcher and her policies; see Skidelsky, 1989, p. 45), she tried to get her way by bullying the cabinet and party.

Thatcher's jarring personality and sheer force of will, coupled with her Churchillian rhetoric, were formidable political tools (Beckett, 2006). Where others sought to build a consensus, Thatcher attempted to dominate allies and adversaries into submission. "I am not ruthless," she once said, "but some things have to be done, and I know when they are done one will be accused of all sorts of things" (Young, 1990, pp. 104–105).

Thatcher's style of leadership was unique when compared with the styles of her predecessors. Thatcher was generally more ambitious, more of a centralizer, more autocratic, less collegial, more confrontational, and more ideological than her predecessors. As Anthony King (1986) notes, Thatcher "leads from the front. She stamps her foot, she raises her voice. For a British prime minister, she is extraordinarily assertive" (p. 118). This assertive style was essential to Thatcher's success. Not only did she take her cabinet and party by storm, she also took them by surprise. Thatcher was different, and the difference often worked.

LEADING IN THE CABINET

Thatcher's aggressive style was very evident in her dealings with her cabinet. The tradition of collegial decision making gave way to prime ministerial rule. Thatcher's vision of collegiality saw her cabinet falling into line behind her. With her early cabinet, Thatcher moved cautiously but later adopted a bullying style when the cabinet was "hers" (Harris, 1989, p. 109). And after she solidified her power, Thatcher chose her cabinet more on the basis of loyalty and obedience than on ability and experience. It was to be a *conviction cabinet*.

Her first cabinet was a mixture of old traditional Tory Conservatives sprinkled with a few true believers. But over time, Thatcher replaced the traditionalists with a cabinet more loyal to her. "Is he one of us?" was the question often asked by Thatcher; or, Is he "wet" or "dry"? (Harris, 1989, p. 128; Young, 1990, pref.) It was *her* cabinet, *her* party, *her* government. Decisions were not generally agreed to after debate and discussion. Often,

Thatcher would tell her cabinet what she wanted, then try to bully them into submission. She was frequently successful.

Cabinet meetings were often tense and conflictual. Former cabinet minister David Howell remembered that "some arguments just left such acrimony and ill-feeling . . . I think the general atmosphere in the government of which I was a member was that everything should start as an argument, continue as an argument and end as an argument" (quoted in Young & Sloman, 1986, p. 14). Thatcher controlled her cabinet through fear and intimidation, by controlling the agenda, by sheer force of personality and conviction, and by creatively using cabinet committees for her purposes. But even with her formidable skills, when matters reached the cabinet level for decisions, Thatcher was on the losing end of the cabinet vote" on more numerous occasions than any other post-war prime minister" (Jenkins, 1988, p. 184). Thus, Thatcher's bullying style proved a two-edged sword. She was sometimes able to force her will upon her cabinet, but, when given the opportunity, the cabinet often struck back.

Thatcher often seemed an outsider in her own cabinet. She once referred to herself as "the cabinet rebel." This allowed or compelled her to overpersonalize everything, and to look upon cabinet meetings as contests to be won. And how was one to win in cabinet? Usually by bullying. Thatcher saw the cabinet as a group organized to endorse her policies, not as a collegial body designed to discuss issues and arrive at decisions.

While Thatcher had not significantly altered the machinery of cabinet government, she did succeed in bending it to her will. She increasingly surrounded herself with weak men, to the point where Denis Healey called the cabinet "neutered zombies." And Shirley Williams remarked after one of Thatcher's periodic cabinet reshuffles, "She has replaced the Cabinet with an echo chamber" (Ogden, 1990, pp. 176, 197).

THATCHER AND PARLIAMENT

In general, when the cabinet collectively decides, the Parliament usually follows. As leader of her cabinet *and* party, Thatcher commanded a good deal of power. This was heightened by the inability of the opposition, Labour, to mount any sustained challenges to Thatcher's leadership. Being able to bully her cabinet, dominate her party, and usually ignore or scoff at her opposition made Thatcher the preeminent force in government. While she did not structurally alter the government, she dominated it. All of this adds up to a style of leadership more *presidential* than prime ministerial in nature, and while one is cautioned against stretching the analogy too far (British power is "fused" or "unified"; U.S. power is separate and often divided), Thatcher clearly preferred the presidential operating style (Thatcher, 2011).

For both the style and the ideological substance of what Thatcher accomplished, an *ism* has been created: Thatcherism. It refers to force of will, depth of conviction, and personal drive. It is also about bullying, rigidity, and close-mindedness. Thatcherism includes dogged determination, clarity of theme, Victorian values, and a crusading approach; it is also about a combative style and a rejection of consensus, about radical economic conservatism and jingoistic patriotism, about promoting inequality and rough justice (Riddell, 1985, chap. 1). Thatcher earned a variety of caustic nicknames, from "the Iron Lady" to "Leaderene," from "Her Malignancy" to "Attila the Hen," from "Boadicea" to "Virago Intacta." But regardless of how one views her, no one can doubt that she made an enormous difference.

THE FALL

The fall of Thatcher came, as falls so often do, not as the result of a single dramatic event, but as a culmination of a series of smaller acts that, one by one, opened the political window of opportunity for Thatcher's critics, and eventually pulled her down.

Thatcher had been vulnerable before, but she always managed to fight off potential challenges and retain power. This was partly a function of her being blessed with a weak and divided opposition party, but also a function of Thatcher's political skill and savvy. By 1989, however, time and good fortune seemed to be running out for Thatcher. She had been in office nearly a dozen years, and many were tiring of her bullying style of leadership. The economy, which during the 1980s was one of her claims to fame, worsened as unemployment and inflation were rising, and economic growth was declining. In this atmosphere, a series of blows to Thatcher's power occurred that led to her downfall.

Having been in power so very long, a form of hubris seemed to over-take her political judgment. As would be the case toward the end of Tony Blair's premiership, the lengthy exercise of power may, at first, fine-tune one's political judgment, yet there may be a point when excessive pride and arrogance overwhelm judgment. This happened to Margaret Thatcher.

One can trace the beginning of the end to the resignation in protest of Nigel Lawson, chancellor of the exchequer, in October of 1989. From that point on, criticism of Thatcher became harsher and more biting, especially relating to the widely unpopular poll tax and Thatcher's intransigence over European unity. When, on November 1, 1989, former Thatcher loyalist and Deputy Prime Minister Sir Geoffrey Howe resigned from the cabinet and, on November 13, made a devastating House of Commons speech in which he attacked Thatcher, saying that her style of leadership was leading to "a very real tragedy" for herself and "running increasingly serious risks for the future of our nation," and accusing her of a failed policy toward European unity, the floodgates of Thatcher-busting broke loose. In resigning, Howe invited "others to consider their response" to his "conflict of loyalty." This invitation to insurrection was not lost on Michael Heseltine, who saw this as his opening to challenge Thatcher for leadership of the Conservative Party.

The flamboyant Heseltine (referred to as Tarzan), a former defense minister under Thatcher, sensed the rumblings of discontent within the Conservative Party, and after five years of quietly but unceasingly campaigning for Thatcher's job, made his move, and openly challenged Thatcher for control of the party. Thatcher accepted the challenge. Heseltine's challenge proved viable not merely on policy differences (which were rather insignificant), but on political grounds. Increasingly, Conservatives came to believe, and their opinion polls verified this, that the Conservative Party was likely to lose the next general election with Thatcher at the helm.

After a very brief leadership campaign, the party voted. Of the 372 votes, Heseltine won 152 to Thatcher's 204. Under the party's leadership selection formula, Thatcher did not receive enough votes for a win (falling 2 votes short), and was forced into a runoff. Vowing that she would "fight on. I fight to win," Thatcher retreated and prepared for the next battle. But the momentum was shifting, and Thatcher soon found her top ministers deserting her sinking ship.

In spite of her pronounced intent to "fight on," it soon became clear that the party was deserting Thatcher. Minister after minister met with

Thatcher and finally persuaded her that the only way to stop Heseltine, whom she detested, was to pull out of the race and allow a cabinet ally to enter. She reluctantly did so, announcing, "Having consulted widely among colleagues, I have concluded that the unity of the party and the prospect of victory in a general election would be better served if I stood down to enable Cabinet colleagues to enter the ballot for leadership." Two did: Douglas Hurd and John Major. Thatcher let it be known that she supported Major, who eventually won.

Major, Thatcher's 47-year-old chancellor of the exchequer, became the youngest British prime minister since 1894. He was, in many ways, a Thatcher clone. He was not born of privilege but worked his way up. This self-made man appeared to be a true believer in the Thatcherite creed. But it was not long before Major began to undo some of the more extremist of Thatcher's policies, including an abandonment of the poll tax in March of 1991.

THATCHER'S PERFORMANCE

It is especially difficult to evaluate Thatcher's performance in office because (a) she is so controversial, (b) her style was so abrasive, and (c) the long-term consequences of many of her actions are still quite mixed. Few people are neutral about Margaret Thatcher. She evokes strong emotions. One thing, however, is quite clear. Thatcher is, as King (1986) has noted, a person of "extraordinary personal force." She has gotten her way. She has imposed her will. She has won.

But how deep is Thatcher's success? Was she good or merely important? By almost all accounts, Thatcher's victories were personal victories, not party or ideological victories, and some were quite ephemeral. She changed Britain's policies but did not win the hearts and minds of the people. As Ivor Crewe (1989) notes, "She is *both* intensely admired and deeply loathed" (p. 45). People respect Thatcher but do not like her. In short, the electorate *has not* become Thatcherite. She has won few converts with her missionary style. Her effort to transform the British people from a dependency culture to an enterprise culture has not succeeded in any deep sense. There was no revolution in social values.

One can examine Thatcher's success in political, policy, and personal terms. Politically, Thatcher was in office nearly 12 years, won three general elections, and utterly humiliated the opposition. In policy terms, the re-cord is mixed, but she did elevate Britain's international reputation, moderate the pace of British decline, and establish the conservative agenda in the political sphere. In personal terms the record is also mixed. It is true she has won, but she did not sell Thatcherism to the British people. She was powerful, but there was a shallowness in many of her victories. She was respected, but unloved; powerful, but a temporary force.

Thatcher was one of the most powerful prime ministers in this century, and she succeeded in implementing almost all of her agenda. She changed Great Britain, remaking it partly in her image. As Harris (1989) writes, "Only Gladstone, perhaps, has had such a profound personal effect on government and politics, on shaping society according to vision" (pp. 288–289). There has indeed been a "Thatcher revolution," and while her contemporaries are mixed (generally along partisan lines) regarding its long-term impact, it is clear that the revolution has changed Britain.

The nation is more prosperous, but the prosperity is not evenly spread. The rich are richer, the poor poorer; the south of England is strong, the north weak. The unions have been weakened, and a sense of "acquisitive individualism" has spread. Market liberalism has been increased; so too have poverty and unemployment. Inflation is down; inequality is up. Local governments became less powerful, the central state more powerful. Whatever long-term results, one knows whom to praise or blame: it has indeed been a Thatcher revolution.

THE GENDER FACTOR

To what extent did gender matter in Thatcher's rise to power and in the way she exercised power? How did this nonfeminist (many would say anti-feminist) woman rise in a male society, male party, male political system, to govern a nation? Thatcher is, in Webster's (1990) words, "a conspicuous figure in the world of sexual politics." She adds:

> Gender has been central to the way in which she has been seen and understood, to the images and narratives which have been shaped around her, and to the cult which surrounded her for much of the 1980s. Her presence at the centre of the national stage has raised in a dramatic form questions

and meanings about masculinity and femininity, public and private life. In the discussions which have circulated around these, what it is to be a "real woman" and a "real man" has been a prominent theme, reflected in two paradoxical and common judgments: that "she isn't really a woman," and that "she is the best man in the country." (p. 1)

Feminists are torn when it comes to Thatcher. After all, Thatcher benefited from the repercussions of the women's movement, without which she could never have achieved the prime ministership. But at the same time, Thatcher rejected, even vilified, the women's movement. Webster (1990) writes of Thatcher:

> For women Mrs. Thatcher has often been an ambivalent figure. Some feminists have found little difficulty in reaching a verdict: she is an ardent servant of patriarchy, colluding with male power and male violence. She is not, and never has been, one of us. Others have felt the problems of attacking her, the dangers of a slide into misogyny, the need to disassociate themselves from sexist slogans like "Ditch the Bitch." Those who have written about her from a feminist perspective have often felt a need to recognize that she has proved that a woman can be Prime Minister, that she is capable, well-organized, articulate and courageous, that she has coped extremely effectively with the demands of the jobs, and in that sense has not "blown it for women." (pp. 1–2)

Thatcher's rise was made possible by the strides of the women's movement, but she often chided and denigrated that movement. Two representative quotes from Thatcher illustrate:

> The battle for women's rights has been largely won. The days when they were demanded and discussed in strident tones should be gone forever. And I hope they are. I hated those strident tones you hear from some "women's libbers." (from a speech to the Institution of Electrical Engineers, July 26, 1982)
>
> The feminists have become far too strident and have done damage to the cause of women by making us out to be something we're not. You get on because you have the right talents. (quoted in the [London] *Times*, May 10, 1978)

Thatcher used her femaleness when it suited her interests, but women were not a part of the Thatcher revolution. Thatcher's political agenda was decidedly lacking in proposals designed to advance the cause of women's rights to Britain. In fact, Thatcher often enjoined women to stay at home, to raise families, to assume traditional roles—Do as I say, not as I do. There is, in the Thatcher revolution, room for no more women.

Gender is important to Thatcher, and she has used it repeatedly and in a variety of ways. As Barbara Castle has noted:

> She's . . . shown almost a contempt for her own sex in the way she has used her power as Prime Minister. Of course she has sex consciousness . . . she wouldn't bother so much about her appearance, her grooming . . . if she weren't sexually conscious. But that's different from what I mean. Her treatment of the services that matter so much to women, that liberate them from the domestic servitudes, all the social services . . . these don't arouse her interest at all. (quoted in Little, 1988, pp. 110–111)

She surrounded herself with men but rarely strong, independent men. Thatcher's cabinet, and even her closest advisers, were usually fairly weak men, willing not only to take orders, but to suffer blistering public humiliation at the hands of Thatcher. Throughout her public life there seems to be only one woman whom Thatcher admired: India's Indira Gandhi (Young, 1990, p. 120).

Through her career, Thatcher was very adept at sexual style flexing, using a variety of different approaches to her femaleness as circumstances dictated. Early in her career she assumed the public role of devoted housewife and mother, though in fact she spent little time at either task (Young, 1990, pp. 306–312). Later, she assumed the roles of mother to the nation, firm nanny, wartime dominatrix, and, still later, androgynous leader. This style flexing allowed Thatcher to pick and choose sexual roles to fit perceived needs. "I don't notice that I'm a woman," she once remarked, "I regard myself as the Prime Minister" (*Daily Mirror*, March 1, 1980).

How did Thatcher's gender affect her sense of self? Some argue that she "discarded most of the significant gender traits and became for all practical purposes, an honorary man" (Young, 1990, p. 304). Governing in a "man's world" of politics, it is argued, forced her to jettison all aspects of femininity and "act like a man." In fact, her style of leadership, domination, and bullying is often characterized as a male style. As prime minister, she led almost a womanless existence. Practically no one on her staff or in her cabinet was female, and she spent her time in the company of men. She was almost always the lone woman, surrounded by men.

Thatcher was a "gender bender," floating back and forth between what are conventionally seen as male and female roles, producing a synthesis, or a type of political cross-dressing. But if Thatcher's career was a tribute to the "manly qualities" of toughness, aggressiveness, and power, how did she escape the scorn of society for being "unfeminine"? The fact of the matter is that by her style flexing, Thatcher was seen as different things at different times.

Often, Thatcher used gender differences as a political tool. In a way, being a woman proved to be one her greatest advantages. Women have a great deal of experience dealing with men who hold positions of power, but men have virtually no experience dealing with women who are in positions of political power. Men were not accustomed to being in subordinate positions politically, and Thatcher exploited this situation. Melanie Philips has noted, "If she'd been a man, she would never have got away with half of it; she understood this and played it for all she was worth." She continued:

> Mrs. Thatcher simply didn't behave as men thought a woman should behave. She was rude, she shouted, she interrupted, she was tough, she was ruthless—male qualities that she used more effectively than the men who thought all this just wasn't cricket. If a male Prime Minister had behaved like this, it would have been thought entirely normal and his colleagues and opponents would have had no difficulty in using the same tactics against him. (quoted in Harris, 1989, p. 66)

Just as being a woman helped Thatcher gain some early political appointments (the Conservative Party had few women in Parliament, and thus Thatcher was tapped for ministerial appointments prior to proving her ability), it also helped her in dealing with the men in her government. Many of the men in her cabinet simply did not know how to deal with an assertive woman, especially one in a position of political superiority. Thatcher's bullying style got the best of a number of her cabinet appointees. One, Jim Prior (1988), wrote an almost apologetic biography, in which he confesses his inability to stand up to an aggressive woman. Even opposition leader Neil Kinnock noted that "Mrs. Thatcher is more difficult for me to oppose . . . I've got, however much I try to shrug it off, an innate courtesy towards women that I simply don't have towards men" (quoted in Little, 1988, p. 109).

Thatcher often showed men up and, by all intentions, derived a great deal of pleasure from such encounters. Webster (1990) notes that Thatcher enjoyed demonstrating to an audience "what they [men] really were—the weaker sex. Conventional sex roles were reversed as men were lumped together as feeble and fumbling, a gang of 'wets' and craven yes-men, while Mrs. Thatcher alone carried the banner of masculine virtues—strong, decisive, determined, courageous" (p. 117).

In dominating her cabinet and colleagues, Thatcher would, and could, engage in a variety of different styles and roles depending upon her approach to the situation. She thus kept her cabinet off balance, and often at her mercy. She was indeed different, and the men around her did not know how to deal with her. Even the few skilled and strong men who would sometimes fly into the Thatcher orbit (e.g., Michael Heseltine) had trouble dealing with the prime minister. As Webster (1990) notes of the men in Thatcher's cabinet, "They simply did not know how to handle her" (p. 118).

Overall, the gender factor helped Margaret Thatcher. From her early political rise, when the Conservatives needed "a woman," to her tenure as prime minister, Thatcher used gender issues with skill and cunning. She used her gender, sometimes relying on feminine wiles, sometimes as nanny, sometimes as bully, sometimes to coax, cajole, and flatter, but always calculatedly. As Young (1990) notes, "Without discarding womanhood, she has transcended it" (p. 312).

But Thatcher's success and her style of governing were not merely a result of gender. Clearly, she was driven by unbending ideological conviction. She was a crusader whose forcefulness mixed with the gender issue to produce a truly unusual politician. As she noted, "If a woman is strong, she is strident. If a man is strong, gosh, he's a good guy" (quoted in Young, 1990, p. 543). This represents a paradox of women in power. If they are strong, they are criticized for not being "womanly"; if they are weak, they "prove" that women simply cannot govern. It is a no-win proposition.

CONCLUSION

Margaret Thatcher came to power with the cards stacked against her. She had limited experience, did not have the support of a majority of her party's leaders, promoted a new and radical agenda, *and* she was a woman. But while her level of political opportunity was not high upon assuming office, a dozen years later one is struck by just how many of her key agenda items have been implemented. Historians, looking back on the Thatcher years, will note that, more than most prime ministers, she left her mark. She was powerful and purposeful, a force for change, a woman who dominated the political landscape of Britain. There is no question that Thatcher made a difference. She won. But were Thatcher's victories also Britain's victories? She won, but did Britain?

Long-term evaluations must be left to historians, but from the vantage point of 2012, Thatcher's record seems decidedly mixed. She left Britain more prosperous, but it is a prosperity not evenly shared. Britain is today still in social disrepair, divided and unequal. The social cohesion and harmony that resulted from the welfare state have deteriorated. The wealthy, who were poised to profit from Thatcher's vision of an opportunity society, have benefited greatly. As Peter A. Hall (1989) has written:

> Nagging doubts remain. There is something ignoble about a regime that preaches the virtues of personal initiative and equality of opportunity while cutting back on the social and educational programs that generally extend such opportunities to those at the bottom of the ladder. If all revolutions have their shadows, this is the shadow that still hangs over Mrs. Thatcher's moral revolution. (p. 14)

Thatcher's philosophy of rugged individualism has opened entrepreneurial doors for the British, but it has also closed other doors. Britain is less a community, is more divided, has less that binds it together. Thatcher saw the choice as either self-interest or society; she chose the former. But clearly self-interest is not enough. The search for community must also be a part of the national quest. However, for Thatcher, the invisible hand guides, the trickle-down theory determines.

Thatcher was the first woman to head the government of a major Western nation, served longer continuously than any modern prime minister, tamed the trade unions, revived Britain's pride and economy, led her country to victory in war, and overwhelmed her opposition. But, as the *Financial Times* wrote as she departed in 1989, "Her flaws were as large as her virtues." She turned a blind eye to the poor and disposed, was overbearing and domineering, and left Britain a harsher, nastier place than she found it. She was a woman of firm conviction and great strength, but she had been running against the "socialist past" for so long, many in Britain wondered if, toward the end, she had a proactive vision. Thatcherism, it appears, may have reached its limits (Berlinski, 2010).

Clearly, Thatcher changed Great Britain. She accomplished a great deal through the force of her will and the power of her ideas. Where most British governments ground to a halt because of failed policies, scandals, lack of leadership, or electoral shifts, Thatcher managed not only to stay in power for a dozen years, but also to dominate her party thoroughly and to demoralize her opposition.

Did Thatcherism survive after Thatcher's departure? While Thatcher did implement a variety of changes, much of her power was built on her persona. Thus, Thatcherism as a style of governing did not survive her. It was too dependent on Thatcher's unique style and drive. But what of Thatcherism as a policy approach? Robert Skidelsky (1988) has doubts:

> Thatcherism may have been necessary to break out of the corporatist and bureaucratic impasse of the late 1970s; but the analysis was over simple, the means crude and mean. More fundamentally, Thatcherism as an economic and social philosophy—as a basis for long-term government of Britain—is seriously one-sided. (p. 23)

One senses that Thatcher herself knew that Thatcherism was coming to an end. Her importance to the revolution is not lost in modesty. Thatcher once remarked, "I think I have become a bit of an institution," and "The place wouldn't be quite the same without this old institution" (quoted in Young, 1990, p. 543). Her handpicked successor, John Major, while a true believer, was up against formidable odds in attempting to reinject Britain with another dose of Thatcherism, not the least of which was Thatcher's apparent reluctance truly to step down from power. After all, shortly after announcing her resignation, Thatcher publicly stated that she would make a "good back-seat driver," leading a Labour critic to charge, when noting that Major's first cabinet contained no women (the only cabinet of all of Western Europe *not* to have a woman minister), "Is the only woman in the Cabinet the back-seat driver?" and other opposition politicians took to calling Major "Mrs. Thatcher's poodle." This prompted Major to fire back, "I am my own man."

Less than two years after assuming office, John Major was required to call a national election. In the midst of the worst recession in Britain since the World War II, but facing weak opposition in Neil Kinnock and the Labour Party, Major and the Conservatives, while losing approximately 40 seats, managed to maintain a slim majority in the Parliament. It was the fourth consecutive national election victory for the Conservatives, and in some ways it served as vindication for Margaret Thatcher. In June 1992, upon the recommendation of John Major, Queen Elizabeth II named Thatcher a "peer of the realm," and she became Baroness Thatcher, a life member of the House of Lords.

Margaret Thatcher was a revolutionary leader, not simply because she was a woman, not simply because she was a powerful woman, but because she was these things and more. She governed for a dozen years, won almost all of her major policy goals, and vanquished her opposition. Unusually, Thatcher was the beneficiary of the gender issue. She used her opportunities wisely and well, and seized power. As Webster (1990) says, there was "not a man to match her."

NOTES

1 This quote is from the mother of one of Margaret Roberts's (Thatcher's) schoolmates to her daughter, quoted in Harris (1989, p. 66).
2 As Indeed Hugo Young (1990, p. 3) claims in the opening sentence of *One of Us*.
3 For reviews of the Thatcher economic policy, see Kavanaugh (1990, chap. 8) and Menford (1989).
4 This was confirmed by Thatcher in a June 7, 1987, television interview with David Frost.

REFERENCES

Beckett, C. (2006). *Thatcher*. London: Haus Publishing.
Berlinski, C. (2010). *There is no alternative: Why Margaret Thatcher matters*. New York: Basic Books.
Campbell, J. (2009). *Margaret Thatcher: Grocer's daughter to Iron Lady*. New York: Vintage Books.
Clayton, D.H., & Thompson, R.J. (1988, Summer). Reagan, Thatcher, and social welfare. *Presidential Studies Quarterly, 3*, 565–581.
Crewe, I. (1987). Has the electorate become Thatcherite? In P. Hennessy & A. Seldon (Eds.), *Ruling performance: British governments from Attlee to Thatcher* (pp. 25–49). Oxford: Basil Blackwell.
Hall, P.A. (1989, October 2). The smack of firm government. *New York Times Book Review*, 8.
Harris, K. (1989). *Thatcher*. London: Fontana.
Hennessy, P., & Seldon, A. (Eds.). (1987). *Ruling performance: British governments from Attlee to Thatcher*. Oxford: Basil Blackwell.

Jenkins, P. (1988). *Mrs. Thatcher's revolution*. Cambridge, MA: Harvard University Press.

Kavanaugh, D. (1990). *Thatcherism and British politics*. Oxford: Oxford University Press.

King, A. (Ed.). (1986). *The British prime minister*. London: Macmillan.

Little, G. (1988). *Strong leadership*. Melbourne: Oxford University Press.

Menford, P. (1989). Mrs. Thatcher's economic reform programme. In R. Skidelsky (Ed.), *Thatcherism* (pp. 93–106). Oxford: Basil Blackwell.

Ogden, C. (1990). *Maggie*. New York: Simon & Schuster.

Prior, J. (1988). *A balance of power*. London: Hamish Hamilton.

Riddell, P. (1985). *The Thatcher government*. Oxford: Basil Blackwell.

Robenson, M. (1989). *Mother country*. London: Farrar, Straus, & Giroux.

Rose, R. (1984). *Do parties make a difference?* Chatham, NJ: Chatham House.

Skidelsky, R. (Ed.). (1989). *Thatcherism*. Oxford: Basil Blackwell.

Thatcher, M. (1993). *The Downing Street years*. New York: Harper Collins.

Thatcher, M. (1995). *The path to power*. New York: Harper Collins.

Thatcher, M. (2011). *In her own words*. Colorado Springs, CO: Dialogue.

Vincent, J. (1987). The Thatcher government, 1979–1987. In P. Hennessy & A. Seldon (Eds.), *Ruling performance: British governments from Atlee to Thatcher*. Oxford: Basil Blackwell.

Wapshott, N. (2008). *Ronald Reagan and Margaret Thatcher: A political marriage*. New York: Sentinel Trade.

Webster, W. (1990). *Not a man to match her*. London: Women's Press.

Young, H. (1990). *One of us*. London: Pan.

Young H., & Sloman, A. (1986). *The Thatcher phenomenon*. London: BBC.

12

Why No Madame President?

Gender and Presidential Politics in the United States

Richard L. Fox and Zoe M. Oxley

The United States has never elected a woman as president. Further, no woman has ever been nominated by a major party to run for president. Hillary Clinton in 2008 was the first woman presidential candidate to ever win a state primary or caucus. In the 2012 presidential contests, President Obama and nine Republican candidates participated in the electoral process. Only one woman ran, Minnesota Congresswoman Michelle Bachmann. She was among the first of the candidates to withdraw from the race after a disappointing performance in the first nominating contest in the state of Iowa. In the history of the United States, two women, Democrat Geraldine Ferraro in 1984 and Republican Sarah Palin in 2008, have been selected by male presidential candidates to run for vice president. Both were part of losing tickets.

Certainly, women's lack of success in attaining the highest office in the United States is not exceptional, as most nations of the world have not had a woman head of state. But what makes the lack of women's success in the United States notable is that the United States ranks very highly worldwide in terms of women's status. According to the World Economic Forum's *Global Gender Gap Report*, the United States is sixth in the world in terms of women's economic opportunity and participation (Hausmans, Tyson, & Zahidi, 2011). An analysis and ranking conducted by Ronald Inglehart and Pippa Norris (2003) ranked the United States ninth in the world in terms of progressive attitudes toward gender equality. Yet, as many of the chapters in this volume illustrate, women leaders in far more traditional and patriarchal cultures than in the United States have been able to do what American women have yet to do—they have made it to the top political position in their country.

In this chapter, we ask the basic question: why has a woman yet to be elected as president of the United States? In exploring this question, we have divided the chapter into three sections. We briefly cover the history of women who have sought the presidency in the first section. In the second section, we identify and examine what we view as the five primary challenges to women's ascension to the highest office in the United States. Here we focus on the masculine nature of the presidency, the unique electoral context in the United States, the shallow pool of potential women candidates, voter attitudes toward women political leaders, and media coverage of women candidates. In the final section and conclusion of the chapter, we evaluate Hillary Clinton's 2008 run for the presidency and draw some lessons regarding women's future presidential candidacies. Ultimately, we advance the central premise that certainly a woman can and will be elected president of the United States, but there are many impediments that make the task more daunting than in other countries.

HISTORY OF WOMEN CANDIDATES FOR PRESIDENT

The first woman to ever publicly declare her intention to run for the presidency was Victoria Woodhull in 1872. Woodhull was supported by the National Woman's Suffrage Association and ran as a member of the Equal Rights Party. Her candidacy took place at a time when women were not allowed to vote. Woodhull did not receive any electoral votes, and it is even unclear how many votes she received as her name was not included on any printed ballots (Goldsmith, 1996). Belva Lockwood, the next woman presidential candidate, was also part of the suffrage movement running under the banner of the Equal Rights Party. Lockwood ran twice, in 1884 and 1888, and is renowned for being one of the first women attorneys in the United States. Ultimately, historians, as well as Lockwood herself, had trouble getting a clear record of how many votes she received in her runs for the presidency. Lockwood claimed that she received thousands of votes, and that she actually won some electoral votes. Her protests of electoral fraud, however, were largely ignored (Norgren, 2007). Political scientist Ruth Mandel (2007) has described Woodhull and Lockwood as "extraordinary women, exhibiting courage and daring" (p. 284), as both took courses of action that were unimaginable for women of that time.

The modern history of women running for the presidency begins with Maine Republican Senator Margaret Chase Smith (see Table 12.1). Smith's candidacy was a landmark because she was the first woman from a major political party to run for president. She announced her candidacy on January 27, 1964, and competed in several of the states that held primaries and caucuses at the time. She did not win any of the state contests, but her name was placed in nomination at the Republican convention. She was the first woman to ever be formally nominated for president within the mainstream electoral process. Smith received only a few votes on the first ballot and then withdrew her name from consideration (Sherman, 2000).

Eight years later, in 1972, African American Congresswoman Shirley Chisholm launched the most organized and serious presidential bid of any woman at that point. She contested primaries in 12 states and won roughly 150 delegates, a record unbeaten by any woman candidate until Hillary Clinton ran for president in 2008. Chisholm herself acknowledged that she did not have a chance to win the race but was hoping to blaze a trail for future women candidates and candidates of color (Smooth, 2010). Two other female Democrats, Patsy Mink in 1972 and Ellen McCormack in 1976, ran for president, but both made little progress toward actually winning the party nomination or even garnering much national attention.

The next notable woman who considered running for office was Democrat Pat Schroeder in 1987. Schroeder began looking at the race after fellow Coloradan Gary Hart's campaign was undone by a sex scandal. Schroeder was considered a serious candidate as she had been elected seven times to the House of Representatives and had become a national figure, speaking out on many issues ranging from abortion to defense policy. After testing the waters as a presidential candidate for several months, Schroeder decided not to run. In the midst of her speech announcing that she was not running, Schroeder began to cry. The political world erupted about what this meant for women candidates. One columnist called Schroeder the "stereotype of women as weepy wimps who don't belong in the business of serious affairs" (Schroeder, 1999, p. 185). The 17 seconds of Schroeder's speech that were tear filled became a symbol of women running for the presidency.

The next major party woman to run for president was Republican Elizabeth Dole in 2000. Though Dole had never held an elected position, she had served in two cabinet positions, Labor and Transportation, and

TABLE 12.1

History of Major Party Women Candidates for U.S. President

Name	Home State	Party	Year of Attempt	Highest Political Position	Outcome of Attempted Run for President
Margaret Chase Smith	Maine	Republican	1964	Senator	Received 22 delegate votes from four states at the Republican National Convention, second only to Republican nominee Senator Barry Goldwater.
Shirley Chisholm	New York	Democrat	1972	House Representative	Received over 400,000 votes in 14 primaries.
Patsy Takemoto Mink	Hawaii	Democrat	1972	House Representative	Convinced by a group of liberal Democrats to run for president, Mink received 2% of the vote in Oregon's primary, coming in eighth out of nine candidates.
Ellen McCormack	New York	Democrat	1976	No Governmental Experience	Appeared on the ballot in 18 states but did not win any primaries. She received 27 delegate votes from five states at the same Democratic National Convention that eventually nominated Jimmy Carter.
Patricia Schroeder	Colorado	Democrat	1988	House Representative	Dropped out in September 1987—just three months after she declared her intention to run.
Elizabeth Dole	North Carolina	Republican	2000	Secretary of Transportation and Labor	Raised almost $5 million before dropping out of the race in October 1999.
Carol Moseley Braun	Illinois	Democrat	2004	Senator	Raised less than $1 million for her campaign and dropped out before the first primary.
Hillary Rodham Clinton	New York	Democrat	2008	Senator	Came in second to Barack Obama, the eventual Democratic presidential nominee.
Michelle Bachmann	Minnesota	Republican	2012	House Representative	Suspended 2012 presidential campaign after placing sixth in Iowa's Republican caucuses.

Compiled by Authors

had served as the president of the American Red Cross, a large national organization. Dole had been a fixture in Washington and in the Republican Party for several decades. Speculation about Elizabeth Dole running as part of a Republican presidential ticket dates back as far as the 1980s (Goodman, 1988). Though Elizabeth Dole clearly had interest in the White House for many years, she was in the awkward position of being married to U.S. Senator Bob Dole, who himself ran for president three times. Bob Dole made his final unsuccessful bid for the presidency in 1996, thus effectively ending his political career and clearing the way for Elizabeth Dole. On March 10, 1999, in Des Moines, Iowa, Elizabeth Dole launched her bid for the presidency. Her candidacy received considerable attention as she campaigned, mostly in Iowa, New Hampshire, and South Carolina. Several early polls had her polling in the top three of Republican candidates. Much of the news coverage and speculation about her candidacy, however, suggested that she was really running for the vice presidency, but Dole brushed this off by repeatedly saying she was "running to win" (Gutgold, 2006, p. 114). While Elizabeth Dole was clearly a very serious and substantive candidate, the party was coalescing around Texas Governor George W. Bush. Dole ultimately pulled out of the race seven months after she began, and before any votes were cast. Her campaign claimed they had not been able to raise enough money to compete with Bush, being out-raised at that point $57 million to $4.7 million (Gutgold, 2006). Despite all of her credentials and effective public speaking, Elizabeth Dole was not able to break through and become a serious contender for the U.S. presidency.

In 2004, former Illinois Senator Carol Moseley Braun ran for the presidency. She very explicitly wanted to identify as the woman candidate in a field of seven men. An early *Time* magazine article about Moseley Braun's chances states: "The smart money bets the 55-year-old will never rise higher than an asterisk in the polls" (Cooper, 2003). Ultimately, this analysis proved correct and as with previous women presidential candidates, when Mosley Braun failed to catch on as a candidate, she withdrew from the race before a single vote was cast.

When former First Lady and New York Senator Clinton announced her candidacy for the presidency in January 2007, she was by far the best positioned of any woman to make a run for the presidency. She was the clear front-runner for the Democratic nomination—a *Washington*

Post/ABC News poll (2007) placed Clinton in the lead, with 41% of the vote. Her closest rival was Senator Barack Obama, with 17% of the vote. While Clinton maintained her front-runner status for most of 2007, the Obama campaign was gaining momentum and popularity. As the voting began in January 2008, Obama won the first contest in Iowa, and Clinton countered with a win in New Hampshire. The two candidates were locked in a tight battle for the Democratic nomination that lasted until June, when Clinton ultimately conceded to Obama. Across the campaign, Clinton received more than 18 million votes and won 21 states. A great deal has been written about the Clinton campaign and the degree to which gender played a role in the campaign and ultimate defeat (Carroll & Ditmar, 2010). Ultimately, most analysts blamed her defeat on being out-organized and -strategized by the Obama campaign. However, as we detail elsewhere in this chapter, Clinton's gender was not an irrelevant factor.

In 2012, Michelle Bachmann, a third-term congresswoman from Minnesota, sought the Republican party nomination to challenge incumbent president Barack Obama. Bachmann, a conservative firebrand, was a hero among the far-Right Tea Party movement that rose to prominence in the 2010 midterm elections. Bachmann formally announced her candidacy on June 26, 2011. Early in the presidential campaign, Bachmann performed very well, earning praise for some of her debate performances and winning the Ames Straw Poll, a major campaign event prior to the Iowa caucus. Polls by the *Wall Street Journal* and NBC News in July 2011, had Bachmann in second place behind eventual nominee Mitt Romney (Murray, 2011). Ultimately, Bachmann could not sustain her early success. Her campaign faded, and she finished sixth in the Iowa caucuses. Bachmann pulled out of the race a few days later. Overall, Bachmann did not receive a great deal of attention for being a woman, and few people questioned the appropriateness of her candidacy. Bachmann's candidacy was similar to the trajectory of many of the male Republican candidates who ran in 2012, as almost everyone in the field had a moment when he or she was near the top of the pack. In this regard, Bachmann's candidacy could be seen as a mild normalization of women running for president, with her performance mirroring many of the men in the race and little attention being paid to the fact that she is a woman.

CHALLENGES FACING WOMEN PRESIDENTIAL CANDIDATES

As this brief history of women's presidential candidacies demonstrates, women have had a very difficult time presenting themselves as viable leaders of the country. Clearly, early attitudes about the role of women in public and political life have changed dramatically, even in the last 40 years. At least one woman has sought the presidency in every election since 2000. While that is an important trend, the number of women who have run for president pales in comparison to that of men. Across U.S. history, only nine women have sought the presidential nomination for one of the major political parties. In 2012 alone, eight men mounted serious campaigns for the Republican nomination.[1] The road for women presidential aspirants remains challenging. In this section of the chapter, we identify the primary impediments for women's presidential candidacies that remain in place early in the 21st century.

The Masculine Nature of the Institution of the Presidency

The institution of the U.S. presidency is distinctly masculine space. Of the 44 people to serve in the White House, all have been men. The original conception of the U.S. presidency is heavily associated with the founding of the United States. Men such as George Washington, John Adams, and Thomas Jefferson, referred to affectionately as the Founding Fathers, helped design the government and served as the nation's first three presidents. These men, as well as others, are the iconic figures who forged the presidency and the government. The conception of a masculine ethos begins with the founding and the notion that the presidency is a place for great leaders—great male leaders. Since the founding period, the United States has faced many challenges to the survival of the nation, including the Civil War, World War I, the Great Depression, World War II, and the Cold War. Male presidents have guided the country through all of these challenges. Since the founding, hundreds of men have sought the office of the presidency, and, as noted above, only a small handful of women have ever sought the office. Many political scientists and analysts have identified the strong cultural association among masculinity, leadership, and politics as one of the greatest hurdles to women's ascension in U.S. politics (e.g., Duerst-Lahti, 2010; Enloe, 2004.).

But what does it mean in the modern era to say that the presidency is masculine space? In the words of political scientist Mary Anne Borrelli (1997), "the traditionally masculine schema" of the presidency includes traits such as "toughness, competitive drive, incisiveness, and displaying initiative." Georgia Duerst-Lahti (2010) identifies "the test of executive toughness, a preference for military heroes, the sports and war metaphors of debates" as a few examples of the masculine space of presidential elections. The language in the U.S. Constitution that recognizes the president as "commander-in-chief" of the armed forces during times of war certainly connotes masculinity. Women have been generally prohibited from commanding anything for most of U.S. history, much less military forces. The hurdle for any woman who seeks the presidency is to meet the test of masculinity and show she has the mettle for the position. To be successful, a woman presidential candidate has to be able to convince a broad swath of the public that she is up to this task. This is not a hurdle that male candidates face as it is usually assumed that men have what it takes to be the leader of one of the world's most powerful countries.

Still, the importance of demonstrating masculinity in presidential politics has been a central aspect of several campaigns even between men. Caroline Heldman (2007) has shown that the "feminizing" of male candidates has been evident in recent campaigns. In 1988, Michael Dukakis put on an oversized military helmet to ride around in a tank. As Heldman notes "opponents used this picture to feminize Dukakis, making reference to his lack of 'manliness.'" In 2004, in the race between John Kerry and George W. Bush, Kerry was maligned in conservative media for using tanning products and getting a manicure prior to a presidential debate. Popular FOX News anchor Bill O'Reilly commented, "What do you think Osama bin Laden's going to think about this spray on tan? Is that going to frighten him? (23–24)"

The U.S. presidency is fully masculine space. For a woman to be successful in pursuit of the presidency, she must be able to overcome the deep cultural expectation that men are the natural fit for the position. These tropes are particularly evident in voter reactions to and media coverage of women candidates, discussed more fully below.

The U.S. Electoral Environment

From a comparative context, the U.S. electoral system is unique. Beyond the masculine nature of the institution of the presidency described above, the process of electing presidents in the United States is more complex, onerous, and candidate driven than in almost any other advanced democracy. At a general level, the United States has a presidential system of government whereby a candidate for the presidency must run as a political entrepreneur. To start, winning one of the two major party's nominations entails building a candidacy from the ground up—hiring staff, building an organization, raising substantial sums of money, and mapping out a strategy to run in the nominating contests of all 50 states (Wayne, 2011). The political parties in the United States run the nominating elections, but the parties do not select the candidates. Compared with most democratic systems, the United States has a very weak party system, whereby the parties cannot even control candidate nominations. In running for president, there is the early process of the invisible primary schedule where candidates scurry around behind closed doors trying to attract endorsements, key fund-raisers, and party activists to their campaign. Certainly, the invisible primary worked against women for many election cycles as the top strategists and behind-the-scenes political figures were men. More recently, Melissa Haussman (2003) argues that since the 2000 elections, women have been able to work more effectively in the political parties and behind the scenes.

In the current presidential election system, the process of procuring a major presidential party nomination is a one- to two-year endeavor. For instance, in 2012, after spending many months laying the groundwork for his candidacy, Mitt Romney, the eventual Republican party nominee, formally announced his candidacy on June 2, 2011. This was a full 17 months before the general election. After a lengthy primary battle against eight other candidates, he secured his party's nomination in early April 2012. After the primary battle comes the general election, which is consumed by presidential debates, voter mobilization efforts, and intensive campaigning in the 10 to 12 swing states that have been decisive in winning recent presidential elections.

As part of the endeavor of running for office, fund-raising is critical for both the primary and general elections. Early projections about the 2012 election suggest that the two major party candidates will each have to raise between 500 million and 1 billion dollars. Raising money at this level requires candidates to be well connected with the types of communities that can make substantial contributions. Evidence from previous women's candidacies suggests that women may have had trouble breaking into fund-raising networks. Despite her previous political experience and strong standing in the polls, for example, raising campaign funds did not come easily for Elizabeth Dole when she ran for the 2000 Republican nomination. "I couldn't believe it was so hard to get people to contribute $500 to attend a political dinner for Dole," stated one of her campaign staffers. "If I was working for [George W.] Bush, I could get people to contribute $1,000 to eat with Barney, his dog" (quoted in O'Connor, 2003, p. 214). Since Dole's race, Victoria Farrar-Myers (2007) has looked in depth at the fund-raising of women House and Senate candidates. She did not uncover any differences in the challenges faced by women compared to men. She argues that the only burden left for women running for president is to navigate the notion of viability. Viability, or the belief that a candidate can win, might very well be something that is more difficult for women. Furthermore, showing viability is certainly part of the invisible primary, as candidates try to convince party leaders they can win.

The system of running for president in the United States is marked by its length, the amount of money that candidates must raise, and weak parties. This process stands in marked contrast to the parliamentary electoral systems employed in most democratic regimes. In terms of time and money, elections in countries with parliamentary systems tend to last anywhere from four to eight weeks. Typical is the Canadian or Italian system, where elections last six weeks. To become the head of state in a parliamentary system, a candidate only has to become the leader of the party, usually determined by a vote of all of the elected members of the parliament. While certainly wrangling to become the head of a political party in a parliamentary system poses challenges, it pales in comparison to the length and intensity of the process in the United States. As Table 12.2 reveals, of the 18 women leaders in the world as of mid-2012, 11 were elected in parliamentary systems. Only 5 faced direct elections by the people, and none of those faced anything like the gauntlet of the U.S. electoral system.

Ultimately, the election process in the United States almost requires candidates to be national figures and financially well connected. These attributes alone make the ascension of a woman more difficult in the United States than in most other countries. But this difficult electoral process is even further compounded for aspiring women candidates by the masculine nature of U.S. political culture, described above. Finally, because U.S. parties do not have a system of gender quotas for national officeholders, such as those employed in a number of Western democratic countries, there is a smaller pool of women to serve as possible candidates—a topic we now turn to in greater detail.

TABLE 12.2

Electoral Process in Countries Where Women Are Currently Heads of State

Name	Country	Title	Year Elected	Electoral Process
Angela Merkel	Germany	Chancellor	2005	Elected by parliament
Ellen Johnson Sirleaf	Liberia	President	2006	Directly elected by simple majority of voters
Pratibha Patil	India	President	2007	Indirectly elected by majority vote of electoral college
Cristina Fernandez de Kirchner	Argentina	President	2007	Directly elected by 45% of voters, or 40% with a 10% margin of victory over second-place candidate
Sheikh Hasina Wajed	Bangladesh	Prime Minister	2009	Elected by parliament
Jóhanna Sigurdardóttir	Iceland	Prime Minister	2009	Elected by parliament
Dalia Grybauskaite	Lithuania	President	2009	Directly elected by plurality of voters, in open-list proportional representation system
Laura Chinchilla	Costa Rica	President	2010	Directly elected by qualified majority of voters
Kamla Persad-Bissessar	Trinidad & Tobago	Prime Minister	2010	Elected by parliament
Julia Gillard	Australia	Prime Minister	2010	Elected by parliament
Iveta Radicová	Slovakia	Prime Minister	2010	Elected by parliament
Dilma Rousseff	Brazil	President	2011	Directly elected by absolute majority of voters in a two-round system
Cissé Mariam Kaïdama Sidibé	Mali	Prime Minister	2011	Appointed by the elected president
Atifete Jahjaga	Kosovo	President	2011	Elected by parliament
Yingluck Shinawatra	Thailand	Prime Minister	2011	Elected by parliament
Helle Thorning-Schmidt	Denmark	Prime Minister	2011	Elected by parliament
Eveline Widmer-Schlumpf	Switzerland	President	2012	Elected by parliament
Portia Simpson Miller	Jamaica	Prime Minister	2012	Elected by parliament

Compiled by Authors

The Shallow Pool of Eligible Candidates

What are the qualifications to become president? Since the 1960 election of John F. Kennedy, the resume for those elected president has included service as a U.S. senator, a state governor, vice president, or a combination of these three offices. Specifically, among the most recent ten U.S. presidents (1960–2008), the last elected positions they held prior to becoming president were U.S. senator (two), governor (four), and vice president (four). These three elected positions represent the modern pathway to the presidency. Yet, this political career path poses a serious constraint on women's ability to ascend to the presidency. First, there has never been a woman vice president. The position that most visibly serves as the training ground to become president does not provide any potential women candidates. Second, in terms of U.S. senators, women have never held more than 17 of the 100 seats. Despite the relatively open democratic electoral process in the United States, the move toward gender parity in high elective office has been very slow. At the beginning of 2012, the U.S. ranked 94th in the world in the number of women serving in the national legislature (statistic adapted from Inter-Parliamentary Union, 2012). Finally, in 2012, women held only 6 of the 50 state governorships. The reasons for women's difficulties in getting elected to high-level office have been well chronicled in the literature on gender and elections (e.g., Lawless & Fox, 2010; Dolan, 2004). Regardless of the explanation for women's continued lack of underrepresentation in high-level U.S. politics, the result is that there is currently a very limited pool of women who are well positioned to run for president.

As Table 12.3 shows, there are only roughly 20 women in contemporary politics with the credentials for a White House bid, three of which—Hillary Clinton, Sarah Palin, and Condoleezza Rice—have significant national name recognition. Certainly the political environment in the United States is very fluid. The sudden rise of Sarah Palin in 2008, from little-known first-term governor of a small state to national political figure, demonstrates how quickly political dynamics can change. Having said that, in looking toward the 2016 presidential election, there are only 11 women U.S. senators and three women state governors who would be younger than 70 years old by the time of that election. Furthermore, none of them have ever publicly spoken of presidential ambitions. In fact, as of 2012, the only woman in the United States who appears to have the stature and popularity

TABLE 12.3

Shallow Pool of Eligible Women Candidates with Presidential Profile Heading into 2016 Elections

Name	Home State	Party	Age	Outlook on Presidential Potential
SENATORS				
Kelly Ayotte	New Hampshire	Republican	44	First elected to the U.S. Senate in 2010. Was mentioned as a possible running mate for 2012 Republican presidential candidate Mitt Romney.
Maria E. Cantwell	Washington	Democrat	54	Has not publicly indicated whether she would ever consider running for president.
Susan M. Collins	Maine	Republican	56	Has not publicly indicated whether she would ever consider running for president. In 2006, *O Magazine* named her one of six women who could run.
Kirsten Gillibrand	New York	Democrat	46	Has not publicly indicated whether she would ever consider running for president.
Kay Hagan	North Carolina	Democrat	59	Has not publicly indicated whether she would ever consider running for president.
Amy Klobuchar	Minnesota	Democrat	52	Has not publicly indicated whether she would ever consider running for president.
Mary Landrieu	Louisiana	Democrat	57	Has not publicly indicated whether she would ever consider running for president.
Claire McCaskill	Missouri	Democrat	59	Has not publicly indicated whether she would ever consider running for president.
Patty Murray	Washington	Democrat	62	Has not publicly indicated whether she would ever consider running for president.
Jeanne Shaheen	New Hampshire	Democrat	65	Has not publicly indicated whether she would ever consider running for president.
Deborah A. Stabenow	Michigan	Democrat	62	Has not publicly indicated whether she would ever consider running for president.

TABLE 12.3

(Continued)

Name	Home State	Party	Age	Outlook on Presidential Potential
GOVERNORS				
Mary Fallin	Oklahoma	Republican	57	Has not publicly indicated whether she would ever consider running for president.
Nikki Haley	South Carolina	Republican	40	Was mentioned as a possible running mate for 2012 Republican presidential candidate Mitt Romney.
Susana Martinez	New Mexico	Republican	52	Was mentioned as a possible running mate for 2012 Republican presidential candidate Mitt Romney.
OTHER NOTABLES				
Janet Napolitano	Arizona	Democrat	54	In 2006, O Magazine named her one of six women who could run for president. The former governor of Arizona was named Director of Homeland Security in the Obama administration in 2009.
Sarah Palin	Alaska	Republican	48	After serving as Republican vice-presidential nominee in 2008, she was widely considered a potential candidate for the 2012 presidential nomination until she formally announced she was not running in October 2012. Former governor of Alaska.
Hillary Rodham Clinton	New York	Democrat	64	After narrowly losing the Democratic Party nomination in 2008, Clinton was appointed Secretary of State. She is widely touted as the possible Democratic Party nominee in 2016, though claims she is no longer interested in running for president.
Condoleezza Rice	Alabama	Republican	58	Appointed National Security Advisor in 2001 and became Secretary of State in 2004 in the George W. Bush Administration.

Note: Table only includes women who are 65 or younger as of the 2012 elections.

to make a presidential bid in 2016 is Secretary of State Hillary Clinton. An ABC News/*Washington Post* poll from April 2012 showed Clinton with a favorability rating of 65% positive and 27% negative, making her one of the most popular politicians in the country and the most popular member of the Obama administration (Langer, 2012). Clinton would be 69 years old at the time of the 2016 election, the same age that Ronald Reagan was first elected president. Clinton has said that she is through running for president, but she will undoubtedly receive a great deal of pressure from Democrats to jump into the 2016 race (Leonhardt, 2012). Time will tell whether she would agree to a second presidential run.

In the United States, serious presidential candidates do not emerge out of thin air. To mount a successful campaign, candidates need to have prior political experience, ideally by serving as the chief executive of a state or in a national elective office. Until a point in time at which more women are elected to high-level office in the United States, there will remain only a very small group of women who have the résumé of recent presidents.

Voter Attitudes

Do American voters support female candidates? Widespread sexism among the electorate would, of course, spell doom for any woman attempting to be elected to the highest office in the land. There is little evidence, however, of such extensive opposition to a female president today. In fact, since 1975, large majorities of voters have been supportive of a woman in the White House (see Figure 12.1). Beginning in 1937, the Gallup Organization has surveyed adults on this topic, usually by asking the following question: "If your party nominated a generally well-qualified person for president who happened to be a woman, would you vote for that person?"[2] In 1937 and 1945, only one-third of the public would have. Support has grown significantly since then, with a slight majority of voters indicating they would vote for a female presidential candidate in 1955. Nearly three-quarters showed support in 1975. Since 1999, the percentages of adults supporting women's candidacies for president have hovered in the high 80s or low 90s, reaching the highest level ever recorded (93%) in 2011 (Saad, 2011). Certainly in a close election, if 5% to 10% of the public would not vote for a candidate because she is a woman, it would be difficult for a woman to be elected to the White House. Having said this, public support for a female president in the abstract has never been higher.

FIGURE 12.1

Support for Women Presidential Candidates, 1937–2011

Source: Saad, L. (2011, June 20). In the United States, 22% are hesitant to support a Mormon in 2012. Retrieved from www.gallup.com/poll/148100/Hesitant-Support-Mormon-2012.aspx.

At first glance, this trend seems encouraging for women's presidential candidacies. Yet, as we peer more closely, a somewhat less favorable image emerges. First, it can be difficult to assess people's *true* attitudes toward nontraditional presidential candidates, such as women, blacks, Jews, and so on. Why? Some people who would never vote for a qualified female presidential candidate from their own party would not admit to this in a survey interview for fear of appearing sexist. In other words, they would provide a socially acceptable response rather than a truthful one. Because such social desirability pressures exist when people answer questions such as Gallup's, the results in Figure 12.1 certainly overestimate public support for a woman in the White House.

To get around this, and thus attempt to measure more accurately support for women presidential candidates, Matthew Streb, Barbara Burrell, Brian Frederick, and Michael Genovese (2008) employed an alternative approach. They provided survey respondents with a list of items and then asked how many of the items make the respondent "angry or upset." Sample items included "The way gasoline prices keep going up" and "Large corporations polluting the environment." Half of the respondents were given a list of four things that might make them angry. The other half received the same four plus one more: "A woman serving as president." When comparing the average number of items that made individuals angry or upset across the two groups, Streb and his colleagues conclude that the prospect of a female president aroused anger in approximately 26% of their respondents. Because respondents did not have to say *which* items made them angry but instead only state *how many* made them angry, pressures toward offering socially acceptable responses are greatly minimized. The survey interviewer would not know, after all, which items provoked angry responses and which did not. In the end, Streb and his coauthors' conclusions remind us that hidden within the 90-plus percent of Americans who say they would vote for a well-qualified woman is a not-insignificant portion who would, in reality, be angered if a woman were elected president. Overcoming the hostility of a quarter of the electorate to win election to the White House would certainly be a tall order for any candidate, of either sex.

After finding steady increases in voter's willingness to vote for a woman presidential candidate, the Gallup poll found support was a bit lower in 2003 and 2007 than it had been in 1999 (refer to Figure 12.1). In fact, if Gallup's question had been included on surveys in late 2001 or 2002, they very likely would have registered an even larger drop in support. Another poll did query the American public on this topic in 2002, finding that only 80% would have voted for a well-qualified woman from their party (Lawless, 2004).[3]

This change of heart among the public was primarily due to the specific issues that were confronting the nation in the first decade of this century, most especially threats to national security, and the stereotypical perception that men are better able to handle these issues. This finding is consistent with the masculine expectations regarding the presidency discussed above. More specifically, voters have long employed gender stereotypes when evaluating political candidates. This process consists of applying general stereotypes about women and men to female and male candidates. In particular, voters ascribe to candidates specific personality traits and issue competencies. Female candidates are assumed to be more honest, willing to compromise, emotional, and compassionate, whereas male candidates are viewed as stronger leaders as well as more aggressive, decisive, and assertive (Alexander & Andersen, 1993; Huddy & Terkildsen, 1993a; Lawless, 2004; Sapiro, 1981/1982). In terms of issues, voters have the tendency to assume male candidates are better able to handle military and defense matters, terrorism, crime, economic management, and agriculture. Areas of female candidates' presumed expertise include health care, education, poverty, child care, and women's issues (Alexander & Andersen, 1993; Dolan, 2010; Huddy & Terkildsen, 1993a; Lawless, 2004; Rosenwasser &

Dean, 1989; Rosenwasser et al., 1987; Sanbonmatsu, 2002; Sapiro, 1981/1982).

What are the implications of gender stereotyping for women's candidacies? In some situations, women can be advantaged. When voters are in a mood to support candidates who are honest and trustworthy or when an electoral contest focuses on issues such as health care or education, female candidates fare better than their male counterparts (Dolan, 2004; Fox, 1997; Fridkin & Kenney, 2009). More often, however, gender stereotyping is detrimental to women. This is certainly the case for women who vie for the White House. When asked which traits and areas of issue expertise candidates for national-level offices *should* possess, voters prefer stereotypic male traits and issues (Huddy & Terkildsen, 1993b; Rosenwasser & Dean, 1989). Indeed, "'[m]ale' traits tend to overlap with 'leadership' traits (e.g., leadership, strength, intelligence, and toughness), and these traits are often valued more highly by voters when they are evaluating competing candidates for electoral office" (Kittilson & Fridkin, 2008, p. 386). Furthermore, voters who stereotype female candidates as less able than males to handle foreign affairs or terrorism express a more general willingness to vote for men rather than women (Dolan, 2010; Sanbonmatsu, 2002) as well as less willingness to support a well-qualified woman for the presidency (Lawless, 2004). Because voters, on average, believe men are better suited to address these issues, female candidates, in general, are disadvantaged. Furthermore, when the national issue agenda is dominated by terrorism, war, military crises, or similar matters, as was the case in the early 2000s, voter support for a woman in the White House falls off (recall Figure 12.1). As one scholar concluded, "a clear bias favoring male candidates and elected officials accompanie[d] the 'war on terrorism'" (Lawless, 2004, pp. 479–480).

Because gender stereotyping occurs, women presidential candidates face difficult choices on the campaign trail. Voters expect (heretofore male) presidents to possess stereotypically male leadership traits and expertise in male policy areas. Yet, portraying themselves as too masculine can invoke criticism of women for not being feminine enough. This is known as the double bind (Jamieson, 1995), and there are many examples of women candidates who have found themselves in this bind during their presidential campaigns. When she announced her candidacy for the Republican nomination, Margaret Chase Smith emphasized her political experience and independence. She also distributed to those in the audience her blueberry muffin recipe along with muffins she had baked. Her attempt to remind voters of her femininity while at the same time outlining her credentials for the presidency seemed to undermine her candidacy—on that day and throughout her campaign (Sherman, 2000). Elizabeth Dole adopted a different approach: she campaigned by not mentioning her sex or by trying to divert attention away from her femininity. One result of this approach was press criticism that she was not doing enough to reach out to and attract women voters (Heith, 2003; Kennedy, 2003).

Finally, Hillary Clinton's campaign strategy and reactions to it well illustrate difficulties female candidates face when running for the ever-so-masculine office of the presidency. Clinton's strategy purposely highlighted masculine traits of expertise, strength, and decisiveness, and the issue area of national security, on the assumption that these are the traits voters expect their presidents to have, but are traits that women are presumed not to possess. Clinton wanted to leave no doubts in the voters' minds as to what characteristics she would bring to the White House. At the same time, Clinton often downplayed feminine traits and areas of issue expertise, especially once the contest between her and Barack Obama became very close (Lawrence & Rose, 2010). One consequence of this dual strategy of emphasizing the masculine while de-emphasizing the feminine was negative commentary that Clinton was cold, distant, and unemotional (Carroll, 2009; Sykes, 2008). These gender dynamics were keenly on display in the days surrounding the New Hampshire primary. A few days before balloting, Clinton choked up a bit in response to a voter's question. Even though she did not shed any tears, it was widely reported that Clinton had cried in public. Reactions to this episode were mixed. Some New Hampshire voters evaluated Clinton more favorably than they had before "the cry," seeing a side of her that they had not before. In fact, this increased favorability contributed to her victory in the New Hampshire primary (Traister, 2010). Criticism also followed, some of which directly pointed to the danger of placing a (crying) woman in the White House. Other negative commentary, such as the following from then FOX News host Glenn Beck, mocked Clinton and contrasted the episode with her public persona: "Big news from New Hampshire tonight is, 'It cries' . . . After spending decades stripping away all trace of emotion, femininity and humanity, Hillary Clinton actually broke down and actually cried yesterday on the campaign trail" (quoted in Traister, 2010, p. 94). Clinton thus faced the typical double bind: criticized for not being feminine enough when she was emphasizing masculine traits, yet also criticized for being weak and insincere when she displayed emotion on the campaign trail.

Undoubtedly, American voters are much more supportive of a woman in the White House than in past decades. Yet the climate is not such that women candidates are evaluated on the same terms as men are. The public continues to expect its presidents to possess masculine traits and issue expertise, expectations that affect how women campaign for the presidency and that make electoral success more elusive for women. Breaking the link between the presidency and masculinity is not on the immediate horizon in U.S. political culture. Until this link is broken, women vying for the White House will face obstacles that male candidates do not.

Media Coverage

> In this country still, thank heaven, some people are born strong and some are born girls. Some people are born intelligent and some are born girls. Some are born of good character and some are born girls. (quoted in Sherman, 2000, p. 187)
>
> A woman is not emotionally or physically capable of assuming the obligations of the most powerful office in the world . . . we'd be in mortal danger with a female president. (quoted in Falk & Jamieson, 2003, p. 50)

Both of these quotations appeared in newspaper coverage of Margaret Chase Smith's campaign for the 1964 Republican presidential nomination. The implication of both is clear: Smith, or, for that matter, any woman, is not suited for the presidency. Other features of her press coverage were also problematic for Smith's candidacy. One political cartoon, for example, featured two of her opponents carrying boxes labeled with their ideological leanings. In contrast, "Smith is mostly out of the frame; all that's left to represent her is a muffin tin and a portion of ankle and a high-heeled shoe" (Sherman, 2000, p. 186). In addition to focusing on her appearance or sexualizing Smith, questioning her ability to provide foreign affairs leadership was also a common theme. Images of Smith interacting with Nikita Khrushchev, the leader of the Soviet Union, include her flirting with him or bypassing him entirely to discuss cooking and other domestic matters with his wife (Sherman, 2000).

Running for president was challenging enough for Smith; the last thing she needed was unfair treatment by the news media. If the press did not take her candidacy seriously, how could she expect voters to? Of course,

Smith ran in 1964 and it is tempting to assume that media coverage of female candidates has improved since then. Press treatment of women is noticeably better today but, importantly, sex differences in coverage patterns do still exist, especially for presidential candidates.

Because very few women have run for president, our knowledge of media treatment of female candidates comes largely from examinations of other offices, typically state governorships and U.S. Senate seats. During the 1980s, women running for these offices fared much worse in the press than men did (Kahn, 1996). The quantity of coverage, such as the number of times the candidate was mentioned in newspaper stories, was higher for men than women, especially in Senate contests. Differences in coverage content were also apparent. For example, attention to candidates' appearance, personal life, and personal traits was more frequent for women than men. In contrast, men's issue positions appeared in news stories more often than women's issue stances did. Furthermore, questions about a candidate's likelihood of winning were more often raised in news stories of women than men. Kim Fridkin Kahn (1996), who conducted this research, concludes that journalists "hold certain preconceptions about women candidates that lead them to consider those candidates less viable than their male counterparts" (p. 13). These preconceptions undoubtedly contributed to the reality that stories about male candidates were more common and also more likely to focus on core matters related to electoral contests, especially issue positions. Too often, women's coverage highlighted tangential matters, such as appearance or personality, or intimated that the female candidate was unlikely to win.

Today, the media environment is less hostile toward some women's candidacies. Throughout the 1990s and into the 2000s, gender disparities in coverage of candidates running for governor or the U.S. Congress were much less common than in prior decades (Bystrom et al., 2004; Devitt, 2002; Fowler & Lawless, 2009; Kittilson & Fridkin, 2008; Smith, 1997). Similar improvements in news coverage have not occurred among women who run for the presidency, however. Indeed, one thorough analysis of newspaper coverage of eight female candidates, from Victoria Woodhull (1872) to Carol Moseley Braun (2004), offered the following conclusion: "Press coverage is often biased and prejudiced, and it is not much better today than it was in 1872" (Falk, 2008, p. 14). Compared to male presidential candidates with similar credentials and levels of popular support, media stories were more likely to discuss the women's viability, family status, emotionality, personal traits, appearance, and gender. Examples of these coverage features are presented in Table 12.4. At the same time, the female candidates appeared less often in print, saw their issue positions receive less attention, and were less likely to be referred to by their professional titles. Margaret Chase Smith, for example, was identified by her marital status ("Mrs. Smith") rather than her political office ("Senator Smith") 32% of the time. How often was "Governor" replaced with "Mr." for her closest competitor, New York Governor Nelson Rockefeller? Only 5% of the time (Falk & Jamieson, 2003).

The two female presidential candidates whose media coverage has been examined the most thoroughly are Elizabeth Dole and Hillary Clinton. In the case of Dole, her coverage closely resembled that of other female presidential candidates: fewer stories, more attention to her viability and personal details, and less attention to her issue positions (Aday & Devitt, 2001; Bystrom, 2005; Heith, 2001, 2003; Heldman, Carroll, & Olson, 2005). Clinton's coverage in 2008, however, contained notable departures from these trends (Lawrence & Rose, 2010; Miller, Peake, & Boulton, 2010). First, Clinton actually received more coverage than her male Democratic counterparts. Second, attention to Clinton's appearance was not more common than most of her male opponents. Third, Clinton's issue positions were featured in articles as often as or more often than her male competitors.

One area in which Clinton's coverage did differ from the male candidates was its tone. Her coverage was unquestionably more negative. One examination of the traits used to describe Clinton and her chief rival for the Democratic nomination, Barack Obama, found not only that negative traits were more commonly applied to Clinton but also that the nature of the negative traits differed (Miller, Peake, & Boulton, 2010). Negative trait mentions for Obama were most likely related to the job of the presidency; a majority of Clinton's negative trait descriptors were related to her personal character. More specifically, "[w]hereas Obama was largely portrayed as inexperienced [and unqualified], Clinton was largely portrayed as secretive, cold, [calculating,] and even 'scary'" (Miller, Peake, & Boulton, 2010, p. 185). Furthermore, Clinton's campaign tactics and strategy received more critical commentary in the press than did either Obama's or the 2008 Republican nominee, John McCain's (Lawrence & Rose, 2010). Part of the reason for this discrepancy was Clinton's front-runner status; presidential front-runners typically receive more negative coverage than other candidates. Yet, Clinton seems to have faced a higher level of press scrutiny than

TABLE 12.4

Media Coverage of Women Presidential Candidates

Candidate	Examples of Press Coverage
Victoria Woodhull (1872)	Philadelphia campaign stop was described as the "intended visit of Mrs. Woodhull to lecture the women of that city on the blessing of free love."
	"She is rather in advance of her time. The public mind is not yet educated to the pitch of universal woman's rights."
	Described as "seductive," "soiled," "naughty," and "notorious"; also "shallow-headed," "foolish," and "without the light of reason."
Margaret Chase Smith (1964)	"I would hope that a woman President and the Queen of England would not vie with each other in hat or dress styles. It might result in a diplomatic break."
	"[N]ot too many on the legislative scene will take her candidacy seriously."
Shirley Chisholm (1972)	"The presidential candidacy of Representative Shirley Chisholm, the second-term Congresswoman from Brooklyn, is not a venture in practical politics. She candidly recognizes that she is not going to win."
	"Many blacks and women are supporting her because of her race and sex."
Patricia Schroeder (1988)	"Many observers have said that Schroeder, because she is a woman . . . doesn't have a serious shot at the nomination."
	"There's a sense that the candor and humor and down-home style that Pat has that is so terrific and attractive speaking from the House floor isn't the best way to speak as a potential candidate."
	Described as "fuming," "upset," "irked," "angry," and "tearful."
Elizabeth Dole (2000)	"My gut feeling is that she has a good chance at the Vice Presidency. My gut is that the country is not ready for a woman president."
	"Elizabeth Dole, clad in peach silk and perfect lipstick, glided smoothly through a throng."[a]
	"Some men call her a 'Stepford wife,' an over-programmed perfectionist. And women from outside the South found her deep-fried effusiveness off-putting; they could not identify with a woman who calls her husband precious, an adjective they might give a baby but never a husband."[b]

(Continued)

TABLE 12.4

(*Continued*)

Candidate	Examples of Press Coverage
Carol Moseley Braun (2004)	"Hers seems more a personal crusade for rehabilitating her image than a substantive campaign for the public office."
	"[D]ivorced and the mother of a 15-year-old son."
	"Carol the Ideal is the politician with charisma, a megawatt smile and an articulate seriousness of purpose . . . Carol the Real has been different, a politician clouded by bad judgment, inattentiveness to detail and lack of follow-through that has left a trail of disillusioned aides and supporters."

Sources: Unless noted below, all examples were quoted in Falk, E. (2008). *Women for president: Media bias in eight campaigns*. Urbana: University of Illinois Press.

[a] Heith, D. J. (2003). The lipstick watch: Media coverage, gender, and presidential campaigns. In R. P. Watson & A. Gordon (Eds.), *Anticipating madam president* (pp. 123–130). Boulder, CO: Lynne Rienner Publishers, p. 127.

[b] Heldman, C., Carroll, S. J., & Olson, S. (2005). "She brought only a skirt": Print media coverage of Elizabeth Dole's bid for the Republican presidential nomination. *Political Communication, 22*, p. 328.

most past (all male) front-runners. Weeks before Iowans turned out to vote in the first nomination contest of the 2008 season, for example, "themes of Clinton['s campaign] stumbling, losing, and even dying" were present in the media, "leaving [some] to wonder if 'exit talk' is another form of viability talk, another way of casting doubt on the ability of women to rise to high political office" (Lawrence & Rose, 2010, p. 203).

These conclusions were drawn from analyses of Clinton's coverage in traditional media outlets (e.g., newspapers, broadcast television evening news). Regina Lawrence and Melody Rose (2010; see also Carroll, 2009) perused portrayals of Clinton on new media formats, such as cable television talk shows and Internet sites, and uncovered much higher levels of gendered and sexist commentary. One frequent narrative appearing in the new media was that Clinton belonged in her house, not in the White House. "Get Hillary Back in the Kitchen," and "Hillary, Iron My Shirt" slogans exemplify this sentiment (Lawrence & Rose, 2010, p. 201). While clearly sexist, this trope seems rather quaint in contrast to other Clinton narratives found in the new media. Violent imagery appeared, sometimes implying that Clinton's presidential ambitions, or even Clinton herself, should be killed. There were references to Glenn Close's *Fatal Attraction* character never giving up, even appearing to emerge from death. Also, "I Wish Hillary Had Married O.J." bumper stickers were available online (Lawrence & Rose, 2010, p. 201). Another narrative placed Clinton as a would-be killer: a killer of men or a killer of manhood. She was described as a "she-devil," intent on attempting to "strangle [the Obama campaign] in the crib before there's any chance he catches on" or wanting to stab him in the back (Lawrence & Rose, 2010, p. 199). Finally, there were multiple references to Clinton as a "ball buster" or "castrator," including the oft-repeated line by conservative talk show host Rush Limbaugh that Clinton has a "testicle lockbox . . . big enough for the entire Democratic hierarchy" (Lawrence & Rose, 2010, p. 200). Hillary Clinton nutcrackers were also widely available from online retailers as well as airport gift shops. To put it mildly, such sexist, even misogynistic, narratives demeaned Clinton and her candidacy.

Gone are the days when all women candidates receive decidedly worse media coverage than their male opponents. At the same time, we are not yet at the day when the media playing field is completely level across all elective offices. When running for the highest and, not coincidentally, most masculine office in the land, the media landscape is still unfair to women. To be sure, Hillary Clinton's media coverage was much improved in some respects compared to prior women presidential candidates. What should we make of this improved coverage, alongside evidence of contin-ued media bias that Clinton faced, especially in new media outlets? Have we entered a new era, one in which female and male presidential aspirants will be treated more similarly by the press? Whether this is a lesson to be drawn by Clinton's presidential bid is one of the topics we turn to in the next section. Before moving on, we conclude this section with two obser-vations. First, media coverage of candidates matters. Because voter infor-mation about, and images of, candidates can be greatly shaped by media stories, how and how often a candidate is covered by news reporters and whether certain candidates face unequal treatment is a topic that merits continued attention. Second, there is one other important consequence when the media treat female candidates unfairly: even fewer women will vie for the presidency. "By framing women candidates as not serious and not viable and by giving extra measure to their hairstyles, clothing, and general appearance, the press may dissuade potential women candidates from entering the political arena" (Falk, 2008, p. 157).

CONCLUSION: HILLARY CLINTON'S RUN FOR THE PRESIDENCY AND FUTURE PROSPECTS FOR WOMEN CANDIDATES

Without question, Hillary Clinton came closer than any other woman to obtaining her party's nomination for the presidency. She will go down in history recording many path-breaking achievements: first woman to be a front-runner for a major party nomination; first woman to win a state's presidential primary or caucus; and the first woman to come close to actually becoming president of the United States. Because of her candidacy, the prospect of a woman as a viable contender for the highest office in the land became a reality. For the first time, many citizens began to visualize a woman in the White House. The symbolic benefits of Clinton's candidacy should not be underestimated. She not only helped to normalize women's presidential candidacies but also serves as a role model for current and aspiring female politicians.

What other lessons can be drawn from Clinton's campaign, especially for future women's candidacies? We highlight two, both of which reinforce the difficult task that women presidential candidates continue to face. First, Clinton entered the 2008 Democratic nomination contest with significant advantages. As a former first lady and sitting U.S. senator, she had high levels of national name recognition. A large network of donors and fundraisers was available to her—the network that her husband Bill Clinton had established during his two successful runs for the White House. From that start, Hillary Clinton was able to build an even larger base of donors, enabling her to raise over $200 million. By virtue of the attention she received while serving as first lady and her own campaign experiences, Clinton was positioned to mount a viable national campaign for the presidency. These resources and visibility are simply not available for most candidates, male or female. Given women's slow ascension up the ladder of elective office in the United States, female candidates are even less likely than men to have the initial advantages that Clinton possessed. In fact, there is currently not another female politician in the country that comes close to being as well positioned as Clinton was to run. She is the exception that proves the rule: in an electoral environment that privileges entrepreneurship and connections, nontraditional candidates such as women have difficulty breaking through.

While Clinton's background and specific history made her unique among female candidates, her experiences on the campaign trail were in many ways very typical for a woman. The continued presence of gender stereotyping coupled with voter preferences for masculinity in their president constrain how women run for the White House. Not only are campaign strategies influenced, but women presidential candidates face higher scrutiny than do men. Clinton certainly did. And, just as traditional media outlets appear to be treating women candidates more equitably, new media formats can undermine these improvements. The "Wild West" of new media (Lawrence & Rose, 2010, p. 198), where political commentary is less subject to editorial standards of traditional media, has added a new frontier for women candidates to conquer. Navigating these mediums, and the discriminatory and sexist commentary that they readily permit, will not be easy.

In the end, Hillary Clinton's historic candidacy opened the door a bit wider for other women. After 2008, the notion of a woman making a serious bid for the presidency no longer shocks or challenges the sensibilities of most voters. Yet, it is too optimistic to conclude that the door is open wide enough for a woman to march to the White House with the same ease that a male candidate might. Structural features of running for president and cultural expectations regarding women and the masculine office of the presidency will continue to pose challenges for women candidates. In short, while we are closer to seeing a woman in the White House, thanks to Hillary Clinton's campaign, the path to this goal still contains significant obstacles.

Authors Note: We would like to thank Alixandra Greenman for compiling the tables.

NOTES

1   These eight were Mitt Romney, Rick Santorum, Ron Paul, Newt Gingrich, Jon Huntsman, Herman Cain, Tim Pawlenty, and Rick Perry.
2   The earliest Gallup surveys measuring this attitude asked respondents if they would support a qualified woman for the presidency but did not specify her political party. The condition that the female candidate be nominated by "your party" has been included since the late 1940s (Streb et al., 2008).
3   The wording of the question on the 2002 survey was very similar, but not identical, to Gallup's. Specifically, the 2002 survey asked respondents, "If your political party nominated a woman for president, would you be willing to vote for her if she were qualified for the job?" (Lawless, 2004, p. 485). Further, as with Gallup, the 2002 survey presented respondents with only two response options: yes and no. When respondents were explicitly told that they could answer yes, no, or don't know, support for a woman in the

White House dropped from 80% to 65% with 28% of respondents indicating they were unsure of their attitudes toward female presidential candidates.

REFERENCES

Aday, S., & Devitt, J. (2001). Style over substance: Newspaper coverage of Elizabeth Dole's presidential bid. *Harvard International Journal of Press/Politics, 6*, 52–73.

Alexander, D., & Andersen, K. (1993). Gender as a factor in the attributions of leadership traits. *Political Research Quarterly, 46*, 527–545.

Borrelli, M. (1997). Gender, credibility, and politics: The Senate hearings of cabinet-secretaries-designate, 1975 to 1993. *Political Research Quarterly, 50*, 171–197.

Bystrom, D.G. (2005). Media content and candidate viability: The case of Elizabeth Dole. In M.S. McKinney, L.L. Kaid, D.G. Bystrom, & D.B. Carlin (Eds.), *Communicating politics: Engaging the public in democratic life*. New York: Peter Lang.

Bystrom, D.G., Banwart, M.C., Kaid, L.L., & Robertson, T.A. (2004). *Gender and candidate communication: VideoStyle, WebStyle, NewsStyle*. New York: Routledge.

Carroll, S. (2009). Reflections on gender and Hillary Clinton's presidential campaign: The good, the bad, and the misogynic. *Politics & Gender, 5*, 1–20.

Carroll, S. & Dittmar, K. (2010). The 2008 candidacies of Hillary Clinton and Sarah Palin: Cracking the "highest, hardest glass ceiling". In S. Carroll & R.L. Fox (Eds.), *Gender and elections: Shaping the future of American politics*. Cambridge: Cambridge University Press.

Cooper, M. (2003, February 19). Can Carol Moseley-Braun be president? *Time Magazine*. Retrieved from http://www.time.com/time/nation/article/0,8599,424385,00.html.

DeConde, A. (1999). *Presidential machismo: Executive authority, military intervention, and foreign relations*. Boston: Northeastern University Press.

Devitt, J. (2002). Framing gender on the campaign trail: Female gubernatorial candidates and the press. *Journalism and Mass Communication Quarterly, 79*, 445–463.

Dolan, K. (2004). *Voting for women: How the public evaluates women candidates*. Boulder, CO: Westview Press.

Dolan, K. (2010). The impact of gender stereotyped evaluations on support for women candidates. *Political Behavior, 32*, 69–88.

Duerst-Lahti, G. (2010). Presidential elections: Gendered space and the case of 2008. In Susan J. Carroll & R.L. Fox (Eds.), *Gender and elections: Shaping the future of American politics*. Cambridge: Cambridge University Press.

Enloe, C. (2004). *The curious feminist*. Berkeley: University of California Press.

Falk, E. (2008). *Women for president: Media bias in eight campaigns*. Urbana: University of Illinois Press.

Falk, E., & Jamieson, K.H. (2003). Changing the climate of expectations. In R.P. Watson & A. Gordon (Eds.), *Anticipating Madam President*. Boulder, CO: Lynne Rienner Publishers.

Farrar-Myers, V.A. (2007). Money and the art and science of candidate viability. In L.C. Han & C. Heldman (Eds.), *Rethinking Madam President: Are we ready for a woman in the White House?* Boulder, CO: Lynne Rienner Publishers.

Fowler, L.L., & Lawless, J.L. (2009). Looking for sex in all the wrong places: Press coverage and the electoral fortunes of gubernatorial candidates. *Perspectives on Politics, 7*, 519–536.

Fox, R.L. (1997). *Gender dynamics in congressional elections*. Thousand Oaks, CA: Sage Publications.

Fridkin, K.L., & Kenney, P.J. (2009). The role of gender stereotypes in U.S. Senate campaigns. *Politics & Gender, 5*, 301–324.

Goldsmith, B. (1998). *Other powers: The age of suffrage, spiritualism, and the scandalous Victoria Woodhull*. New York: A.A. Knopf.

Goodman, E. (1988, April 5). A Dole on the national ticket? *Minneapolis Star Tribune*.

Gutgold, N.D. (2006). *Paving the way for Madam President*. Lanham, MD: Lexington.

Hausmann, R., Tyson, L.D. & Zahidi, S. (2011). *Global gender gap report 2011*. Geneva, Switzerland: World Economic Forum.

Haussman, M. (2003). Can women enter the "big tents"? National party structures and presidential nominations. In R.P. Watson & A. Gordon (Eds.), *Anticipating Madam President*. Boulder, CO: Lynne Rienner Publishers.

Heith, D.J. (2001). Footwear, lipstick, and an orthodox Sabbath: Media coverage of nontraditional candidates. *White House Studies, 1*, 335–347.

Heith, D.J. (2003). The lipstick watch: Media coverage, gender, and presidential campaigns. In R.P. Watson & A. Gordon (Eds.), *Anticipating Madam President*. Boulder, CO: Lynne Rienner Publishers.

Heldman, C. (2007). Cultural barriers to a female president in the United States. In L. Cox Han (Ed.), *Rethinking Madam President: Are we ready for a woman in the White House?* Boulder, CO: Lynne Rienner Publishers.

Heldman, C., Carroll, S.J., & Olson, S. (2005). "She brought only a skirt": Print media coverage of Elizabeth Dole's bid for the Republican presidential nomination. *Political Communication, 22*, 315–335.

Huddy, L., & Terkildsen, N. (1993a). Gender stereotypes and the perception of male and female candidates. *American Journal of Political Science, 37*, 119–147.

Huddy, L., & Terkildsen, N. (1993b). The consequences of gender stereotypes for women candidates at different levels and types of offices. *Political Research Quarterly, 46*, 503–525.

Inglehart, R., & Norris, P. (2003). *Rising tide: Gender equality and cultural change around the world*. Cambridge: Cambridge University Press.

International Parliamentary Union. (2012, March 31). *Women in parliaments: World classification*. Retrieved from http://www.ipu.org/wmn-e/arc/classif310312.html.

Jamieson, K.H. (1995). *Beyond the double bind: Women and leadership*. New York: Oxford University Press.

Kahn, K.F. (1996). *The political consequences of being a woman: How stereotypes influence the conduct and consequences of political campaigns*. New York: Columbia University Press.

Kennedy, C. (2003). Is the United States ready for a woman president? Is the Pope protestant? In R.P. Watson & A. Gordon (Eds.), *Anticipating Madam President*. Boulder, CO: Lynne Rienner Publishers.

Kittilson, M.C., & Fridkin, K. (2008). Gender, candidate portrayals and election campaigns: A comparative perspective. *Politics & Gender, 4*, 371–392.

Langer, G. (2012, April 25). Michelle Obama, Ann Romney, Hillary Clinton: In personal popularity, the women rule. *ABC News/Washington Post*. Retrieved from www.langerresearch.com/uploads/1127a24FavorabilityNo24.pdf.

Lawless, J.L. (2004). Women, war, and winning elections: Gender stereotyping in the post September 11th era. *Political Research Quarterly, 53*, 479–490.

Lawrence, R.G., & Rose, M. (2010). *Hillary Clinton's race for the White House: Gender politics and the media on the campaign trail.* Boulder, CO: Lynne Rienner Publishers.

Leonhardt, David. (2012, February 3). The 2016 election, already upon us. *New York Times.*

Mandel, R.B. (2007). She's the candidate! A woman for president. In B. Kellerman. & D. Rhode (Eds.), *Women and Leadership: The state of play and strategies for change.* San Francisco: Jossey-Bass.

Miller, M.K., Peake, J.S., & Boulton, B.A. (2010). Testing the *Saturday Night Live* hypothesis: Fairness and bias in newspaper coverage of Hillary Clinton's presidential campaign. *Politics & Gender, 6,* 169–198.

Murray, M. (2011, July 19). NBC/WSJ poll: Bachmann surges to 2nd place in '12 GOP Field. *First Read.* Retrieved from http://firstread.msnbc.msn.com/_news/2011/07/19/7113880-nbcwsj-poll-bachmann-surges-to-2nd-place-in-12-gop-field?lite.

Norgren, J. (2007). *Belva Lockwood: The woman who would be president.* New York: New York University Press.

O'Connor, K. (2003). Madam president: Sooner or later? In R.P. Watson & A. Gordon (Eds.), *Anticipating Madam President.* Boulder, CO: Lynne Rienner Publishers.

Rosenwasser, S.M., & Dean, N.G. (1989). Gender role and political office: Effects of perceived masculinity/femininity of candidate and political office. *Psychology of Women Quarterly, 13,* 77–85.

Rosenwasser S.M., Rogers, R.R., Fling, S., Silvers-Pickens, K., & Butemeyer, J. (1987). Attitudes toward women and men in politics: Perceived male and female candidate competencies and participant personality characteristics. *Political Psychology, 8,* 191–200.

Saad, L. (2011, June 20). In U.S., 22% are hesitant to support a Mormon in 2012. Retrieved from www.gallup.com/poll/148100/Hesitant-Support-Mormon-2012.aspx.

Sanbonmatsu, K. (2002). Gender stereotypes and vote choice. *American Journal of Political Science, 46,* 20–34.

Sapiro, V. (1981/1982). If U.S. Senator Baker were a woman: An experimental study of candidate images. *Political Psychology, 3,* 61–83.

Schroeder, P. (1998). *24 years of house work—and the place is still a mess: My life in politics.* Kansas City, MO: Andrews McMeel.

Sherman, J. (2000). *No place for a woman: A life of Senator Margaret Chase Smith.* New Brunswick, NJ: Rutgers University Press.

Smith, K.B. (1997). When all's fair: Signs of parity in media coverage of female candidates. *Political Communication, 14,* 71–82.

Smooth, W.G. (2010). African American women and electoral politics: A challenge to the post-race rhetoric of the Obama moment. In S.J. Carroll & R.L. Fox (Eds.), *Gender and elections: Shaping the future of American politics.* Cambridge: Cambridge University Press.

Streb, M.J., Burrell, B., Frederick, B., & Genovese, M.A. (2008). Social desirability effects and support for a female American president. *Public Opinion Quarterly, 72,* 76–89.

Sykes, P.L. (2008). Gender in the 2008 presidential election: Two types of time collide. *PS: Political Science and Politics, 41,* 761–764.

Traister, R. (2010). *Big girls don't cry: The election that changed everything for American women.* New York: Free Press.

Washington Post-ABC News poll. (2007, October 1). *The Washington Post.* Retrieved from http://www.washingtonpost.com/wp-srv/politics/polls/postpoll_100107.html.

Wayne, S.J. (2011). *The road to the White House. 2012* (9th ed.). Independence, KY: Cengage Learning.

13

Conclusion

Women as Political Leaders:
What Do We Know?

Michael A. Genovese

Having examined the lives and careers of the fascinating and important leaders discussed in this volume, what patterns or lessons might we draw? What can we learn from these cases, these stories of lives lived in the private world of the family and public world of politics? Can we draw pre-paradigmatic or pre-theoretical conclusions about women and leadership? Can we bring these seemingly disparate stories together to form patterns and make generalizations about women as political leaders?

From this study, a number of patterns appear to be especially noteworthy.[1] Several patterns stand out when we examine the contexts in which women have emerged as national leaders. Many female leaders have held office in less-developed nations (e.g., Aquino, Badaranaike, Bhutto, Chamorro, Charles, Gandhi, Pascal-Trouillot, and Perón); most rose in nations that maintained some form of democracy; few rose in "stable" times, meaning that most have come to power in times of social or political stress; and most have come to power in secular political regimes.

RISE TO POWER

Why did *these women*, above all others, rise to power in their political systems? What distinguishes their career paths from those of other women? In an examination of the career patterns of the women who have become national leaders, one characteristic seems suggestive: until recently, few of the women rose to power "on their own." Many of the women who have become leaders came to power in periods of social or political turmoil, and "inherited" power from family, father, or husband. Many of these women had little independent political experience on their own. Aquino, wife of the slain opposition leader; Bhutto, daughter of the ousted (and later executed) prime minister; Chamorro, wife of the opposition leader and *La Prensa* editor; Gandhi, daughter of India's first prime minister; and Perón, wife of deceased president—all came to power as a result of family status. Less common is the woman (e.g., Thatcher and Meir) who can rise to power on her own without the aid of powerful family connections. Also, the route to political power varies with level of development: Women in less-developed societies seem more dependent on spousal or family position than are women in more-developed societies.

This is linked to another curious familial factor. Just as many forceful male political figures have had a strong identification with their mothers (e.g., FDR, Lyndon Johnson), so too have many women leaders had very strong bonds to their fathers (e.g., Thatcher).[2] They have tended to come from families where much was expected, where opportunities for personal development abounded, and where the male figure encouraged or pushed the daughter to move beyond role limitations and social stereotypes.

LEADERSHIP STYLE

Are there "male" and "female" styles of leadership? Many researchers, such as Astin and Leland (1991), see men and women as exercising very different styles of leadership, with males using a hard style of leadership that stresses hierarchy, dominance, and order. Women, on the other hand, exercise leadership characterized by a soft style of cooperation, influence, and empowerment. In this sense, have the women who have headed governments exercised more "male" or "female" styles of leadership?

No one would ever accuse Margaret Thatcher, the Iron Lady, of exercising a soft style of leadership, nor could such a thing be said of Golda Meir. On the other hand, Violeta Chamorro and Corozon Aquino were often criticized as being weak or soft. When examining the styles of leadership exercised by the women who have headed governments, no clear pattern (certainly no distinctively feminine leadership style) emerges.

Some of the leaders have exercised a hard style, while others exercised a softer style of leadership. This, of course, raises the question: is there an *androgynous style* of leadership, one that combines elements of what are seen as the male and female styles of exercising power and leadership? Perhaps the empathetic style of Bill Clinton serves as a model for this leadership style. Or, rather than choose one or another style of leadership, should the goal be for the leader to exhibit *style flexing*? Different situations require different styles of leadership. The leader adept at recognizing what the situation requires and adapting his or her style of leadership to fit that situation stands a better chance of achieving success than the leader who rigidly adheres to one style of leadership in all situations.

POLICY CONSEQUENCES

Do women leaders pursue policy agendas that are different from those of their male counterparts? Are women in power more likely to bring other women into power or promote a feminist political agenda? To promote family issues? To promote a leftist agenda? In short, speaking in policy terms, does it make a difference that a ruler is a woman?

In general, the research on women who hold political office reveals a tendency for women to be slightly more liberal than men (see Thomas, 1987; Welch, 1985). Is this also true of women who lead nations? In examining the policy preferences of the women who have served as national leaders, no clear pattern emerges. None of these women has been a "revolutionary" leader, and overall they have tended to be spread across the ideological spectrum.

The concern for "women's issues" likewise has varied from leader to leader, with Margaret Thatcher promoting what many referred to as policies that were hostile to women's interests, and other leaders pursuing a more profeminist agenda.

All leaders face enormous constraints that must be overcome if they are to achieve policy and political success. It is not unreasonable to presume that one of the reasons women leaders have not been more demonstrably profeminist is because such a policy agenda might be considered radically anti-status quo, and pushing these issues would be too politically risky.

PERFORMANCE IN OFFICE

By what standards are women judged? What are the assessments of their tenures in office? How well—or poorly—have these women played the political hands they were dealt? Under what circumstances have these women left office? And to what extent did gender matter?

Overall, the performance of women who have headed governments has been mixed. While some female leaders have achieved a great deal (e.g., Thatcher and Merkel), many other have not been thought of as political successes (e.g., Perón, Aquino, Bhutto). This is so for a variety of reasons, not the least of which relate to gender. Even under the best of circumstances, leaders have a difficult time overcoming barriers to rulership, but when one remembers that most women leaders have risen at times of great societal hardship and systemic stress, and that they have had to confront the great barrier of gender, it is not surprising that their efforts at leadership have sometimes been rebuked.

Very few leaders are considered "great" to begin with; the circumstances under which most women national leaders have risen have clearly contributed to the problems of most to overcome the barriers of gender and prejudice to achieve greatness. A woman in power is unusual; only when it is seen as unremarkable that a woman holds power will we be able to judge women's performance in office adequately.

A WOMAN IN THE WHITE HOUSE

Barriers can be broken and glass ceilings shattered. In the 2008 Democratic presidential primary contest, a black man, Barack Hussein Obama, and a woman, Hillary Rodham Clinton, took the race down to the wire before Obama was able to win the nomination. One barrier broken. He then went on to win the general election and become president. Another barrier broken. The next barrier will be a woman securing the presidential nomination of one of the major parties. The next, a woman in the White House.[3]

What does this study of women who have headed governments suggest for the first female United States president? First of all, the fears and suspicions still harbored by some voters are unfounded. There is no rational reason to oppose a woman for president simply because she is a woman. The leaders examined in this book governed in good times and bad, during peace and war, and their overall performance was at least as good and many would argue, slightly better than their male counterparts.

That is not to say that gender does not matter. Clearly it does, both in the pathway to leadership, and in the efforts to govern. But gender *is not* an impenetrable barrier to effective governing. As we noted at the outset of this book, context matters greatly. A truer guide to determining the effectiveness of a leader is the context in which he or she governed. Yes, skill and judgment matter, but context sets the parameter of power. If the country is experiencing economic growth or a recession, for example, context will matter more than skill in determining options and outcomes. Thus, in order to evaluate the effectiveness of a leader, we must know the conditions under which he or she governed.

Still we must ask: why does the United States lag so far behind the rest of the world in allowing women access to leadership positions in politics?

In our history, about only 20 women have declared themselves a candidate for the presidency. Victoria Woodhull was the first in 1872 (see Tables 13.1 and 13.2). Only two women, Geraldine Ferraro and Sarah Palin, have been a major party candidate for vice president. Why so few?

Even as barriers have fallen, there are still forces that inhibit women from, as Disrelli said, "Climbing to the top of the greasy pole." One of the key barriers can be seen in the "feeding system" or the political minor leagues where politicians get their feet wet, run for office, prove themselves under fire, are road tested, develop a record of accomplishment, build up a resume. The feeder system in the United States still underrepresents women. If women are to be taken seriously in politics, there will have to be more women in the political pipeline of stepping-stone offices. Starting at the local level and building up to statewide offices, governorships (see Table 13.3), the U.S. Senate (see Table 13.4) and cabinet and sub-cabinet posts (see Table 13.5), women must build credibility by developing a record of performance.

TABLE 13.1

Major Female Presidential Candidates

Name	Year	Party
Victoria Woodhull	1872	N/A
Belva Lockwood	1884	National Equal Rights
Margaret Chase Smith	1964	Republican
Shirley Chisholm	1972	Democrat
Patricia Schroeder	1988	Democrat
Elizabeth Dole	1999	Republican
Carole Moseley Braun	2004	Democrat
Hillary Clinton	2008	Democrat
Michelle Bachmann	2012	Republican

TABLE 13.2

Female Vice-Presidential Nominees

Name	Year	Party
Geraldine Ferraro	1984	Democrat
Winona La Duke	2000	Green
Ezola Foster	2000	Reform
Sarah Palin	2008	Republican

TABLE 13.3

Women Governors, 2012

Name	State	Party
Jan Brewer	Arizona	Republican
Suana Martinez	New Mexico	Republican
Beverly Purdue	North Carolina	Democrat
Mary Fallin	Oklahoma	Republican
Nikki Haley	South Carolina	Republican
Christine Gregoire	Washington	Democrat

TABLE 13.4

Women in U.S. Senate, to 2012

Name	State	Party	Years
Rebecca Latimer Felton	Georgia	Democrat	1922
Hattie Wyatt Caraway	Arkansas	Democrat	1931–1945
Rose McConnell Long	Louisiana	Democrat	1936–1937
Dixie Bibb Graves	Alabama	Democrat	1937–1938
Gladys Pyle	South Dakota	Republican	1938–1939
Vera Cahalan Bushfield	South Dakota	Republican	1948
Margaret Chase Smith	Maine	Republican	1949–1973
Eva Kelly Bowring	Nebraska	Republican	1954
Hazel Hempel Abel	Nebraska	Republican	1954
Maurine Brown Neuberger	Oregon	Democrat	1960–1967
Elaine S. Edwards	Louisiana	Democrat	1972
Muriel Humphrey	Minnesota	Democrat	1978
Maryon Pittman Allen	Alabama	Democrat	1978
Nancy Landon Kassebaum	Kansas	Republican	1978–1997
Paula Hawkins	Florida	Republican	1981–1987
Barbara Mikulski	Maryland	Democrat	1987–present
Jocelyn Burdick	North Dakota	Democrat	1992
Dianne Feinstein	California	Democrat	1993–present
Barbara Boxer	California	Democrat	1993–present
Patty Murray	Washington	Democrat	1993–present
Carol Moseley Braun	Illinois	Democrat	1993–1999
Kay Bailey Hutchison	Texas	Republican	1993–present
Olympia Snowe	Maine	Republican	1995–present
Sheila Frahm	Kansas	Republican	1996
Susan Collins	Maine	Republican	1997–present
Mary Landrieu	Louisiana	Democrat	1997–present
Blanche Lincoln	Arkansas	Democrat	1999–2011
Maria Cantwell	Washington	Democrat	2001–present
Jean Carnahan	Missouri	Democrat	2001–2002
Hillary Rodham Clinton	New York	Democrat	2001–2009
Debbie Stabenow	Michigan	Democrat	2001–present
Lisa Murkowski	Alaska	Republican	2002–present
Elizabeth Dole	North Carolina	Republican	2003–2009
Amy Klobuchar	Minnesota	Democrat	2007–present
Claire McCaskill	Missouri	Democrat	2007–present

(Continued)

TABLE 13.4

(*Continued*)

Name	State	Party	Years
Jeanne Shaheen	New Hampshire	Democrat	2009–present
Kay Hagan	North Carolina	Democrat	2009–present
Kirsten Gillibrand	New York	Democrat	2009–present
Kelly Ayotte	New Hampshire	Republican	2011–present

TABLE 13.5

Women Appointed to Presidential Cabinet

Years	President	Appointments	Women
1968–1974	Nixon	31	0 (0%)
1974–1977	Ford	12	1 (8.3%)
1977–1981	Carter	21	4 (19.0%)
1981–1989	Reagan	33	3 (9.1%)
1989–1993	G.H.W. Bush	17	3 (17.6%)
1993–2001	Clinton	29	12 (41.4%)
2001–2009	Bush	47	8 (17.0%)
2009–2012	Obama	23	

CONCLUSION

There is no question that opportunities for women have opened up in the past 40 years. The Women's movement, the spread of democracy, and other factors have coalesced to open doors that have historically been closed to women. But the basic structure and legacy of male domination remains intact. The women who have headed national governments, while a varied lot, do have one thing in common: none of them has challenged in any fundamental way, the patriarchal power structure of her society. To do so would have been political suicide.

If doors have opened for women, enormous barriers still exist. Women remain outsiders and second-class citizens. The hurdles that inhibit the emergence of women in the public sphere are formidable, but, as Alexis de Toucqueville reminds us, "evils which are patiently endured when they seem inevitable become intolerable when once the idea of escape from them is suggested" (quoted in Tavris & Wade, 1984, p. 362). That there is increasingly believed to be an escape from the bondage of patrimony is the essential ingredient in the creation of a just and equal society that liberates both men and women (Cantor & Bernay, 1992).

NOTES

1 In many of the categories to be examined, we can include the other women who have headed governments but whose cases are not presented in this book: Sirimavo Bandaranaike of Sri Lanka, Mary Eugenia Charles of Domincia, and Ertha Pascal-Trouillot of Haiti.
2 This is true for most women who have achieved political success at the subnational level as well. See Astin and Leland (1991, pp. 42–47).
3 Lori Cox Han and Carole Heldman, eds., *Rethinking Madam Presidency: Are We Ready for a Woman in the White House* (Boulder, CO: Lynne Rienner, 2007); and Robert P. Watson and Anne Gordon, eds., *Anticipating Madame President* (Boulder, CO: Lynne Rienner, 2003).

REFERENCES

Astin, H.S., & Leland, C. (1991). *Women of influence, women of vision*. San Francisco: Jossey-Bass.

Cantor, D.W., & Bernay, T. (1992). *Women in power: The secrets of leadership*. Boston: Houghton Mifflin.

Tavris, C., & Wade, C. (1984). *The longest war: Sex differences in perspective*. San Diego: Harcourt Brace Jovanovich.

Thomas, S. (1987). *Explaining legislative support for women's issues*. Paper presented at the annual meeting of the Midwest Political Science Association, Chicago.

Welch, S. (1985). Are women more liberal than men in Congress? *Legislative Studies Quarterly, 10,* 125–134.

Author Index

Subject Index